Running Mac OS X Tiger

Other resources from O'Reilly

Related titles

AppleScript: The Definitive Guide

AppleScript: The Missing Manual

Classic Shell Scripting

Learning the bash Shell

Learning Unix for Mac OS X Tiger

Mac OS X: The Missing Manual, Tiger Edition

Mac OS X Tiger for Unix Geeks

Mac OS X Tiger in a Nutshell

Mac OS X Tiger Pocket Guide

SSH, The Secure Shell: The Definitive Guide

Unix Power Tools

Macintosh Books Resource Center

mac.oreilly.com is a complete catalog of O'Reilly's books on the Apple Macintosh and related technologies, including sample chapters and code examples.

oreillynet.com is the essential portal for developers interested in open and emerging technologies, including new platforms, programming languages, and operating systems.

Conferences

O'Reilly brings diverse innovators together to nurture the ideas that spark revolutionary industries. We specialize in documenting the latest tools and systems, translating the innovator's knowledge into useful skills for those in the trenches. Visit *conferences.oreilly.com* for our upcoming events.

Safari Bookshelf (*safari.oreilly.com*) is the premier online reference library for programmers and IT professionals. Conduct searches across more than 1,000 books. Subscribers can zero in on answers to time-critical questions in a matter of seconds. Read the books on your Bookshelf from cover to cover or simply flip to the page you need. Try it today with a free trial.

Running Mac OS X Tiger

James Duncan Davidson and Jason Deraleau

O'REILLY®

Beijing · Cambridge · Farnham · Köln · Paris · Sebastopol · Taipei · Tokyo

Running Mac OS X Tiger

by James Duncan Davidson and Jason Deraleau

Copyright © 2006 O'Reilly Media, Inc. All rights reserved.
Printed in the United States of America.

Published by O'Reilly Media, Inc., 1005 Gravenstein Highway North, Sebastopol, CA 95472.

O'Reilly books may be purchased for educational, business, or sales promotional use. Online editions are also available for most titles (*safari.oreilly.com*). For more information, contact our corporate/institutional sales department: (800) 998-9938 or *corporate@oreilly.com*.

Editor:	Chuck Toporek
Production Editor:	Adam Witwer
Cover Designer:	Emma Colby
Interior Designer:	David Futato

Printing History:

December 2003:	First Edition, originally published as *Running Mac OS X Panther*.
December 2005:	Second Edition.

 This book uses RepKover™, a durable and flexible lay-flat binding.

ISBN: 0-596-00913-5

[M]

Table of Contents

Preface

Mac OS X is the first real operating system for the 21st century. A stunning achievement not to be confused with Mac OS 9 and its predecessors even as it builds on their legacy, Mac OS X redefines our expectations of what a computer should be. On the surface, Mac OS X has a graphical user interface (GUI) with usability that can't be touched by any other OS on the planet. Under the hood, it has a powerful Unix engine known as Darwin, which was developed through Apple's open source initiative and based on the FreeBSD 5.0 Unix distribution and the fully buzzword-compliant Mach 3.0 kernel. This combination of features gives the system its smooth multitasking behavior and virtual memory management.

This strong foundation provides with the system the stability it needs to amaze, intrigue, and serve you. It is also this foundation that lets you run the Apache web server, the Postfix mail server, and X11 applications next to Microsoft Word, Adobe Photoshop, and Macromedia Dreamweaver—a feat that nobody thought possible a few years ago. For many, Mac OS X has replaced the dual boot systems that they used to have: one partition for Windows so you could run Office and another for Linux for doing Unix-related work. Now, it's all under one roof.

Even better, Mac OS X continues to improve. Each release brings new features, speed improvements, and more polish. This book, *Running Mac OS X Tiger*, will help you master the latest version of Mac OS X. You'll learn how to get the most out of the pretty GUI as well as how to dive into the Unix layer of the system to take fine-grained control when you need to.

Audience

This book is written for users and power users of Mac OS X and assumes that you already have some experience with Mac OS X and with computers in general. For example, this book assumes that you have found and used the System Preferences application, have discovered how to change the way that your windows minimize and how the Dock works, and that you've figured out how to change your desktop background. I'm going to speak to you as somebody who wants to truly master what is going on with your system. Maybe you want to turn your Mac into a web server. Or maybe you want to know the pros and cons of the various filesystem choices that you have. Possibly you want to understand how Mac OS X's networking subsystem makes it possible to switch effortlessly between wired and unwired networks as well as letting you share your connection with others.

The command line will be covered extensively in this book and, while I expect that you are at least comfortable with the idea of the command line, one thing I won't assume is that you are a Unix guru who is knowledgeable about all of the shell's dark corners. I'll give you enough help and explanation of how the command line works so you can accomplish everything you need to. If you decide you like the Unix side of Mac OS X, you can learn more about it by reading *Learning Unix for Mac OS X Tiger*, by Dave Taylor (O'Reilly).

On the other hand, if you are a Unix guru, you may be interested in *Mac OS X Tiger for Unix Geeks*, by Brian Jepson and Ernest E. Rothman (O'Reilly), as a companion book that serves as a magic decoder ring describing the differences between Mac OS X's internals and those of Linux, Solaris, and other variants of Unix.

And, if you really do want to learn how to set your desktop pictures and how to use Stickies, iChat, and iTunes, I suggest you put this book down and pick up *Mac OS X: The Missing Manual, Tiger Edition*, by David Pogue (Pogue Press); surely it's located somewhere nearby in the bookstore. Better yet, buy it at the same time you pick up this book. The two books go well with each other.

There are two other books that you should consider as companion books to this one:

- *Mac OS X Tiger in a Nutshell*, by Andy Lester (O'Reilly), serves as a quick reference to many of Tiger's features.
- *Mac OS X Tiger Pocket Guide*, by Chuck Toporek (O'Reilly), squeezes the most-used features into a pocket-sized quick reference guide.

How This Book Is Organized

This book consists of 14 chapters along with two appendixes.

Chapter 1, *Where It All Came From*
> Mac OS X is the successful hybrid of technologies from Unix and the original Mac OS. On its own, the history would be interesting enough. But the impact of Apple's decisions while fusing these two systems together affects how the system operates to this day.

Chapter 2, *Installing the System and Software*

Whether you're upgrading from a previous version of Mac OS X or doing a fresh install, this chapter helps you get going with Tiger and helps Tiger get going on your Mac. OS installation is covered, in addition to Aqua and Unix software installation.

Chapter 3, *Lay of the Land*

Mac OS X is composed of many different technologies with several different lineages. This chapter starts by examining these diverse tools and how they work together to form Apple's next-gen OS.

The layout of the Mac OS X filesystem is different from that of most other operating systems. It shares history with traditional Unix filesystem layouts, but introduces several concepts that make it easier for the system to keep its data separate from yours. This chapter looks beneath the Finder's presentation of the filesystem and explains how the filesystem is laid out, with details on what is located where.

Chapter 4, *The Terminal and Shell*

The Terminal gives you access to the Unix core of Mac OS X. While it is possible to become a decent user without ever using the Terminal, you'll need a good understanding of it to become a guru and unleash the full potential of the system. This chapter shows how to use the Terminal and how to configure the various shells on the system.

Chapter 5, *System Startup and Login*

Quite a bit happens behind the simple gray Apple logo and spinner that appear when Mac OS X starts up. This chapter looks at what gets executed when and what the various boot options are. In addition, it takes a look at the process by which events happen when you log in and out of the system.

Chapter 6, *Users and Groups*

Thanks to its Unix heritage, Mac OS X is a multiuser operating system through and through. This chapter dives into the question of why there are multiple users on the system and why they are gathered into groups. It also explains how to add users from both the Accounts preference panel and the command line, how user security works, and how to access the functionality of the root user.

Chapter 7, *Open Directory*

Open Directory stores the most important data about your system—the list of users, groups, printers, and so forth. Based on LDAP, it works with NetInfo, flat files, other LDAP servers, and Microsoft's Active Directory. This chapter shows you how this system works and how to modify data contained within it.

Chapter 8, *Files and Permissions*

Most administration tasks that you perform will involve working with files in one capacity or another. This chapter explains the various attributes and permissions that a file can have and how to work with them. It also takes a look at how to effectively find files on the system and how Tiger's new Spotlight makes it a whole lot easier.

Chapter 9, *Disks and Filesystems*

Mac OS X supports many different kinds of disks including: hard drives, removable USB and FireWire drives, floppy drives, CDs, DVDs, and virtual disk images. This chapter gives you the lowdown on the different kinds of filesystems you can use and the pros and cons of each. It also goes into the various network filesystems Mac OS X supports, both as a client and a server.

Chapter 10, *Printing*

The printing architecture that Mac OS X uses is very flexible and supports both local and network printers. This chapter gives you a detailed look at how printing works, how to use print servers, how to connect with Windows-hosted printers, and even how to share your ink jet printer with Windows users. It also offers a look at the Common Unix Print System (CUPS), which serves as the foundation for the rest of the printing system.

Chapter 11, *Networking*

Mac OS X lives to be connected to other machines. This chapter shows you how the networking system works including wireless, spontaneous networking (Rendezvous), and Internet Connection Sharing. It also covers how to connect to corporate VPN networks.

Chapter 12, *Monitoring the System*

The first step to keeping your system in tip-top shape is to know where to go to get information about how the system is running. This chapter covers the Console, System Profiler, Activity Monitor, and many other tools as well as gives you the skinny on what to look for in your system's logfiles.

Chapter 13, *Automating Tasks*

Mac OS X has had a rich toolkit for automating both the Terminal and the GUI. With Tiger's Automator, that automation is coming to a whole new audience. This chapter dives into using Automator and other tools for automating your Mac.

Chapter 14, *Preferences and Defaults*

All user configuration data on Mac OS X is stored in the defaults system. This system is structured, in a way similar to the filesystem, to keep your data separate from the system's data, allowing you to migrate it between machines easily. In addition to discussing how the defaults system works, this chapter shows you how to modify preferences stored in the system in a variety of ways.

Appendix A, *Boot Command Keys*

> While your Mac boots up, you can give it all sorts of commands, and they all involve somewhat cryptic key combinations. This appendix gives you the full reference to all the commands.

Appendix B, *Other Sources of Information*

> There are a wide variety of good resources containing more information about Mac OS X. This appendix serves as a list of resources that will help you develop knowledge about Mac OS X.

How to Use This Book

You should be able to jump into this book wherever you wish. Reading straight through from front to back, however, will ensure that you won't encounter any surprises, as every effort has been made to avoid forward references. If at any time you need to dig deep and find out why something isn't working as you expect, read Chapter 12.

There are a zillion things I'd love to show you about how your Mac operates under the hood. Due to the desire to both get this book into your hands before the end of this century as well as to allow you to carry it next to your PowerBook in your backpack, I'm going to cover the most salient and interesting aspects of each subject and, where appropriate, point you to additional sources of information.

Don't be shy about dog-earing the pages as well as highlighting parts of the book that you find useful. Computer books should not be treated as pristine coffee table books. They should be used. And, it won't be long before Apple releases a new version of Mac OS X, which will prompt a revision of this book that you'll surely want to buy. So go ahead, scribble notes in the margins!

Compatibility

Mac OS X is evolving rapidly. There have been four major releases since it was first released as Version 10.0 in March 2001, and there is no sign that Apple is slowing down. To keep things simple, this book is targeted directly at Mac OS X Tiger (Version 10.4.2 was the most current version when this book went to press). While most of this information may work with previous or later releases of Mac OS X, there is no way to ensure this, and I'm certainly not going to pretend that I'm psychic and that the advice in this book will apply to the next release of Mac OS X (whatever big cat they name it after). Use this book with Tiger and you should be safe.

Conventions Used in This Book

The following is a list of the typographical conventions used in this book:

Italic

Used to indicate new terms, URLs, filenames, file extensions, directories, commands and options, and program names. For example, a path in the filesystem will appear as */Developer/Applications*.

Constant width

Used to show code examples, the contents of a file, or the output from commands.

Constant width italic

Used to show text that should be replaced with user-supplied values.

Constant width bold

Used to show text that is input by the user.

↵

A carriage return (↵) at the end of a line of code is used to denote an unnatural line break; that is, you should not enter these as two lines of code but as one continuous line. Multiple lines are used in these cases due to printing constraints.

$, %, #

The dollar ($) and percent (%) signs are used in some examples to show the prompt of the *bash* or *tcsh* shell; the hash (#) mark is the prompt for the root user.

Menus/navigation

Menus and their options are referred to in the text as File → Open, Edit → Copy, and so on. Arrows are also used to signify a navigation path when using window options; for example, System Preferences → Accounts → Login Items means that you would launch System Preferences, click the icon for the Accounts preference panel, and select the Login Items pane within that panel.

Menu symbols

When looking at the menus for any application, you will see some symbols associated with keyboard shortcuts for a particular command. For example, to create a new project in Project Builder, you would go to the File menu and select New Project (File → New Project), or you could issue the keyboard shortcut, Shift-⌘-N. The symbol is used to refer to the Apple menu in the upper-left corner of the screen.

Directories and folders

In the text, you will see the same thing referred to sometimes as "directories" and sometimes as "folders." The term "directory" is used when referring to directories in the command line or in the Unix part of the OS. When using the

Finder and other GUI applications, however, the traditional Mac OS term "folder" is used.

You should pay special attention to notes set apart from the text with the following icons.

This is a tip, suggestion, or general note. It contains useful supplemental information about the topic at hand.

This indicates a warning or a caution. It will help you solve and avoid annoying problems.

Using Code Examples

This book is here to help you get your job done. In general, you may use the code in this book in your programs and documentation. You do not need to contact us for permission unless you're reproducing a significant portion of the code. For example, writing a program that uses several chunks of code from this book does not require permission. Selling or distributing a CD-ROM of examples from O'Reilly books does require permission. Answering a question by citing this book and quoting example code does not require permission. Incorporating a significant amount of example code from this book into your product's documentation does require permission.

We appreciate, but do not require, attribution. An attribution usually includes the title, author, publisher, and ISBN. For example: "*Running Mac OS X Tiger* by James Duncan Davidson and Jason Deraleau. Copyright 2006 O'Reilly Media, Inc., 0-596-00913-5."

If you feel your use of code examples falls outside fair use or the permission given above, feel free to contact us at *permissions@oreilly.com*.

Safari® Enabled

When you see a Safari® Enabled icon on the cover of your favorite technology book, that means the book is available online through the O'Reilly Network Safari Bookshelf.

Safari offers a solution that's better than e-books. It's a virtual library that lets you easily search thousands of top tech books, cut and paste code samples, download chapters, and find quick answers when you need the most accurate, current information. Try it for free at *http://safari.oreilly.com*.

How to Contact Us

All the people who have worked on this book, including (but not limited to) the author, editor, and copyeditor, have tested and verified the information in this book to the best of their ability, but you may find that features have changed—or even that we have made mistakes! As a reader of this book, you can help us to improve future editions by sending along your feedback. Please let us know about any errors, inaccuracies, bugs, misleading or confusing statements, and typos that you find anywhere in this book.

Please also let us know what can be done to make this book more useful to you. Your comments will be taken seriously, and we will try to incorporate reasonable suggestions into future editions. You can contact us at:

O'Reilly Media, Inc.
1005 Gravenstein Highway North
Sebastopol, CA 95472
(800) 998-9938 (in the U.S. or Canada)
(707) 829-0515 (international or local)
(707) 829-0104 (fax)

You can also send us messages electronically. To be put on the mailing list or to request a catalog, send email to:

info@oreilly.com

To ask technical questions or to comment on the book, send email to:

bookquestions@oreilly.com

There is also a page on O'Reilly's web site dedicated to this book. It lists examples, errata, and plans for future editions. You can find this page at:

http://www.oreilly.com/catalog/runmacx2

For more information about our books, conferences, Resource Centers, and the O'Reilly Network, see our web site at:

http://www.oreilly.com/

Acknowledgments

A few years ago, I never thought I'd be writing the acknowledgments for an O'Reilly book. A lot of people have helped me get to this point, and I'm grateful first to Brian Jepson, for introducing me to Derrick Story and the Mac DevCenter team (*http://www.macdevcenter.com*). Next, of course, is Derrick himself. Derrick's feedback proved invaluable as I first tested my writing chops. And that's to include all of the other wonderful feedback I've gotten on the Mac DevCenter and other O'Reilly sources.

A very big thank you to James Duncan Davidson, for doing an excellent job on the first edition and digging through old backups to find some screenshots that I just couldn't reproduce. Thank you to Chuck Toporek, my editor, for burning the midnight oil and giving me a swift kick when life's other projects took me away from this one. Writing a book is quite a different process from essays and articles; Chuck's patience and guidance were very much appreciated as I made that jump.

I'd like to thank my family and friends for being supportive of my pursuits and not nagging me about spending so much time on the computer. In particular, thanks to Stefan, Eric, Dan, and Willow for helping me stay sane through writing this book. Thanks also to Rich, Fraser, Dave, and Jeff for being excellent companions in my professional life. Shout-outs to the FHP crew and the former RCN CCS department. Finally, the biggest thanks has been saved for Alisa, Dione, and Chris. Thanks for being the best friends anyone could ever ask for and being there to keep me from bouncing off the walls.

P.S. Thanks to John, Paul, George, and Ringo for the great music.

Acknowledgments from the First Edition

First and foremost, I'd like to thank all the people who reviewed the material in this book as it was written: Gabe Benveniste, Mike Clark, Damon Clinkscales, Stuart Halloway, Bethany Jane Hanson, Joseph Heck, Manton Reece, Daniel Steinberg, Dave Thomas, and Glenn Vanderburg as well as a whole lot of people at Apple (you guys know who you are). These people had front row seats to the creative process, watched a book grow, made tons of helpful comments, and asked all the right questions along the way. They even came through when I asked them to review chapters over the Thanksgiving holiday. The book you hold in your hands is, in large part, a result of their input. I owe them all my gratitude and thanks.

Special thanks go to Dave and Daniel who both went way beyond the call of duty. Any time I can repay the favor, guys, and review material for you, I'll be there.

Of course, there's the editorial team without whom an author is just somebody who scribbles random gibberish on paper. Chuck Toporek, who has worked with me on three books and become a friend along the way, brought this idea to me and helped me bring it to fruition. In addition to editing the book, Chuck picked up the pen and authored Appendix A. Jill Steinberg, also a friend, was the copyeditor for the book. She fretted over my use of words and helped turn them into something that I'm proud to put on the bookshelf. In addition to wielding the red pencil, she also offered valuable advice and critique during the early work on this book. Both Chuck and Jill are top-notch. Without them, this would not be a coherent book.

Many thanks to the women and men of the Apple Developer Connection who were of great assistance throughout the project. Without their support, this book couldn't have been written and printed in 2003. Writing about an OS is not an easy task.

Writing about one that is evolving as fast as Mac OS X is and still being timely is even harder. Without the support of the ADC and others at Apple, by the time we got a decent book together, news of the next version of Mac OS X would have made it obsolete.

Great thanks, as always, to Tim O'Reilly for so many things, but most of all for always listening and being willing to try to do what's right, even if it's risky and hasn't been done before. The production of this book was anything but typical. The last chapter was written during the 2003 Thanksgiving holiday and the book should be in stores by the end of the year or just after—in other words, it came together very rapidly. We've bent a few rules along the way and without Tim's support, it couldn't have happened.

David Futato watched as I took a design tuned from years of FrameMaker use and implemented it afresh using Adobe InDesign. Along the way, he offered many helpful suggestions and tips. I may have executed the layout and tweaked it to work well in a new environment, but the design is his and I hope it was implemented to his satisfaction.

During the writing of this book, many things happened in my personal life for which I am thankful. I moved to Portland, Oregon, a fantastic place to live even with the rain. I watched two of my best friends get married: Jason Hunter to Kathlyn in Yosemite; and Jim Driscoll to Sent-si in Hawaii. And, with the help of Dr. Atkins, I weigh less than I have in 10 years. I'm not sure how I managed to do all that while writing a book—a process that found me up until the wee hours of the night and, on more than one occasion, watching the sunrise before going to bed.

The music. Always the music. iTunes shows the following artists as the most frequently played during the creation of this book: Amon Tobin, BT, The Chemical Brothers, Coldplay, The Crystal Method, Electric Skychurch, Everclear, Fatboy Slim (Norman Cook), Filter, Fischerspooner, Fluke, Foo Fighters, Groove Armada, Josh Wink, Juno Reactor, No Doubt, The Orb, Paul Oakenfold, Paul van Dyk, Pink Floyd, Tabla Beat Science, Timo Maas, Tori Amos, Underworld, and Venus Hum. You better believe that I can't write without music.

And finally, many thanks to my family and friends who lent their support to the book writing process and who always encouraged me to chase my dreams.

## CHAPTER 1

Where It All Came From

The original Mac OS defined the basic metaphors that influenced personal computing and, for a decade, was the standard by which all other personal computer operating systems were measured. It was not until Microsoft Windows 95 was introduced that anything else came close. Unfortunately, while Apple made many mistakes, Microsoft continued to improve Windows and ended up owning the user desktop experience for the last half of the 1990s. Now, with the advent of a technological tour de force known as Mac OS X, the Mac is once again setting the standard for what a personal operating system should be.

The Mac OS as we now know it is far different from the version released in 1984. It is a successful hybrid of ideas that were first expressed in the original Macintosh and of technologies that come from a computing philosophy long considered to be the antithesis of the Mac experience: Unix. The fusion of these two very different camps gives us the platform we know and love today.

Instead of giving the same laundry list of features in this chapter that you can get from Apple's web site or from most other books covering Mac OS X, I'm going to take a look at the predecessors to Mac OS X and explore the various origins of the modern system. The intent isn't to tell the story of Apple Computer or Steve Jobs (although those histories are interesting); the focus here is on the technologies at hand, where they came from, and how they influenced the development of the Mac operating system. Each major technology of the current Mac OS X is introduced and its source identified.

The Classic Mac OS

In 1983, after the incredible success of the original Apple II (the first true personal computer for most people) and the later relative disappointments of the Apple III and the Lisa, Steve Jobs organized a group of engineers under a pirate flag to make a computer that could be used by anybody.

The result of their efforts, known as the Macintosh, was introduced to the world a year later accompanied by the fanfare of the famous "1984" commercial (directed by Ridley Scott of *Alien* and *Blade Runner* fame). With a message of empowerment, the Mac redefined what a personal computer could be. What made the Mac different from every other personal computer at the time was its graphical user interface (GUI), inspired by research that originated at Xerox PARC: a desktop where files lived in folders, and you used a mouse to move things where you wanted them. The Mac's original desktop is shown in Figure 1-1.

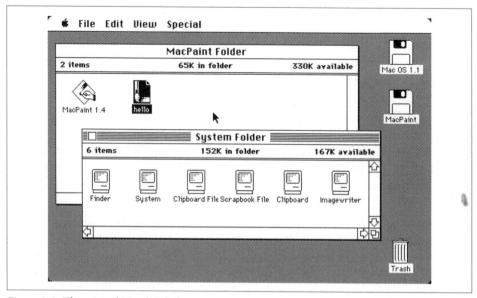

Figure 1-1. The original Mac OS desktop

The desktop metaphor introduced with the original Mac in 1984 lives on today in the current Finder. Sure, today's desktop is rendered in full color and the original was comparatively crudely drawn in black and white, but the basic idea remains much the same: opening disks and folders yields windows that contain icons that represent files.

At the heart of the system was a set of programmatic routines called the Macintosh Toolbox that allowed programmers to implement the various essential interface components—such as windows, menus, alert boxes, scrollbars, and other controls—in their applications. In 1984, the Toolbox was an amazing feat of engineering and contributed to a consistent user experience that was the envy of other operating system vendors. But, over the years after its release, more and more routines were added to the Toolbox as the system developed. This resulted in more features, but those features came with a price—the system became fragile.

System 7

In 1991, Apple introduced System 7, an upgrade that greatly modernized the Mac. It incorporated many features that would guide future development: seamless multitasking (albeit cooperative), color icons, personal file sharing, virtual memory, and a hierarchical System folder to help organize Control Panels and Extensions. The Mac interface also evolved for System 7, growing a bit more sophisticated as shown in Figure 1-2.

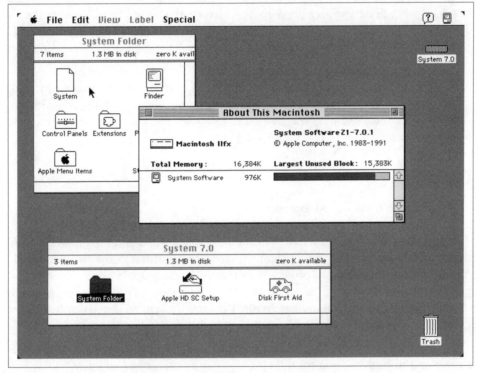

Figure 1-2. The System 7 desktop

System 7 also laid the foundation for three very important technologies:

QuickTime
A powerful multimedia technology for manipulating, enhancing, storing, and streaming video, graphics, sound, and animation.

ColorSync
A set of system routines for color management allowing for graphics to be color managed from editing to print.

AppleScript
An easy-to-use scripting language that allows you to automate tasks on your system.

Although System 7 was years ahead of every other operating system from the ease-of-use perspective, not all was rosy with this release. With all the new functionality, the Toolbox had become even more fragile than its predecessors. It turned out that cooperative multitasking, where applications are expected to play nice with each other, meant that any application could hog all the processor time and, in effect, lock up a system. And, most glaringly, the Mac OS did not provide memory protection between programs. This not only let applications run faster as well as enable all sorts of nifty customizations (also known as hacks), but it also let applications scribble into each other's memory space, inevitably corrupting the system. As Apple released new hardware, developers dreamed up new features that could be implemented only by using system extensions. While extensions had good intentions, they frequently conflicted with each other, which forced users to reboot their Macs several times a day.

At this point, even though development continued on the Mac OS, eventually leading to OS 8, OS 9, and the Classic environment under Mac OS X, it was obvious to Apple that a radical overhaul was needed to provide a more solid foundation for the future.

Copland

To address the need for a more stable operating system, Apple embarked on the development of a new operating system, dubbed Copland, in 1993. With Copland, the focus was on increasing stability, portability, ease-of-use, and performance. Copland was intended to be Apple's stepping stone to a future OS that would include preemptive multitasking and protected memory—keeping applications separate and preventing them from crashing each other or taking the entire system down. Much to the chagrin of Mac users as well as Apple, Copland descended into a death spiral of budget and schedule overruns.

Three years later, in 1996, Copland was cancelled and Apple desperately looked elsewhere for a new foundation for the Mac OS. For a time, it looked like Apple would purchase Be, started by Apple alum Jean-Louis Gassée, and use the technically sophisticated BeOS as the foundation for its next-generation operating system. The BeOS was developed on the PowerPC chip fitting in with Apple's Mac hardware strategy, had impressive multitasking abilities, an advanced filesystem, and provided the memory protection that the Mac OS so desperately needed. The only catch: BeOS was an unfinished work in progress that was unproven in the marketplace.

Several months into negotiations to acquire Be, the two companies were not able to agree on a price. Be wanted $400 million dollars for its unfinished and unproven system, and Apple did not want to take such a risk at that high price. After negotiations fell through late in 1996, Be struggled for several more years and then was eventually acquired by Palm, Inc.

Once again, Apple was left with no direction for its operating system, and many thought that the demise of Apple was near. Then, discussions started with Steve Jobs that led to the purchase in December 1996 of the company that he founded after leaving Apple in 1985: NeXT Computer. With this purchase came the portable and feature-rich NEXTSTEP operating system.

NEXTSTEP

Originally introduced to the world in 1987, along with the elegant NeXT cube, NEXTSTEP was intended to "create the next insanely great thing," as only Steve Jobs could say. The driving mantra was to do everything right, and not to repeat the mistakes that Apple had made. Built on top of BSD Unix and the Mach microkernel, NEXTSTEP had the preemptive multitasking and memory-protected core that Mac OS needed. NEXTSTEP also used Display PostScript from Adobe, allowing developers to use the same code to display documents onscreen and print to paper, enabling truly WYSIWYG applications. NEXTSTEP also featured a rich GUI desktop, as shown in Figure 1-3.

For developers, NEXTSTEP came with a set of libraries, called "frameworks," and tools to enable programmers to build applications using the Objective-C language. Developers loved this mix of technologies. For example, Tim Berners-Lee used NEXTSTEP to write the first few versions of both the client browser and server software that would start the World Wide Web.

NEXTSTEP evolved through many releases and was adopted by many governments and companies as their platform of choice. It made inroads into the military, banking, healthcare, and telecommunications industries and received glowing reviews from the press. Because it was created as a fresh start, avoiding the mistakes of the design of the original Macintosh and yet building on its ideas, it was able to jump far ahead of anything else.

In 1993, NEXTSTEP was ported to the Intel x86 architecture. Subsequently, other ports were performed for the Sun SPARC, Digital Alpha, and Hewlett-Packard PARISC architectures. Later, the development frameworks and tools were revised to run on other operating systems, such as Windows and Solaris. These revised frameworks became known as OpenStep. The NeXT team gained quite a bit of experience in implementing its technology on multiple platforms.

From NEXTSTEP, Mac OS X directly inherits the following:

The Mach kernel
> Descended from a research project at Carnegie Mellon University and first designed by Avi Tevanian (Apple's current chief software technology officer) in the mid-1980s, the Mach kernel performs the critical functions of abstracting the hardware of the computer from the software that runs on it. It provides symmetric multiprocessing, preemptive multitasking, protected and virtual memory, and

On Spelling and Capitalization

Over the years, there's been quite a bit of confusion as to how Copland was spelled, with many using the spelling "Copeland." However, a quick Google search with the term "copland +site:apple.com" turns up many old documents on Apple's web site that set the record straight. It's Copland without an "e."

There's also been quite a bit of confusion about how the word NEXTSTEP is capitalized, with camps of rabid curmudgeons gathered around the variations of NeXTSTEP, NeXTStep, and NEXTSTEP—each claiming their capitalization is correct. Well, the truth of the matter is they are all right. NeXT varied the capitalization over the various releases of the system. This book uses the all-caps form of the word as that's how Apple referred to the operating system in the press release dated December 26, 1996, announcing the merger of Apple and NeXT.

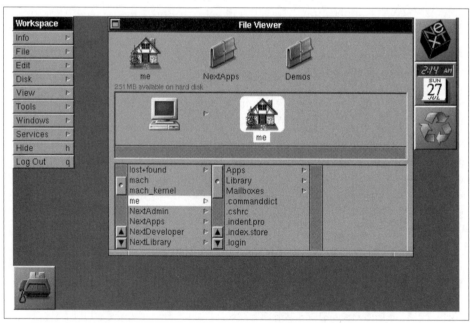

Figure 1-3. The NEXTSTEP desktop

support for real-time applications. Because the kernel is the gatekeeper to hardware and controls each application's view of memory, individual applications can't crash or corrupt the system.

The BSD layer

Derived from FreeBSD, the BSD layer provides the "user visible" part of the Unix layer: the process model, the concept of users, basic security policies, networking, and support for filesystems. This layer allows many Unix applications, such as the Apache web server, to be easily ported and run on Mac OS X.

The NEXTSTEP programming frameworks
Now known as Cocoa, NEXTSTEP defined a rich set of object-oriented APIs, a set of libraries, a runtime, and a development environment for building applications. It provides most of the infrastructure needed to build graphical user applications and to insulate those applications from the internal workings of the core system.

You don't necessarily *have* to ever see this layer if you don't open up the Terminal, but it's there nonetheless, and knowledge of it is *de rigueur* to becoming a power user. Through the course of this book, you're going to get quite familiar with this layer; mastery of the BSD Unix core of Mac OS X is essential to gaining complete mastery of your system.

Rhapsody

At the 1997 World Wide Developer Conference (WWDC), Apple demonstrated an early build of Rhapsody, a version of NEXTSTEP that ran on Macintosh hardware. With NeXT's experience porting the system to multiple hardware architectures, it was easy enough for Apple to get a build up and running on a single Mac model in time for the conference. The development community was invigorated as an ambitious project plan was announced that would supposedly lead to a release in 1998 of a new Mac OS for the PowerPC and Intel platforms.

As part of the project plan, three major components were announced: the Yellow Box, which would run OpenStep-based applications on top of Rhapsody; the Blue Box, which would run a future version of the classic Mac OS as a Rhapsody process; and the Red Box, which would allow OpenStep applications to run on top of Windows with a simple recompile.

Rhapsody brought the integration of the following technologies into the current Mac OS X:

Classic
With the outgrowth of the Blue Box, Classic allows older Mac applications to run unmodified under the new operating system. Essentially an operating system running within a process, it doesn't confer all the advantages of a protected-memory preemptive system to the applications running within it. If an application crashes inside Classic, it can corrupt any other applications also running in Classic. However, Classic allows the old and new operating systems to run at once with the same screen, mouse, and a modicum of cross-platform application utility. It's not a perfect solution, but it allows users to continue using their older Mac OS applications as they migrate to the new system.

Java™

> From the beginning, the Rhapsody team made it a priority to implement good Java support on the platform. This support would allow Java applications and applets to run and operate without modification. As well, a layer of functionality—known as the *Java Bridge*—was implemented, allowing Java and Objective-C to work together. With this functionality, Cocoa applications can be built using Java.

Several problems arose that would keep Rhapsody from ever seeing the light of day as a consumer system. The first problem was getting Rhapsody to run on Apple's entire product line. Each model of Macintosh was very different from other models, and clever engineering hacks had been put into place over time in earlier versions of the Mac OS so it would run on all Macs at the time (including PowerPC- and 680x0-based Macs). This variation of hardware made it harder to port the Mac OS, as each new Mac model required its own port of the OS. This led to the reduction in the number of older Macs that would support the new OS as well as to the introduction of many changes to the hardware platform to ease the marriage of software and hardware.

The second major problem to face Rhapsody was the lack of commitment by the major Mac software vendors, such as Adobe and Microsoft, to rewrite their products using the Objective-C language and the frameworks derived from OpenStep. Without a complete rewrite, their applications were doomed to live as second-class citizens in the new OS by running in the Blue Box (that is, Classic mode). It became clear to Apple that without the support of the major software vendors shipping first-class applications, the new OS would not succeed. Apple rethought its strategy and decided to postpone the new OS as a consumer system. This delay gave Apple more time to make its next-generation OS run on more hardware as well as to develop a compatibility layer that would make it easier for older Mac software to be ported to run on the new system. This layer, called Carbon, was introduced at WWDC 1998 along with the rest of the plan for Mac OS X development after Rhapsody.

Even though Rhapsody wasn't widely released, it wasn't a failure. It represented an important phase of the transition of the old NeXT-based operating system into something that could be the next generation of the Mac OS. Without Rhapsody, all that followed could not have happened. In fact, the major distinction between Rhapsody and Mac OS X is the name change and the integration of Carbon.

Continued Development of the Classic Mac OS

After Apple bought NeXT, not all its development efforts were spent creating Rhapsody and eventually Mac OS X. While development proceeded with the new operating system, several releases of the classic Mac OS bridged the gap between System 7 and Mac OS X.

Rhapsody, Mac OS X, and Intel

Over the years, it had been rumored that there would be an official Mac OS X release for Intel x86 hardware. These rumors started from the day Apple purchased NeXT and were well founded, as NEXTSTEP had run on x86 hardware. They were further fueled by Apple's early confusion about what it was going to do with the raft of technologies acquired from NeXT. And all the talk about boxes—Red, Yellow, and Blue—didn't help matters.

While Apple maintains Darwin (the underlying Unix layer of Mac OS X) to run on x86 processors, there were continued rumors that Apple was secretly working on a version of Mac OS X to run on Intel-based hardware. This project, reportedly codenamed *Marklar* (after the aliens in the *South Park* cartoons), was supposedly being developed somewhere deep inside Apple's Cupertino labs.

On June 6, 2005, these rumors became reality. On stage at Apple's World Wide Developer Conference in San Francisco, Steve Jobs announced that Apple would be transitioning to the Intel platform. Joking about Mac OS X's "secret double life," Jobs revealed that all versions of Mac OS X since its inception had been built and tested on both PowerPC and Intel processors. He also set out a timeline for moving all of Apple's Mac offerings to Intel processors by the end of 2007.

Mac OS 8, which made its appearance on July 22, 1997, was the first of these releases. Hailed at the time as the "Most significant Macintosh operating system since 1984," it brought a new platinum-based look and feel to the desktop (based on the look and feel from Copland), complete with spring-loaded folders that popped up when a file was dragged onto them, and contextual menus activated by holding down the Control key while clicking an icon. Mac OS 8 also made it easier for users to connect to the Internet with an Internet Set Up Assistant and bundled Netscape Navigator and Microsoft Internet Explorer. Finally, Mac OS 8 marked the introduction of the Macintosh Runtime for Java, allowing applications written in Java to run on the Mac.

More important to the migration to Mac OS X, Apple was busy making the modifications required so it would run well both as its own operating system and in Mac OS X's Classic mode. In addition, a lot of work went into the Carbon library so developers could start writing applications that would run on both the old and new systems. This turned out to be a protracted exercise in identifying the system calls that developers were using and resulted in the releases of several versions of the Carbon libraries for the classic Mac OS.

After several releases of Mac OS 8 (8.5, 8.5.1, and 8.6), development of the original Mac OS moved into its final phase with the release of Mac OS 9 on October 23, 1999. This release introduced an updated desktop look and feel, as shown in Figure 1-4; the Keychain application, which allows all of your passwords to be held in one place; automatic software updating over the Internet; and the Network Browser, which allows easy browsing of the servers and computers connected to the local area network. This release came with an updated Carbon library for developers to write against and many more changes to the core of the OS to enable it to run under Mac OS X as Classic. Mac OS 9 also sported many performance enhancements; after all, for a considerable amount of time, it was still the OS that shipped by default on every new Mac.

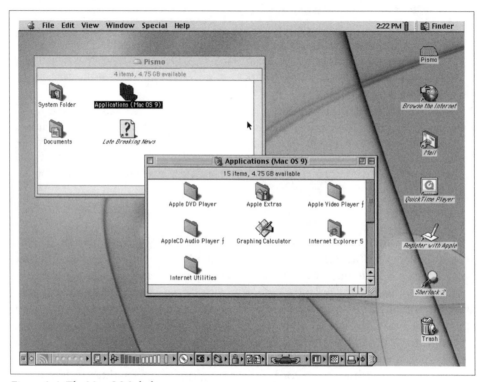

Figure 1-4. The Mac OS 9 desktop

 Development of Mac OS 9 wrapped up with the release of Version 9.2.2 on December 5, 2001. This version ships as Classic in every new Macintosh. At WWDC 2002, Steve Jobs read a eulogy to Mac OS 9, dramatizing the message with a fog-shrouded coffin.

The Introduction of the iApps

October 1999 didn't just bring Mac OS 9, it also produced iMovie, the first of the so-called iApps. Using the Mac's built-in FireWire port, iMovie was the first product of its kind to allow home users to connect a handheld camcorder to a Mac and edit and produce their own movies. Following the success of iMovie, Apple moved forward in

January 2001 with its iApps strategy. iMovie was soon followed by iTunes, for managing digital music, and iDVD for taking the movies created in iMovie and creating DVDs that could be used on any home DVD player.

The release of these three applications marks a turning point for Apple. Not only was the Mac OS being conceived of as an operating system that would help sell Macs, it was also being conceived of as the center of a larger strategy whereby the Mac would enable the so-called Digital Hub. Instead of just being a provider of hardware and the operating system that ran on it, Apple positioned itself as a provider of solutions that pulled together the various digital devices that you might have and made them more useful.

Mac OS X 10.0

Apple shipped Mac OS X Public Beta in September 2000. More than 100,000 people bought the beta, and Apple reported that there were more than 75,000 feedback submissions. Not only did the Public Beta serve to indicate that Apple was going to ship Mac OS X, it helped Apple identify the issues that users needed to have addressed in order to replace the original Mac OS.

After four years in development, the first full release of Mac OS X, known to the engineers who worked on it as *Cheetah* and to the public as Version 10.0, finally shipped on March 24, 2001—17 years and 3 months after the introduction of the original Macintosh. People gathered at stores everywhere to welcome its introduction. The fusion of Mac OS and Unix was complete, and Apple finally had the next-generation operating system that it wanted.

This release brought the following features:

Carbon
> A subset of the original Mac OS Toolbox APIs that could be safely transitioned from the old Mac OS to the new one, Carbon was the lifeline for older Mac OS applications, allowing them to be ported to the new system. This meant that applications essential for attracting users to the new system, such as Microsoft Office and Adobe Photoshop, could be ported to Mac OS X and take advantage of preemptive multitasking and protected memory.

Quartz 2D
> The powerful imaging layer of Mac OS X, Quartz 2D handles all the drawing on the system and delivers a rich imaging model based on PDF (replacing the Display PostScript used by NEXTSTEP), on-the-fly rendering, and anti-aliasing—all managed by ColorSync to ensure graphics look their best.

Quartz Compositor
> The windowing system for the OS and provider of low-level services such as event handling and cursor management, the Quartz Compositor is based on a

"videomixer" model where every pixel on the screen can be shared among windows in real time. This model allows for smooth transitions between the states of a GUI; one of the traits of the Aqua experience.

Aqua

More than a color, and more than something that brings to mind the properties of water, Aqua is an attitude. When Apple set out to design the interface for Mac OS X, it wanted to take all the good parts of the previous Macintosh and mix them with new features made possible by modern computer hardware.

Aqua brings the user interface to life with depth, transparency, translucence, and motion. Aqua also recognizes that it is managing a thoroughly multitasking machine. Instead of popping up dialog boxes in the middle of the screen, Aqua provides sheets that are attached to the window that they pertain to, allowing other tasks to be performed without hindrance and clearly communicating function to the user.

The Aqua interface is pictured in Figure 1-5.

Figure 1-5. The Mac OS X 10.0 desktop and the Aqua user interface

Mail

An easy-to-use mail client, Mail was (and is) compatible with Internet-standard mail servers that use the SMTP, IMAP, and POP protocols, and it shipped with a built-in configuration to seamlessly access iTools-based Mac.com mail.

iTunes and iMovie

Critical to Apple's Digital Hub strategy, the first release of Mac OS X also included ports of the iTunes and iMovie applications, which first appeared on Mac OS 9.

Impressive as it was, by all measures, the first release of Mac OS X was not quite ready for most of the Mac faithful. It lacked DVD playback, and the major applications like Adobe Photoshop and Microsoft Office weren't released yet. Still, it was more than usable for the Unix geeks, who were among the early adopters. Many improvements were to come, but Mac OS X's first consumer release signaled that it would not be another failure like Copland.

Darwin and Open Source

As Mac OS X was developed, Apple made sure the open source foundations of Mac OS X remained open by starting up the Darwin project. Darwin is essentially the non-GUI part of Mac OS X and is a complete operating system in itself. If you are interested in running Darwin separately, you can download it for free from Apple's Darwin site (*http://developer.apple.com/darwin/*) and have a full working operating system. It won't have the Mac OS X Aqua desktop, but you can use Darwin just like you would Linux, from the command line and using the X11 window manager.

The main tree of Darwin is kept under pretty careful control; after all, Apple builds the base to an operating system that it distributes to millions of people from this tree. To provide a place for experimentation, Apple and the Internet Software Consortium run the OpenDarwin project. You can find the OpenDarwin site at *http://www.opendarwin.org/*.

Developer Tools

When Apple released Mac OS X, they made a great decision by also deciding to provide development tools to every Mac user for free, including the Project Builder IDE and the Interface Builder GUI layout application. These aren't just simplified tools to learn development with; they are the same tools that Apple uses to develop the operating system itself as well as its various applications. These tools allow development of Carbon- and Cocoa-based applications, system libraries, BSD command-line utilities, hardware device drivers, and even kernel extensions (known as KEXTs).

The developer tools aren't installed by default, because Apple doesn't think most users will want them and would probably want the almost 500 MB of disk space for something else. But developers, as well as power users who want to compile programs available in source code form on the Internet, can easily find them and install them from a variety of sources. And, since they are free, any user who wants to try developing software can do so purely by investing the time it takes to learn.

Command-Line Access

It is difficult to say what kind of success Mac OS X would enjoy without having access to the command line. According to legend, as Rhapsody developed into Mac OS X, there were many within Apple who didn't want to ship the Terminal command-line tool—or at the very least, wanted it installed only as part of the developer tools. After all, the command line was seen as the antithesis of the Mac experience. However, those who wanted the command line to be present prevailed, and the Terminal shipped in the */Applications/Utilities* directory.

This was a fortunate move indeed, as a large percentage of the early adopters of Mac OS X were not traditional Mac OS users, but switchers from Linux and other flavors of Unix, including Solaris and FreeBSD. Without access to the command line, these users—a market to which many at Apple in 2000 probably didn't expect to sell—would never have moved to the platform.

Mac OS X 10.1

The next release of Mac OS X, Version 10.1 (known to Apple engineers as *Puma*), was released in September 2001, just six months after the initial release of the system. With Puma, Apple focused on performance and ensuring that the critical Carbon layer was robust enough for Microsoft Office and Adobe Photoshop to be released. Puma, along with the large influx of applications that came with it, made it clear that Mac OS X was going to be a success and that the strategy for migrating from the old Classic Mac OS to the new OS was going to work.

The quick release cycle of Puma also indicated that Apple was moving rapidly to improve the OS in ways that were meaningful for both Classic Mac OS users as well as those switching from other platforms such as Windows. As a maintenance release, it was released as a no-charge upgrade—the only version of Mac OS X to date that didn't have a price tag associated with it.

With Puma came the release of the last of the original iApps to make the jump from OS 9: iDVD. Apple's Digital Hub strategy was now fully on Mac OS X, signaling that Apple's application development efforts were now entirely focused on Mac OS X. Apple further strengthened the iApps strategy in January 2002 with the release of iPhoto for managing digital photos, and continued in July 2002 with the release of iTunes 3 as an update to the popular music jukebox application.

Also revealed in July at Macworld New York was .Mac (pronounced "dot-Mac"), a suite of Internet services, including those that used to be part of the older iTools service, and software. The new pay service included the McAfee Virex virus scanner and the new Backup software for making safe backups of critical data to .Mac.

Mac OS X 10.2 Jaguar

The next release took Mac OS X to the next level. Unlike previous versions of Mac OS, Apple decided to put the codename, *Jaguar*, into the name of the product itself. On the box and at its web site, it is known as Mac OS X Jaguar. It is also the first release of Mac OS X to come as the default boot OS on every system Apple sold, marking an important step in the transition between the classic Mac OS and Mac OS X. The Jaguar desktop is shown in Figure 1-6.

Jaguar introduced the following features:

Quartz Extreme
> Building on the already powerful Quartz Compositor, Quartz Extreme performs most of its work in OpenGL, allowing it to take advantage of the enormous potential of modern graphics processors, and offloading the tasks from the computer's CPU. With Quartz Extreme, all applications on the system have easy access to 3D capabilities, and this paves the way for later user interface improvements.

Address Book
> Previous versions of Mac OS X had a rudimentary contact database. Jaguar introduced a new system-wide contact database, along with a management application, called simply the Address Book. With its simple and elegant API, the Address Book can be incorporated into any application, and all the built-in applications on Jaguar, such as Mail and iChat, support it.

Rendezvous
> Built on the work of the IETF Zero Configuration (Zeroconf) effort, Rendezvous enables machines to discover each other without user intervention. This lets you share services with ease between machines on the same network and allows you to seamlessly connect to machines by setting up a local network and just hooking up cables or setting up an ad hoc wireless network. You can find out more about Zeroconf at *http://www.zeroconf.org*. Due to a trademark dispute, Rendezvous was renamed Bonjour with the release of Mac Os X Tiger.

iChat
> Another in Apple's series of iApps, iChat is an elegant AOL Instant Messenger (AIM)–compatible application that leverages the strength of Rendezvous to allow chats between users on the local network. This is handy for ad hoc networks such as those at conferences and other events.

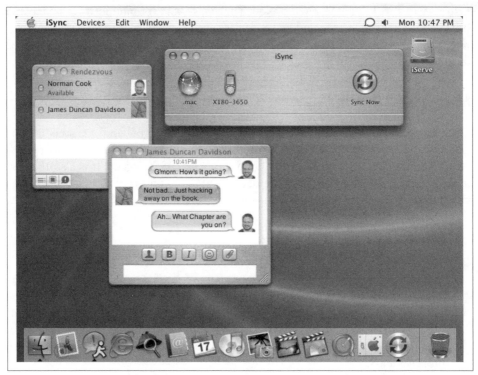

Figure 1-6. The Jaguar desktop with iChat and iSync

Windows-compatible networking

> Leveraging the capabilities of Samba, an open source software package for working with the Windows SMB file-sharing protocol, Jaguar can share its filesystems with Windows clients as well as mount Windows-based filesystems. Jaguar also introduced the capability to integrate with Windows Active Directory to ease the migration of Macs into Windows-dominated networks.

Even though Jaguar shipped with enough features to make most people happy, Apple didn't stop there. After Jaguar was released, Apple released the following products for it:

iCal

> This personal calendaring application handles multiple calendars and enables sharing of those calendars via the Internet. Calendars can be published either through .Mac or to any server that supports the WebDAV protocol.

iSync

> A tool for synchronizing the address book and calendars on a Mac to mobile phones, PDAs, and the iPod. iSync allows information to be kept on multiple machines by synchronizing data against the .Mac service.

iLife

iLife is a bundle of new versions of iPhoto 2, iMovie 3, and iDVD 2, along with already available iTunes 3, as a shrink-wrapped, boxed product available for sale in stores. Even though iLife has a cost associated with it, iPhoto, iMovie, and iTunes remain free downloads. Only iDVD is available exclusively through iLife.

Safari

A brand new browser with a highly tuned rendering engine, Safari replaces Microsoft's Internet Explorer as the browser of choice on Mac OS X. This browser fulfilled a real need as evidenced by the fact that there were 500,000 downloads of the public beta between January 7 and 9, 2003.

Mac OS X Panther

Panther, the name given to Mac OS X 10.3, brought another host of improvements to the system and continued in the Mac OS X tradition of "It's getting better all the time." A few of the improvements made to the system were:

A new Finder

The Finder that shipped with Mac OS X 10.0 through 10.2 was a simplified interpretation of the classic Finder from the original Mac OS that was designed to work on a single-user system. On the multiuser Mac OS X, this meant the files that typical users cared about—those in their Home directories—were located three levels away from the filesystem root.

The Finder in Panther, shown in Figure 1-7, introduced a new Sidebar on the left side of every Finder window that gives you quick access to the various disks attached to your computer, your Home directory, and any other locations that you put there. When you select a disk or a folder from the Sidebar, it becomes the start of what you see in the window view. And, changing a paradigm in place since 1984, Panther's Finder made it so that removable disks can be ejected or disconnected by clicking on an eject icon in the Sidebar, rather than having to drag disks to the Trash.

Exposé

Building on the power of Quartz Extreme, Exposé introduced a new way to work with the dozens of windows that are open on the typical Mac OS X user's desktop. Instead of having to dig through the open windows one by one, you can use either a keystroke or a mouse gesture and perform one of three actions:

* Show all the windows open in miniature so you can see all of them at once.
* Show all the windows belonging to a particular application.
* Clear all the windows off the screen so you can see the desktop.

These actions can be set to a variety of keystrokes and mouse gestures by using the Exposé preference panel in System Preferences.

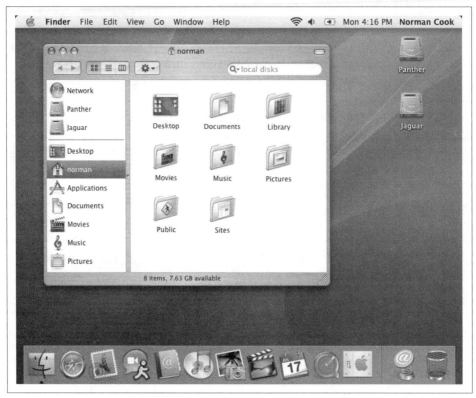

Figure 1-7. Panther's desktop and Finder

Fast user switching

Built on Unix, Mac OS X has always supported multiple users and allows there to be multiple users logged in at once via the command line. Panther took a cue from Windows XP and introduced the capability for multiple users to be logged into the GUI at the same time. When you change users, the new desktop rotates into place, giving a very clear indication that you are entering into another user's desktop; an example of the many ways in which the graphics abilities given to the system by Quartz Extreme have been put to use.

Fast application switching

You can quickly switch between applications using the ⌘-Tab keystroke. This feature was present in previous versions of Mac OS X, but in Panther, it was changed to be similar to the way it is done in Windows, featuring an elegant transparent window that appears onscreen to allow you to see what application you are switching to.

Security

Panther introduced a host of security features designed to make data safe. The FileVault feature can encrypt the contents of your Home directory so even if somebody gets physical access to your disk, the contents of your files aren't exposed. When it's time to empty your Trash, you can choose to overwrite the deleted files with random data so the old files cannot be recovered.

In addition, all the GUI applications included with Panther, and most of the command-line ones, were aware of the Kerberos security services that Panther made available. Kerberos is a cryptographic secure network authentication protocol that enables single sign-on. After entering your password when you log in, all of your network applications, such as Mail, can automatically log into Kerberos-enabled servers.

Font Book

Panther's Font Book application built advanced font management into Mac OS X. Instead of managing fonts via the filesystem, Font Book lets you activate and deactivate fonts on the fly, organize them into collections, and preview fonts. It also allows you to take advantage of ligatures, kerning, and many other font features.

iDisk synchronization

Building on the .Mac online service, Panther made iDisk a permanent fixture in the Finder. Starting with Panther, you can opt to have your iDisk synchronized with your computer. This allows you to work transparently with the same files on multiple machines whether or not you are online at the time you want to work with them. The only catch is that you have to dedicate as much space on your local hard drive as you have on your iDisk, which with a basic .Mac account is 250 MB.

Xcode Tools

As part of Panther, Apple revamped the developer tools, replacing Project Builder with a new IDE called Xcode and dubbing the entire toolset Xcode Tools. Including the Xcode IDE, Interface Builder, *gcc* 3.3, updated documentation, and performance tools. Xcode provides everything you need to develop applications on, and for, Mac OS X.

Mac OS X Tiger

Released on April 29, 2005, the latest installment of Apple's next-generation operating system is Mac OS X Tiger. Mac OS X 10.4 boasts more than 200 new features and improvements over Panther, though a lot of them have been made under the hood. In many ways, Tiger is perhaps the most important release for developers since Mac OS X 10.0. It includes several great new technologies that developers will put to use in their applications in the coming years. However, end users shouldn't feel left out, as Tiger has plenty to offer you as well (Figure 1-8).

Installing the Xcode Tools

You can quickly check to see if you have Xcode Tools installed by seeing if you have a */Developer* folder on your hard drive. If so, you are ready to go. If not, you'll need to install the tools either from the Xcode Tools CD that came with your copy of Mac OS X or from a disk image that you can download from the Apple Developer Connection (ADC) web site. If you bought your Mac with Mac OS X installed on it, you'll find the Xcode Tools disk image on your hard drive.

A special note: Apple provides regular updates (two to three times a year) to the Xcode Tools through the ADC web site. These releases introduce new features, fix bugs, and improve the available documentation. If you don't want to download the rather large files, Apple will send you a copy on CD for a nominal charge. Log into the ADC Member web site and go to the Purchase section.

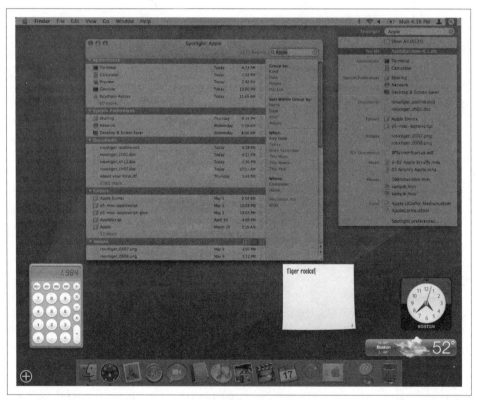

Figure 1-8. The Tiger desktop showing Dashboard and Spotlight

While it would be impractical to describe all of the benefits that Tiger brings to the table, here are some of the more noteworthy technologies Apple has introduced:

Spotlight

Perhaps the most touted feature of Tiger, Spotlight is a mix of several tools that bring powerful searching to the desktop. When first introducing Spotlight, Steve Jobs joked that it's easier to find information on the Internet than it is to find it on your own computer. By creating a system-wide index of a user's files and metadata, Spotlight empowers fast, convenient searches of all the data on your computer. By opening up that index to software developers, Apple has paved the way for future applications to harness this powerful technology. Spotlight has already been used to improve several of Mac OS X's bundled applications, such as the Smart Folders found in the Finder and Mail.

Automator

Though AppleScript and, in recent years, shell scripting provide for the automation of many tasks on your Mac, they can be quite intimidating to new users. With Tiger, Apple has created a new application—simply dubbed Automator— that significantly lowers the learning curve. Automator allows you to create *workflows* that can quickly perform a variety of tasks, all without having to learn tricky syntaxes and arcane commands. By dragging and dropping actions provided by applications installed on your system, you can easily create workflows that do everything from creating birthday emails to organizing your pictures and music.

Dashboard

Another feature in Tiger that's sure to become popular is Dashboard. The Dashboard is a new component, built into Exposé, that provides a workspace for keeping *Widgets*. Widgets are small web applications that are designed to provide users with tidbits of information at a glance. Based around HTML, CSS, and JavaScript, Dashboard Widgets can be developed by web designers for download over the Internet and by application developers for inclusion with their software.

iChat AV

While Apple's AOL Instant Messenger (AIM)–compatible messaging client has had audio and video conferencing features for quite some time, those features have been significantly beefed up in Tiger. iChat AV now supports up to 10 participants in audio chats. Where it really shines, however, is with video conferencing. Tiger's iChat has support for four simultaneous participants in a video chat. At the same time, its video quality has been improved through the use of the new H.264 video codec. In addition to improvement of its audio and video aspects, iChat AV has added support for the Jabber IM protocol.

The hardware requirements for using iChat AV with multiple participants may exclude some Mac users from taking advantage of video
and audio conferencing, especially if they intend to host. While one-
to-one video conferences can still be accomplished on 600MHz G3s
and newer processors, hosting a four-person video conference requires
at least Dual 1GHz G4. For more information on iChat AV's requirements, see *http://www.apple.com/macosx/features/ichat/*.

.Mac synchronization

Synchronization of your contacts, bookmarks, and calendars has been a core feature of iSync since its introduction. In Tiger, however, Apple has moved the .Mac
synchronization services out of iSync and into a system library. By using this
library, developers can synchronize their software's settings between multiple
Macs over the .Mac service. Tiger's Mail and Keychain Access have both made use
of the .Mac SyncServices, allowing .Mac users to sync their Keychains as well as
mail accounts, signatures, and rules.

What Does the Future Hold?

It's been more than four years since Apple unleashed Mac OS X upon the masses. In
that time, the operating system has developed rapidly and fruitfully. Each release has
brought increases in speed, refinements, and powerful new technologies. At the same
time, the success of the iPod and iTunes and the failures of Microsoft have put Apple
and its colorful OS in the limelight. Mac OS X is poised to continue raising the bar as
more and more people are exposed to Tiger.

It will take some time for developers to harness all of Tiger's power and release the next
generation of applications to amaze us. However, few outside Apple's headquarters in
Cupertino know how the next generation of Mac OS X itself will evolve. While it's
likely we'll see improvements to the new technologies introduced in Tiger and continued refinement of the OS and its applications, my crystal ball doesn't offer many peeks
at the groundbreaking features Mac OS X Leopard (Version 10.5) is sure to bring.

With the introduction of Apple's transition to the Intel processor, one of the features slated to make an appearance in Leopard is Rosetta. Rosetta is an emulator that
allows software compiled for the PowerPC processor to run on Intel Macs without
requiring a recompile. While not every application will be compatible with Rosetta,
it is certainly a useful shim for those developers who won't be able to port all of their
code to Intel-based Mac OS X in time for its launch.

One thing's for sure, when WWDC 2006 comes around, all eyes will be on Apple as
it prepares the OS that will compete with Microsoft's Windows Vista (formerly
known by its codename, Longhorn) in late 2006 or early 2007. Now that we've taken
a look at the Mac OS of our past and glimpsed at its future, let's focus on the Mac
OS of today: Tiger!

## CHAPTER 2

Installing the System and Software

If Tiger came preinstalled on your Mac, congratulations. You can probably skip about half of this chapter and move onto the section that covers software installation. However, if you're upgrading from Panther or another version of Mac OS X, or if you've come to a point where you want to (or need to!) reinstall Tiger on your Mac, then these first few sections are for you.

This chapter provides you with the details you need to successfully install Mac OS X Tiger on your Mac. It also has information on how to install other software on your Mac, including ways to install Unix applications.

Preparing to Install Tiger

While Apple's installer for Mac OS X is pretty straightforward, there are some things you need to think about (quite seriously) before you gut your system and install Tiger. If you have a new Mac that's fresh out of the box, your slate's pretty clean. However, if you have a Mac that you've been using for some time, you need to think about backing up your existing system, and more important, how you want to reconfigure your system for running Mac OS X in the future.

Backing Up Your Life

When you back up your computer, you're not just backing up raw bits of data; you're backing up your life. Why do I put it that way? Well, think about what's on your computer. Email, bookmarks to your favorite web sites, contacts in your Address Book, your music, pictures, documents, and projects you're working on, and most important, passwords stored in your Keychains file that you use to access everything. If you don't have a regular backup ritual, you should really think good and hard about implementing something now. Not tomorrow or next week. Now. You never know when your Mac is suddenly going to get hit with stray solar radiation and go all wacky like Screwball Squirrel in a Tex Avery cartoon (and that's pretty darn wacky).

Where to back up

If you have a .Mac account, you can backup up to 1 GB of data to your iDisk, but this depends on how much storage space you allocate for email usage as well. If needed, you can expand your online storage to 2 GB (for an extra $50 per year), but at that price, you may as well go out and buy an external FireWire drive. Plus, FireWire drives are much faster than uploading all of that data over most Internet connections.

FireWire drives are relatively inexpensive, but do your homework before you run out to pick something up. Things to look for in a drive include:

Size
> Because the need for space is insatiable, you should always get the largest drive you can afford.

Portability
> Think hard on this one. Do you want or need to take your FireWire drive around with you? Or is a larger drive that sits on your desk but that doesn't fit in your backpack okay? If you want a portable drive, make sure to get a drive that doesn't require an external power source (usually called "bus-powered").

Speed
> For a portable drive, you'll have to settle for a slower disk. If, however, you've opted to get a bigger desktop-sized drive, be sure to get something nice and fast. 5400 rpm is okay, 7200 rpm is much better. When you're storing as much data as modern drives can hold, you'll want to be able to get to it right away. The faster, the better.

Backup software and other utilities
> Some FireWire drives come with tools that you can use for backing up data from your Mac to the drive. Frankly, buy a drive for the drive and not for any packaged extras it might come with.

Take the time to read the reviews of various drives, their specs, and any software that might come with them before you make your final decision. The best advice when it comes to buying a backup drive is: don't be cheap. Remember, this is your life you're backing up. Don't end up with a cheap FireWire drive that you'll regret purchasing.

What to back up

Okay, so now that it's pretty clear that you need to pay attention to what you're backing up your data to, it's time to look at what you should really back up before you install Tiger.

You don't need to worry about backing up the System folder and all the Unix utilities that came with Mac OS X. The Tiger installer will take care of making sure that stuff ends up in the right place. Just focus on what's most important to you: stuff in your Home folder, any shell scripts or AppleScripts you may have written, configuration files, and application preferences.

If you have a .Mac account, you should consider using it for part of your backup needs. Considering that the .Mac sync services store the contacts in your Address Book, calendar and to-do items from iCal, bookmarks from Safari, your Keychains, Mail settings, etc., you can save a lot of time. As a matter of fact, you can configure your .Mac syncing to back up (that is, sync) your data to the .Mac servers hourly if need be. Also, with Mac OS X Tiger, the libraries that are used for syncing data through .Mac have been made available to developers, so expect to be able to back up more and more data in this manner in the future.

Here is a list of things you should seriously consider backing up before you thrash your system:

- Application data (*~/Library/Application Support*)
- Safari bookmarks (*~/Library/Safari/Bookmarks.plist*)
- Preferences (*~/Library/Preferences*)
- Keychains (*~/Library/Keychains*)
- Email, message sorting settings, and junk mail database rules from Mail.app (*~/Library/Mail*)
- Stickies (*~/Library/StickiesDatabase*)
- Fonts you've added to the system, either in your local domain (*~/Library/Fonts*) or for global use on your system (*/Library/Fonts*)
- Any shell scripts you have created
- Any AppleScripts you have created
- Any databases you run and access frequently, including FileMaker Pro and MySQL databases

In addition to these specific items, you'll want to look for anything stored in these folders in your Home folder:

- Documents (files you've created and saved locally)
- Movies (movies you've saved or created with iMovie, Final Cut Express, or Final Cut Pro)
- Music (music stored in iTunes)
- Pictures (pictures stored in iPhoto)
- Sites (any local web site you've created and are serving from your Mac)
- Files saved to your desktop

Also, you'll want to make sure that you have the following information somewhere safe:

- QuickTime Pro's registration number (you can find this by going into the QuickTime preference panel)
- The registration codes for all your software as well as your install media (or the URLs you need to use to download applications from the Internet)

Again, this is just a rough list. You should use this as a guide, and then look good and hard at all the data stored on your Mac before you back it up. Once you've started installing Mac OS X on your Mac, even if you use one of the archive and install options that you can select, you should assume that there's no going back to recover the data. Make sure you have a good, solid backup before you pop in the Tiger install DVD and restart with the C key held down.

Tips for Upgrading

In addition to making sure you have a good backup of your data, if you're upgrading from a previous version of Mac OS, you'll want to check on a few other things. First, make sure your system meets the Tiger hardware requirements:

- PowerPC G3, G4, or G5 processor
- Built-in FireWire
- At least 256 MB of memory
- A built-in display or one that is connected to an Adle-supplied video card
- A DVD drive

 If your Mac doesn't have a DVD drive, you can order CD media from Apple by filling in and mailing out the form available at *http://images. apple.com/macosx/pdf/tigermediaexchangev3.pdf.*

Next, you'll want to be sure you have enough free disk space on your system. Mac OS X Tiger requires 3 GB of disk space, plus another gigabyte if you plan on installing the Xcode Tools. Sometimes an installer will use up a bit more space as it writes temp files and moves data around. This is particularly true if you're planning on doing an archive and install. To be safe, you might want about 5 GB of free space, just in case.

Once you're sure your machine meets the hardware and disk space requirements, it's a good idea to run some diagnostics on your existing OS install to help ensure that any existing problems are not propagated onto your new install. A good start is to boot from the Tiger install DVD and use Disk Utility (it's available from within the Tiger installer at Utilities → Disk Utility) to verify the disk's integrity and its permissions.

It also wouldn't hurt to take a little bit more time and run the hardware diagnostic disc that came with your Mac. If you've purchased AppleCare, you could use the TechTool disc as well. It's imperative that your machine is in healthy condition before you upgrade to Tiger, and every extra little step you take now can help prevent headaches down the road.

Installing Tiger

Assuming that you've taken the time to back up your data and check it to make sure that everything you need is there, it's now time to think about installing Tiger on your Mac. The important word there is "think"; there's nothing wrong with a default Mac OS X installation, it's just that you should really think about how you're going to use your Mac.

- Are you going to run Classic? If so, you should consider setting up a separate partition in which to install Mac OS 9.

- Are you going to run more than one version of Mac OS X on your Mac for testing purposes? If so, you'll need separate partitions for them, too.

- Are you running an application that can benefit from a scratch disk, such as Final Cut Pro or Photoshop? Consider setting aside part of your hard drive as a partition just for that purpose. It won't be as good as a dedicated separate drive, but it's better than nothing.

The next thing you'll need to decide is how you will install Tiger: clean, archive, or (if applicable) upgrade?

- A clean install is recommended, since it wipes your drive and checks it for errors (and attempts to fix said errors) before installing the operating system.

- If you opt to archive and install, all the data in the */Users* directory will be archived and retained in a buffer during the install, then dropped back into the */Users* directory once the installation has completed. Then it's up to you to go back and pull what you want out of the archive and trash the rest.

- The upgrade option upgrades your existing Mac OS X installation, removing unneeded files, installing new ones, and overwriting old versions with the latest and greatest. This option has the most chance of sullying your new install with problems from your current one.

The archive and install option works well in many cases. However, many people are paranoid enough about software, and how various versions of software interact with each other, that they always go for the clean install.

Partitioning Your Hard Drive

If you're planning to partition your hard drive into more than one big partition, you should jot down how big you want those partitions to be. Keep in mind that the largest partition should be used for the system you boot into most. Also keep in mind that re-partitioning your drive erases all the data on it, so be extra sure that you have a good backup and realize that you'll be forced to clean install (which isn't necessarily a bad thing).

As an example, say you have a 80 GB drive and you want to have separate partitions for your primary Tiger installation, a test Mac OS X installation (for playing with other versions of the system—something that happens all too often in the *Running Mac OS X* labs), Classic, and a scratch disk for Photoshop. If you aren't going to be using the test installation and Classic for much more than testing, you can get away with devoting a bare minimum of space on this partition. Classic will fit in under 2 GB, and 3 GB will do in a pinch for a Mac OS X installation. You'll also want to size your scratch disk appropriately; for Photoshop work, 2 GB is usually sufficient unless you are working with poster-sized images. So, for this example, the partition scheme for an 80 GB drive might look like that shown in Table 2-1.

Table 2-1. A sample partition scheme

Partition	Size	Use
1	73	Primary OS installation (Mac OS X Tiger)
2	3	Test Mac OS X installation
3	2	Classic
4	2	Scratch disk

Once you have decided that you need to partition your drive, you'll need to do it before or during the installation process. You can't wait until after you finish and repartition your drive without losing the data on your drives and having to start all over.

To partition your drive during the installation process, follow these steps:

1. Insert the Tiger install DVD and reboot your Mac, holding down the C key as it starts up.
2. From the menu bar, select Utilities → Disk Utility; this launches the Disk Utility program from the installation disc.
3. In the left pane, select the hard drive you want to partition.
4. Click the Partition tab button to the right to examine the partitioning scheme for the hard drive.

5. In the Volume Scheme section, the pop-up menu should probably be set to Current. From this, select the number of partitions you want to create on your hard drive. You can have up to 16 partitions on a single drive.

6. Set up your partitions by either grabbing the slider bar between the partitions in the Volume Scheme side or in the Volume Information section to the right.

7. In the Volume Information section, make sure you install the Mac OS 9 drivers if you plan to install Mac OS 9 to run Classic. Depending on how much space you need for Classic, give yourself at least 2 GB of space (and maybe more if you can) for installing Mac OS 9 and the applications you'll need to run in Classic mode. If you think you'll need more space for Mac OS 9, allocate the amount of space the apps require.

8. When you click on a partition in the Volume Scheme section, details about that partition show up in the Volume Information section, including its Name, Format, and Size. For example, when you set up new partitions, the partitions will have a name of Untitled 1, Untitled 2, and so on. If you want to change the name of a partition, click the partition block in the Volume Scheme section and then give the partition a new name by typing something into the Name field (for example, Tiger).

9. For Mac OS X partitions, set the Format to "Mac OS Extended (Journaled)."

10. For Mac OS 9 partitions, set the Format to "Mac OS Extended."

11. When you're done changing the information in the Volume Information section, click the Partition button.

12. A warning sheet pops up, letting you know that by partitioning, you will destroy all the information on the drive. If you're certain that you have a good backup from which to reload your data, click the Partition button on the sheet to split up your drive.

Your hard drive will be erased, and the drive will be reformatted with the number of partitions you selected. You'll know Disk Utility is done when you see the partitions show up in the left side of the window. Now that your drive has successfully been partitioned, quit Disk Utility with ⌘-Q to resume the installation process.

If you'd like to learn more about disks, partitions, and filesystems, take a look at Chapter 9.

Step-by-Step Installation

Okay, so you've backed up your data, you've figured out how you're going to install Tiger (clean, right?), and you've evaluated how you need to slice up your hard drive during the install. Now it's time to roll up your sleeves and get on with the process of installing the latest in Mac OS X goodness on your Mac.

Once you've decided how you want to partition your drive—or even that you want to leave it all as one big partition—the next step is to actually break out the install disc and do the deed. Here's the step-by-step process, including pointers to the places in the installation process where you'll want to make some decisions.

1. With your Mac running, insert the Install DVD in your DVD drive.

2. Restart your computer.

 A faster way to restart your Mac is to hold down the Option key and use the → Restart menu. By holding down the Option key, you're forcing your Mac to restart without it prompting you first.

3. As your Mac is starting up (in other words, when you hear the famous *booonnnnnng!* sound), hold down the C key. This forces your Mac to boot using the Install disc and starts you on your way to installing Tiger on your Mac.

 If you've decided to repartition your drive, here's the point at which you'll want to follow the step-by-step directions from the previous section, "Partitioning Your Hard Drive."

4. After your Mac starts up, you will be welcomed to the Mac OS X Installer. The Installer uses a set of screens to help you configure your system and then the Mac OS X installation. You'll encounter the following screens:

Select Language
The first screen you see asks you to select the primary language you'll use on your Mac. This sets the language defaults for the system, as well as the applications you later install.

Welcome to the Mac OS X Installer
This is just a warm little greeting to let you know that you're on your way to installing Mac OS X; just click the Next button to advance.

Software License Agreement
This is Apple's standard license agreement for Mac OS X. If you have the time, you should read through this before clicking the Continue button, but chances are you could read through (and understand) *Moby Dick* faster. After clicking the Continue button, a sheet will flop out of the window's titlebar asking you to confirm that you've read the license agreement and you agree to be persecuted to the fullest extent of the law should you be found in violation of said agreement. If you agree to be banished to the Land of Misfit Toys, click the Agree button to proceed with the installation process.

Select a Destination

Here, you need to decide where you're going to install Mac OS X. If you haven't yet partitioned your hard drive, now's the time to do that before you select a drive to install Mac OS X on. For more information on how to partition your hard drive, see the section "Partitioning Your Hard Drive" earlier in this chapter.

After selecting the drive or partition on which you're going to install Mac OS X, you will see that the Options button is now clickable. Clicking the Options button gives you, well, the option to choose how you want Mac OS X to be installed on the drive. The three options you have to choose from are:

Upgrade Mac OS X

This allows you to upgrade an earlier version of Mac OS X that exists on the disk to the new version you're installing.

Archive and Install

This option moves all the system files into a folder named Previous System and then installs the new version of Mac OS X. Beneath this option is a checkbox with the label, Preserve Users and Network Settings. If you click this checkbox, all the user data and any network settings will be saved. This is a handy option to use if you don't want to gut the entire system and want to make it (sort of) easier for users to get up and running (sort of) quickly after the install.

Erase and Install

This final option completely erases the hard drive or partition before installing Mac OS X. This is known as a clean install, and is recommended for any type of major release upgrade.

Also on the Options page is a pop-up menu that lets you select the filesystem type for your install. Here you have just two options to select from, and the one to choose is Mac OS Extended (Journaled). Unless you really know what you're doing, do not select Unix File System from this menu.

Easy Install on HardDiskName

This is where the proverbial fork in the road comes in during the install. If you take the right fork, you can go with the default Easy Install; if you take the left fork, you can click the Customize button to pick and choose the items that will be installed.

If you select Easy Install, the standard applications like iCal, iSync, Safari, Mail.app, and all the possible language support packages will be installed on your Mac. The one thing that won't get installed on your Mac with the Easy Install method is Apple's version of X11; if you want that, you'll need to click the Customize button (or install it later).

If you click the Customize button, you'll be taken to another screen that's labeled, "Customize Install on *HardDiskName*." Below that, you'll see a list of the packages that can be installed. Items that have a checkmark in their box will be installed as part of the Easy Install. These items include:

- Essential System Software (this item is grayed out and cannot be unchecked)
- Printer Drivers
- Additional Fonts
- Language Translations
- X11 (unchecked by default)

 If you didn't opt to install X11 from the Customize install screen, you can always install it later by inserting the Install DVD in your Mac and double-clicking the Optional Installs package. Within the Installer is an option for X11 that you must enable (it's found under the Applications listing).

Things you can uncheck include:

Language translations
> The language you've selected at the beginning of the installation process will be installed by default, but why install Dutch, Japanese, and French (to name a few) if you don't need them? By deselecting this item, you will free up 695 MB of hard drive space for other things.

Printer drivers you won't need
> If you have only one brand of printer attached to your Mac, there really isn't a need to install the other brands. However, if you are installing on a laptop, you might want to keep all the drivers so that you can print to any random printer you might come across in your travels.

5. When you've finished selecting the items you want to install, click the Install button to begin the installation process. A progress bar appears with messages telling you what's being installed. When prompted, quit the installation and click the Restart button to boot into your Tiger system.

Configuring the System

Once you've made it through the Install phase of Tiger, your Mac will restart and you'll be presented with a series of setup screens to help you configure your Mac at a very basic level. You'll set up the first user account, configure network settings, and more.

The following list describes the configuration screens you'll encounter:

Welcome

Based on information you provided on the Select Language screen during installation, this screen asks you to select the region or country you live in. For example, if you selected English as your language, you will be asked to choose one of the following: United States, Canada, Australia, Ireland, or the United Kingdom. There is also a checkbox on this page to reveal other countries from which you can select.

Migration Assistant

A new feature that started shipping on all new Macs a while back is now included with Tiger. The Migration Assistant makes it easy to move data from an old Mac to a new one. Or, if you're installing Tiger on its own partition and keeping your old Mac OS X install around, it can copy the data from another disk partition in the same Mac. If desired, the Assistant will walk you through the process of connecting your old Mac with a FireWire cable and booting it into FireWire target disk mode. In this state, the Tiger Installer searches through the old Mac's Mac OS X installs and copies over applications, user data and files, and other system settings. You can also run the Migration Assistant at any time by double-clicking it in the */Applications/Utilities* folder.

Personalize Your Settings

Based on the country you selected on the Welcome screen, you'll be asked here to choose a keyboard layout to match your language needs. Like the previous screen, there is a checkbox to reveal all the other countries.

Your Apple ID

If you have an Apple ID, you can enter that here along with its password. If you have a .Mac account, your .Mac email address (for example, *runningosx@mac. com*), as well as its password, will be your Apple ID by default. If you don't have a .Mac account, you can select the option "Create an Apple ID for me," and the Installer will build an ID for you based on your username.

Registration Information

Here you get to enter your name, address, phone number, and email address. This information gets transmitted back to Apple when you register Mac OS X at the end of the installation process. The information you provide is used only by Apple, and if you have any concerns about how the company might use this information, you should click the Privacy button to reveal Apple's Privacy Policy.

A Few More Questions

There are three options for you to select from here to provide additional information about yourself (or, more important to Apple, how you intend to use Mac OS X). The first two options are found in pop-up menus, where you're asked to answer where you will use your computer and to describe what you do for a living. The third option just asks whether you'd like to receive Apple news and other information about its products, as well as services from other companies.

Thank You

Now that you've filled out the basic information about who you are, click the Continue button to transmit that data to register your Mac and Tiger with Apple.

Create Your Account

The first and last name you entered on the Registration Information screen will be combined and placed in the Name and Short Name fields on this screen. The only exception is that your Name appears as it normally would (for example, Norman Cook), and your Short Name appears as all lowercase text, run together (for example, norman). Fortunately, these fields are editable, so you can go back and tweak these to your heart's content. There are also spaces to enter and verify a password for your account, as well as to provide a Password Hint, and to select a picture that will be used on the login screen if you set up your account to require a login password.

Since this is the first user you're setting up on your Mac, this user will have administrator privileges by default. Other users can be set up later using System Preferences → Accounts, and they too can be assigned administrator privileges, if you think they're worthy.

Get Internet Ready

This screen gives you two simple options to select from: to either use your existing Internet service or to not configure your Mac to connect to the Internet. If you select the second option, you'll be asked to verify that you really don't want to connect your Mac to the Internet. If this is really what you want to do, you'll skip the next four steps and find yourself at the Select Time Zone screen, described later.

How Do You Connect?

Depending on the connection capabilities of your Mac, you will have one of five options to choose from:

- Telephone modem
- Cable modem
- DSL modem
- Local network (Ethernet)
- Local network (AirPort wireless)

Select the connection you'll use most and click the Continue button to configure your Mac to connect to the Internet.

If you select Cable modem or DSL modem, you are taken to the Your Internet Connection page, where you need to fill in information about the network to which you will connect. For the most part, leaving the TCP/IP Connection Type menu set to Using DHCP should be all you need to do here before clicking the Continue button, but check with your ISP first to see if it has anything specific for you to enter in the following fields:

- DHCP Client ID
- DNS Hosts
- Domain Name
- Proxy Server

If you select Local network (either Ethernet or AirPort), you are taken to the Your Local Area Network screen. If the network to which you're connecting uses DHCP, your Mac will obtain its IP address from the DHCP server. If you want to use this configuration, make sure that the radio button next to the Yes option is selected and then click the Continue button. If you don't want to use DHCP (maybe you get to have a static IP address?), click the radio button next to the No option and then click Continue to go back and configure your network settings.

Now You're Ready to Connect

With all your settings in place, it's now time to establish a connection with Apple's servers to send off your registration information. Click the Continue button to register and proceed. You'll see a Connecting... screen with a twirling progress meter as your registration information is sent along to Apple.

Select Time Zone

Here you're shown a map of the world, from which you can select the city nearest you for establishing the date, time, and the time zone your Mac is located in.

Thank You

If you've made it to this screen, your job is done. Tiger has been successfully installed on your Mac and you're ready to start using it. Well, as soon as you click the Go button.

Finally, after about an hour or so of installing Tiger, you're ready to embark on using your Mac. It's up to you to set up and configure your Mac's preferences (through the System Preferences application) however you'd like. If you're in need of information on how to tweak and use Mac OS X Tiger (other than the information you'll find in this book), you should check out the following books:

Mac OS X Tiger Pocket Guide, by Chuck Toporek (O'Reilly Media, Inc., 2005)

Revised and expanded to cover Tiger, this handy little book covers all the basics you need to know about using Mac OS X Tiger. The book includes keyboard shortcuts and a 45-page guide that you can use to further configure your Mac. The book's small size makes it easy to carry around in your computer bag, and it doesn't clutter up your desk either.

Mac OS X: The Missing Manual, Tiger Edition, by David Pogue (O'Reilly Media, Inc./ Pogue Press, 2005)

> David Pogue's Missing Manuals have shown Mac users the light, and this newly revised edition continues to lead the pack. If you're new to Mac OS X, you should read this book before you read the book you now hold in your hands.

Mac OS X Tiger in a Nutshell, by Andy Lester, et al. (O'Reilly Media, Inc., 2005)

> More of a geek's treasure trove, *Mac OS X Tiger in a Nutshell* drills right down to Mac OS X's Unix core. About a third of the book is the Unix command reference, listing over a third of the approximately 1,000 shell commands you can issue under Mac OS X. This book makes a great companion to *Running Mac OS X Tiger* and should be by your side as you explore the depths of your Mac.

It's time to install some software to put your Mac to good use, which is covered in the next section.

Back It Up Again

It might seem like a strange concept, but once you've installed Mac OS X, loaded up all of your programs, and copied your data back onto the hard drive, you may want to perform a full disk backup. By backing up your pristine install, you can always restore from that checkpoint if (when) any problems occur in the future, thereby avoiding having to start from scratch all over again.

The Software of Mac OS X

There are many different kinds of applications available for Mac OS X. As you'll learn in Chapter 3, there are Carbon apps, Cocoa apps, native Unix programs, Java apps, the list goes on. Mac OS X is a very versatile operating system and it can run a variety of different programs. Most of that software breaks down into one of the following categories:

Mac OS X GUI applications

> These are software applications that are written using Cocoa, Carbon, or Java and run right in the Aqua user environment. Some examples include Microsoft Office, Apple's iLife suite, Adobe Photoshop, and NetNewsWire.

Classic GUI applications

> Software that was written for Mac OS 9 and earlier. These apps run in the Classic environment, which is essentially Mac OS 9 running on top of Mac OS X. Most software written for older versions of the Mac OS has been Carbonized to run on Mac OS X. However, you might still have some stragglers that you need to use.

Unix-based GUI applications

> Applications that are written to use the X11 window system. While this book mostly discusses Unix as it pertains to the command-line environment, Unix has its own graphical user interface. The popular open source desktop environments KDE and GNOME have given a home to a plethora of free software apps with graphical interfaces, such as the GIMP and GAIM.

Unix-based CLI applications

> Daemons and utilities for use on the command line. This includes many parts of Mac OS X itself.

For most users, the majority of applications installed on their Macs are GUI apps. Some people will have some older Classic applications that have either not been ported or will never be. Even fewer people will have Unix-based software of either the GUI or CLI variety. Each of these categories has its own unique operating environment with a slightly different set of rules and procedures.

For example, Mac OS X GUI applications are the simplest to use. You locate the program in your */Applications* folder, double-click its icon, and go to work using it. Software that requires the Classic environment works in a similar manner, with the caveat that the Classic Environment must be launched before the program runs successfully.

For Unix-based GUI applications, you'll need to have Apple's X11 environment installed, which is an optional package during the Tiger install (and can be installed after the fact, as described earlier). In the case of Unix-based CLI applications, you'll have to open up the Terminal to make use of them (the Terminal is discussed in Chapter 4).

Software Installers

Not only are there several different types of software available for Mac OS X, there are several different ways to install those applications. Each of these is discussed in detail below.

Drag-and-drop install

Perhaps the easiest method of installation, but the most frequently botched, is the drag-and-drop install. Mac OS X has given rise to the popularity of using disk images for distributing software. A Disk image is essentially a single file that contains a virtual disk full of files. Software distributed on a disk image is usually of the drag-and-drop variety, though some developers will distribute a *.pkg* file for the Mac OS X Installer to use or some sort of custom software installer. Figure 2-1 shows an application distributed on a disk image.

Figure 2-1. An application distributed by disk image

Finding Software

There is a lot of good software out there for Mac OS X. Commercial vendors such as Microsoft, Adobe, and Quark develop software for Mac OS X, and their wares are available through a variety of channels. Mac OS X also has a very healthy shareware and freeware community, with many of the most popular apps for the platform being developed by mom-and-pop kind of operations. In addition, Mac OS X's Unix under-pinnings open up the world of open source software to Mac users.

With all of these choices, it can be tough to pick the right tool for the job. Luckily, sites like MacUpdate (*http://www.macupdate.com*) and VersionTracker (*http://www. versiontracker.com*) come to the rescue, giving users and developers a place to get together and find, share, and review software. So the next time you're looking for a great new app to use (or even the latest updates for your favorite apps), point Safari in the direction of those sites to get the scoop.

A lot of confusion arises from the use of disk images, as some users will download an application and never copy it off of the disk image. Instead, the application is run from the disk image. The user won't notice a problem until she restarts the machine and then has difficulty locating the app again. So, to successfully install software dis-tributed on a disk image, you must drag it from the disk image and drop it into your Applications folder, as shown in Figure 2-2. This copies the application from the disk image to your Applications folder. You may then eject the disk image and run the app by double-clicking its icon, found in your Applications folder.

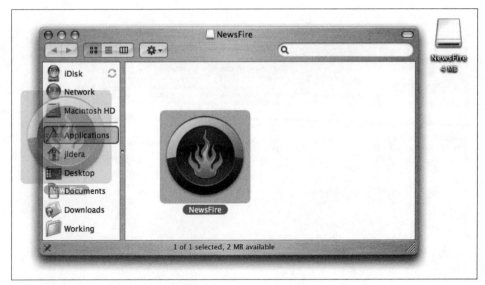

Figure 2-2. Performing a drag-and-drop install

It's worth noting that drag-and-drop is also used by many applications that are distributed on CD or DVD. Disk images are just an intangible analog of distribution on media.

Mac OS X's Installer

Another popular method of distributing software for Mac OS X is to use Mac OS X's own Installer. The Mac OS X Installer is located in */Applications/Utilities*, though it's unlikely you'll ever need to launch it by hand. Instead, you'll find it is launched for you when you double-click a *.pkg* file. These package files are actually bundles (discussed in more detail in Chapter 3) that contain the software being distributed, as well as some files to help the Installer along. Figure 2-3 shows Apple's iWork suite being installed using the Mac OS X Installer.

One of the nice things about the Mac OS X Installer is that it provides consistency for the user; each install is virtually identical, even though the software being installed differs. Another advantage of the Mac OS X Installer is that it leaves records behind. When an application is installed using the Installer, a Bill of Materials (*.bom*) file is placed in */Library/Receipts*. These *.bom* files are used by the system for a variety of purposes. For example, the feature of Disk Utility that repairs permissions is based around reading what a file's permissions are supposed to be, according to the Installer's receipt. It's also worth noting that applications that use drag-and-drop install or are installed using a custom installer don't have this same benefit.

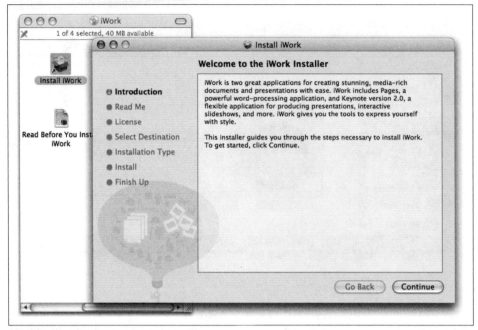

Figure 2-3. Mac OS X's Installer

Custom installers

Some applications written prior to Mac OS X are still distributed using custom installers. These are small applications whose sole purpose in life is to take files from point A and place them at point B on your Mac. Point A is usually some kind of install media (such as a DVD or even a disk image), and point B is most likely your Applications folder. Custom installers have little uniformity between vendors, though some software developers will use an installer developed by another company. For example, a popular iPhoto plug-in, FlickrExport (*http://www.connectedflow.com*), uses an installer developed by Wincent software (*http://www.wincent.com*). Figure 2-4 shows a custom installer for the venerable database application FileMaker.

Installing Unix Software

Now that the various methods of installing common Mac applications have been covered, let's take a look at Unix applications. Most Unix software is distributed as raw source code. This means that the files you download when you get a Unix app are not in a form that your computer can interpret. They must first be *compiled* into machine language before they can be executed.

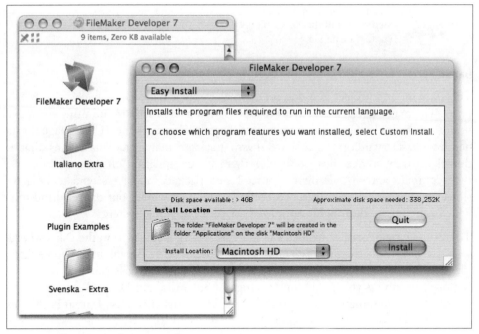

Figure 2-4. A custom software installer

In reality, most software exists in this state at some point. It's just that in the case of most popular Unix apps, the software is released under an open source license. The most prevalent open source licenses actually require that the source code be included when distributed. For commercial applications like Microsoft Office, it would actually be to their disadvantage to include the source code. By preventing others from accessing their software's source code, commercial development houses can ensure they stay in business. Who would buy Word if you could just download the source and compile it yourself?

If you're not a software developer or a Unix veteran, the concept of compiling your own software might seem a bit foreign. Luckily, other software developers have created tools to make the process of downloading, compiling, and installing open source software as easy as a few commands on the command line. These tools are known as *package managers*.

On Mac OS X, there are two main package management projects. While other projects exist, the Fink and DarwinPorts projects are the most popular and most mature. These projects not only develop the tools to facilitate the installation of open source apps, but they also port and test these apps on the Mac OS X platform to ensure they work properly. The following sections below go into detail on each of these projects.

If you will be compiling and installing Unix apps on your Mac, you'll need to install the Xcode Tools. See the sidebar "Installing the Xcode Tools" in Chapter 1.

DarwinPorts

The DarwinPorts project is based on another popular package manager: FreeBSD's ports. The major difference is that FreeBSD's system is based around using the *make* utility for the bulk of its tasks. In contrast, DarwinPorts uses the Tcl language for its handiwork. DarwinPorts is a *source-based* package manager. This means that it downloads raw source files, configures them for compilation on your system, and then compiles and installs them. Source-based package managers tend to be a bit slower when installing software (compiling can take a while), but the resulting software is often more thoroughly optimized for your individual system.

To install DarwinPorts, download the Mac OS X *.pkg* installer from the DarwinPorts web site (*http://darwinports.opendarwin.org*). Once you've downloaded the package file, double-click it to have the Mac OS X Installer install the base DarwinPorts distribution. Something you might find strange about installing DarwinPorts is that it doesn't leave anything in your Applications folder. This is because DarwinPorts uses a special directory in the filesystem to keep its files and software.

The DarwinPorts distribution is kept in */opt/local*, with several different subdirectories of that folder being reserved for various purposes. In effect, this is a separate filesystem domain (discussed in Chapter 3) from the rest of Mac OS X, which keeps the OS and DarwinPorts from stepping on each other's toes. However, it can make life a little more confusing for you, as you'll need to either specify the absolute path to run a DarwinPorts package, or add the */opt/local/bin* and */opt/local/sbin* paths to your shell's default path. You can learn more about file paths and your shell in Chapter 4.

After you have DarwinPorts installed, you should execute the following command to synchronize its package information:

```
$ sudo /opt/local/bin/port -d selfupdate
```

You should also use the previous command periodically, to help keep your Darwin-Ports infrastructure current. Once this command has completed, you can enter this command to get a list of available software packages in the DarwinPorts distribution:

```
$ /opt/local/bin/port list | more
```

When something catches your eye, you can install it using the following command:

```
$ sudo /opt/local/bin/port install packagename
```

In this example, **packagename** is the name of the desired port you want to install on your Mac. DarwinPorts first checks to see if any packages upon which your desired package depends are also installed. This means it looks for requisite libraries, checks that they are the proper versions, and if not, queues them to be installed first. Once all of the dependencies have been met, the *port* command downloads the source code for the port and begins to compile and install it. As each of these steps is processed, DarwinPorts gives you an update, as shown in Example 2-1.

Example 2-1. Installing a port using DarwinPorts

```
$ sudo /opt/local/bin/port install bladeenc
---> Fetching bladeenc
---> Attempting to fetch bladeenc-0.94.2-src-stable.tar.gz from http://bladeenc.mp3.no/
source/
---> Verifying checksum(s) for bladeenc
---> Extracting bladeenc
---> Applying patches to bladeenc
---> Configuring bladeenc
---> Building bladeenc with target all
---> Staging bladeenc into destroot
---> Packaging tgz archive for bladeenc 0.94.2_0
---> Installing bladeenc 0.94.2_0
---> Activating bladeenc 0.94.2_0
---> Cleaning bladeenc
```

Congratulations. You've just installed your first piece of ported open source software. DarwinPorts (and Fink, for that matter) takes all the complication out of the compiling process and does all of the work for you. If you're a do-it-yourself kind of person, you can read the section "Compiling Unix software" later in this chapter to see what kind of dirty work you're spared by using a package manager.

Removing a package from your system is as easy as installing it. To remove a Unix app that you no longer use, enter this command:

```
$ sudo /opt/local/bin/port uninstall packagename
```

Heard about a great new feature in a new release of your favorite package? First, synchronize your DarwinPorts infrastructure as discussed above. Then, issue this command to update the port:

```
$ sudo /opt/local/bin/port upgrade packagename
```

If you'd like to upgrade all of your installed ports in one go, you can use the *-a* switch when calling *port*:

```
$ sudo /opt/local/bin/port -a upgrade
```

Before upgrading all of the ports at once, you should probably check out which ports are out of date by using the *outdated* keyword with *port*:

```
$ sudo /opt/local/bin/port outdated
```

Fink

The Fink project also draws inspiration from an existing package management system. In this case, it is Debian GNU/Linux's *apt* and *dpkg* tools. While DarwinPorts is solely a source-based package manager, Fink can use either source-based or binary-based packages. Binary-based packages are compiled before they are put into the package system, so when your Mac goes to install the package, it doesn't have to compile from source code. This results in a much faster install process, though the resulting package may not be customized for your particular Mac.

In practice, that's not as big a deal as it sounds. Still, the Fink project will use a source-based system in most cases, requiring an extra switch to have it use the binary distribution.

To get started using Fink, download its installer from the Fink web site (*http://fink. sourceforge.net*). Once you've downloaded the disk image, opened it, and run the installer, you'll find you have a new folder at the top of your Macintosh HD. The */sw* folder is where Fink keeps its installed packages and configuration data. Fink uses a very similar syntax to DarwinPorts, but here's a breakdown on some of the commands used to perform common package management tasks.

Once you have Fink installed, you'll want to see what packages are available. To view them, enter the command:

```
$ /sw/bin/fink list | more
```

To install a package, the command is:

```
$ sudo /sw/bin/fink install packagename
```

If you'd like to save some time and use the precompiled, binary version of a package, add the *-b* option, as in:

```
$ sudo /sw/bin/fink -b install packagename
```

When you want to remove a package, just call Fink with the *remove* keyword:

```
$ sudo /sw/bin/fink remove packagename
```

To upgrade a package, you first need to synchronize Fink with its *selfupdate* option, as follows:

```
$ sudo /sw/bin/fink selfupdate
```

The first time you run this command, it asks you whether you want to use *rysnc*, CVS, or if you'd rather stick to point releases. If you're aiming for stability, you'll want to stick to the point releases. If you're more accustomed to being on the bleeding edge, go for the *rsync*. The Fink project prefers that CVS access be used only by their developers, but leaves the option there for those who have problems using the other two methods.

Once you've finished synchronizing Fink, enter the command:

```
$ sudo /sw/bin/fink update packagename
```

To update the desired package, or to update all of your installed packages:

```
$ sudo /sw/bin/fink update-all
```

Compiling Unix software

While Apple has included many great open source applications with Mac OS X and the package manager projects offer hundreds more, there are thousands of open source projects out there. It's impractical to expect any project to encompass all of them, let alone keep them all updated with the latest releases. For this reason, you might find yourself needing to install one of these apps by hand.

Installing open source software can be broken down into the following stages:

1. Download the software source code and expand it.
2. Read any available installation documentation.
3. Configure the source code for your system.
4. Compile the source code into application binaries.
5. Install the application binaries in the proper location on your system.
6. Profit.

As an example, here are the steps you'd take to configure *nmap* (*http://www.insecure.org/nmap*), a popular tool for identifying services on a network host. First, you'll need to download the *nmap* source code from the web site. Most source code is distributed in a *tarball*, which is just an archive created using the *tar* utility and then compressed using *gzip* or *bzip2*.

 As of this writing, the current release of *nmap* is 3.93. If these commands give you problems, double-check the *nmap* site for the latest version and substitute it for 3.93.

To download the tarball, you can use Safari or, if you're feeling particularly Unix-ish, *curl*:

```
$ curl -O http://download.insecure.org/nmap/dist/nmap-3.93.tar.bz2
```

Once the download has completed, you'll need to expand the resulting archive with the *tar* command. Depending on whether the archive was compressed using *gzip* or *bzip2*, you'll need to use a slightly different syntax. Check the *tar* manpage for more information:

```
$ tar xvjf nmap-3.93.tar.bz2
```

After the tarball has been expanded, change to the resulting *nmap-3.93* directory and take a look at the *README* and *INSTALL* files. Take note of any specific instructions for compiling the software on Mac OS X as well as any other caveats the developers wish to make you aware of. Assuming there aren't any hitches on the way, the next step is to configure the source code for compiling by using the software's *configure* script.

The *configure* script is a strange beast; each application has its own unique script. Depending on the software you're installing and its features, the script might just check for a few simple system libraries or a variety of tools and other dependencies. A good place to start when using *configure* is with its *--help* option. This option displays the *configure* script's help information, which details the various options and libraries that the script looks for. If the script requires any libraries that are not on your system, you'll need to compile and install them first.

 One of the most frequently used configure switches is *--prefix*. This switch is used to tell the script where it should install the software on your system. Traditionally, the install prefix is the root directory (*/*). However, on Mac OS X, there's a good chance that using a root prefix will cause you to overwrite system files and cause other incompatibilities. To avoid this calamity, you should use another path on the filesystem, like */usr/local*, as the prefix.

Once you've determined which *configure* options you'll need to use, run the script with those options to get started:

```
$ ./configure --prefix=/usr/local
```

If the *configure* script fails, take a look at the last line printed to the screen. Chances are it was unable to find a requisite library or command. Compile and install the dependency and then try running the *configure* script again.

When the *configure* script has finished preparing the source code for your system, use the *make* command to compile the code into binaries:

```
$ make
```

This is usually the lengthiest part of the install. Depending on the speed of your machine and amount of installed memory, compiling an application can take anywhere from a few minutes to several hours. Assuming the software compiles without any errors, the final step is to install the resulting binaries in the proper location:

```
$ sudo make install
```

If compiling fails, try running the *configure* script again and take note of any errors. Then, attempt to contact the developer, a support forum, or a mailing list related to the software about the problem. Include as much detail as possible, including any errors the *configure* script and *make* might have given you, details about your system, etc. Not all open source apps will compile cleanly on Mac OS X, but most developers are helpful in making it so they will.

Staying Up-to-Date

Computer software is a constant work in progress. No developer has ever written a bug-free, perfectly secure, blazing fast application, and it's highly unlikely anyone ever will. Luckily, we're not working in a static world. As developers release updates and patches to their software, it's important to put them on your Mac. Just like backing up your data is a rather boring necessity, so too are software updates.

Mac OS X's Software Update

For Apple-supplied software, Mac OS X uses Software Update, which you can launch by selecting → Software Update. When launched, Software Update connects to Apple's servers, retrieves a list of available updates, and then checks which ones have not yet been installed. Once this process has completed, the Software Update window displays the available updates and allows you to select which ones you want to install, as shown in Figure 2-5.

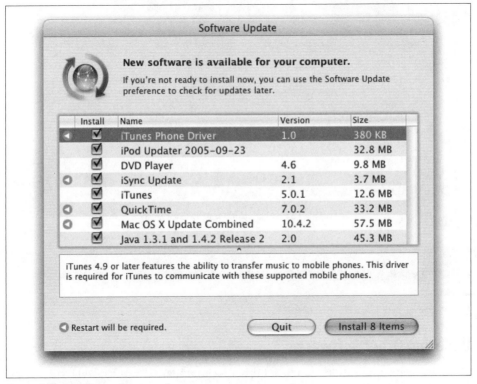

Figure 2-5. Installing software updates

Each available update is listed, including its size, version, and an icon indicating whether the update requires a restart. Selecting an individual update displays some brief notes about what the update contains and affects. In most cases, you'll want to install all of the available updates; the system detects which ones are actually needed. However, if there's an update you don't need (e.g., you're not an iPod user and thus don't want the iPod Updater), you can have Software Update ignore it by selecting the update and then choosing Update → Ignore Update.

Software Update is configured using its preference panel in System Preferences (→ System Preferences → Software Update), as shown in Figure 2-6. Here, you can set whether Software Update should check for updates automatically, how often it should check, and whether it should download the updates automatically before prompting to install them. Using the Installed Updates tab, you can quickly tell which updates have been installed, which version was installed, and when the installation took place.

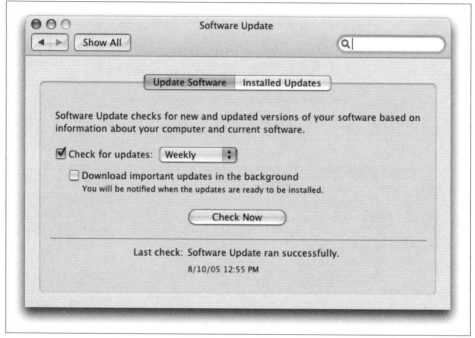

Figure 2-6. Software Update preferences

Updating Other Software

Other software applications can be a bit harder to update. Unfortunately, there is no convenient utility to update all of your apps at once. Some apps come with an updater for that particular application. For example, Microsoft Office comes with the Microsoft AutoUpdate application, which only checks for updates to Microsoft products. Many applications are written to check for updates themselves, though the process for acquiring and installing the update may not be automated. Still other applications have no built-in update mechanism at all, forcing you to go to the developer's site to find updates.

To help alleviate some of this burden, sites like MacUpdate (*http://www.macupdate. com*) and VersionTracker (*http://www.versiontracker.com*) carry software updates. If you're having problems finding an update on the manufacturer's site or don't want to spend your day shuffling around between several different sites to retrieve the updates for all of your software, you might want to start on one of those sites. VersionTracker and MacUpdate each also offer a subscription-based service that comes with an application that will scan your hard drive for installed software and notify you when updated versions are available.

Further Explorations

This chapter has covered quite a bit about installing software on your Mac. For the most part, installing software is much harder to explain than it is to actually do. However, if you'd like some more information on getting Mac OS X and applications onto your machine, take a look at the *Getting Started* manual that was included in the Mac OS X retail box.

You might also want to take a look at the manpages for the following commands:

- *make*
- *softwareupdate*
- *tar*

## CHAPTER 3

Lay of the Land

When you first log into Mac OS X, you see a user interface that is the end result of 20 years of development; quite a bit of work has gone into making it an elegant and usable interface for your computer. Underneath it all, however, Mac OS X is a structured environment based on Unix, and to truly master it, you'll need to know how it all fits together. This chapter discusses the architecture of Mac OS X: how the various layers work together to create what Apple calls the world's most advanced operating system.

This chapter also discusses how the filesystem in Mac OS X is organized and how to navigate through the system using the Finder and the Terminal. Each of these programs gives access to different layers of the system. For some tasks, the Finder is the best tool for the job. For others, using the Terminal is a way of life. Read on to find out which tool is best in various situations.

The World's Most Advanced Operating System

As discussed in Chapter 1, Mac OS X is the convoluted product of two parents: the original Mac OS and the NEXTSTEP operating system. For the most part, however, NEXTSTEP had the dominant genes, giving Mac OS X its Unix underpinnings and a significant portion of its system libraries. From the Mac OS of yesterday, Mac OS X inherited QuickTime, Carbon, and many other tools. Plus, Apple has developed several technologies that have made their debut on Mac OS X, like Spotlight, CoreAudio, and Quartz Extreme.

To understand how Mac OS X is structured, it's helpful to have an understanding of its components and their relationships with one another. Operating systems are made up of many small blocks that fit together like bricks in a wall, arranged in rows or layers. Figure 3-1 shows what a wall made of Mac OS X "bricks" might look like.

While Chapter 1 approached many of these topics from a historical perspective, the following sections will dissect and discuss Mac OS X from the bottom up.

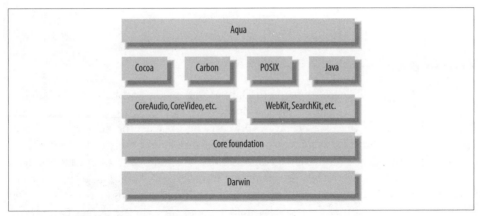

Figure 3-1. A layered view of Mac OS X

Darwin

If you were to strip away all of the beauty of Aqua and all of the programming librar-ies Apple includes with Mac OS X, you'd be left with Darwin. As a matter of fact, you can even acquire Darwin in this raw form from Apple. While you won't be able to run iTunes on it without the rest of Mac OS X, Darwin still provides a capable—though spartan—computing environment, similar to a very basic install of Linux or FreeBSD.

At the core of Darwin is the Mach kernel. Mach is responsible for most of the low-level tasks on your system. It manages the CPU, scheduling, prioritizing, and send-ing instructions to your Mac's processor. It handles your Mac's memory, employing virtual memory when needed and ensuring applications can't overwrite each other's address spaces. It uses device drivers—or *kernel extensions*, in Mach parlance—to access hardware devices like hard disk drives and network cards. Essentially, the Mach kernel provides the bridge between the logical and the physical. It is the inter-mediary between the software and hardware that make up a Macintosh.

Around this powerful core, Apple has employed a highly modified version of FreeBSD. Although Mach has raw access to system hardware, it still needs some sort of abstraction to turn those raw bits into something meaningful. This is where the BSD components of Darwin take charge and provide logical structures such as net-working sockets and process threads. This BSD wrapper provides the same kind of structure to Mach's raw data as consonants and vowels provide to the raw sounds of your voice box.

Darwin is what sets Mac OS X apart from previous generations of the Mac OS and makes it a Unix. Even though the Finder and other applications may look familiar from the Mac OS 9 days, what's going on behind the scenes has drastically changed, all the way down to the way the operating system talks to the hardware. Darwin provides a stable and reliable foundation for the rest of Mac OS X, much like the lowest layer of a brick wall supports the crushing force of the layers above it.

Core Foundation

Similar to how the BSD components of Darwin make sense of the raw bits handled by the Mach kernel, the Core Foundation of Mac OS X provides structure to the bytes coming out of the Darwin layer. Or, carrying on with the analogy of speech, this layer of the operating system structures data similar to how words are made up of letters. Part of Core Foundation's responsibility is to employ a set of common data types to be used by the various programming libraries, allowing data to move seamlessly between different processes on the system. In addition, the Core Foundation layer implements features like process management and simple access to network and I/O data streams.

Application and Multimedia Services

Sitting above the Core Foundation layer is a series of technologies designed to make programmers' lives easier. These interfaces provide developers with an optimized, standardized, and robust set of tools to accomplish common programming tasks. For example, prior to Mac OS X 10.2, many applications kept a unique and often proprietary set of information pertaining to a user's contacts. When you opened your email client, its address book was a separate affair from any other application's address book. By including a centralized repository for contact information and giving programmers a way to access and extend it, Apple made life easier for the user, who no longer has to detail his contacts within each program, and for developers, who get all of that information and capability "for free."

Mac OS X includes a lot of these complimentary and complementary tools. You can find some information on the more prevalent ones below:

CoreAudio

Introduced with Mac OS X Panther, CoreAudio offers developers a way to get great audio out of the Mac without having to reinvent the wheel. Apple designed CoreAudio to have a very low latency as well as to be extensible. CoreAudio is a modular system for which programmers can create special *Audio Units*. Audio Units provide effects processing, such as reverberation or equalization. And since CoreAudio has such a low latency, these types of effects can be applied in real time to an audio signal. CoreAudio also includes libraries for sequencing MIDI data, encoding and decoding audio streams, and converting between different audio formats.

CoreImage and CoreVideo

New to Tiger, CoreImage does for pictures what CoreAudio does for sound. CoreImage's *Image Units* can be used to apply various types of filters to an image, such as sharpening an image or making it black and white. Like CoreAudio, these filters are applied in real time to the image. As a matter of fact, Mac OS X can apply these filters so quickly that CoreImage's sibling, CoreVideo, can take advantage of the effects in real time as well. While still a nascent technology, it's not difficult to see how CoreImage and CoreVideo can give new power to applications like Adobe's Photoshop or Apple's own Final Cut Pro.

QuickTime

Apple's venerable media player is more than just an application sitting on your Mac's hard drive. Developers can work the power of QuickTime into their own applications using the QuickTime APIs. Capable of handling a variety of audio, image, and video formats, QuickTime is used heavily within many applications, including the popular iTunes and iLife suite.

Spotlight

Not all of the services present in Mac OS X are based around multimedia. Also new to Tiger, the Spotlight libraries enable programmers to not only harness the power of Spotlight searching in their applications, but also to extend Spotlight to work with their custom file formats. Looking ahead, Mac users may reach a point where a file's location on a drive simply won't matter, much as iLife users don't have to worry about where their audio files or digital pictures are stored. No more having to remember where you stored that important document— future Spotlight-enabled applications will extract the files from the filesystem.

Sync Services

Another library making its debut in Tiger, Sync Services are used by developers to synchronize an application's data using Apple's .Mac service. While iSync was used by Apple's apps in the past for this purpose, Sync Services are now exposed to developers and can be employed within their applications as well.

WebKit

WebKit is the powerful HTML processing engine that the Safari web browser uses to render web sites. Many applications in Tiger have taken advantage of WebKit as well, such as the new Mail. In addition, third-party developers have started to employ WebKit, for example, the Omni Group's OmniWeb browser.

Application Environments

Mac OS X includes several different application environments that developers can use to create their software. Application environments make up the most basic libraries and data structures that programmers can use. In many ways, the application environment is where the magic of Mac OS X development happens. Programmers pick an environment with which they are familiar or, in some cases, one that works best for a given task. For programmers coming from Mac OS 9 and earlier, they're likely used to using Carbon. Since Carbon is available on both Mac OS 9 and Mac

OS X, applications written using Carbon can be run on either underlying OS, making it easy for developers to port an app from the OS of yesteryear.

For those developers who are new to Mac programming, Apple recommends using Cocoa. Cocoa was the application environment used in NEXTSTEP and is perhaps more "native" to Mac OS X. Before Mac OS X was on Apple's radar, NEXTSTEP was hailed for its easy programming environments. As mentioned in Chapter 1, NEXTSTEP was used by Tim Berners-Lee to create the first web browser and web server.

In addition to the Cocoa and Carbon application environments, Mac OS X has Java and POSIX environments. For many computer users, their only exposure to Java comes in the form of applets found on the Web. However, full-fledged applications can be written in Java and can run alongside other Mac OS X apps. Apple also includes a bridge between Java and Cocoa, though it hasn't been used in many applications.

The POSIX environment is provided for developers who are writing applications that conform to the POSIX standard. This includes software that runs in the X11 environment and other software that can trace its roots in Unix programming. The inclusion of a POSIX environment is what enables Mac OS X to run Unix applications after a simple recompile and what empowers projects like Fink and DarwinPorts (both discussed in Chapter 2).

Aqua

The top-most layer of Mac OS X is that with which you are most familiar. Mac OS X's user interface has been described as "lickable," and even if it might not pleasure one's taste buds, it's certainly a joy to look at. This beauty is provided by Aqua, Mac OS X's graphical user interface and the successor to Platinum. Aqua is rendered using the Quartz engine, which uses PDF technologies to move data to the screen. On Macs that support it, Quartz is accelerated using your Mac's video card, and thus is known as Quartz Extreme.

Filesystem Hierarchy

Like most other filesystems, the Mac OS X filesystem is conceptually a hierarchical tree-based structure that branches from a root. In the case of Mac OS X, the filesystem is rooted on the drive partition from which the system boots. In the typical case where you boot off the single partition of the hard drive that is in your machine, your filesystem is rooted there. If you have more than one disk drive, then the filesystem is rooted on whichever partition you boot from. Likewise, if you boot from an external disk drive or even a disk image on a network server, the filesystem will be rooted from there. Figure 3-2 shows a Finder window displaying the boot disk's filesystem.

The structure of the Mac OS X filesystem at the root level is very strict, and almost every file that Mac OS X needs to run has a specific place within it. Some of the folders at the root of the filesystem are visible in the Finder when you click on your boot drive; others are not.

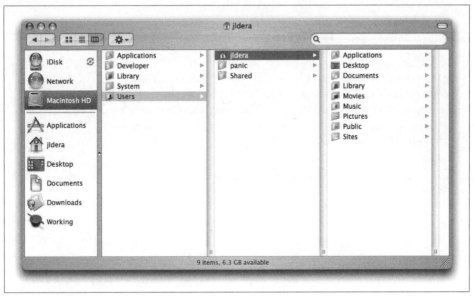

Figure 3-2. The Finder showing the boot disk

The Filesystem Through the Finder

The folders at the root of the filesystem that are visible in the Finder are:

Applications
> This folder contains applications that are available to all users on the system. Most applications that Apple ships for Mac OS X (such as iCal, iPhoto, and Safari) are located here. In addition, a large number of useful utility programs, such as the Terminal and Activity Monitor, are installed in the Utilities subfolder.

Developer
> If you have installed the developer tools on your system, most of the applications, documentation, examples, and other files needed for building applications for Mac OS X are located here.

Library
> This folder contains application- and system-specific resources, such as fonts and application preferences, that are needed by all the users on the system. In some respects, this folder is like its namesake in that it holds a lot of useful information for the various parts of the system.

System

This folder contains the resources used by the operating system itself. Mac OS X is very particular about the files in this directory and will prevent you from messing with them. It's best to consider this directory strictly Apple's domain.

File Extensions and the Finder

By default, file extensions, the part of a filename that comes after the dot, are hidden in the Finder. This means a file named *DialUpNumbers.txt* will appear in the Finder, by default, as *DialUpNumbers*. Some folks, especially old-time Mac OS 9 users, prefer this approach as they wish to look at the icon to determine what kind of file it is. Others, however, including most of us who cut our teeth on Unix, prefer to see the file extensions intact.

To make file extensions viewable all the time, use the Finder → Preferences menu (⌘-,), click on the Advanced button in the toolbar, and then click on the checkbox next to "Show all file extensions."

Users

This folder contains the Home folders for the users on the system. Within a Home folder, a user is the master of her domain. Outside a user's Home folder, the ability to make changes is greatly limited and depends on the type of user she is.

If the Classic Mac OS 9 environment is installed on your machine, you'll also see the following folders:

Applications (Mac OS 9)

This folder contains applications that aren't designed to run on Mac OS X.

Desktop Folder

This folder contains all the files and folders that are part of the Mac OS 9 desktop. This folder is useful when you boot back and forth between Mac OS 9 and Mac OS X and need to get to the files that you left on the Mac OS 9 desktop.

Documents

This is the traditional folder in Mac OS 9 for storing your documents and is placed here for convenience. In Mac OS X, you should always use the Documents folder in your Home folder instead of this folder.

System Folder

This folder contains the Mac OS 9 system and supporting files.

These folders aren't part of Mac OS X but are located at this level of the filesystem for ease of use when you boot into Mac OS 9 from the drive.

The Filesystem Under the Hood

The Finder's view of the filesystem doesn't reveal everything that's there. The Finder is just one view, and for most users, it is sufficient because it keeps hidden system files, sometimes known as *dot files*, from view. The Terminal (*/Applications/Utilities*), however, lets you dive beneath the pretty GUI view and see everything in the filesystem. Example 3-1 shows the output of the *ls* command.

 Chapter 4 will give you a little bit more grounding in the Terminal. For now, just play along.

Example 3-1. The command-line view of the filesystem root

```
$ ls /
Applications    Network      bin      mach.sym       tmp
Desktop DB      System       cores    mach_kernel    usr
Desktop DF      Users        dev      opt            var
Developer       Volumes      etc      private
Library         automount    mach     sbin
```

As you can see, this is a much different view of the filesystem than you'll see in the Finder. Some of the folders—Applications, Library, Network, System, and Users—are the same as those in the Finder, but many aren't exposed. You'll see this kind of difference time and again in Mac OS X. The GUI gives you a filtered view of the system, and most of the time, this filtered view is exactly what you want. The Terminal, on the other hand, gives the raw view of the system, providing you with unfettered access to the depths of the system.

Some of the folders and files visible using the command line at this level, but hidden in the Finder, are:

Desktop DB and Desktop DF
> These are the hidden files behind Mac OS 9's desktop. The Desktop folder in the Finder view uses these files to present your Mac OS 9 desktop to you while you are booted into OS X.

Network
> This virtual filesystem allows you to browse the filesystems shared from servers on your network.

Volumes
> This directory contains all the disks, other than the boot disk, that are attached to your computer. For example, external FireWire disks (including an iPod), as well as CDs, will show up here.

automount
> This directory contains links to any filesystems mounted from network file servers using network protocols such as AFP, NFS, and SMB.

bin

This directory contains many of the executable Unix programs that your system needs.

cores

This directory contains crash files for the various Unix programs. This is the traditional location in which Unix programs write out their crash data.

dev

This directory contains the various device nodes for the system. One of the core ideas of Unix is that the various devices can be treated as files—including some devices that you normally wouldn't think of as being a file. The *dev* tree contains the "files" that represent everything attached to the operating system.

etc

This directory contains configuration files used by the various Unix components of the system.

mach, mach.sym, and mach_kernel

These files make up the kernel, the core part of the operating system that manages everything else.

opt

This directory is used to store optional Unix tools and libraries that may not be an integral or included part of Mac OS X itself. For example, Mac OS X Server places the Apache 2 web server in this folder but uses an earlier version of Apache as its default web server daemon.

private

This is the directory that actually contains the *etc*, *var*, and *tmp* directories. These directories actually don't live at this level of the filesystem but are linked into the root (/) directory.

sbin

This directory contains system executables needed at startup as well as some configuration utilities for the system.

tmp

This is a place for the temporary files that some Unix programs create.

usr

This directory contains the Unix tools and libraries that are intended for all users on the system.

var

This directory contains data that changes frequently such as mail spools and logfiles. The disk files that implement the backing store for virtual memory are also held here.

More hidden files

There's actually another layer of hidden files beyond what you see with the *ls* command. If you change the command and add an *-a* option (to show all files), you'll see the extra files shown in Example 3-2.

Example 3-2. Hidden files in the root directory

```
$ ls -a /
.                 .vol           Network      cores       opt
..                Applications   System       dev         private
.DS_Store         Desktop DB     Users        etc         sbin
.Spotlight-V100   Desktop DF     Volumes      mach        tmp
.Trashes          Developer      automount    mach.sym    usr
.hotfiles.btree   Library        bin          mach_kernel var
```

The *.DS_Store* file contains the Finder settings and the comment text for the various files within the folder. The rest of these files are, well, files that you really don't need to see. They are hidden from the command-line view, which indicates that you should mess with them only if you really need to and you know what you are doing.

Opening hidden directories in the Finder

Even though the Finder hides these directories from you, there is an easy way to get to them. Simply use the Go to Folder command (Go → Go to Folder, or Shift-⌘-G) and enter the path to the folder you want to see. An example of this is shown in Figure 3-3.

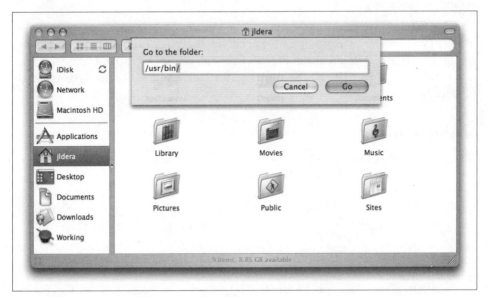

Figure 3-3. The Go to Folder sheet

If you want to see every file on your system all the time, you can do so by typing the following command in the Terminal:

```
$ defaults write com.apple.Finder AppleShowAllFiles YES
```

Then, either log out and log back in, or just give the Finder a few minutes to pick up the change. This seems cute at first (and some people may find it useful), but it can quickly become irritating, so you might find yourself preferring the Finder's regular view instead. To reverse this setting, use the following command:

```
$ defaults write com.apple.Finder AppleShowAllFiles NO
```

This command uses the defaults system, which is covered in more detail in Chapter 14.

 If you'd rather not log back in or wait for the Finder to pick up on your changes, you can relaunch the Finder by holding down the Option key and using the Finder's Dock menu. When holding Option, a new choice will appear labeled Relaunch.

The Many Roots of the Finder

The Mac OS X Finder allows you to ignore the way the filesystem is structured at the command-line level and look at it in a variety of ways that are more relevant to everyday tasks. By selecting one of the items in the Sidebar (shown in Figure 3-4), the view to the right of the Sidebar changes to reveal that folder's contents, or specific details about a selected file.

The most useful feature about this tool in the Finder is that it gives you quick access to your Home folder (which is usually the center of activity on your computer), or to any other folder that you place in the Sidebar. You can even place a Desktop Printer (discussed in Chapter 10) in the Sidebar, for quick access to its drag-and-drop functionality.

The Home Folder

All the files, applications, preferences, and resources that are yours and yours alone are located within your Home folder. This is where you should make all your modifications and additions. If you are an old-school Mac OS 9 user, this is where you should feel like customizing your system. And, even better, if you play by the rules, you'll be able to move to a new machine simply by copying your Home folder.

The folders you'll find inside your Home folder are:

Desktop
> Contains all the files and folders that appear on the Mac OS X desktop for the user.

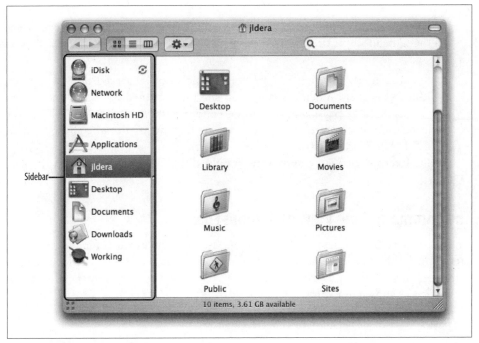

Figure 3-4. The Finder's Sidebar

Documents

    Intended to contain your documents. Of course, you can save your documents anywhere in your Home folder, but this is the recommended location. It is also the default location that will be proposed for you when you save a document from an application.

Library

    Contains application- and user-specific resources that belong to a single user only. This allows you to have fonts on the system that nobody else can use. It also allows your applications to save your preferences separate from those of other users.

Movies

    Intended to contain your movies. This is where iMovie creates its project files.

Music

    Intended to contain your music. This folder is where iTunes keeps its datafiles as well as your MP3 and AAC files. It is also the default save location for Garage-Band audio projects.

Pictures

    Intended to contain your digital photographs. iPhoto keeps its data here—including photos you upload from a camera.

Public

> Intended to contain the files that you are willing to share with other users, either on the same machine or across the network.

Sites

> Intended to hold your personal web site, which can be served by Mac OS X's built-in web server. When personal web sharing is turned on, these documents can be accessed by passing a path of the pattern *~username*. For example, a user with the username *norman* could access these documents from his machine with the URL *http://localhost/~norman/*. Even if you don't run a web server on the public Internet, this is a handy way to publish files to other people on the network.

The Command-Line View of a Home Folder

Unlike the base of the filesystem, the command-line view of the Home folder looks pretty much the same as what you see in the Finder. The only difference is, using the command line, you can see the hidden "dot" files that you can't (by default) see in the Finder, as shown in Example 3-3.

Example 3-3. The command-line view of the Home folder

```
$ ls -a
.                       Documents       Pictures
..                      Library         Public
.CFUserTextEncoding     Movies          Recycled
Desktop                 Music           Sites
```

These dot files are either self-explanatory or are files that you usually don't need to worry about. The one thing you should notice is the ~ symbol when you first open a Terminal window. This symbol is shorthand for your Home directory. From anywhere on the system, you can construct a path using the ~ symbol, and the operating system will automatically use the full path to your Home directory.

Filesystem Domains

In our discussion about the filesystem, you've no doubt identified a certain amount of redundancy. There's a Library folder at the root of the filesystem, one in your Home folder, and one in the System folder. And if you create an Applications folder in your Home folder to store applications that aren't for use by others, you'll note that it automatically gets the same folder icon as the Applications folder at the root of the filesystem, as shown in Figure 3-5.

This is the result of a concept known as *filesystem domains* and is structured to allow multiple users to share the same system or to be hosted on a server so they can use multiple systems and yet provide a consistent experience.

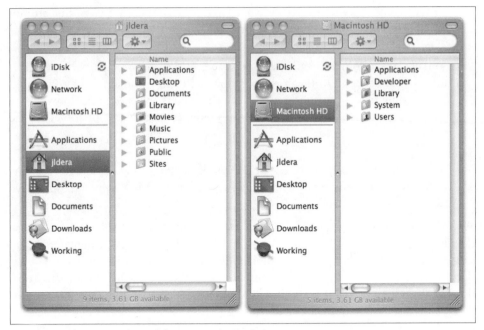

Figure 3-5. The User and Local domains in the Finder

Where to Put Your Applications

The various filesystem domains give you a choice as to where to put your applications. If you are the only user on a system that is going to be using an application, you should consider putting it into an Applications folder in your Home folder. This keeps your applications separate from all of the applications that come on the system in the */Applications* folder. However, there are many applications—typically older applications that have been migrated from Mac OS 9—that have to be installed in the */Applications* folder. There's no winning sometimes, but at least for many applications, what domain you place them into is your choice.

There are four domains in Mac OS X:

User

> Contains the resources for a user logged into the system. As you would expect from the similarity of descriptions, this domain is contained within the user's Home folder.

Local

> Contains the resources that users of a particular system share with each other. The Local domain consists of the Applications and Library folders at the root of

the filesystem. These resources are available to users of the system but are not available to users on networked computers.

Network

Contains the resources available to all users of a local area network. Applications, documents, and other resources located in this domain are available on any machine that is part of the network. The folders that hold this domain vary according to network setup but typically appear as a Network folder in the Finder.

System

Contains the resources required for the system to run. These resources are part of the operating system installation and can be modified only by administrative users.

When a resource is requested by an application, Mac OS X searches these domains—in the order above—to satisfy the request. For example, when an application requests a particular font, the system will search the Fonts directory in the User domain first. If the system doesn't find the font there, it will look in the Local domain. If it doesn't find it there, it will look in the Network domain, and finally it will look in the System domain.

This hierarchical search allows a user's configuration file to override a system-wide preference. Furthermore, the consistency in naming of directories between the domains, such as the Library directory that appears in each domain, allows for easy management of resources.

The Library

I've made lots of references to the Library directory and have indicated that it is for the storage of resources. Any kind of resource that an application needs can be located in the Library. Here's a list of some of the most common directories you'll find in the Library and the kinds of resources they contain (and remember, you can create one of these directories in a domain in which it doesn't exist):

Application Support

Contains third-party plug-ins, helper applications, templates, and even data for the applications on your system. You'll usually find the resources for an application in a subdirectory named after the application.

Audio

Contains drivers, plug-ins, and sounds for Mac OS X's audio subsystems.

Caches

Contains temporary data used by the applications on your system. For example, Safari will keep web page data here so when you revisit a page, you don't have to download all the content on it again.

Calendars
> Contains the ICS files used to store the calendar data for a user. This directory is used by iCal and appears only in the User domain.

ColorSync
> Contains profiles and scripts used by Mac OS X's ColorSync color management subsystem.

Documentation
> Contains documentation for various parts of the system. Also, the Help application uses this folder to hold files that it displays.

Favorites
> Contains aliases to frequently accessed folders, files, or web sites. This directory appears only in the User domain.

Fonts
> Contains fonts for applications to use. The fonts in this directory are easily managed using Font Book (*/Applications*).

Frameworks
> Contains the frameworks and shared libraries that applications need to operate.

Internet Plug-Ins
> Contains the various helper applications, such as the Flash Player, that extend the functionality of your web browsers.

Mail
> Appearing only in the User domain, this directory contains the mail for a user.

Preference Panes
> Contains applets that will appear in the System Preferences application.

Preferences
> Contains the preferences for an application.

Printers
> Contains printer drivers and printer definition (PPD) files. The drivers are organized by vendor name.

Scripting Additions
> Contains scripts and scripting resources to extend AppleScript's capabilities.

StartupItems
> Contains scripts and programs that are run at boot time. This appears only at the Local and System levels.

WebServer
> Appearing in the Local domain, this directory contains the content and CGI scripts for the system's web server. When you turn on web sharing on your machine, you can access the documents from your local machine using the URL *http://localhost/*.

Many other directories may appear in your Library, but as you can see, the files that you find here affect, control, and configure your experience on Mac OS X.

Bundles

A unique concept introduced with Mac OS X is that of the bundle. Bundles take many different forms: frameworks, applications, and software plug-ins can come packaged as bundles. A bundle is essentially a directory structure in the filesystem that is treated by the Finder as a single entity. For example, the Backup application included with a .Mac subscription will appear in the Applications folder as a single, double-clickable item. If you were to view the same application from the Terminal, you'd see that it is actually a directory, as shown in Example 3-4.

Example 3-4. Viewing the contents of an application bundle

```
$ ls -la /Applications/Backup.app/
total 0
drwxrwxr-x    3 root   admin    102 May 17 09:09 .
drwxrwxr-x   57 root   admin   1938 Aug 31 08:52 ..
drwxrwxr-x    8 root   admin    272 Apr 23  2004 Contents
```

While the Finder hides this fact, you can expose it by right-clicking (or Control-clicking) the application and choosing Show Package Contents. This will show you the bundle's contents, as shown in Figure 3-6.

Not all bundles are applications. Some software programs use bundles as their file formats (for example, the Mac OS X Installer's *.pkg* files) as well as the development frameworks that are included with the OS. One of the nicest things about bundles is that they work behind the scenes, enabling a complete application to be presented as a single icon in the Finder. This makes removing, moving, and installing a piece of software a simple drag and drop operation.

Further Explorations

A great resource for expanding your understanding of the way in which the system is put together can be found on the Web. Apple has extensive documentation about the design of Mac OS X available on the Apple Developer Connection (*http://developer.apple.com/documentation/*). A great place to start is the Mac OS X Technology Overview, which can be found at *http://developer.apple.com/documentation/MacOSX/Conceptual/OSX_Technology_Overview/index.html*.

Figure 3-6. The contents of an application bundle shown in the Finder

CHAPTER 4

The Terminal and Shell

The Terminal application (*/Applications/Utilities*) is the portal to the internals of Mac OS X. You can use—and become proficient with—the operating system without ever touching the Terminal. But if you truly want to dig deep and learn how to unleash the full potential of the underlying Unix capabilities of the system, the command line is essential. And once you know how to use it, the Terminal becomes a tool so valuable that many power users keep it in their Dock or in the Finder's Sidebar for quick access.

Tempting as it may be to think of the Terminal as the Unix part of Mac OS X, it's simply an interface to the underlying Unix operating system, and specifically to those programs that give the system its Unix character.

This chapter makes the assumption that you have at least a passing familiarity with the idea of the command line. Maybe you remember using a shared system at a school somewhere. Or maybe you had a DOS-based machine that required you to go sleuthing into the depths of the *C:* world. In any case, the aim of this chapter is to familiarize you with the Terminal, the shell, and some of the other tools you'll need through the rest of the book.

 If this chapter goes over your head and you need more of a grounding on the subject, you should pick up *Learning Unix for Mac OS X Tiger*, by David Taylor (O'Reilly).

Terminal Overview

When you launch the Terminal application, shown in Figure 4-1, you are greeted with a single, rather plain-looking window. What you see here is essentially the same command-line interface that Unix users have been seeing since the days when eight-track tapes were en vogue. The system greets you with a friendly "Welcome to Darwin!" message and then gives you a prompt for the *bash* shell, indicated by the dollar sign ($). This is your cue that you are interacting with the command line. At this point, you have direct access to the internals of Mac OS X. And, if you have administrator privileges and a little bit of know-how, you can do everything you ever wanted to, and more.

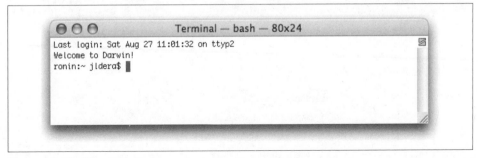

Figure 4-1. The Terminal window

The prompt displayed in the Terminal is the output from a program known as the *shell*. The shell is the mediator between you and the internals of the Unix system. The shell's job is to interpret the commands you type and invoke the various programs on your system to satisfy those instructions. Each command you enter typically consists of a program name and some parameters to pass to that program. When the shell executes the program, its results are displayed in the Terminal window. Example 4-1 shows the use of the *date* command, which returns the current date and time.

Example 4-1. Using the date command

```
$ date
Thu Jul 14 13:52:36 EDT 2005
```

After the *date* command exits, the shell resumes control of the display and outputs another prompt enabling you to enter your next command.

What Can I Execute?

To quickly list all the command-line utilities available—in other words, those utilities that are in directories listed by your PATH environment variable—hit Shift-Esc twice in a row. When you do, the following message appears:

```
Display all 1311 possibilities? (y or n)
```

Answer yes, and you can page through all of the commands.

Essential Filesystem Commands

In the Finder, it's easy to find your way around; after all, it was designed to be easy. The command line isn't such a walk in the park. It's just you and the prompt. So, how do you find your way around? Quite simply, by using a set of commands at the prompt. Table 4-1 lists the commands that you will most often use to navigate your way around.

Table 4-1. Common shell navigation commands

Command	Description
pwd	Displays the current working directory
ls [options] filename	Lists the files in the given directory
cd directory	Changes directory
mkdir dirname	Makes a directory
rmdir dirname	Removes a directory
cp from to	Copies a file
mv from to	Moves a file
rm file	Removes a file
sudo [command]	Invokes the *command* with root privileges

Getting around the filesystem

As Chapter 3 began to explain, Mac OS X's filesystem (and most—if not all—other filesystems) can be visualized as a tree-based structure. At the very top of this tree is the root directory, which is represented by a simple / in the Unix shell. The root directory is the partition from which the system has been booted, usually named Macintosh HD. Beneath the root directory, you'll find the filesystem domains that were discussed in Chapter 3. You'll also find a folder named Volumes. The Volumes directory is where Mac OS X mounts any filesystems besides the root filesystem. For example, if you had a FireWire disk drive named *Taco*, it would be mounted in the Volumes folder as *Taco*.

When you're working in the Terminal, there are two ways to refer to a file or directory's location. The first is the *absolute path*. An absolute path lists every directory that must be traversed to reach the file (or directory) to which you're referring. The absolute path starts at the filesystem root (/) and then lists each subdirectory in order, from top to bottom. As an example, the Documents folder in the user *alisa*'s Home directory has an absolute path of */Users/alisa/Documents*. The Applications folder at the top of Macintosh HD is simply */Applications*.

The other way to refer to a file's location is by using its *relative path*. The relative path of a file (or directory) starts at the current working directory. For instance, if you are working in the user *alisa*'s Home directory, the Documents folder is just *Documents*. A file within that folder has a relative path of *Documents/SomeFile.doc*.

Many times when working with relative paths, you need a way to refer to either the current directory or its parent directory.

There are two entries reserved in each directory for just this purpose. By using the *ls* command with the *-a* option, you can see these two special entries. One is named dot (.), and the other is dot-dot (..).The dot directory always refers to the current directory. For example, the path *./foo.txt* refers to the *foo.txt* file in the current directory. The dot-dot directory always refers to the parent of the current directory. The path *../bar.txt* refers to the *bar.txt* file in the parent directory of the current directory.

Using a combination of absolute and relative paths, you can navigate around the filesystem more quickly than you can with the Finder. While changing to the */Applications/ Utilities* folder in the Terminal takes only one command, it takes quite a few clicks in the Finder to get to the same location. This speed is why many Unix users feel more comfortable dealing with file operations in the Terminal than they do in the Finder.

The command you'll use most often when moving around your Mac's disk is the *cd* command, which is short for *change directory*. The *cd* command is dead simple to use. Like most Unix commands, you invoke the command by its name, followed by a space and any parameters you're passing to the command. The *cd* command uses an absolute or relative path for its parameter. To change into the */Users* folder, type *cd* in the Terminal window, followed by a space and then the folder's path (*/Users*). Finally, to execute the command, press the Return key. The results look something like Example 4-2.

Example 4-2. Changing directories on the command line

```
ronin:~ jldera$ cd /Users
ronin:/Users jldera$
```

If you've never used a Unix system before, it may seem like nothing has happened. No text is presented to confirm that it worked; no new windows pop up. Instead, the shell faithfully prints out another prompt, waiting for your next command. When working with many command-line tools, you won't receive much feedback from a command. And, in just about every case, that means the command executed successfully.

You can tell that the *cd* command was successful, because your shell prompt has changed. Where there was previously a ~, you can see that the path */Users* is shown. You can also confirm what your current directory is by using the *pwd* command, as shown in Example 4-3.

Example 4-3. Using pwd to see the current directory

```
ronin:/Users jldera$ pwd
/Users
```

At this point, you may be wondering what the ~ was for. When you first open a Terminal window, you are placed in your user's Home directory. The ~ symbol is used as a shorthand way of referring to your Home directory. You can use this shortcut to construct a file's relative path from your Home directory. For instance, the Documents folder in *alisa*'s Home directory could have a path of */Users/alisa/ Documents*, *~/Documents*, *./Documents*, or just plain *Documents*. However, the absolute path of */Users/alisa/Documents* will always work, regardless of the current directory or user. It's important to remember that the ~ shortcut is valid only for your own Home directory. If you're moving another user's files around, you'll need to forego its convenience.

Viewing a directory's contents

Another potentially confusing caveat of using the Terminal is that a directory's contents are not immediately shown when you change to that directory. In the Finder, you can tell right away what files are in which folders. It's a visual environment that easily conveys the concept of a container. The command line isn't quite so simple. To see what files are in a directory, use the *ls* command, as shown in Example 4-4.

Example 4-4. Using ls to view a directory

```
$ ls
Desktop        Library        Music          Public
Documents      Movies         Pictures       Sites
```

There is a myriad of options and switches available for the *ls* command. You can get a lot more detail on them from the *ls* manpage (enter the command *man ls* to take a look). However, there are only a few that are used on a regular basis. The common *ls* options are listed in Table 4-2.

Table 4-2. Common ls options

Option	Function
S	Sorts files by size, largest first
R	Recursively lists the contents of subdirectories
l (lowercase L)	Displays detailed data for each item (similar to the Finder's List view)
a	Shows all files, even hidden ones
h	When used with the -l option, shows file sizes using familiar units (for example, M for megabytes, K for kilobytes, and so on)

Viewing a file's contents

The *ls* command is great for viewing the contents of a directory, but it will do little to help you view the contents of a file. For this purpose, the command line has several different utilities. The following list discusses each of these in brief, while their manpages contain more detailed information, in case you need a more advanced feature.

An important thing to remember when working on your Mac is that not all files are the same. Most applications use a binary format that may not be viewable on the command line. Many other applications, however, use plain old text files for storing their data. Keeping this difference in file formats in mind, some of the commands that follow may not present the output you'd expect.

cat

The *cat* command is perhaps the simplest way to view the contents of a file. However, the command prints out the entire contents of the file at once, which might cause the contents to scroll by too quickly for you to read. You could always use the scrollbars on your Terminal window, but you'd probably be better off using a pager, such as *less*.

more

more is a pager. The basic purpose of a pager is that it lets you view the contents of a file without actually having to open the file. The pager displays the contents of the file, screen by screen, waiting for your input before displaying each screen of content. The original *more* could only go forward through a file. To view part of the file that had just been scrolled by, you had to run the command again.

less

less is another pager. According to its manpage, *less* is the opposite of *more*. On Mac OS X, they are essentially the same. The binaries for */usr/bin/more* and */usr/bin/less* are identical and behave similarly. What sets *less* apart from *more* is that *less* gives more control over navigation through the file's contents, enabling you to scroll up and down through the file.

open

You can use the *open* command to have Mac OS X open a file in its native application. This is great for use with binary file formats, whose contents would be unreadable using a command like *cat*.

Working with files and directories

Now that you're more comfortable with moving around the filesystem, you're probably wondering how to move your files and directories around as well. Once again, the Finder does a better job of visualizing file operations. Dragging a file to move it from one folder to another gives an excellent indication of the process. However, given the Finder's somewhat limited view of the filesystem (see Chapter 3 for more discussion of hidden files and folders), you'll find yourself having to perform file operations on the command line whenever you want to work with the innards of the OS.

 If you're used to the Finder's progress indicators, you may want to use the *-v* option with the command-line examples that follow. When supplied with the *-v* option, the command will be verbose in its output, displaying each file operation as it is processed. To do so, simply insert the *-v* option immediately after the desired command and before any other options or parameters.

Perhaps the simplest task you'll want to perform on a file is deleting it. For this purpose, the command line supplies the *rm* command. One extremely important difference between deleting a file in the Finder and deleting it on the command line is that the *rm* command does not send the file to the Trash. It is immediately removed from the system once you press the Return key. To remove a file on the command line, enter the command:

```
rm SomeFile.txt
```

 The section on shell aliases later in this chapter has some tips for making the *rm* command a bit safer.

Removing a directory is very similar, except you use the *rmdir* command. The directory must be empty to be removed, so you should use the *rm* command to remove its contents before removing the directory. Or, you can use the *rm* command's switch for recursion, *-R*, to remove the directory and its contents all in one go:

```
rm -R SomeDirectory
```

The *rmdir* command's counterpart is *mkdir*, which you use to create new folders. A convenient switch you can use with *mkdir* is the *-p* option. When using *-p*, you can specify that *mkdir* create a series of nested folders. For example, the command:

```
mkdir -p Folder1/Folder2/Folder3
```

creates *Folder1* in the current directory, *Folder2* within the *Folder1* folder, and *Folder3* within the *Folder2* folder.

Another common file operation you'll want to perform is copying a file. To copy a file, use the *cp* command:

```
cp OriginalFile FileCopy
```

The *cp* command also has a switch for recursion, *-R*, which you should use when copying a directory and its contents.

For moving files and directories, use the *mv* command. Unlike the *cp* and *rm* commands, there is no special option for recursion when using *mv*. Even if you pass it a folder for its source, it simply moves the folder and its contents:

```
mv SomeDirectory NewLocation/
```

Wildcards

Quite often when you use the command line, you will want to perform operations on groups of files at one time. For instance, you may want to copy all the files in a directory that start with a particular prefix. Or, you may just want to see all the files in a directory that end with the *.jpg* extension. Fortunately, the shell provides a painless way to accomplish this with the help of some wildcards. Table 4-3 lists the most common wildcards.

Table 4-3. Common wildcards

Wildcard	Matches
?	Any single character
*	Any string of characters
[set]	Any character in the set
[!set]	Any character *not* in the set

By far, the most widely used wildcard is the asterisk (*). As an example, to find all the files ending with *.plist* in the *~/Library/Preferences* directory, use the following:

```
$ ls ~/Library/Preferences/*.plist
```

You can also use the asterisk by itself as an argument. This selects every file in a directory. For example, the following command can be dangerous indeed:

```
$ rm *
```

This will remove every file in the current directory. Even more dangerous is combining wildcards with the *rm* command's *-r* option, which puts *rm* into recursive mode and removes every directory as well as every file in a directory. Execute such a command at the root of the filesystem, and you could lose everything. Wildcards are powerful, so use them with care.

Terminal User Interface

In many ways, the command-line environment and the GUI are as diametrically opposed as possible. One stresses exactness while the other emphasizes ease of use. However, Apple has provided several features in the Terminal application to help it work better with the Aqua side of Mac OS X.

One of these features is the ability to drag and drop files from the Finder to the Terminal. When you do so, the full pathname of the file is inserted on the command line. This means instead of trying to remember a long path to a file, you can quickly find it in the Finder, compose a command in the Terminal, and then drag and drop the file or folder icon into the Terminal window.

Also, while using the Terminal, there's a plethora of keystrokes you can use to whiz through tasks with ease. Table 4-4 lists the most commonly used ones.

Table 4-4. Commonly used Terminal keyboard shortcuts

Key	Description
⌘-N	Create a new Terminal window.
Shift-⌘-N	Connect to server via SSH, SFTP, FTP, or Telnet.
⌘-.	Send a break character (equivalent to Control-C).
Shift-⌘-V	Paste selected text (similar to the middle mouse button in X Window).
⌘-Home	Jump to the top of the scrollback buffer.
⌘-End	Jump to the bottom of the scrollback buffer.
⌘-Page Up	Scroll one page up in the scrollback buffer.
⌘-Page Down	Scroll one page down in the scrollback buffer.
⌘-up arrow	Scroll one line up in the scrollback buffer.
⌘-down arrow	Scroll one line down in the scrollback buffer.
⌘-left arrow	Switch to the next Terminal window when you have multiple windows open.
⌘-right arrow	Switch to the previous Terminal window when you have multiple windows open.

One keystroke that should be mentioned in particular—once you start using it, you'll never stop—is Shift-⌘-V, which copies whatever text you have highlighted in the buffer and instantly pastes it at the prompt. If you've ever used an X Window application, you'll recognize this as the equivalent of selecting text with the mouse and using the middle mouse button to copy and paste the text.

In addition to the keyboard shortcuts supplied by the Terminal application, the *bash* shell has some shortcuts for making keyboard input easier. Some of the most common shortcuts are listed in Table 4-5.

Table 4-5. Common bash keyboard shortcuts

Key	Function
Control-A	Move the cursor to the beginning of the current line.
Control-E	Move the cursor to the end of the current line.
Control-U	Delete the beginning of the current line (from the beginning to the cursor).
Control-K	Delete the remainder of the current line (from the cursor to the end).
Control-W	Delete the previous word on the current line.
Control-Y	Undo a deletion performed by Control-U, Control-K, or Control-W.
Control-T	Transpose the current character with the one immediately preceding it.

Another useful feature of the Terminal is the ability to split the window, as shown in Figure 4-2, and use the top part to scroll back through the buffer while working in the bottom part. You activate and deactivate this feature by using the button directly above the scrollbar.

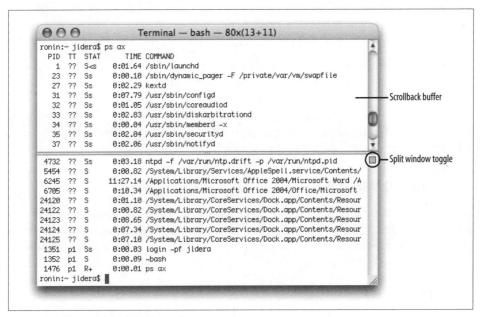

Figure 4-2. The Terminal's split window

You can change the colors used by the Terminal, including the background and foreground colors, as well as the transparency of the Terminal window. When you are staring at nothing but text, it's nice to be able to set it up with colors that are comfortable for you to use. Just select the Terminal → Window Settings menu item and tweak away. Once you're done, you can have your new settings be the default for all subsequent Terminal windows, or you can make changes and then save them (using File → Save) as a *.term* file. When double-clicked, the resulting *.term* file will open a new Terminal window with your custom settings.

Configuring and Using bash

As mentioned earlier, *bash* is Mac OS X's default Unix shell. Apple made the switch from *tcsh* to *bash* because of its support for Unicode text, something that's very important in the international market. Another logical reason for switching to *bash* is that it is the default shell for most Linux distributions and is easier to script with than *tcsh*. Because *bash* is now the default shell, this book focuses on its use, with an occasional nod to the other shells where appropriate.

The default configuration of *bash* is perfectly adequate for casual usage, but you'll inevitably want to configure it to your own liking. This section takes a look at the various configuration files for *bash*, its environment variables, how to set up command aliases, and how to use *bash*'s history to your advantage. You'll also learn a bit about redirecting output between commands and into files, as well as some basic shell loops.

Environment Variables

Every program on the system runs in an *environment*. The environment consists of a set of name-value pairs, known as *environment variables*, which communicate a variety of configuration settings to a program. For example, the shell uses the PATH environment variable to find a program to execute in response to a command. To get an idea of what kinds of data are stored in environment variables, execute the *set* command, as shown in Example 4-5.

Example 4-5. Examining environment variables with set

```
$ set
BASH=/bin/bash
BASH_VERSINFO=([0]="2" [1]="05b" [2]="0" [3]="1" [4]="release" [5]="powerpc-apple-darwin8.
0")
BASH_VERSION='2.05b.0(1)-release'
COLUMNS=80
DIRSTACK=( )
EUID=501
GROUPS=( )
```

Example 4-5. Examining environment variables with set (continued)

```
HISTFILE=/Users/jldera/.bash_history
HISTFILESIZE=500
HISTSIZE=500
HOME=/Users/jldera
HOSTNAME=ronin.local
HOSTTYPE=powerpc
...
```

When you execute the *set* command, you'll see quite a bit of output—probably around 40 lines. Some of the environment variables may make sense when you first look at them, and some won't. Table 4-6 lists some of the environment variables you are likely to use on occasion.

Table 4-6. Commonly used bash environment variables

Variable	Description
BASH	Location of the *bash* shell program
BASH_VERSION	Version of *bash* currently running
COLUMNS	Number of columns to use in Terminal view
DIRSTACK	List of directories used by the *pushd* and *popd* commands
GROUPS	Various groups with which the user is associated
HISTFILE	File containing the shell history
HOME	Home directory for the user
HOSTNAME	Name of the system on which the shell is running
LINES	Number of lines currently being used by the shell
PATH	List of directories the shell uses to resolve commands
PS1	String used as the primary prompt
PS2	String used as the secondary prompt
SHELL	Shell program being used
SHELLOPTS	Options in effect for the shell
TERM	Type of terminal that the shell is displaying its content to
UID	User ID of the currently logged-in user
USER	Username of the currently logged-in user
_ (underscore)	Previously executed command

To see the value of a single environment variable such as PATH, you can use the *echo* command, as shown in Example 4-6.

Example 4-6. Using the echo command to examine an environment variable

```
$ echo $PATH
/bin:/sbin:/usr/bin:/usr/sbin
```

The dollar sign in front of PATH means you are referring to an environment variable. If you had just entered **echo PATH**, the shell would return PATH, as shown in Example 4-7.

Example 4-7. Results of using the echo command without a dollar sign

```
$ echo PATH
PATH
```

To set or change an environment variable for the lifetime of the shell, use the *export* command. For example, to change the PATH variable so that you can run your own commands in *~/bin*, you could use the following command:

```
$ export PATH=$PATH:~/bin
```

This sets the PATH variable to the currently existing PATH with the *~/bin* directory appended to it. An important thing to remember here is that you need to use a colon (:) as a delimiter between command paths. These commands will last for the lifetime of the current shell, which is as long as that Terminal window is open. To add these paths to the shell permanently, you'll have to edit one of *bash*'s configuration files, described next.

Configuration Files

When *bash* first starts, it looks for *run command* files. Commonly called *rc* files, Unix apps use these files to store basic configuration data that is used as the program loads. As a matter of fact, there are some special *rc* files in the */etc* folder that are involved with the initial setup and loading of Mac OS X itself. You can learn some more about them in Chapter 5.

The *bash* shell first looks at the */etc/profile* file for its initial state. This is a system-wide set of default settings that are superseded by any other files subsequently loaded by *bash*. Next, three files in the Home directory, if they exist, are used to configure *bash*:

.bash_profile
> Contains environment variables and commands that are read and executed every time you create a new Terminal window and a shell is created for it, or when you SSH into your machine and are presented with a prompt. This allows you to customize the shell to your liking. If *bash* doesn't find this file, it looks for *.bash_login* and *.profile* respectively to fill in for it.

.bashrc
> Contains environment variables and commands that are read and executed only when you create a subshell by typing **bash** in an already running shell.

.bash_logout
> Contains commands that are read and executed when you log out of a shell. You could use this to clean up files before you log out.

By default, these files don't exist as part of a user's Home directory until you create them. The most useful of these three files is *.bash_profile*, which is used to customize the shell. For example, if you wanted to permanently modify the PATH that the shell uses to resolve commands, you could create a *.bash_profile* file in your Home directory and add the following line:

```
PATH=$PATH:~/bin:/Developer/Tools
```

This causes the PATH environment variable to be set to the given string each time you open a new Terminal window. Because *.bash_profile* is only read when the shell is created, any changes you make to it won't take effect until you start the next shell. If you don't want to close your shell and start a new one, you can use the *source* command to load the contents of the *.bash_profile* file:

```
$ source ~/.bash_profile
```

Aliases

In addition to searching the PATH for commands, the *bash* shell lets you define a set of aliases. Aliases are commonly used to create a shorter command name for long command strings so that they're a bit more manageable or to rename commonly used commands. It's important to note that these are not the same aliases as those defined in the Finder. Finder aliases are closer to the Unix concept of a symbolic link. It's a shortcut to a file instead of a shortcut for a command.

To define an *alias* for a command, use the following syntax:

```
alias name=command
```

Where *name* is the name of the *command* alias you are defining, and *command* is the command that's actually executed by the shell when you invoke the alias. One common use of aliases is to accommodate fat-fingering of commands. For example, if you are always typing *sl* instead of *ls*, you could define the following alias so that you don't get scolded by the shell again:

```
$ alias sl=ls
```

Another use for aliases is to create a simple command for a longer one. For example, if you are often changing directories to somewhere deep in the hierarchy, you can set up an alias that will allow you to go there quickly:

```
$ alias fdocs="cd ~/Documents/Corporate/Master/Forecasts"
```

Notice the use of quotes around the command. This is required when a command consists of more than one word.

Yet another use for aliases is to redefine a command to add some default options. For example, if you're constantly forgetting about the hidden dot files on your machine, you can redefine the way the shell handles the *ls* command:

```
$ alias ls="ls -a"
```

As another example, if you're still getting used to the fact that the shell doesn't make use of the Trash can, you can make the *rm* command ask you to confirm file deletions by using its *-i* switch:

```
$ alias rm="rm -i"
```

To get a list of all the aliases currently defined, use the *alias* command by itself, as shown in Example 4-8.

Example 4-8. Examining the currently defined shell aliases

```
$ alias
alias sl=ls
alias fdocs="cd ~/Documents/Corporate/Master/Forecasts"
```

You can even make aliases to GUI applications. For example, if you wanted to create a quick shortcut to open the Safari browser while on the command line, you could define the following alias:

```
$ alias safari="open -a Safari"
```

With this alias in place, to launch Safari, you simply need to type **safari** into the command line. And remember, to make an alias permanent, you'll need to create a

.bash_profile file and place the alias into it or edit your existing *.bash_profile* file and then *source* it so the change takes effect.

History

As *bash* runs, it keeps a history of the commands that you've executed. This feature is quite handy as it lets you look at and reuse commands that you've previously entered. Where the shell's history is particularly useful is when you need to invoke a command that has a lengthy set of parameters that you can't remember.

The simplest way to use the history is to use the up and down arrows on your keyboard. This will step back and forth through the commands that you've executed and display each in turn at the prompt. To get more out of the history, you can use the *history* command, which displays a list of previously executed commands. Example 4-9 shows some output from *history*.

Example 4-9. Using the history command

```
$ history
1 cd Documents
2 ls
3 open -a Safari
4 history
```

The commands are listed in the order in which they were executed. To reuse a particular command, type **!** (exclamation point; also called "bang" by Unix geeks), followed by the number of the command you want to reuse. Example 4-10 shows how to use this command.

Example 4-10. Using a command from the history

```
$ !2
ls
Adobe SVG 3.0
Installer Log
Music
Desktop
Pictures
Documents
Public
Library
Sites
Movies
Work
```

Note that the shell tells you which command is running as it runs the command. This is useful because you can tell what arguments are being used. Another way to navigate the history list is to use the first few letters of the command instead of the command number. Example 4-11 shows how to quickly execute the last command that started with an *o* character.

Example 4-11. Executing a command from the history based on character

```
$ !o open -a Safari
```

Whenever you exit *bash*, it writes its history to the *~/.bash_history* file. Likewise, whenever you start *bash*, it populates its history with the contents of the *~/.bash_history* file. This allows you to quit and restart your shell and still have your history available to you. By default, the history file is set to retain up to the last 500 commands. To change this value, set the `HISTFILESIZE` environment variable to the number of lines that you want to keep. For example, to change it to remember 1,000 commands instead of 500, you would use the following:

```
$ export HISTFILESIZE=1000
```

Once again, if you'd like to make this change permanent, you'll have to add it to your *~/.bash_profile* file.

Redirecting Output

If you've been using the shell for a while, the *history* command might have so many entries to display that they scroll by too quickly for you to read them. Earlier in the chapter, you learned about the *more* command. It might have occurred to you that this would be a perfect opportunity to use *more* to paginate the *history* command's output. However, it may not have been immediately obvious how to do so.

This is where one of the most powerful features of the Unix shell comes into play. The shell allows you to redirect the output from one command and pass it along to another command. It also enables you to redirect a command's output to a file for later perusal. For example, if the *history* command's output is scrolling too quickly for you, you could redirect its output to the *more* command as follows:

```
$ history | more
```

The pipe (|) character is used for passing the data between commands. For saving the output to a file, you'd use the greater than character (>). So if you wanted to save a directory listing of your */Applications* folder to a file on your Desktop, use the command:

```
$ ls -l /Applications > ~/Desktop/DirectoryListing.txt
```

You can even append output from a command to the end of a file by using two greater than symbols (>>). If you want to add the directory listing of your */Applications/Utilities* folder to the file on your desktop:

```
$ ls -l /Applications/Utilities >> ~/Desktop/DirectoryListing.txt
```

For some fun with redirecting data between commands, try using the *ls* command to send a directory listing to the *say* command. Just make sure your speakers are on to hear the results.

Loops

Another powerful feature the shell gives you is the ability to loop through commands. This will come into play more in Chapter 13 when shell scripts are covered, but for now, here's a basic example of a loop. Let's say that you have several text files on your Desktop that you want the *say* command to read aloud to you. After reading the discussion of wildcards earlier in the chapter, you might think the following command would work:

```
$ say ~/Desktop/*.txt
```

However, executing that command will make *say* merely speak the files' names, not read the files' contents to you. To have each file read aloud, you need to supply each file's name to the *say* command, using only one file each time you issue the command. This can quickly become tedious if you have several files you want to have read aloud.

If you enter the shell commands shown in Example 4-12, you can make the shell do all of that work for you:

Example 4-12. A simple shell loop

```
$ for i in $(ls ~/Desktop/*.txt)
> do
> say -f $i
> done
```

The first line of this loop starts with the *for* command, which tells *bash* that we're defining a loop. The next value, *i*, is a temporary variable to hold a single file's name. The *in* portion tells *for* that the part that follows, *$(ls ~/Desktop/*.txt)*, is where it should look for the values to place in *i*. The *$()* convention is used to have the shell place the output of one command (in this case, *ls ~/Desktop/*.txt*) into another, but isn't quite the same as redirecting the output using a pipe.

The *do* line indicates to the shell that the commands that follow are the contents of the loop. The loop is closed with a simple *done* command. When executed, the shell will use the *ls* command to find all files in *~/Desktop* that end in *.txt*. The shell will then take the first result, store it in the variable *i*, and process the commands between *do* and *done*. Once the commands have been executed, the shell takes the next value from the directory listing results, places it in the *i* variable, and then loops through the commands again.

Shell Scripts

One of the true powers of the shell is that you don't always have to type in your commands by hand, tediously one after the other. When you find a set of tasks that you perform often, you can consolidate them into a *shell script*. A shell script is nothing more than a collection of shell commands that is saved in a file on the filesystem. For more information on shell scripts, as well as some examples, take a look at the section on shell scripts in Chapter 13.

Using Other Shells

Essentially, all the shells on the system (*sh*, *bash*, *ksh*, *tcsh*, and *zsh*) do the same thing: they take input from you and translate it into commands that are run on the system. However, each shell differs in the specifics of how you interact with it and the special features that it offers. If you've never used the Unix shell, you'll do just fine sticking with the default *bash* shell. But if you've become accustomed to the *tcsh* shell that was the default on earlier versions of Mac OS X, or if you are an old-hand Unix user who simply prefers another shell, you may want to change the default shell to suit your preferences.

Because a shell is a program like any other, all you have to do to use a different shell temporarily is type its name at the command line. For example, if you want to use the *tcsh* shell, execute the following:

```
$ tcsh
```

The prompt changes to a percent sign (%), which is the default prompt for the *tcsh* shell, and will be in effect until you exit out of it.

The Secure Shell

There's another popular shell found on Unix systems: *ssh*. The secure shell allows you to connect to a remote Unix system and execute commands on it as if you were sitting at its console. *ssh* is primarily made up of two components. One is *sshd*, which is dubbed Remote Login on Mac OS X. This is the server component of *ssh* that handles incoming shell requests.

The other half of *ssh* is the *ssh* command, which is kept in */usr/bin*. You can learn more about the Secure Shell in Chapter 12.

Changing the Shell

To change the default shell used by the Terminal when it launches, simply open the Terminal preferences (Terminal → Preferences), then specify the shell you want to execute in the "Execute this command" text field, as shown in Figure 4-3. Now, whenever you open a Terminal window, you'll get the shell that you want.

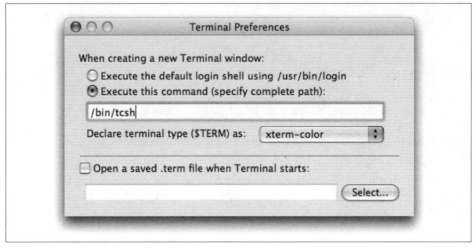

Figure 4-3. Changing the shell using the Terminal preferences pane

Note that this setting doesn't change your default shell when you remotely log in. To change your default shell at the system level rather than only in the Terminal application, you'll need to modify your user account's *shell* value. You'll need to use Net-Info Manager to do so, as shown in Chapter 7.

Using Other Terminals

In addition to having many different shells to choose from, there are alternative terminal applications available. If you find that Apple's Terminal doesn't get the job done, you can try out an application such as iTerm (*http://iterm.sourceforge.net/*). iTerm, a freeware application, fulfills the same purpose as Apple's Terminal, but it has a few extra niceties, such as a tabbed window interface and graphical flourishes, such as using an image as your Terminal window background.

If you're a Unix veteran, you may be looking for the tried-and-true *xterm*. When you install Apple's X11 package, *xterm* is installed as well and will open by default upon launching the X11 application in */Application/Utilities*. Unix vets might also seek out *rxvt*. While *rxvt* is not included with Mac OS X or the X11 package, you can install it using a package manager such as Fink or DarwinPorts (both of which were discussed in Chapter 2).

Getting Help

The *bash* shell provides a *help* command that will give information about all its built-in commands. Example 4-13 shows how to get information about the *alias* command.

Example 4-13. Getting help for alias

```
$ help alias
alias: alias [-p] [name[=value] ... ]
'alias' with no arguments or with the -p option prints the list
of aliases in the form alias NAME=VALUE on standard output.
Otherwise, an alias is defined for each NAME whose VALUE is given.
A trailing space in VALUE causes the next word to be checked for
alias substitution when the alias is expanded. Alias returns
true unless a NAME is given for which no alias has been defined.
```

If you want to get a list of commands that *help* can help you with, use the command by itself.

To get help about any other command in the Unix shell, use *man*, the all-purpose, Swiss Army knife for getting information for most commands on the system in a form known as a *manpage*. For example, to see the manpage for *man*, type the following:

```
$ man man
```

When you execute this command, you'll see the output shown in Figure 4-4. Notice that there's a colon (:) at the bottom of the window with the cursor next to it. This indicates that there's more content to be seen in the manpage. At the prompt, you can:

- Hit the spacebar or the F key to page down.
- Hit the B key to go back a page.
- Type a / (slash) followed by a word to search forward for that word.
- Hit the Q key to quit.

When you quit out of viewing a manpage, the information goes away and you are left with the same contents in your window as you had before you executed the *man* command. This is because *man* actually uses the program configured in your environment to be the pager—a program that can take output and step through it a page at a time. By default, the pager is the *less* tool, which is the application that allows you to use the keystrokes listed above. If you want, you can use the *more* pager by setting your PAGER environment variable as follows:

```
$ export PAGER=more
```

The *more* pager isn't as full-featured as *less*, but it does leave the contents of the manpage onscreen when you exit. All things being equal though, I suggest you open

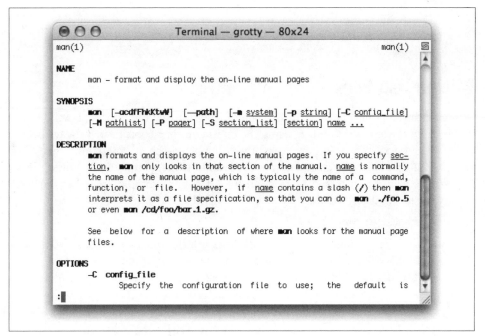

```
         Terminal — grotty — 80x24

man(1)                                                        man(1)

NAME
       man - format and display the on-line manual pages

SYNOPSIS
       man [-acdfFhkKtwW] [--path] [-m system] [-p string] [-C config_file]
       [-M pathlist] [-P pager] [-S section_list] [section] name ...

DESCRIPTION
       man formats and displays the on-line manual pages. If you specify sec-
       tion, man only looks in that section of the manual. name is normally
       the name of the manual page, which is typically the name of a command,
       function, or file.  However, if name contains a slash (/) then man
       interprets it as a file specification, so that you can do  man ./foo.5
       or even man /cd/foo/bar.1.gz.

       See below for a description of where man looks for the manual page
       files.

OPTIONS
       -C config_file
              Specify the configuration file to use; the default is
:
```

Figure 4-4. The man command

a second Terminal window rather than change your pager to browse the manpage documentation.

The real trick to using *man* is knowing which command might be the one that you want information on. To help you find the right manpage, use the *apropos* command. For example, if you want to find the manpages containing information about power management, use the following command:

```
$ apropos power
```

This returns six manpages, with one for *pmset* that has a summary indicating that it's for modifying power management settings.

Other Places to Find Help

Of course, there are other resources for helping you out with the command line. In addition to the books listed in the "Further Explorations" section toward the end of this chapter, you can find help online. A good place to start is Google (*http://www. google.com*). If you're having trouble with a specific command, enter it into the Google search box and see what comes up. Chances are, one of the first few hits will either have a tutorial or some pointers to get you in the right direction.

O'Reilly's own Mac DevCenter (*http://www.macdevcenter.com*) often has tips on using the command line or provides other articles related to Mac OS X's Unix subsystem. Also, it's worth remembering that there are very few practical differences between the shell on Mac OS X and on other Unixes. So most articles you find for FreeBSD, Linux, and other Unix flavors will prove helpful as well.

Editing Text Files

While editing text files in the GUI is straightforward using the built-in TextEdit program (*/Applications*), editing files using the command-line tools hasn't always been a walk in the park, unless you are comfortable with old-school text editors like *vi* or Emacs. But thanks to the *open* command, several of the command-line editing tasks that you need to perform can be done in the GUI. For example, to open your *bash* history file in TextEdit, use the following command:

```
$ open ~/.bash_history
```

For most text-file editing, however, TextEdit is a little underpowered. Also, it can't be used as the command-line editor program (via the EDITOR environment variable), and it can't be used to edit files while you are logged in remotely.

Alternatives to TextEdit

While Mac OS X's built-in TextEdit can certainly get the job done, there are text editors that are far more robust. The venerable BBEdit (*http://www.barebones.com*) has been a popular text editor on the Mac for many years now. Recent versions of BBEdit have added support for script editing, allowing you to modify and run a script without having to move back and forth between the BBEdit application and the Terminal. The only downside to BBEdit is its cost: $150. However, BareBones software also offers TextWrangler, which is a lighter-weight text editor and best of all, it's free.

A newer text editor that's gained some popularity is SubEthaEdit (*http://www. codingmonkeys.de*). SubEthaEdit offers many of the features found in BBEdit, but touts its collaboration abilities. Using Bonjour, SubEthaEdit users can share and modify documents on the fly.

Both SubEthaEdit and BBEdit include a command-line tool for easy integration with Mac OS X's shell.

---

nano

If you do need to edit text files on the command line—say you are logged in remotely or need to edit a file owned by root—the easiest text editor to use on the system is *nano*. To use *nano* to edit a file, use the following command:

```
$ nano filename
```

When you use *nano*, you'll see the user interface shown in Figure 4-5. In place of a toolbar, there is a series of commands at the bottom of the screen. The caret (^) character prefixing all those lines stands for the Control key on your keyboard. Simply press the Control key plus the letter of the command to perform some action. For example, to save a file, which *nano* refers to as "WriteOut," hit Control-O. To open, or "Read" a file, hit Control-R. And to exit, hit Control-X.

 Versions of Mac OS X prior to 10.4 used *pico* for a simple text editor. On Tiger, *nano* is used instead, and the command */usr/bin/pico* has been replaced with a link to */usr/bin/nano*.

Aside from the Control key combinations, *nano* is fairly straightforward to use. Arrow keys move the cursor up and down, and whatever you type is inserted wherever the cursor is located.

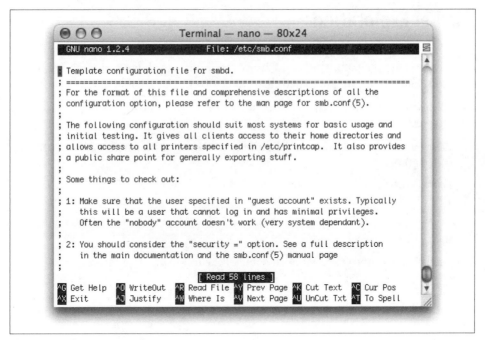

Figure 4-5. The nano text editor

vi and Emacs

Mac OS X also ships with the two venerable Unix powerhouses of text editing: *vi* and Emacs. Each of these tools has a long history and feature sets that are even longer. These tools are powerful indeed and up to the task of any amount of text editing that you want to do—including hardcore development—but in many ways, they are more complicated than what you need for everyday tasks. However, if you are already a user of either of these two editors, they are available for use on the system.

 In Mac OS X Panther, the default *vi* was switched to *vim*, a *vi* replacement that duplicates all the functionality of the original *vi* and extends it in many useful ways, adding unlimited undo and syntax highlighting.

This isn't the place for a full tutorial on how to use *vi* or Emacs, but you should be able to exit either of these shells if you find yourself in one. To exit *vi*, type the following:

    :q!

To exit Emacs, type Control-X, and then Control-C.

Further Explorations

This chapter's aim was to give you enough knowledge of how the shell works to successfully execute the commands that are covered through the rest of the book. However, this chapter has just scratched the surface of what is possible with the shell.

The following books are recommended to help you learn more about the subjects in this chapter:

- *Learning the bash Shell,* Third Edition, by Cameron Newham (O'Reilly Media, Inc., 2005)
- *Learning the vi Editor,* Sixth Edition, by Linda Lamb, et al. (O'Reilly Media, Inc., 1998)
- *Learning GNU Emacs,* Third Edition, by Debra Cameron, et al. (O'Reilly Media, Inc., 2004)

You might also want to take a look at some of the following manpages:

- *man*
- *apropos*
- *ls*
- *mkdir*
- *rmdir*
- *cd*
- *rm*
- *mv*
- *cp*

## CHAPTER 5

System Startup and Login

Usually, the first thing you do when you sit down at your computer is either hit the Power-On button or—for those who leave their machines on all the time—log in. Most of the time, you probably don't think much about what happens behind the Apple logo and spinner as the system boots up or about the events that happen between the time you enter your username and password and the time Mac OS X's desktop appears.

Booting a Mac is not a single-step process; over 100 programs take part in the process of transforming your machine from an inert collection of plastic and metal into a running system. In general, though, the process can be broken down into three major steps. First, the hardware powers up and organizes itself. Next, the hardware launches the operating system, and *then* the operating system finally starts up. This chapter removes the veil of mystery and shows what goes on behind the scenes as your Mac starts up—from the time you press that Power-On button, right up to the login screen.

The Hardware Boot Process

When you press the Power-On button on your Mac, a small hardware program embedded in the main logic board of your machine, known as the POST (Power-On Self Test), is activated. The first thing the POST does is power up and then initializes the CPU. Next the POST performs some tests on the core system components, such as the memory, to make sure the system can boot. If everything checks out OK, the POST starts a program called Open Firmware, located on a reprogrammable chip on the motherboard. It's at this point in the boot process that you hear the famous Mac chime.

Open Firmware's first job is to find the various hardware devices attached to the motherboard of the machine. This includes internal hardware such as video cards and hard drives as well as external hardware connected via the FireWire, USB, and SCSI buses. As Open Firmware discovers the various hardware devices, it organizes them into a device tree, which makes it easier for the higher levels of the system to access those devices.

So What's Open Firmware?

You're no doubt familiar with the terms *software* and *hardware*. But *firmware*? Well, when chip designers make a mistake in a hardware program, they pretty much have to throw away the chip and start over. This is quite unlike software, where all you need to do is replace the instructions without throwing away a physical device. The solution that hardware designers came up with is to create a chip that can be reprogrammed. The instructions on the chip are permanently stored on it, so it's not quite software. But they can be changed. Being neither hardware nor software, they settled on the name *firmware*.

Open Firmware is the name given to the IEEE standard for a machine-independent BIOS that grew out of the boot code used in workstations and servers from Sun Microsystems. What separates it from other BIOS implementations is that it uses a bytecode representation of the Forth language. This allows the same code to run on different processors without change, which lets hardware makers provide on-card drivers that will work on PowerPC, Sparc, and Intel x86 architectures. In addition, Open Firmware provides a mechanism for each piece of hardware to describe itself so that the host system can best use it.

You can find out more information about Open Firmware at *http://www. openfirmware.org*.

After Open Firmware finds the hardware, it looks for an operating system to boot. It first checks its own configuration for the boot device. Assuming the configured device is a disk and is attached, Open Firmware then looks on the disk for the blessed operating system booter and loads and boots the system. If a bootable operating system isn't present on the configured device, Open Firmware conducts a search of any other drives attached to your system. Finally, if no boot device is found, you're presented with a folder icon with a blinking question mark indicating that no boot system could be found.

 If you previously used Mac OS 9 (or earlier versions of the Mac OS), chances are you've seen the flashing question mark a few times. It wasn't uncommon for something to get corrupted, causing Open Firmware not to find Mac OS 9's System folder on startup. This doesn't happen as often—if ever—with Mac OS X, thankfully.

Taking a Peek at Open Firmware

Even though you will rarely (if ever) need to deal directly with Open Firmware, you can take a quick peek at its configuration using the *nvram* command-line tool. Example 5-1 shows the use of this command and a bit of its output (slightly abbreviated).

Example 5-1. Looking at Open Firmware's configuration

```
$ nvram -p
oem-banner? false
boot-script
virt-size -1
output-device screen
output-device-1 scca
input-device keyboard
input-device-1 scca
mouse-device mouse
selftest-#megs 0
boot-volume 3
boot-device mac-io/ata-4@1f000/@0:10,\\:tbxi
boot-screen
boot-args
default-server-ip
default-gateway-ip
default-router-ip
default-client-ip
default-subnet-mask
default-mac-address? false
screen-#columns 100
screen-#rows 40
scroll-lock true
skip-netboot? false
diag-switch? false
boot-command mac-boot
ram-size 0x30000000
```

Notice the boot-device line in the output. This tells Open Firmware what device it should boot from. In this case, Open Firmware is set to boot from the ATA-based disk drive. This string is different depending on what kind of bus (ATA or SCSI) your hard drive is attached to and what partition on the drive you are booting from.

The *nvram* command can also be used to set these values if you have an administrator account on the system. To set a particular value in Open Firmware, you would use the following syntax:

```
sudo nvram name=value
```

If you want to set a large number of values at once, you can load them from a text file. The file must consist of a list of *name=value* statements. The syntax for loading the contents of the file into Open Firmware is:

```
sudo nvram -f filename
```

Resetting Open Firmware

It should go without saying, but mucking about with your Open Firmware settings can put your system into a fairly odd state. Luckily, if you go overboard and your Open Firmware settings get messed up, there's an easy way to reset things, commonly referred to as "Zapping the PRAM." To do this, hold down Option-⌘-P-R while booting your machine. Hold these keys down until you've heard the system startup chime two or three times, and then let go of the keys to boot your system.

Updating Firmware

Every so often, an update to Mac OS X is released that requires a firmware upgrade for certain machines in order to work correctly. Since Open Firmware is used primarily at boot time, not having up-to-date firmware can result in a machine that won't boot—it'll get stuck at a gray screen instead. You should be sure to read the release notes for any major update to Mac OS X to see if you need a firmware update before installing it.

Another place to look for documentation about firmware updates is on Apple's support web site at *http://www.info.apple.com*. To quickly see the pages dealing with firmware updates required for Mac OS X, enter `Mac OS X Firmware Update` in the Search Apple Support box. These pages tell you how to determine whether the firmware on your Mac needs to be upgraded before you install a new operating system.

There are two ways to determine the firmware version you have:

- The first is to use the System Profiler application (see Chapter 12 for details on System Profiler).
- The second is to access Open Firmware directly.

Accessing Open Firmware

If the *nvram* command doesn't give you enough access to the firmware of the system, you can access it directly by holding down the Option-⌘-O-F keys as you boot your machine. This drops you right into Open Firmware's command line, as shown in Example 5-2.

Example 5-2. The Open Firmware command-line interface

```
Apple PowerBook3,1 4.1.8f5
BootROM built on 03/21/01 at 11:49:53
Copyright 1994-2001 Apple Computer, Inc.
All Rights Reserved
Welcome to Open Firmware, the system time and date is: 22:51:00 09/21/2003
To continue booting, type 'mac-boot' and press return.
```

Example 5-2. The Open Firmware command-line interface (continued)

```
To shut down, type 'shut-down' and press return.
ok
0 > _
```

The first line of output tells you the model of your computer, followed by the version of your firmware. In this case, the computer is an Apple PowerBook3,1, and the firmware version is 4.1.8f5.

Macintosh Model Names

When you see your Mac's model name in Open Firmware or in System Profiler as something like "PowerBook3,1" you might wonder how that maps to its more well-known name of "PowerBook G3 (FireWire)." It refers to the machine using the latter name while Open Firmware and the system internals know it as the shorter, more concise name—and there's no direct mapping between the two names to be found on the Apple web site.

There is a file, however, on your hard drive that gives the mappings between these names (*/System/Library/SystemProfiler/SPPlatformReporter.spreporter/Contents/Resources/English.lproj/Localizable.strings*). This is a Unicode file, so you'll need to open it in TextEdit (using the *open -e filename* command, which forces a file to be opened in TextEdit) or some other editor that understands the Unicode text encoding.

After the banner is printed, you are at the Open Firmware prompt (>), a pretty limited place unless you really know what you are doing. Table 5-1 lists a few of the commands that you can use. If you get yourself in a real jam, Example 5-3 shows how to reset your firmware and restart the system.

Table 5-1. Open Firmware commands

Key	Description
printenv	Prints all the variables held in firmware
namevalue	Sets a variable to the given value
password	Sets an Open Firmware password
reset-nvram	Clears the variables in firmware and replaces them with default values
reset-all	Causes the machine to reboot
mac-boot	Causes the machine to continue booting into the configured system
shut-down	Shuts down the machine

Example 5-3. Resetting Open Firmware and restarting the system

```
0 > reset-nvram
0 > reset-all
```

Setting the Boot Disk

To set the disk that you want to boot from, use the Startup Disk preference panel in System Preferences. When you launch this tool, as shown in Figure 5-1, it will allow you to choose from all of the Mac OS system folders on the hard drives attached to your machine. If there is a Mac OS X Server offering NetBoot or NetInstall services, you will see its available bootable images as well. If such a server is not detected, you still have the option to boot from a network volume by choosing the Network Start-up item.

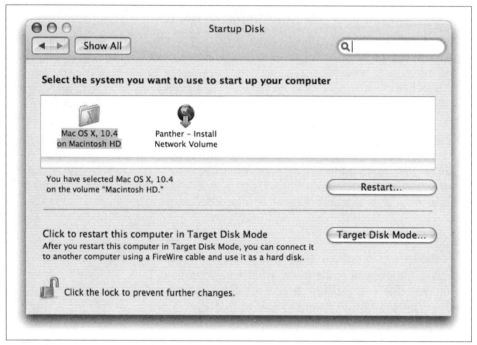

Figure 5-1. The Startup Disk preference panel

When you select an operating system to boot from in the Startup Disk preference panel, two things happen. First, Open Firmware is programmed with the location of the boot device. Second, a small bit of information is written to the boot blocks of the hard disk that contains the system indicating where on the drive the boot program for the operating system is located. This second step, known as *blessing the system*, allows more than one OS to be installed on a hard drive or partition. This means you can boot into either Mac OS X or Mac OS 9, even if they are both installed on the same volume.

Booting Mac OS 9

In January 2002, Apple began shipping all new Macs with Mac OS X as their default operating system. Shortly thereafter, at Apple's World Wide Developer Conference (WWDC), Steve Jobs gave a mock eulogy for Mac OS 9, stressing to developers the importance of Mac OS X. However, in January 2003, the final change was made: new Macs would only boot into Mac OS X, leaving Classic the only way to run older Mac apps. While this change might have left some users with legacy Mac software in the cold, it reflects Apple's dedication to the Mac OS X platform. Sometimes, you just have to give up the past and move on to bigger and better things.

Blessed system disk

To look at the startup settings for your machine from the command line, use the *bless* command. For example, to take a look at the various settings of the drive from which you are currently running, execute *bless* as shown in Example 5-4.

Example 5-4. Executing bless to examine boot settings

```
$ sudo bless -info -bootBlocks
finderinfo[0]: 2483 => Blessed System Folder is /System/Library/CoreServices
finderinfo[1]: 0 => No Startup App folder (ignored anyway)
finderinfo[2]: 0 => Open-folder linked list empty
finderinfo[3]: 0 => No OS 9 + X blessed 9 folder
finderinfo[4]: 0 => Unused field unset
finderinfo[5]: 2483 => OS X blessed folder is /System/Library/CoreServices
64-bit VSDB volume id: 0x1BD7BA028DDA6A89
```

Try changing the settings around in your Startup Disk preference panel and reentering this command to see what changes. You may have to switch out of the Startup Disk preference panel for it to save your modifications. There's quite a bit more you can do with the *bless* command, such as blessing a particular folder or partition on your disk. See the *bless* manpage for details.

Changing the Boot Disk at Boot Time

Sometimes you will want to boot from some device other than the default. Usually this happens when you need to boot from a DVD or a FireWire drive to replace or repair your primary OS installation. You can use the following options to choose the boot disk you want to use:

- To boot from a DVD, hold down the C key as you boot.
- To boot from a NetBoot server, hold down the N key as you boot.

- To see the local drives that contain a bootable partition, hold down the Option key as you boot, which invokes an Open Firmware program called the *OS Picker*, as shown in Figure 5-2.

- If you have one disk that contains Mac OS 9 and one disk that contains Mac OS X, you can boot into Mac OS X by holding down the X key while the system boots. If you have more than one Mac OS X system installed, however, this trick won't work.

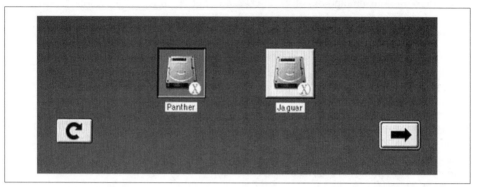

Figure 5-2. The OS Picker

The OS Picker duplicates some, but not all, of the functionality of the Startup Disk preference panel. While it will show all bootable partitions available to your Mac, it is limited in that it can only see the blessed operating system on a partition. This means that if you have both Mac OS X and Mac OS 9 installed on the same partition, OS Picker shows only the one that was configured for boot in the Startup Disk preference panel. If you want to boot into the non-blessed operating system on a partition, you'll have to make the change in Startup Disk and not with the OS Picker.

Locking Down Open Firmware

Since Open Firmware controls the boot process and accepts input from the keyboard during system boot time—either in the form of boot-key combinations or by accessing the Open Firmware prompt—it is easy for anybody to make your Mac boot from any other drive. For most personal users, this isn't a problem. In fact, it allows great flexibility in starting up your system with multiple versions of Mac OS. In corporate or academic settings, however, you may not want people to be able to muck about with the settings of the computer, or the data it contains, quite so easily.

There are two ways to enable an Open Firmware password. The first is to download the Open Firmware Password utility from Apple through its support web site at *http://docs.info.apple.com/article.html?artnum=120095*. The second way is at the Open Firmware command line using the following process:

Single-User and Verbose Modes

There are two other useful modes you can use while booting your Mac: *single-user mode* and *verbose mode*. Single-user mode is a special Unix system state in which system startup is stopped and a login prompt is offered, allowing for administrative and maintenance activities to be performed without ever seeing Mac OS X's Aqua interface. Historically, single-user mode has been used when a system becomes unstable and needs critical areas to be fixed. To boot into single-user mode, hold down ⌘-S at startup. When the system has booted, you are presented with a simple command-line prompt. To exit single-user mode, type **exit** or **reboot**; *exit* causes the system to go multiuser and complete the boot into the GUI environment.

To start your Mac in verbose mode, hold down ⌘-V at startup. Instead of the gray-on-gray Apple logo and spinner, you'll see a plain-text printout of the various things going on as you boot your system. If you want to see this every time you boot your system, you can use the *nvram* command to set the Open Firmware variable *boot-args* to -v.

1. Boot into Open Firmware (Option-⌘-O-F).
2. At the Open Firmware prompt, type your password; you are prompted to enter your password twice.
3. Set a security mode for Open Firmware by typing *setenv security-mode full* or *setenv security-mode command*. The first option totally locks down your machine and requires a password to be entered to boot the system. The second option lets the system boot as configured, but requires a password to either access the Open Firmware or use any boot key options.
4. Restart the machine using the *reset-all* command.

To turn off password protection, boot into Open Firmware and type **setenv security-mode none**. You will be asked for your password, if one is set, to make this change.

If you have a password-protected machine for which you've forgotten the password, there is a way to reset the password: open the machine and change the total amount of RAM in your system. Then reset the PRAM by using Option-⌘-P-R at boot time.

It should be noted that being able to lock down the system with an Open Firmware password is not a total security feature. If somebody can open up the machine and reset the memory in it, then Open Firmware will disable the password protection. Sure, you can padlock desktop machines, but there is no way to keep people out of the memory expansion slots on a laptop. This matches a truism in computer security—if somebody has physical access to a machine, then he can gain access to the data on it. Though if that data is encrypted with a tool like FileVault (discussed in Chapter 9), an intruder won't be able to read it.

The Operating System Boot Process

When Open Firmware boots Mac OS X, it does so through *BootX* (located in */System/ Library/CoreServices*). It's important to note that Open Firmware doesn't know that it's booting Mac OS X, nor does it have any concept of the filesystem that contains *BootX*. All it knows is that there is a program at a particular location on a drive that it can load and run. It is the job of *BootX* to boot the system from there.

The first thing *BootX* does is display the "boot" image on screen. This is the monochrome gray-on-gray screen with the Apple logo and spinner on it that you see after your computer chimes. It then loads the kernel from the disk and the essential kernel-level device drivers (such as those for accessing disk drives) necessary to get things running. Once loaded, the kernel's initialization procedure is called.

The kernel loads device drivers for all the devices connected to the computer and then finds the boot drive. It may seem a bit odd that the kernel has to find the drive that it was loaded from, but remember that it was loaded from the drive and then started. The kernel determines the drive it was loaded from by consulting Open Firmware. Once the kernel finds the boot drive, it mounts the drive at the Unix filesystem root (*/*), starts its internal process server, which allows processes to communicate with each other, and then starts the *launchd* daemon, which takes over for the BSD */sbin/init* program previously used by earlier versions of Mac OS X.

Launch Control

Prior to Tiger, Mac OS X used a very traditional Unix startup process. After initialization, the kernel would load *mach_init* and *init* before passing control to the */etc/rc* script. The *rc* script did the bulk of preparing your Mac for everyday use, and it continues to on Tiger. It starts the virtual memory system, mounts filesystems, loads kernel extensions, and launches service daemons. Finally, pre-Tiger Macs would launch *SystemStarter* to finish booting the system.

For Tiger, Apple reinvented Mac OS X's startup procedure. However, the repercussions of these changes extend beyond the boot process. On a Unix system, there are several daemons tasked with launching other applications. Some of these "super daemons," like *xinetd* and *inetd*, launch a daemon in response to a network connection. Others, like *cron* and *at*, run software based on time schedules. Tiger's *launchd* replaces not only *init* and *SystemStarter*, but these other daemons as well.

When loaded by the kernel, *launchd* scans through */System/Library/LaunchDaemons* and */Library/LaunchDaemons* for items that need to be loaded. Like *SystemStarter* before it, *launchd* uses XML-formatted property list (*plist*) files to store configuration information for each daemon. Using these files, *launchd* determines which services are enabled, their dependencies, and whether they can be launched on demand. Next, *launchd* loads the services in an order that satisfies all dependencies and, when possible, uses parallel execution. This allows Tiger to load what it needs—and only what it needs—as quickly as possible, resulting in shorter boot times and a leaner system.

Daemons and agents

The *launchd* daemon breaks background processes into two types: agents and daemons. An agent is an application that runs within the context of a user session. That is, it is designed to stay in the background and handle requests for the length of a user's use of the system. When the user logs in, the agent is started. When he logs out, the agent is stopped. A daemon, by contrast, is designed to provide services for the entire time the system is running, regardless of which user is logged in; daemons are started at boot and stopped at shutdown. In short, agents are for users, daemons are for the system.

launchd is capable of handling both daemons and agents. On Tiger, the majority of system services that were formerly started by *SystemStarter* have been migrated to use *launchd*. In addition, services and tasks started by *xinetd* and *cron* have also been migrated. Though Mac OS X is the only Unix system to use this new launcher so far, Apple has made *launchd* open source, paving the way for adoption by other Unix systems. Apple also plans to extend *launchd* to handle other types of launch tasks. For example, a future version of *launchd* could sense hardware changes and load an application in response, similar to how plugging in a digital camera launches iPhoto with the current system.

Inside a launchd property list file

Configuration files for each of the services handled by *launchd* are kept in either */System/Library/LaunchDaemons* or */Library/LaunchDaemons* (following the filesystem domains discussed in Chapter 3). Agents keep their configuration files in similar locations, but within a folder named LaunchAgents. Each service's *launchd* configuration file is an XML-formatted property list similar to that shown in Example 5-5.

Example 5-5. A launchd service property list file

```
<?xml version="1.0" encoding="UTF-8"?>
<!DOCTYPE plist PUBLIC "-//Apple Computer//DTD PLIST 1.0//EN"
"http://www.apple.com/DTDs/PropertyList-1.0.dtd">
<plist version="1.0">
<dict>
    <key>Label</key>
    <string>com.apple.syslogd</string>
    <key>ServiceDescription</key>
    <string>Apple System Log Daemon</string>
    <key>OnDemand</key>
    <false/>
    <key>ProgramArguments</key>
    <array>
```

Example 5-5. A launchd service property list file (continued)

```
            <string>/usr/sbin/syslogd</string>
    </array>
    <key>ServiceIPC</key>
    <false/>
</dict>
</plist>
```

Example 5-5 shows the property list file for *syslogd*. Since most of Tiger's services have been configured to work with *launchd*, you can find a number of other examples in the */System/Library/LaunchDaemons* folder.

Working with launchd services

To control *launchd* services by hand, Apple has provided the *launchctl* command (short for "launch control"). Using *launchctl*, you can start and stop services, load and unload configuration files, and view running services on your system. Because *launchd* has been written to handle both user and system daemons and agents, you'll need to call *launchctl* with root privileges to access services run by the system. Example 5-6 shows how to use *launchctl* to list *launchd*'s active system services.

Example 5-6. Viewing launchd's active services

```
$ sudo launchctl list
com.apple.KernelEventAgent
com.apple.mDNSResponder
com.apple.nibindd
com.apple.periodic-daily
com.apple.periodic-monthly
com.apple.periodic-weekly
com.apple.portmap
com.apple.syslogd
com.vix.cron
org.postfix.master
org.xinetd.xinetd
com.openssh.sshd
```

SystemStarter

Though *launchd* is the primary launch mechanism for applications on Tiger, not all daemons and agents have been updated to make use of it. Because of this, you may still end up using *SystemStarter* to launch custom daemons. *SystemStarter* determines the services it should start by scanning */System/Library/StartupItems* and */Library/ StartupItems* for items to be started when the system starts up, and then launches them. To help reduce boot time, *SystemStarter* attempts to run as many startup items as possible in parallel. This means startup tasks that take a little while to complete, such as setting up the network, don't stop all the other startup tasks from starting. This parallel process lets the boot process take advantage of dual processor machines.

The hostconfig file

Many startup items need some amount of input as to whether they should be launched or not. For example, if Personal Web Sharing is turned off on your machine, then the Apache startup item should not activate. To control these startup items without moving them out of their StartupItems folder, Mac OS X provides the */etc/hostconfig* file—a simple file consisting of a set of name-value pairs indicating which services should be run and which ones should not. This file is shown in Example 5-7.

Example 5-7. An example /etc/hostconfig file

```
##
# /etc/hostconfig
##
# This file is maintained by the system control panels
##
# Network configuration
HOSTNAME=-AUTOMATIC-
ROUTER=-AUTOMATIC-
# Services
AFPSERVER=-YES-
AUTHSERVER=-NO-
AUTOMOUNT=-YES-
CUPS=-YES-
IPFORWARDING=-NO-
IPV6=-YES-
MAILSERVER=-NO-
NETINFOSERVER=-AUTOMATIC-
NFSLOCKS=-AUTOMATIC-
NISDOMAIN=-NO-
RPCSERVER=-AUTOMATIC-
TIMESYNC=-YES-
QTSSERVER=-NO-
WEBSERVER=-NO-
SMBSERVER=-NO-
DNSSERVER=-NO-
COREDUMPS=-NO-
VPNSERVER=-NO-
CRASHREPORTER=-YES-
```

By looking at this file, you can see that many of the various servers available on the system aren't started at boot time. If you use the System Preferences application to enable a service and come back to this file, you'll see that the -NO- next to a service name has changed to -YES-.

 The *SystemStarter* doesn't use */etc/hostconfig* to make its decisions about which services to start; individual services use this information to decide that for themselves. For example, *SystemStarter* always runs the *RemoteDesktop* startup item, but when the *RemoteDesktop* startup item is invoked, it checks */etc/hostconfig* to see whether it should run or not.

Anatomy of a startup item

So what does a startup item look like? At a basic level, a startup item is a folder with the name of the startup item that contains the following two files:

- A program; typically a shell script, whose name matches the name of the startup item.

- A configuration property list (*plist*) file named *StartupParameters.plist* declaring the services provided by the item and its dependencies. Table 5-2 lists the keys that must appear in the configuration property list.

Table 5-2. StartupParameters.plist key descriptions

Key	Description
Description	A short description of the startup item. This string appears in the Boot panel at startup.
Provides	A list of services provided by the startup item. A service typically provides only one kind of service. *SystemStarter* runs only the first startup item it finds for any service provided.
Requires	A list of the services that this service depends on and that must be started before this item can be started. Note each item on this list must contain the service name, not the startup item name, of the service.
Uses	A list of services that this item uses but that aren't required for this item to be started.
OrderPreference	A string that lets *SystemStarter* determine in which order to start items that are equal in the dependency tree. This string can be one of the following: "First," "Early," "None," "Late," and "Last." This preference is advisory and might be ignored by *SystemStarter*.

Creating your own startup item is easy; much easier than actually writing a program that provides a useful service, although simple shell scripts that delete old files are useful services, too. Here's the step-by-step process to create your own startup item:

1. Create a directory in */Library/StartupItems* for your startup item. The name of the directory is the name of the item and should give some clue as to its function. Never create startup items in */System/Library/StartupItems*—that's the domain of Mac OS X.

2. Create an executable in the directory and name it the same thing as your startup item. The executable can be a shell script or a compiled program.

3. Create the *StartupParameters.plist* file in the directory. This file must be a valid property list file and contain values for the Description, Provides, Requires, Uses, and OrderPreference keys. You can create this file either by using a text editor and following the format shown in Example 5-8, or by using the Property List Editor application (*/Developer/Applications/Utilities*).

Example 5-8. The StartupItems.plist file for the Apache web server

```
{
    Description = "Apache web server";
    Provides = ("Web Server");
    Requires = ("DirectoryServices");
```

```
    Uses = ("Disks", "NFS");
    OrderPreference = "None";
}
```

SystemStarter is not just responsible for starting up startup items; it can also be used to restart or stop them. Because of this, *SystemStarter* passes in an argument to a startup item's executable, indicating the desired action. The valid strings for this argument are: "start," "restart," or "stop." A startup item is responsible for checking this argument and acting accordingly. Example 5-9 shows a sample startup script that can handle this. You can use this sample script as a template for your own startup items.

Example 5-9. A simple startup item executable

```
#!/bin/sh
# This script includes the /etc/rc.common file which provides useful
# functions that make the job of creating a startup item easier.
. /etc/rc.common
StartService( )
{
    "Starting my service"
    # insert code to start service here.
}
RestartService( )
{
    ConsoleMessage "Restarting my service"
    # insert code to stop service here.
}
StopService( )
{
    ConsoleMessage "Stopping my service"
    # insert code to stop service here.
}
# This should be the last line of your startup item. It calls the
# RunService function defined in rc.common which will in turn call
# the appropriate function in this script.
RunService "$1"
```

Starting and stopping startup items

You can start and stop Startup Items at any time using the *SystemStarter* command-line tool. To use this tool, use the following syntax:

```
    SystemStarter action service
```

where *action* is either *start*, *stop*, or *restart*, and *service* is the kind of service the startup item provides. Example 5-10 shows how to manually start the Apache web server.

Example 5-10. Manually starting the Apache web server

```
$ sudo SystemStarter start "Web Server"
Starting Apache web server
Processing config directory: /private/etc/httpd/users/*.conf
 Processing config file: /private/etc/httpd/users/colpanic.conf
 Processing config file: /private/etc/httpd/users/jldera.conf
 Processing config file: /private/etc/httpd/users/panic.conf
/usr/sbin/apachectl start: httpd started
```

The output from *SystemStarter* lets you know what's going on. In the case of the example here, the alert indicating that the server's fully qualified domain name couldn't be found is normal. To stop the Apache web server, use the command shown in Example 5-11.

Example 5-11. Manually stopping the Apache web server

```
$ sudo SystemStarter stop "Web Server"
Stopping Apache web server
/usr/sbin/apachectl stop: httpd stopped
```

Booting into Safe Mode

At some point you may experience a problem with a kernel extension crashing during system startup, which causes a kernel panic before startup is complete. To start your machine and remove or repair the offending item, Mac OS X can be booted into *Safe Mode*. To boot into Safe Mode, hold down the Shift key as you boot your Mac; this loads only the absolute minimum number of kernel extensions and only the most crucial daemons and services.

Because of Safe Mode's restrictions on kernel extensions and startup items, you are quite limited in what you can do. You can't use a DVD player, capture video, use an AirPort wireless network, or many other things. Therefore you should really use Safe Mode only when you need to troubleshoot a startup issue.

Logging In

When the system has booted and starts the *loginwindow* program, the system displays the user login screen, as shown in Figure 5-3. You won't see the login screen, however, if you've enabled the auto-login preference in the Accounts preference panel. With auto-login turned on, the selected user is automatically logged into her user account as the system starts up.

When you log in, the following things happen:

- Your environment, including preferences, environment variables, and Keychains, are loaded.
- The *SystemUIServer* is launched and handles the menu bar and menu extras (those little applets up in the upper-right area of the screen).

- The pasteboard server (*pbs*) is launched.
- The mouse, keyboard, sound, and display are configured according to your preferences.
- Any user-defined login items are processed.
- The Dock and Finder are started.

Figure 5-3. The Login panel

Bypassing the GUI Login Window

If for some reason you are at the login window and want to bypass it and get straight to the command line, there's a quick and easy way to do so. Simply enter `>console` (include the greater-than symbol) as your username in the login dialog box. The GUI exits and dumps you off at the black and white text-based console. Don't worry, the GUI comes back after you log out of your console session.

The only catch to this trick is that you must have your login screen set to display the username and password boxes instead of a list of users. However, if you have just the list of users, you can hold Option-Shift-Down Arrow and then press Return to reveal the username and password boxes.

Once the Finder is started and your login items have completed, login is finished and you can use your Mac. After a user has logged in, the *loginwindow* process has the following responsibilities:

- Monitors the Finder and Dock applications and restarts them if they unexpectedly exit for some reason.
- Displays alert dialogs from hidden applications.
- Manages the Force Quit window (→ Force Quit or Option-⌘-Esc).
- Manages the logout process.

 If the Finder or Dock processes die for some reason, they are automatically restarted by the *loginwindow* process. And if, for some reason, the *loginwindow* process itself dies, *launchd* restarts it so the login window is displayed and the system isn't left in an unusable state.

User Authentication

While the *loginwindow* process manages the login window and the process of logging a user into the machine, it doesn't actually perform the authentication of the user's credentials (usually a password). Instead, it passes off authentication to Directory Services. Only if a user's authentication credentials are accepted by Directory Services will the login process continue. Otherwise, the login window shakes—resembling somebody shaking her head and saying no—and won't log the user into the system until the user's password is entered correctly. Directory Services are covered in depth in Chapter 7.

Login Items

After they log in, users can specify applications to launch automatically by using the Accounts preference panel. A list of these applications can be found and configured through the Startup Items tab of the Accounts preference panel, as shown in Figure 5-4. For example, in the figure, you can see that both Address Book and Mail are set to start up automatically on login. You can put pretty much any application you want into this list.

If you want an application to run but not show up in your Dock, click the Hide button next to the item. Many support applications, such as the Palm Desktop HotSync manager, will run hidden using the functionality provided by this panel.

Customizing the Login Screen

You can customize the login window through the Login Options tab of the Accounts System Preference panel, shown in Figure 5-5. The Login Options pane lets administrators define how the list of users are displayed in the login window, among other

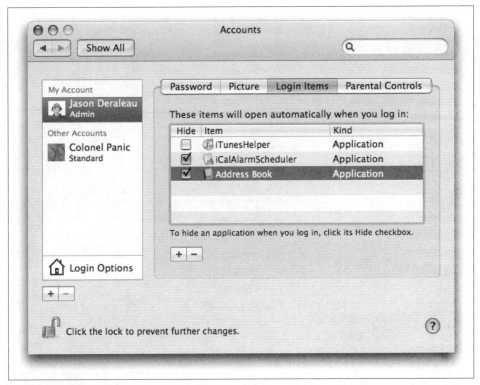

Figure 5-4. Login items

options such as whether or not the Restart, Sleep, and Shut Down buttons are displayed, and whether or not password hints will be displayed if a user fails to correctly enter his password three times in a row.

Tiger brings two important enhancements to the login window for international and handicapped users. International users can enable the Input menu on the login window, allowing easy language selection during login. For users with visual impairment, Mac OS X offers the VoiceOver feature for use at login. When enabled, VoiceOver describes aloud the elements of the login window, including the username and password fields.

This panel also lets you enable Fast User Switching, a feature that lets you have multiple users logged in at the same time. When you activate this, the Accounts menu shows up in the upper-right corner of the screen, to the left of the Spotlight icon. Depending on what you set on the Login Options screen preference panel, this menu bar item appears as either an icon, or with users' short or full names. You can click to the item to reveal a menu that allows you to log in as another user, to present the login panel, or to access Account Preferences, as shown in Figure 5-6.

When another user logs in, either through the login window or Fast User Switching, the same login process described in this section occurs.

Figure 5-5. Login Options

Figure 5-6. Fast User Switching menu

Logging Out

You can log out of your session using any of the following methods:

- Use the Log Out menu.
- Use the Shift-⌘-Q keystroke combination while using any application.

When you use either of these methods, the system displays a dialog box making sure that you really want to quit. If you don't want to see this dialog box, hold down the Option key while using the menu item or use the Option-Shift-⌘-Q key combination.

When you log out, all programs that you started while logged in quit automatically (if you haven't already quit them). However, if an application window has unsaved changes, you will be prompted to save those changes first before the application quits.

Shutting Down the System

When you shut down the system or reboot, a controlled process occurs so that the system is left in a good state. This process is:

- All running startup items are called with the stop parameter, giving them a chance to shut down gracefully.
- All running processes are stopped.
- The system syncs the filesystems with their in-memory caches.
- The system hands off control back to Open Firmware.
- Open Firmware either shuts down the system or reboots, depending on the instructions that the system handed to it as it shut down.

Normally, you'll shut down the system by selecting ⌘ → Shut Down. You can also shut down from the command line using either the *reboot* or the *shutdown* command. To reboot the system, simply enter the following:

```
$ sudo reboot
```

To shut down the system:

```
$ sudo shutdown -h now
```

 When you reboot or shut down from the command line, all running applications are automatically and promptly terminated. This means any unsaved changes will be lost, so make sure this is what you want to do before issuing either of these commands.

Energy Preferences

Apple's portables are more popular than their desktop siblings. While features like integrated wireless networking, DVD burners, and looks usually make the list, one of the most touted features is battery life. The Energy Saver preference panel in System Preferences is where you can make adjustments to get the most out of your laptop's battery. And don't you desktop users feel left out; there are some nice options for you to use as well.

Sleep

One of the best ways to conserve energy is to make use of the Sleep function ( → Sleep). When your Mac is put to sleep, it shuts down almost every one of its components (although no running applications are quit). When it's in this low power mode, the system isn't off. However, it isn't exactly usable either. To return your system to its normal state, wake it by pressing its Power-On button. The machine quickly springs back to life without requiring you to sit through another boot.

In addition to putting the system to sleep, you can put your display to sleep. Since the display is one of the largest drains on your battery, it's a good idea to put your display to sleep when it is not in use. To configure your system's sleep settings, use the Energy Saver preference panel, as show in Figure 5-7.

Scheduling

Another nice feature found in the Energy Saver preferences is the Schedule. Using the Schedule, you can have your Mac automatically power on and off at certain times of the day. This is a great option for classroom and corporate environments, where systems may not be properly turned off every day. You can access the Schedule by clicking the Schedule button in the lower-right corner of the Energy Saver preference panel.

Further Explorations

For more information about the topics in this chapter, see the *System Startup Programming Topics* book. It's installed on your system as part of the Xcode Tools package and is located at */Developer/ADC Reference Library/documentation/MacOSX/Conceptual/BPSystemStartup/*.

You may also want to look at the following manpages:

- *nvram*
- *bless*

- *rc*
- *launchd*
- *launchd.plist*
- *launchctl*
- *SystemStarter*

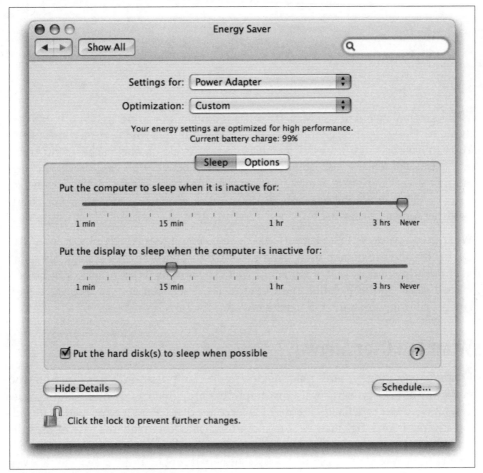

Figure 5-7. The Energy Saver preference panel

CHAPTER 6

Users and Groups

Thanks to its Unix heritage, Mac OS X is a multiuser operating system through and through. This simple fact means there can be more than one user of your system. You can have accounts for every member of a household on one machine, and everyone's stuff will remain independent and safe. Even better, with Fast User Switching, multiple users can be logged into the same machine at the same time. While only one user at a time can use the screen, with a quick click of a menu, you can switch effortlessly between user sessions.

What isn't obvious at first glance is that the concept of users runs quite deep in Mac OS X. Not only are human users treated as separate entities by the system, but many nonhuman users exist on the system as well. This means different tasks can be performed safely and in isolation from other tasks. Users can also be associated with groups, allowing the system to treat many users the same way.

What Is a User Anyway?

From the operating system's point of view, a user isn't necessarily a real person who taps away at the keyboard. A user is simply an entity that can own files and execute programs. A user is defined in terms of an account that has a set of properties including a numeric user ID, such as 501, and a username. Internally the system uses the user ID to keep track of the files and processes that belong to a user. The username is a more human-readable form that is used heavily throughout the system so that you don't have to think in terms of numbers.

Each user is also part of one or more groups. A *group* is a collection of users that the system can treat as a unit. Like a user, the system defines a group in terms of a numeric group ID and a more readable group name. Associating users with groups gives you the ability to control various resources of the system, and not just on a case-by-case basis. For example, the system uses the *admin* group to indicate users that can administer the computer. If your user ID is associated with the *admin* group, you have the ability to perform administrative tasks on the system.

To take a look at your user and group IDs, log into the command line and execute the *id* command, as shown in Example 6-1.

Example 6-1. Using the id command

```
$ id
uid=501(jldera) gid=501(jldera) groups=501(jldera), 80(admin)
```

The results of this example tell us that the currently logged-in user is named *jldera*, has a user ID of 501, and is a member of the *jldera* and *admin* groups. If you take a look at a non-administrative user, you will see something like the output shown in Example 6-2.

Example 6-2. Using the id command for a specific user

```
$ id panic
uid=502(panic) gid=502(panic) groups=502(panic)
```

This user isn't part of the *admin* group and therefore won't be allowed to administer the computer. Typical users have access to their Home folders and to the System Preferences panels that customize their user experience, but the rest of the system will be off limits (at least it will be if they don't know an administrator's username and password).

You'll notice in the examples above that the user IDs are 501 and 502. And if you are the only user on your machine, you'll notice that your user ID is also 501. This pattern is not coincidental; it follows the numbering scheme that Mac OS X uses to separate out users that should appear in the login window from those that should not. The rule is that users with an ID less than 500 won't appear. Those with an ID greater than 500 will appear.

Administrative Users

Administrative users represent a special class of users on the system. Here are just a few things that they are allowed to do that users without administrative privileges aren't:

- Install new programs in the */Applications* folder
- Add items to the */Library* folder such as startup items that take effect when the system is booted
- Change network settings using the Network preference panel
- Change the system time using the Date & Time preference panel
- Add users to or remove them from the system
- Set up or remove printers

Without administrative privileges, users are pretty much restricted to their Home folders and are only able to change the settings in System Preferences that relate to their desktops such as screen backgrounds and Finder preferences. The various System Preferences panels that require administrator access have a closed padlock on them, indicating that the user is not able to change the settings.

When you first install Mac OS X, the user that you create during the installation process automatically has administrative privileges. However, users created after that time will not have administrative privileges unless the person who creates their accounts (an administrator) grants the users admin privileges in the Accounts panel of System Preferences. You should consider your security needs and determine whether the user ID that you use for your normal work on the machine should have administrative privileges.

Managing Users

Traditional Unix systems typically store their user and group information in the */etc/ passwd* and */etc/group* files—and if you go looking, you can find these files on your Mac. However, after Mac OS X boots, it does not use these files. Instead, it uses Open Directory (discussed in Chapter 7) to store its user and group information. This allows the system to work equally well in home setups where there is only one machine and in enterprise environments where there might be hundreds of machines that use a central server for authentication.

While there are many ways to manage users on Mac OS X, the simplest and most direct by far is to use the Accounts preference panel.

Managing Users from the Command Line

Many hardcore Unix users are used to being able to manage users from the command line using tools like *useradd, usermod, userdel, groupadd, groupmod, groupdel, gpasswd, grpconv,* and *grpunconv*. Unfortunately, these commands don't exist on Mac OS X. The only tool of this kind on Mac OS X is the *passwd* command, which is used to change a user's password.

While it is possible to perform some user management from the command line through direct manipulation of the NetInfo database using the *niutil* command (covered in Chapter 7), several pieces of data in a user's NetInfo record, such as the *generateduid* property, don't have command-line tools to manage them. For almost all purposes, and unless you really need to manage users from the command line, you should use the Accounts preference panel to manage users.

Managing Users with the Accounts Panel

When you open the Accounts preference panel, you are presented with a list of users on the system and a set of tabbed panes to modify users, as shown in Figure 6-1.

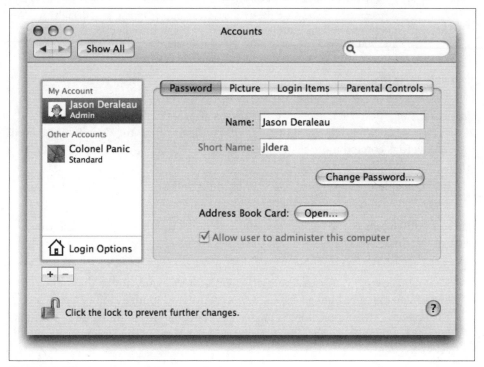

Figure 6-1. The Accounts preference panel

Creating a user

To create a user, click the plus (+) button. A sheet drops down asking for information about the new user. The various fields are:

Name
> This is the full name for the user. This name shows up in most places where Mac OS X displays user information, such as the log in panel and any of the alert screens that prompt you for an administrator password.

Short Name
> This is the Unix-style name for the user and is what you'll typically see on the command line. The default short name runs your first and last names together with no spaces in it (e.g., *jasonderaleau*) and is represented in lowercase letters. Unix usernames of yore used to be limited to eight characters or less, while Mac OS X allows short usernames up to 255 characters.

Don't feel like you have to stick with the Short Name that Mac OS X gives you. Having to type in your full name to login can be a bit of a pain, so if you want, change the Short Name to just your first name (e.g., *jason*), or something else (such as *jldera*) that makes sense to you.

Remember, just because the system gives you something as a default doesn't necessarily mean that you have to use it. If the field is editable and you'd rather use something different, change it.

Password & Verify
> This is where you set the password for the user.

Password Hint
> This is where you define a hint that will be displayed to the user if an incorrect password is entered more than three times.

Allow user to administer this computer
> If you enable this checkbox, the user account will be added to the *admin* group and given administrative privileges on the machine.

There are three tabs of the Accounts preference panel that allow you to fine-tune the settings for a user. They are:

Password
> This tab allows you to view the user's name, short name, and address book card entry. You can also change the user's password and grant administrative access. Remember, when you allow somebody to become an administrator, that user becomes a member of the *admin* group and can modify the system however she sees fit.

Password Assistant

When you click the Change Password button, a sheet drops down prompting you for your current password and the password you want to change it to. Next to this New Password field, you'll find a small button with a key on it. Clicking the key will launch the Password Assistant in a separate window. Using this Assistant, you can have Mac OS X generate a password for you to use for your account.

The Password Assistant offers several different types of passwords. Some of them are designed to be easy to remember while others are intended to be extremely difficult to crack. In today's age of identity theft, it's important to have a secure password, and the Password Assistant can be quite helpful in creating one. If you'd like to create your own password (or test an existing password's security), select Manual as the Type of password. Then, type in your password in the Suggestion field.

As you create passwords, the Password Assistant will fill the Quality bar, indicating the security of the password. In addition, the Assistant offers you tips on how to make your intended password more secure.

Picture

This allows you to associate a picture with a user, which is handy for the various user lists. You can either use one of the Apple provided pictures or choose one of your own. Also, if you have an iSight camera connected to your computer, the Add Picture dialog box will let you take a snapshot, which you can use for this picture.

Login Items

Shown only when viewing the current user's account, this list of applications is launched every time you log into your Mac. You can also specify that an application should load at login by enabling the Open at Login option on the app's Dock menu.

Parental Controls

A new feature in Tiger, the Accounts panel's Parental Controls tab is used to restrict a user's access to various Mac OS X applications. While administrator accounts cannot be controlled through this means, it is quite useful for protecting younger Mac users from some of the dangers of the Internet. You can read more about their configuration in the "Parental Controls" section found later in this chapter.

When you've finished setting up a user, his Home folder is created in the */Users* folder, and he will be able to log into the system.

 When you create an account using the Accounts preference panel, all properties about that user are stored in the local NetInfo database managed by Open Directory. To see the contents of this database, use NetInfo Manager (*/Applications/Utilities*), which provides a barebones view of the NetInfo database and will allow you to make substantial changes. You'll see more about NetInfo Manager and how user records are stored in Open Directory in Chapter 7.

Deleting a user

To delete a user, select the name of the user from the list and click the minus button (–). You are presented with a dialog box asking whether you really want to delete the user and what you want to do with the contents of the user's Home folder. You can either archive the user's folder to a disk image (*.dmg*) file in the */Users/Deleted Users* directory or quickly and permanently erase it, as shown in Figure 6-2.

If you choose to save the contents, you can browse through them at any time by double-clicking the *.dmg* file. This mounts a temporary drive from which you can restore a user's data. Another option is to save the disk image and then burn it to CD or DVD for historical purposes. When you have decided that you no longer need the files for the user, you can delete the disk image from the */Users/Deleted Users* directory as long as you have admin privileges.

Disabling a User

Some operating systems allow you to disable a user's account so it can't be used but the user's Home directory remains intact. Mac OS X doesn't let you disable a user per se. However, you can always accomplish the same thing by changing the user's password to something that only you, the administrator, will know. The user will be locked out, but the Home directory will still be intact.

Figure 6-2. Deleting a user with the Accounts preference panel

Parental Controls

Though earlier versions of Mac OS X included a means to restrict a user's access to the Finder, Tiger takes restricting the user environment a step further with Parental Controls (see Figure 6-3). Parental Controls allow you to easily limit a user's experience in several bundled Mac OS X applications. While most of these controls are presented as a means for parents to protect their children, they could be just as useful in a business environment. Corporate systems administrators, however, will find that Mac OS X Server's Workgroup Manager provides a more flexible means of managing preferences.

Figure 6-3. A user account's Parental Controls

As shown in Figure 6-3, the applications that can be managed are:

Mail

Mail can be configured to allow correspondence only with addresses that you specify. Additionally, permission emails can be sent to a parent's email address for review.

Finder

You can choose to restrict the user to a version of Finder that provides a somewhat limited experience, or enable the Simple Finder and specify the exact documents, folders, and applications a user can access.

iChat

Much like Mail, iChat can be configured with a list of users who may instant message the child's account.

Safari

After enabling a user's Parental Controls for Safari, you cannot browse to pages that are not on the user's Bookmarks Bar, as shown in Figure 6-4. Attempting to modify the Bookmarks Bar will prompt you for an administrator's password, allowing for finite control of the user's browsing experience.

Dictionary

Enabling Parental Controls for Dictionary prevents searches for words that may be considered inappropriate for children (just think of George Carlin's "Seven Words You Can't Say on Television" routine, and you get what I mean).

Figure 6-4. The restricted Safari in action

Nonhuman Users

Even if you are the only human user of the system, there are well over a dozen accounts on the system. Most of these user accounts are not intended for use by you or any user on the system but are set up for use by various services and programs on the system. These nonhuman accounts let applications, such as the Apache web server and the Postfix mail server, run in a controlled environment so if they are breached by a hacker, the potential damage is limited. Table 6-1 lists some of the nonhuman users that are defined on the system.

Table 6-1. Some of Mac OS X's nonhuman users

Username	User ID	Description
root	0	The administrative user
daemon	1	Core system daemons
lp	26	Printing service
postfix	27	The Postfix SMTP server
www	70	The Apache web server
nobody	99	A user with greatly restricted access

Many of the nonhuman users, such as *cyrusimap* and *qtss*, aren't used on the average person's system but instead are defined for use on Mac OS X Server. Others, such as *postfix* and *www*, are used only when you run the Postfix mail server or the Apache web server. Under most conditions, you'll notice only processes owned by either your own ID or by the *root* user when viewing processes in the Activity Monitor or with the *ps* command.

Creating a Nonhuman User

If you need to create a nonhuman user for some reason (for example, to run some server program securely), you shouldn't create that user account with the Accounts preference panel; nonhuman users don't need a Home folder and the other folders a normal user gets when an account is first created. Instead, you should create the account by directly editing the NetInfo database. For details on how to create a nonhuman user account, see Chapter 7.

The Root User

As in all Unix systems, Mac OS X has a special user, named *root*, that is not subject to the control of the permissions structure. The *root* user, sometimes called the superuser, can modify any part of the filesystem as well as execute any program. It can also stop the execution of any running program on the system.

The *root* user is a dangerous one. Some commands executed as *root*, such as *rm -rf /*, can immediately disable a system; you really have to think about what you are doing with every command you issue using *root*. To help prevent mishaps, Mac OS X is configured by default to allow access to the *root* user only through the *sudo* (super*u*ser *do*) program. To use this program, you must be an administrative user, and simply preface the command you want to enter with *sudo*. Example 6-3 shows how to use *sudo* to print out some of the contents of *secure.log*, a file that is visible only to the *root* user and that contains the records of the various actions of Mac OS X's security systems.

Example 6-3. Using sudo

```
$ sudo tail /var/log/secure.log
Password: ********
Jun 11 14:04:42 ronin SecurityAgent[447]: Showing Login Window
Jun 11 14:04:46 ronin SecurityAgent[447]: User Authenticated: continue login process
Jun 11 14:04:46 ronin com.apple.SecurityServer: authinternal authenticated user jldera
(uid 501).
```

Because *sudo* keeps an internal timer, you can execute multiple commands without typing your password each time. It also logs each use in */var/log/system.log*, so you can go back and see a list of commands that were executed (a procedure covered in Chapter 12). This is handy when you have multiple users with administrative privileges on a system.

If you prefer to live a bit more dangerously, you can get a shell as the *root* user by issuing the following command:

```
$ sudo -s
Password: ********
#
```

The prompt changes to # indicating that every command typed will be run as the *root* user.

 Even though it takes more work, you should avoid opening root shells using the *sudo* command. By doing so, you are less likely to make a horrific mistake and hose your system. If you do make a mistake, each command will still be logged, allowing you to figure out what went wrong.

Enabling the root user

Some people really want to be able to log into their system as *root*. For some reason having administrative privileges and the ability to execute any command using *sudo* isn't enough. If you are one of these people, you can enable the *root* user so that you can log in either to the GUI or the command line and have unfettered and unmonitored access to your system. I don't recommend that you do this, but if you insist, here's how:

1. Launch NetInfo Manager (*/Applications/Utilities*).
2. Authenticate yourself using the Security → Authenticate... menu.
3. Enable the *root* user using the Security → Enable Root User menu.
4. Give the *root* user a password; one that is as secure as any password you would give an admin user of the system.

If you follow this procedure, you will have a fully functional *root* user. You can even log out of your system and log in as the *root* user. Remember: you should stick to using *sudo* instead of using the *root* user.

If you want to enable the *root* user from the command line, you can do so by executing the following command:

```
$ sudo passwd root
```

After setting the password, the *root* user account is active.

Further Explorations

While the core concepts of users and groups have been presented in this chapter, the intricacies and history of group and user management on Unix systems are covered in much more detail in *Essential System Administration* by Aeleen Frisch (O'Reilly). You may also want to check out the following manpages:

- *id*
- *passwd*
- *sudo*

CHAPTER 7

Open Directory

Open Directory, the directory services layer of Mac OS X (see Figure 7-1 for a detailed view), offers the essential service of providing information to the system about users, machines, printers, and more. It's also something that most people know very little about. To many, Open Directory is mysterious because its name connotes a tie to the idea of a filesystem directory. In reality, Open Directory doesn't have much at all to do with the filesystem other than the fact that its data is arranged in a hierarchical tree.

For the most part, however, Open Directory is an enigma, because the role it plays is central enough to the system that it's hard to distinguish what it's doing. At Apple's 2003 Worldwide Developer's Conference (WWDC), an Apple employee retold a story about how management always wanted to see a demo of directory services. His response was simply, "Did you make it past the login window? [If so,] well, that's the demo."

Every time you log in, whether through a local or a network account, and every time you browse for Macintosh- or Windows-based file servers, you are using Open Directory. When you log into your Mac using the login window, the login window consults Open Directory to see whether you have a valid username and password for the system. If Open Directory indicates that the username and password are okay, login proceeds. If not, you're challenged until you either get it right or your entry is refused. When you want to connect to a server, the Finder consults Open Directory for a list of server-based filesystems. In large networks, Open Directory can be used to configure printers, mail settings, and much more.

This chapter gives you an overview of what directory services are, where they came from, and what problems they solve. It also shows you how directory services are used in Mac OS X by Open Directory and how to connect to servers that provide directory information like Mac OS X Server, Active Directory, and NetInfo.

Open Directory in Action

To help explain how Open Directory is used in Mac OS X, let's look at a few examples. When you enter your username and password into the login window, the following steps happen:

1. The login window calls Open Directory with a request to authenticate the user.
2. Open Directory takes the username and password and, if the user exists, looks up the authentication method.
3. Using the proper process governed by the authentication method, Open Directory attempts to validate the password.
4. Open Directory indicates whether the user was authenticated to the login window.
5. If the user was authenticated, the login window proceeds to create a GUI session for the user.
6. As the GUI session is created, Open Directory is queried to give the location of the user's Home folder.

This basic process of querying Open Directory for user information is followed by all parts of the system that either know how to use Open Directory or are using it behind the scenes by using the PAM (pluggable authentication modules) functionality built into many Unix-based applications. For example, when you log into your computer remotely via SSH, the following steps occur:

1. *sshd* (the SSH server daemon) gets the username and password for the user requesting to log in.
2. *sshd* then makes a PAM call to authenticate the user. This is handled by Open Directory.
3. Open Directory takes the username and password and, if the user exists, looks up the authentication method.
4. Using the proper process governed by the authentication method, Open Directory attempts to validate the password.
5. Open Directory indicates whether the user was authenticated to *sshd*.

In addition, the act of browsing the network for filesystems when you use the Finder's Go → Connect to Server (⌘-K) menu causes a lookup into Open Directory, which then presents the information that it finds using LDAP, NetInfo, Bonjour, SMB, SLP, and AppleTalk. Open Directory is also used by Terminal's File → Connect to Server (Shift-⌘-K) command, which allows you to create a connection to Bonjour-enabled computers that advertise SSH and Telnet services.

Directory Services Defined

Historically, Unix systems have stored user and password information in "flat" text files located in the */etc* directory and let applications access that data directly. This works well enough when you only have to administer one machine. However, in the 1980s, with the advent of the Unix-based workstation and the proliferation of personal computers allowing mass deployments of computers in offices and universities, managing user information on each machine became a serious administration problem. The problem only became worse as administrators tried to cope not just with setting up users, but setting up printers, servers, and other network resources.

Various solutions have been invented over the years to alleviate this problem. Sun introduced Network Information Services (NIS, also known as "Yellow Pages"), NeXT developed NetInfo, Novell built a business around NetWare (and failed), and Microsoft ended up taking it away from Novell with Active Directory. All these solutions have a common goal: to centralize the information needed so that a group of users across a variety of machines can be managed effectively.

When development on Mac OS X started, Apple inherited the NetInfo code that came with NEXTSTEP. The company knew it was not going to be enough to just provide for management of homogenous networks of Macs, so Apple set out on a path to build a set of technologies collectively known as Open Directory. These technologies brought support for the Lightweight Access Directory Protocol (LDAP) and Kerberos (a network authentication standard developed at the Massachusetts Institute of Technology) to the operating system. Starting with the release of Panther, Mac OS X interoperates with all the major directory services systems in use including Active Directory, as shown in Figure 7-1.

The way in which applications use Open Directory is illustrated in Figure 7-1. When a native Mac OS X application, such as the login window, needs to authenticate a user, it calls into Open Directory. It then authenticates the user information against whatever data store it is configured to use. To accommodate Unix-based command-line applications, the BSD authentication routines have been modified to use PAM, which then uses Open Directory to authenticate against. Likewise, whenever any system component needs to find a resource, such as a network file share, it uses Open Directory.

The end result is a system in which the applications that need authentication and configuration data can get it without knowing, or even caring, where that data is stored. It should be noted that it's not just end-user applications that use this abstracted data. The data about a user that's obtained from Open Directory is used by every part of the system. For example, the filesystem permissions scheme described in Chapter 8 relies on the user and group information stored in Open Directory.

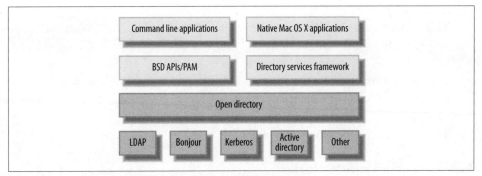

Figure 7-1. How applications and Open Directory fit together

Kinds of Directory Information

Open Directory can handle many different kinds of information. The following are the most common types of data that Mac OS X looks to Open Directory to provide:

- User identification data including real name, username, and user ID
- Authentication information used to verify passwords given by a user
- Group identification data
- The location of a user's Home folder, either on a local machine or on a network server
- Network filesystems
- Quotas for disk, print, and mail usage
- Network-enabled printers that are either shared by other machines or are directly connected to the network

Sources of Directory Information

Open Directory is a flexible bridge allowing information to be obtained from many different sources. These sources fall into roughly three categories: configuration information, authentication services, and discovered services.

Sources of configuration information

LDAP
> The open standard used in many mixed environments and the native Open Directory database in Mac OS X Server 10.4.

NetInfo
> As mentioned earlier, NetInfo is the legacy directory service picked up from NEXTSTEP and earlier versions of Mac OS X. It is the standard local directory service for the client version of Mac OS X.

Active Directory
> This is Microsoft's LDAP-based directory service provided by Windows 2000 and Windows 2003 servers.

hNIS
> Network Information Services servers are still used by many Unix shops but less frequently since LDAP hit the street.

BSD flat files
> These files are located in the */etc* directory.

Sources of authentication information

To authenticate users, Open Directory supports the following technologies:

The Shadow Password Database
> The default authentication mechanism used in Mac OS X. Passwords are stored in the */var/db/shadow* directory, which is accessible only by directory services and the *root* user.

Apple Password Server
> This authentication server ships only as part of Mac OS X Server.

Kerberos
> A network authentication protocol developed at MIT, Kerberos ships as part of Mac OS X Server as well as a standalone server implemented in many large government, educational, and corporate networking environments.

Active Directory
> This is the directory services layer of Windows 2000 Server and Windows 2003 Server. It uses Kerberos to perform authentication.

Sources of discovered services

Open Directory obtains information about network filesystems, printers, and other network devices from the following services:

Bonjour
> Formerly named Rendezvous, this is the Internet Engineering Task Force's (IETF) Zeroconf-based protocol for discovering services on the local network.

SMB
> Service Message Block is used to announce and connect to Windows-based shared filesystems and printers.

SLP
> Service Location Protocol is an open service discovery protocol used on some networks.

AppleTalk
> Apple's legacy Mac OS–based protocol for discovering shared filesystems and printers.

Directory Domains

The advent of network-based directory services did not totally obviate the need for local configuration data. As much as it was necessary to make networks of machines work well together, it was also necessary for computers to be able to work well in standalone situations. Open Directory solves this problem by using a set of domains:

- The *local domain* that every installation of Mac OS X has. It is the first domain to be consulted by Open Directory.
- Any number of *shared domains* an installation of Mac OS X can be configured to use so that it can participate in a networked environment.

These features enable Mac OS X to run just fine in standalone mode while allowing it to be configured to run in large network environments. It can work well in enterprise-wide configurations with multiple platforms that are woven together with various standards. Interoperability has been the Holy Grail for many network administrators. With its range of directory integration, Mac OS X is a first-class citizen in such environments.

The Local Domain and NetInfo

The local domain is the default directory domain of the system. It consists of the following parts:

- The local NetInfo database that is created when the operating system is first installed. It is located in the */var/db/netinfo* directory.
- The local Shadow Password database, created when the operating system is first installed, located in the */var/db/shadow* directory.
- Bonjour, SLP, and SMB for discovery of shared filesystems and other network services.

The Shadow Password database was a new feature in Panther. In prior versions of Mac OS X, the passwords were encrypted (using the *crypt* command-line tool) into a hash form and stored directly in the NetInfo database. However, because the information in the NetInfo database is available to anybody on the machine, the passwords were vulnerable to decryption attempts. All you had to do was dump out the NetInfo database (you'll see the commands to do that later in this chapter) to a flat file and then run any number of password-cracking utilities against the file. You could even do so on a separate machine once you had the flat file.

The Shadow Password database changes this, locking passwords into a directory where they can be accessed only by the *root* user of the system, thereby closing this security vulnerability. When the system needs to authenticate a user, Open Directory looks at the user's NetInfo record, sees that the password is in the Shadow Password database, and then compares the information given to it against the user's

> ## NetInfo Is Dead, Long Live NetInfo
>
> Since the first release of Mac OS X, Apple has been slowly putting together all the pieces to move away from NetInfo and use LDAP for directory services. Panther marked the completion of the migration on the server side. When you install Mac OS X Server, the directory server in use is LDAP, and the only options in the Server Admin tools related to NetInfo are to migrate the data from a NetInfo database to LDAP.
>
> However, on the client side, NetInfo is still the default local directory. So, the rumors of NetInfo's death are still premature.

password. Unless you have root privileges on the machine, there's no way to get to the data that Open Directory uses to authenticate a user.

 The move to shadow passwords breaks some Unix-based tools that still expect to be able to find a crypt-based password. These tools need to be updated to use the PAM-based authentication libraries. The Unix tools that ship as part of the default Mac OS X installation use PAM. However, if you are compiling your own tools, you'll need to be sure they use PAM in order to avoid authentication problems.

To modify information about users and groups in the local domain, typically you use the Accounts preference panel. Whenever you create or modify a user, the user information is stored in the local NetInfo database. Whenever you modify a password, either with the Accounts preference panel or the *passwd* command-line tool, that password is updated in the local Shadow Password database. In addition to these easy-to-use GUI tools in the System Preferences, Mac OS X provides the GUI-based NetInfo Manager (*/Applications/Utilities*) and a set of command-line tools to manipulate NetInfo data.

Examining NetInfo Data with NetInfo Manager

When you first launch NetInfo Manager, you see an interface with two parts, as shown in Figure 7-2. The top part of the interface is a browser that allows you to navigate through the tree hierarchy of the NetInfo database. The leftmost column of the browser displays /, which is the root of the NetInfo database tree. The column to the right of / is the set of top-level directories (not to be confused with filesystem directories!) that are in the database. Unlike other Apple applications, NetInfo Manager doesn't have a help system (⌘-?). This is a sign that this tool isn't for beginners but has given NetInfo a rap that it's a gnarly beast, when in fact it's rather easy to use, you just have to get used to it.

Each directory node in the database can, in addition to holding subdirectories, hold a set of properties. These properties are displayed in the bottom part of the NetInfo

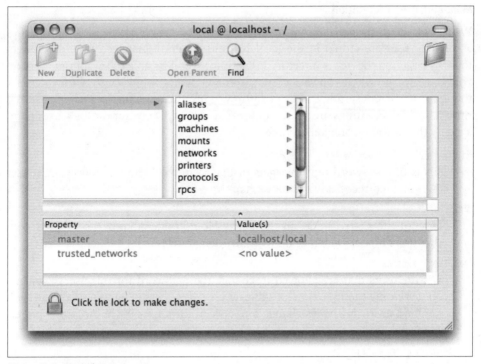

Figure 7-2. NetInfo Manager

Manager interface. As shown in Figure 7-2, the *users* directory contains subdirectories for each user on the system as well as a single property, *name*, that contains the name of the directory.

Because the NetInfo database is inherited from NEXTSTEP and is designed to serve as both a local and distributed directory, it contains many entries that you won't typically use on a single local system. The top-level subdirectories of greatest use on a local system are:

groups
> Contains a listing of the groups and the users that belong to each group. The information in this subdirectory is analogous to the information stored in the classic Unix */etc/group* file.

users
> Contains a listing of the users and the various properties associated with those users. This information serves the same purpose as the Unix */etc/passwd* file.

> By directly using NetInfo Manager to edit the local directory services domain, you could potentially create many problems and cause your system to start up incorrectly or not at all. Exercise great care before making changes.

Managing user information

When you create an account with the Accounts preference panel, all the properties about that user are stored in the local NetInfo database managed by Open Directory. By selecting the */users* directory in NetInfo, you'll be able to see all the users on your system, and when you select your username, you should see something similar to Figure 7-3. Every setting that controls how a user behaves on the system is stored right here. These settings are (in the order that they typically appear for a user managed by the Accounts preference panel):

hint
> This is the password hint that gets displayed in the login window when a user enters an incorrect password more than three times.

sharedDir
> Name of the shared folder in the user's Home folder that can be shared with other users on the system or network. By default, this is the *~/Public* folder.

_writers_passwd
> Lists the users that are allowed to change the password for this user. Typically you'll see only the username of the user record this setting applies to. However, an admin user can always change a password for a user in the Accounts preference panel.

authentication_authority
> Indicates the authentication resource against which to authenticate the user. By default in Tiger, this will be ;ShadowHash;, indicating that the system should authenticate the user against the Shadow Password database in */var/db/shadow*. If you created an account with Jaguar or a previous release of Mac OS X and migrated it to Tiger, this setting might be basic.

name
> The Unix username for the user. This is the same thing as the Short Name field in the Accounts preference panel.

home
> The location on the filesystem of the user's Home folder.

passwd
> By default, when the authentication_authority is set to ;ShadowHash;, the property contains a set of asterisks. If the authentication_authority is set to basic, this property contains the password for the user in a hashed form.

_writers_hint
> Lists the users that are allowed to change the hint of the user's password. By default, this will only contain the name of the user's record.

_shadow_passwd
> A legacy key left from older versions of Mac OS X and NEXTSTEP. Currently it's not used.

Figure 7-3. Examining a user subdirectory in NetInfo Manager

`_writers_picture`

Lists the users that can change the picture for this user.

`realname`

The long name of the user. This property corresponds to the Name field in the Accounts preference panel.

`uid`

The numeric user ID of the user.

`shell`

The default shell of the user; by default, this will be */bin/bash* on Tiger.

`generateduid`

A string that serves as a unique identifier for the user, not only on the local system but anywhere in the world. This string is used inside the Shadow Password database as a key to find the information to validate passwords.

`gid`

The primary group ID of the user.

`_writers_tim_password`
> A legacy key left from older versions of Mac OS X and NEXTSTEP. Currently it's not used.

`picture`
> The user's picture.

`_writers_realname`
> Lists the users that can change the real name for this user.

Given access to this information, it becomes very easy to make substantial changes to the user records on your system. For example, if you want to change the default shell for a user from */bin/bash* to */bin/tcsh*, you can edit the shell property as follows:

1. First, make sure you are authenticated by clicking the padlock at the lower-left corner of NetInfo Manager's window. If the padlock is closed, you'll need to authenticate as an administrative user.

2. Select the user that you want to modify.

3. Find the `shell` property and double-click the name of the shell (*/bin/bash* by default), as shown in Figure 7-4.

4. Change the value to */bin/tcsh*.

5. Click the padlock icon to prevent further changes from being made, or use Security → Deauthenticate.

6. Save the change with Domain → Save Changes (⌘-S).

Managing group information

The only way to affect the group settings for a user in the Accounts preferences panel is to grant the user administrator privileges. No other group manipulation is exposed. However, using NetInfo Manager, you can define new groups on the system and associate users with them. For example, to give the user *alisa* administrative privileges, follow this process:

1. Navigate to the */groups/admin* subdirectory using the browser window at the top of the NetInfo Manager interface.

2. Select the `users` property, as shown in Figure 7-5.

3. Use the Directory → New Value (Option-⌘-N) menu to create a new value in the `users` property.

4. Change the `new_value` string that was inserted to `alisa`.

5. Save the change with Domain → Save Changes (⌘-S).

When you check the "Allow user to administer this computer" checkbox in the Accounts preference panel, the system is simply adding the user to the *admin* group (just as was done here). Likewise, when you uncheck the administration checkbox in the Accounts preference panel, the system removes the user's name from the */groups/ admin* list in the NetInfo database.

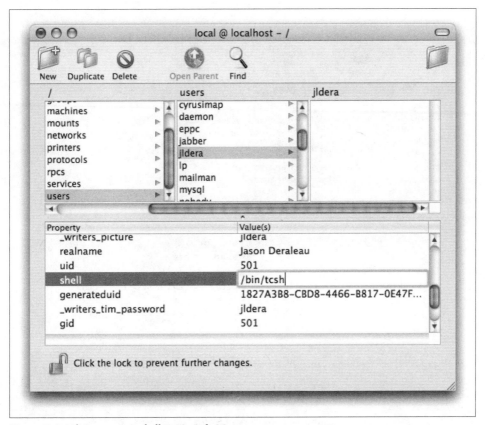

Figure 7-4. Editing a user's shell in NetInfo Manager

Creating a nonhuman user

If you need to create a nonhuman user, meaning an account that is used to run some server program securely (not an account for a dog or a fish), it's best not to create that user with the Accounts preference panel, as a nonhuman user doesn't need to have a Home folder created. Instead, you can create an account by directly editing the NetInfo database. Usually, it's easiest to duplicate an existing user and then edit the various properties to give your new user the correct setup. Here's the step-by-step guide:

1. Launch NetInfo Manager and authenticate as an admin user by clicking the padlock or using Security → Authenticate. When prompted, enter your password and hit Return.

2. In the directory browser at the top of the window, click the *users* entry in the second column and then select the *unknown* user as shown in Example 7-6.

3. Click the duplicate button in the toolbar or use Edit → Duplicate (⌘-D). A duplicate of the unknown user will be created after you accept the dialog box challenge.

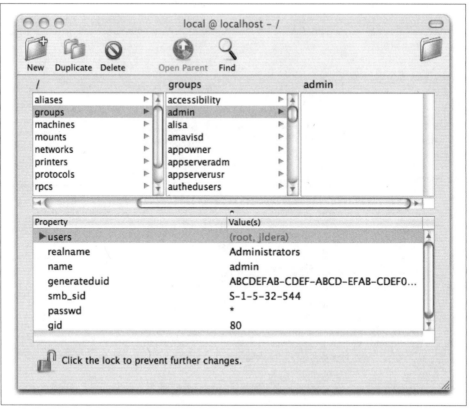

Figure 7-5. Editing the /groups/admin subdirectory in NetInfo Manager

4. In the property-value editor at the bottom of the application window, change the uid (user ID) property to a number that isn't already assigned to some other user. By convention, you should use an ID between 100 and 500. IDs less than 100 are reserved for use by Mac OS X, and IDs greater than 500 appear in the login window. Be sure not to use an ID already in use. To be safe, check the various other user entries to make sure you aren't using their IDs before proceeding. Although NetInfo Manager is perfectly happy allowing you to create multiple user entries with the same user ID, the system itself won't be happy with this situation.

5. Assign a group ID that is the same number as the user ID. You'll create the group for the user in a minute.

6. If the user needs a Home directory (not likely for a nonhuman user, but the documentation for the software that you are creating the nonhuman user for may indicate that it is needed), set the home property to the filesystem location of the directory. If you do assign a Home directory, you are responsible for creating that directory. You can always add or change the home property later.

7. If the user needs to use a shell (once again, not likely, but consult the documentation for the software that you are creating the nonhuman user for), set the shell property to the shell you'd like to use (for example, *bash*, *tcsh*, *zsh*). */usr/bin/false*, a program that doesn't do anything but return a nonzero exit code, is a good choice when you want to make sure that the user can't use a shell.

8. Set the `realname` property to something that makes sense.

9. Move to the groups entry in the browser.

10. Duplicate the *unknown* group.

11. Change the name of the group to be the same as the name of the new user.

12. Change the `gid` (group ID) number to match the user ID number.

Figure 7-6. Duplicating a user entry

Configuring Shared Domains

For many users, especially those who use their Macs at home, the default local NetInfo-based domain is all that's needed. However, users in corporate settings will want to take advantage of the ease of administration and flexibility that using shared domains allows. When a shared domain is in use, any user can log into any machine that is part of the domain and access her Home folder from a network server. All the settings and data for all the computers on the network can be centralized. Also, because there is no user data stored on an individual machine, the data can be replaced or upgraded with ease. When the user logs into the new machine, all of her data is just where she left it.

To enable a Mac to participate in a shared domain, you need to perform a two-step process. The first step is to set up the shared domain directory server that you want to use. The second is to set up the authentication rules for your system. Both steps can be performed with the Directory Access utility (*/Applications/Utilities*), shown in Figure 7-7.

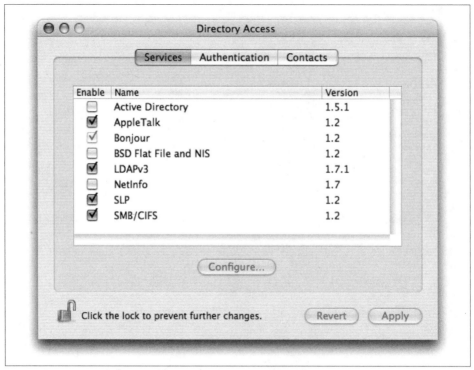

Figure 7-7. The Directory Access application used to configure Open Directory

Configuring Open Directory Sources

When you launch Directory Access, the first thing you'll see is the Services configuration, as shown in Figure 7-7. This gives you a list of directory sources that can be used with Open Directory. These are the same sources of information discussed earlier in the chapter. By using Directory Access, you can enable and disable these sources as well as configure them.

Using Mac OS X Server's Open Directory Server

To configure a client to use the LDAP-based directory services provided by Open Directory Server, select the LDAPv3 entry and click the Configure button. Even if the padlock icon at the lower-left of the window is unlocked, you may still be challenged for an administrator password. After you authenticate, you'll see the panel shown in Figure 7-8.

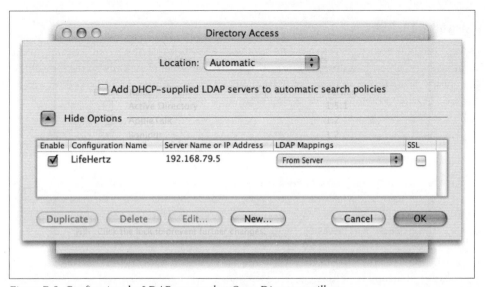

Figure 7-8. Configuring the LDAP servers that Open Directory will use

The "Use DHCP-supplied LDAP servers" box is checked by default. This means that if the system obtained an IP address from a DHCP server that also is set to provide information on where to find an LDAP server, it will go ahead and use it as a directory service. If you are on a network where an LDAP server isn't configured through DHCP, or if you are using a fixed IP address, you'll need to add your server manually. To do this, click the New button and enter the following information:

Configuration Name
   This can be any name you want to assign to your LDAP configuration.

Server Name or IP Address
   The hostname or IP address of the LDAP server.

LDAP Mappings

> The type of LDAP mappings to use. For most purposes, the default "From Server" setting is appropriate. You'll see how to use the other options in this list in the next section.

SSL

> Indicate whether or not to use SSL to contact the LDAP server. This secures the LDAP connection using the certificate credentials provided by the server.

This procedure works for most network environments that use Mac OS X Server's LDAP services. However, it's a good idea to verify this information with the administrator of the Mac OS X Server to which you are trying to connect.

Using other LDAP servers

Since Open Directory Server uses the standard LDAP protocol with no special modifications, the Open Directory client is already LDAP savvy. The only thing that Open Directory needs to know to use any other LDAP server is how data in the directory is stored. This is known as the server's data mappings. The LDAP servers you may use fall into three categories:

- The server is already configured to provide seamless integration with Mac OS X.
- The server is set up to use standard Unix RFC 2307 mappings.
- The server requires you to configure your mappings on Mac OS X.

Trusting the Network

As this book was being prepared for publication, a story broke in the press about a security vulnerability in Mac OS X. It stated an attacker could take over a machine by exploiting Open Directory. To perform this attack, an attacker sets up a DHCP server for a network (shutting down any other operational DHCP servers), and then configures LDAP through DHCP to let him log into any machine that boots on the network.

This isn't a new exploit, but rather is symptomatic of the changes in networking. It used to be that it was rare to move your machine between networks. You always knew the DHCP server or at least knew your admins took care of such things. Therefore picking up LDAP settings from DHCP settings aided easy system configuration. Now, with mobile computing being such a pervasive part of life, it's more questionable to make this assumption.

If you have a laptop that you carry between networks, uncheck the "Use DHCP-supplied LDAP servers" box shown in Figure 7-8, and you won't be subject to this kind of attack.

Unless your setup falls into the first category, you'll most likely need to get some information from your system administrator to configure the LDAP directory service. If you do need to configure your own mappings, select the Custom option from the LDAP mappings pull-down menu. How you set up these mappings depends on your LDAP server and is beyond the scope of this book.

Configuring Active Directory domain servers

Mac OS X Panther brought the ability to use Active Directory, the native directory service used by Microsoft Windows 2000 or Windows 2003 Server. This support relies on the fact that Active Directory uses standard LDAP and Kerberos protocols. In fact, if you wanted to, you could connect to an Active Directory server simply by configuring it as an LDAP server. However, the mappings of data in an Active Directory server don't match up with the mappings needed by Mac OS X. Fortunately, Apple has provided Active Directory–specific functionality in Open Directory that seamlessly maps between the data mappings used by Microsoft Windows and the mappings that Mac OS X expects to see.

What Is Active Directory?

Active Directory is Microsoft's directory that is provided as part of Windows 2000 Server and Windows 2003 Server. It performs the same kinds of duties for a Windows-based network that Apple's Open Directory in Mac OS X Server can provide for Macintosh systems. Since Active Directory is widely deployed in enterprise environments, Apple built in the ability to run from Active Directory into Mac OS X to make it easier for the admins of Windows-based networks to work with Macs. Hopefully it will inspire some of the employees of those companies to switch to the Mac.

At this time, it's a one-way street. Open Directory on Mac OS X can't provide all the functionality for a Windows-based machine that Active Directory can. Being able to run a Mac on an Active Directory–based network, however, is a great step forward for interoperability.

Active Directory comes with a slew of its own terms like *forest*, which refers to a group of Active Directory trees. It reuses terms like *domain* for its own purposes. For the most part, your system administrator will provide the information you need to know. You can also get more information from *Active Directory,* Second Edition, by Robbie Allen, et al. (O'Reilly).

To configure Open Directory to use an Active Directory server, select the Active Directory entry in Directory Access and click the Configure button. You'll be presented with the panel shown in Figure 7-9. Fill in the directory forest, domain, and computer ID fields with the values provided by your network administrator and then click the Bind button.

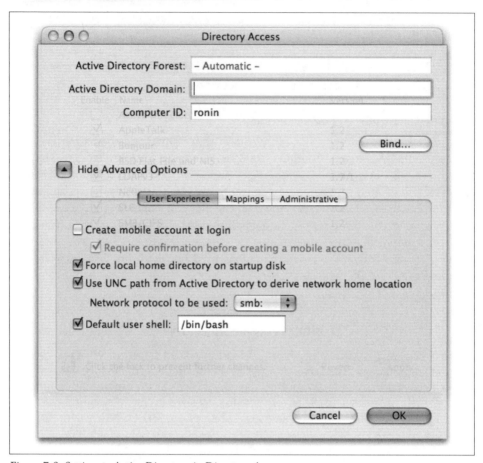

Figure 7-9. Setting up Active Directory in Directory Access

Depending on your setup, you may also want to set the following advanced options:

Create mobile account at login
> Mac OS X will store your Active Directory user account information as an account on your portable. This lets you log into your machine even if the Active Directory domain controller isn't available.

Force local home directory on startup disk
> This option will force Mac OS X to keep users' Home directories on the local filesystem, instead of using a network-based Home directory.

Use UNC path from Active Directory to derive network home location
> A UNC path is similar to a URL. Windows networks and the SMB protocol make use of UNC paths to specify the locations of network resources. Enabling this option will tell Mac OS X to use the UNC path when accessing users' Home directories.

Default user shell

There's only one command-line shell on Windows. Since it's not included with Mac OS X, use this value to set which shell should be used as the default Unix shell for Active Directory users on your Mac.

Map UID to attribute, Map user GID to attribute, Map group GID to attribute

By default, Active Directory doesn't use user IDs, but prefers to use longer GUIDs (Globally Unique ID). If your Active Directory server has been configured to store a user ID for each user (typically when Active Directory has already been configured to support Unix computers), you can specify the attribute within Active Directory that is used to store the UID. If you don't select this option, then a user ID is automatically generated for you based on the GUID attribute in Active Directory. Similarly, the user and group GIDs can also be stored in Active Directory and mapped here.

Prefer this domain server

Lets you specify the hostname of the Active Directory server that you want to use by default. If this server is unavailable, Open Directory automatically uses another server that is part of the forest if available.

Allow administration by

Specifies a list of Active Directory groups whose members are considered to have administrative privileges by Open Directory.

Allow authentication from any domain in the forest

Lets users from any domain in the Active Directory system for your network log into your computer.

Configuring NetInfo-based domain servers

If your network directory services are based on NetInfo, you can configure Open Directory to use it by selecting the NetInfo service type and clicking the Configure button. You'll be presented with the NetInfo configuration panel shown in Figure 7-10. As with LDAP, Open Directory is configured to automatically discover any NetInfo server set in DHCP. In addition, you can set Open Directory to try to contact a NetInfo server via a network broadcast attempt, or you can configure it to contact a specific NetInfo server. Since directory information in NetInfo is always stored the same way, there's no further configuration to perform.

Configuring NIS domain servers

To configure the use of NIS-based directory services, select the checkbox next to the BSD Flat File and NIS entry in Directory Access (refer back to Figure 7-7). Next, click the Configure button. You'll be presented with a panel where you can enter the NIS domain name of your network and, optionally, a list of NIS servers. You can also configure Open Directory to attempt to locate an NIS server by using network broad-

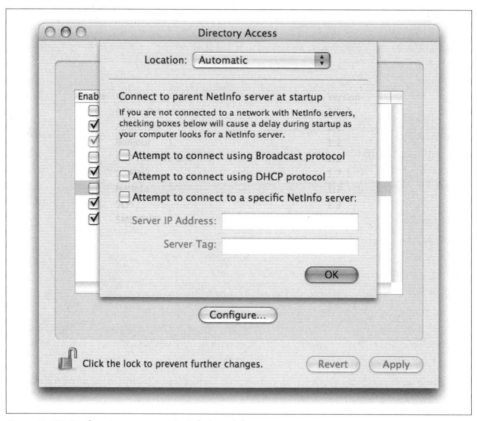

Figure 7-10. Configuring access to NetInfo-based directory services

casts. As with NetInfo, since there is only one way to store data in an NIS server, there is no further configuration to be performed.

Configuring Shared Domain Authentication

Once you have set up the various servers that provide shared domain directory services to your machine, you'll be able to access the resources defined by those servers. However, to use those servers for authentication and to let users defined by those servers log into your machine, you need to configure Open Directory's authentication settings. When you click the Authentication tab, you'll see the interface shown in Figure 7-11. By default, you'll see one entry: */NetInfo/root*. This indicates that your machine is set up to use only the local domain for authentication.

To add a shared domain directory service to be used for authentication, change the search pull-down menu to "Custom path," as shown in Figure 7-11. You'll then be able to click the Add button to use any of the servers you've configured in the Services panel. In Figure 7-11, I've set up Open Directory to use the LDAPv3 server

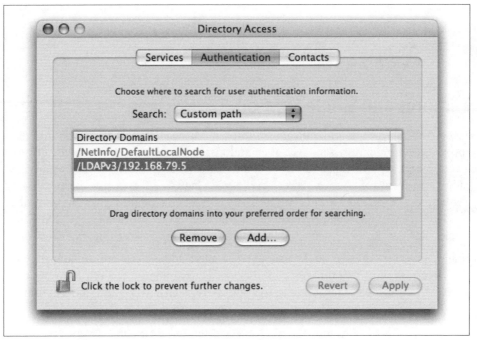

Figure 7-11. Configuring directory services used for authentication

located at 192.168.79.5 to serve as an authentication directory service. This means any user with an account defined by that server will be able to log onto the machine. If you have configured multiple servers, you can drag them into the order in which you want them to be consulted for authentication purposes.

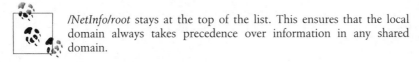 */NetInfo/root* stays at the top of the list. This ensures that the local domain always takes precedence over information in any shared domain.

When you click the Add button, you'll also notice an entry for */BSD/local*. This sets up Open Directory to use the classic Unix */etc/passwd* and */etc/group* files for authentication. It lets you use these files if you wish, but for all the reasons stated at the beginning of the chapter, you most likely don't want to use this option.

Configuring Shared Domain Contacts

Not only does Open Directory handle network services and authentication duties, but it can also provide contact information to the Address Book. To use shared domain servers for contact data, simply change the search pull-down menu to "Custom path" (just as you did for Authentication) and add the servers you would like to use.

Configuring shared contacts in Open Directory isn't the only way to take advantage of LDAP servers from the Address Book. You can set any number of LDAP servers in Address Book's preferences to use as sources of contact information.

Kerberos and Single Sign-on

Kerberos is a network authentication protocol that was developed at MIT to allow applications to identify users over open and insecure networks. It is used by governments, large corporations, and higher education. Kerberos is also the native authentication protocol of Active Directory. Since Jaguar, Apple has been moving aggressively to support Kerberos in both Mac OS X Server and Mac OS X—as well as all of the password-using applications in Mac OS X such as Mail, FTP, SSH, and Apple File Sharing. The reason Apple is making this push is to enable *single sign-on*.

Single sign-on means that after a user enters a name and a password in the login window, every application on the system that needs to authenticate itself for a network service—for example, Mail wanting to log into the mail server—can do so automatically without requiring the user to enter a different username and password.

For users of Mac OS X, either Kerberos is configured for your network and it just works out of the box, or there is a bit of configuration work to be accomplished. If your network falls into the second category, you'll need to get some information from your system administrator.

Command-Line Open Directory Tools

Mac OS X provides a suite of command-line tools to view and manage the information in Open Directory. The most useful of these tools are:

dscl
> A general-purpose interactive command-line tool for working with data in any Open Directory data source, including LDAP, NetInfo, SMB, and Bonjour. This tool can also be used in single-shot mode.

nicl
> An interactive command-line tool for working with data in a NetInfo database. Unlike *dscl*, this tool will not work with any other data source. This tool can also be used in single-shot mode.

nidump
> Extracts data from a NetInfo database into either legacy Unix flat file formats (such as the files found in the */etc* directory) or into a NetInfo-specific raw format.

niload

Loads data from a flat file, either a Unix */etc* format file or a NetInfo raw format file.

niutil

A single-shot tool used for reading and writing information to a NetInfo database. You should consider using *nicl* in single-shot mode instead of this tool.

nifind

Searches through a NetInfo database for directories that match a pattern.

nigrep

Searches through a NetInfo database for directories or properties that match a particular pattern.

Of these commands, the most useful are *dscl*, *nicl*, *nidump*, and *niload*.

Backing Up and Restoring a NetInfo Database

Before you get too creative with your NetInfo database, you should make sure you have a good backup of it. You can create a backup simply by copying the */var/db/netinfo/local.nidb* directory. For example, you can use the following to create a backup:

```
sudo cp -R /var/db/netinfo/local.nidb /var/backups/backup.nidb
```

If you manage to get the NetInfo database into a state where it can't be used, you can boot into single-user mode by holding down ⌘-S as the computer starts up. When you are presented with the single-user prompt (#), execute the commands in Example 7-1.

Example 7-1. Restoring the NetInfo database in single-user mode

```
# /sbin/fsck -y
# /sbin/mount -uw /
# mv /var/db/netinfo/local.nidb /var/backups/damaged.nidb
# cp -R /var/backups/backup.nidb /var/db/netinfo/local.nidb
```

The first command makes sure that the filesystem is safe. The second command mounts the filesystem in read/write mode. The third command moves the damaged database out of the way. The fourth copies the backup copy of the database back into place.

Using dscl

The *dscl* command-line tool is an interactive program like the shell, which means that when you run it, it stays active. And, like the shell, it features tab-completion and a history. This lets you navigate through the large amounts of data that can be present in Open Directory. The best way to learn how to use this tool is to go on a guided tour. Example 7-2 shows how to launch *dscl* so it connects to Open Directory running on your local system.

Example 7-2. Launching dscl

```
$ dscl .
/ >
```

The dot is important; it means connect to Open Directory on the local system. You'll notice that the prompt changes to the greater-than (>) symbol. This means that *dscl* is ready to accept your commands. Table 7-1 lists the various commands you can use. The top level of the directory tree that you are at when you start *dscl* contains the various directory sources that Open Directory has access to. To see these sources of directory information, use the *list* command, as shown in Example 7-3.

Table 7-1. dscl commands

Command	Description
help	Prints out the various commands for *dscl*.
list [*path*]	Lists the subdirectories of the given directory. If no path is given, the subdirectories of the current directory will be listed.
cd path	Changes the working directory to the path given.
read [*path* [*key*]]	Reads the properties in a directory. If no path is given, the current path is used. You can specify a particular key of a property to read. If no key is given, all the properties of the path will be printed.
search path key val	Searches for records that match a pattern at the given path.
auth user [*password*]	Authenticate to the system as a user. You can either specify a password or let *dscl* prompt you for one.
create path [*key* [*val*]]	Creates a path or a property with the given key and value at a path. This command will overwrite any existing path or property.
append path key val	Appends a property value to the property at the given path.
merge path key val	Appends a property value to the property at the given path if the value does not already exist.
delete path [*key* [*val*]]	Deletes a path or a property value at the given path.
change path key oldval newval	Changes the property value at the given path.
changei path key index val	Changes the property value at a given index for the given path.
passwd userPath [*newPassword*]	Changes the password for the user whose record is at a given path.
quit	Quits *dscl*.

Example 7-3. Using the dscl list command

```
/ > list
NetInfo
LDAPv3
PasswordServer
Bonjour
SLP
```

Example 7-3. Using the dscl list command (continued)

```
SMB
Search
Contact
/ >
```

To take a look at the NetInfo database that serves as the local directory service domain, use *cd* and then the *list* command, as shown in Example 7-4.

Example 7-4. Using the dscl cd and list commands

```
/ > cd NetInfo/
/NetInfo/root > list
AFPUserAliases
Aliases
Config
Groups
Hosts
Machines
Networks
Users
/NetInfo/root >
```

You'll notice the exact same set of subdirectories in the NetInfo tree here as you saw in NetInfo Manager, with one key difference, the initial letter in each directory name is in uppercase. This reflects a mapping from the lowercase names that NetInfo uses to the new naming convention used by Open Directory. You can view the properties of a subdirectory record with the *read* command, as shown in Example 7-5.

To take a look at the NetInfo database that serves as the local directory service domain, use the *cd* and then the *list* commands as shown in Example 7-4.

Example 7-5. Using the dscl read command

```
/NetInfo/root > read Users/jldera
_shadow_passwd:
_writers_hint: jldera
_writers_passwd: jldera
_writers_picture: jldera
_writers_realname: jldera
_writers_tim_password: jldera
naprivs: -2147483137
sharedDir:
AppleMetaNodeLocation: /NetInfo/root
AuthenticationAuthority: ;ShadowHash;HASHLIST:<SALTED-SHA1,SMB-NT,SMB-LAN-MANAGER>
AuthenticationHint:
GeneratedUID: 1827A3B8-CBD8-4466-B817-0E47FB30D441
NFSHomeDirectory: /Users/jldera
Password: ********
Picture: /Library/Caches/com.apple.user501pictureCache.tiff
PrimaryGroupID: 501
RealName: Jason Deraleau
```

Example 7-5. Using the dscl read command (continued)

```
RecordName: jldera
RecordType: dsRecTypeStandard:Users
UniqueID: 501
UserShell: /bin/bash
```

Once again, you should notice that this is basically the same information that you saw in NetInfo Manager, but some of the names are different. You'll also notice the difference in capitalization due to a bit of translation behind the scenes between the older NetInfo style of naming and the newer Open Directory style. Table 7-2 provides a mapping of these properties. If you just want to read a single property from a user record, you can use the *read* command, as shown in Example 7-6.

Table 7-2. Mapping Between Open Directory– and NetInfo-style user property names

Open Directory property key	NetInfo property key
AuthenticationAuthority	authentication_authority
AuthenticationHint	hint
GeneratedUID	generateduid
NFSHomeDirectory	home
Password	passwd
Picture	picture
PrimaryGroupID	gid
RealName	realname
RecordName	name
UniqueID	uid
UserShell	shell

Example 7-6. Reading a single property from a user record

```
/NetInfo/root/Users > read jldera UserShell
UserShell: /bin/bash
```

So far, you've only been reading values from the database. To write a value, you'll first need to authenticate and then use the *create* command. For example, if you wanted to set the AuthenticationHint property, you would use the set of commands shown in Example 7-7.

Example 7-7. Writing a property to a user record

```
/NetInfo/root/Users > auth jldera
Password:
********
/NetInfo/root/Users > create jldera AuthenticationHint "Name of my pet"
```

Now, when you take a look at the AuthenticationHint property, you'll see that it has changed, as shown in Example 7-8.

Example 7-8. Checking a modified property

```
/NetInfo/root/Users > read jldera AuthenticationHint
AuthenticationHint: Name of my pet
```

 One important thing to note about the *auth* command is that it will authenticate you only in the directory database in which you are working. For example, if you have an LDAPv3 directory configured in Open Directory, when you authenticate in the NetInfo database, you are not authenticated in the LDAPv3 database.

When you are ready to leave the *dscl* shell, use the *quit* command.

You can also use *dscl* in single-shot mode—this is where you can enter a command directly at the shell prompt and it won't result in an interactive shell. For example, from the command line, we can read the AuthenticationHint property, as shown in Example 7-9.

Example 7-9. Using dscl in single-shot mode

```
$ dscl localhost -read /NetInfo/root/Users/jldera AuthenticationHint
AuthenticationHint: Name of my pet
```

nicl

The *nicl* command works in much the same way as the *dscl* command. The major difference between the two is that *nicl* presents only data in the NetInfo database and presents property names in NetInfo format. To run *nicl*, use the command shown in Example 7-10.

Example 7-10. Starting nicl

```
$ nicl .
/ >
```

When you are at the *nicl* prompt, you can use the same commands as *dscl*, listed in Table 7-1. For example, to list the directories at the top of the NetInfo tree, use the *list* command, as shown in Example 7-11.

Example 7-11. Using the nicl list command

```
/ > list
1          users
2          groups
3          machines
4          networks
5          protocols
6          rpcs
7          services
```

Example 7-11. Using the nicl list command (continued)

```
8          aliases
9          mounts
10         printers
```

You can see from the output in Example 7-11 that each directory in the NetInfo database has a number associated with it as well as a name. To read the properties associated with a user, use the *read* command, as shown in Example 7-12. The property names are quite similar to those used when viewing the data with *dscl*. Table 7-2 lists mappings of some major properties.

nidump

Example 7-12. Using the nicl read command

```
/ > read /users/jldera
name: jldera
home: /Users/jldera
gid: 501
picture: /Library/Caches/com.apple.user501pictureCache.tiff
uid: 501
hint:
sharedDir:
shell: /bin/bash
passwd: ********
authentication_authority: ;ShadowHash;HASHLIST:<SALTED-SHA1,SMB-NT,SMB-LAN-MANAGER>
realname: Jason Deraleau
generateduid: 1827A3B8-CBD8-4466-B817-0E47FB30D441
naprivs: -2147483137
_writers_passwd: jldera
_writers_tim_password: jldera
_writers_picture: jldera
_writers_hint: jldera
_shadow_passwd:
_writers_realname: jldera
```

The *nidump* command is used primarily for outputting the contents of the NetInfo database in standard Unix formats and for making backups of the database. For example, to output the user information in the database in the traditional format used by */etc/passwd*, you would use the *nidump* command, as shown in Example 7-13.

Example 7-13. Using the nidump command

```
$ nidump passwd .
nobody:*:-2:-2::0:0:Unprivileged User:/var/empty:/usr/bin/false
root:*:0:0::0:0:System Administrator:/var/root:/bin/sh
daemon:*:1:1::0:0:System Services:/var/root:/usr/bin/false
unknown:*:99:99::0:0:Unknown User:/var/empty:/usr/bin/false
lp:*:26:26::0:0:Printing Services:/var/spool/cups:/usr/bin/false
postfix:*:27:27::0:0:Postfix User:/var/spool/postfix:/usr/bin/false
```

Example 7-13. Using the nidump command (continued)

```
www:*:70:70::0:0:World Wide Web Server:/Library/WebServer:/usr/bin/false
eppc:*:71:71::0:0:Apple Events User:/var/empty:/usr/bin/false
mysql:*:74:74::0:0:MySQL Server:/var/empty:/usr/bin/false
sshd:*:75:75::0:0:sshd Privilege separation:/var/empty:/usr/bin/false
qtss:*:76:76::0:0:QuickTime Streaming Server:/var/empty:/usr/bin/false
cyrusimap:*:77:6::0:0:Cyrus IMAP User:/var/imap:/usr/bin/false
mailman:*:78:78::0:0:Mailman user:/var/empty:/usr/bin/false
appserver:*:79:79::0:0:Application Server:/var/empty:/usr/bin/false
clamav:*:82:82::0:0:Clamav User:/var/virusmails:/bin/tcsh
amavisd:*:83:83::0:0:Amavisd User:/var/virusmails:/bin/tcsh
jabber:*:84:84::0:0:Jabber User:/var/empty:/usr/bin/false
xgridcontroller:*:85:85::0:0:Xgrid Controller:/var/xgrid/controller:/usr/bin/false
xgridagent:*:86:86::0:0:Xgrid Agent:/var/xgrid/agent:/usr/bin/false
appowner:*:87:87::0:0:Application Owner:/var/empty:/usr/bin/false
windowserver:*:88:88::0:0:WindowServer:/var/empty:/usr/bin/false
tokend:*:91:91::0:0:Token Daemon:/var/empty:/usr/bin/false
securityagent:*:92:92::0:0:SecurityAgent:/var/empty:/usr/bin/false
jldera:********:501:501::0:0:Jason Deraleau:/Users/jldera:/bin/bash
panic:********:502:502::0:0:Colonel Panic:/Users/panic:/bin/bash
```

To make a backup of the NetInfo database, handy for when you want to make potentially harmful changes, use the following command:

```
$ nidump -r / . > nibackup.txt
```

niload

The *niload* command is complementary to *nidump*. This command can accept a variety of Unix */etc* file formats as input to add data to a NetInfo database. For example, the following command loads a */etc/passwd*-style file named *userlist* into the database:

```
$ niload passwd . < userlist
```

To perform a full database restore from the output of an *nidump* command, you would use the following command:

```
$ niload -r / . < nibackup.txt
```

Further Explorations

Several resources are available to help you deepen your understanding of directory services and the technologies behind Open Directory. These are:

- *Essential Mac OS X Panther Server Administration*, by Michael Bartosh and Ryan Fass (O'Reilly Media, Inc., 2005)
- *Mac OS X Server Open Directory Administration*, by Apple Computer; available at *http://www.apple.com/macosx/server*.

- *LDAP System Administration*, by Gerald Carter (O'Reilly Media, Inc., 2003)
- *Kerberos: The Definitive Guide*, by Jason Garman (O'Reilly Media, Inc., 2003)
- *Active Directory*, Second Edition, by Robbie Allen, et al. (O'Reilly Media, Inc., 2003)

Also, you may want to refer to the following manpages:

- *DirectoryService*
- *netinfo*
- *dscl*
- *nicl*
- *nidump*
- *niload*
- *fsck*

## CHAPTER 8

Files and Permissions

While most computer use revolves around files, files are particularly central to Unix-based systems. Commands are executable files. Devices and disks are identified as files. Even most interprocess and network communication occurs through what appear to be files. This Unix view of the world permeates the lowest levels of Mac OS X, even to the point that many system privileges and permissions are controlled, in part, through access to files. Access to files is organized around the concepts of ownership and permissions.

This chapter starts out by looking at how to find files, an area in which Tiger's Finder and Spotlight bring tremendous improvements over previous versions of Mac OS X. You'll also learn more about how to work with files: their permissions, metadata, attributes, and more!

Finding Files

When you are working on your Mac, most of the time it's not a matter of having the correct permissions to access a file that gets in your way; it's being able to find the file in the first place. With Mac OS X Tiger, Apple brings us Spotlight technology, a great new tool for helping you find the right file. Spotlight works by indexing the data contained not only within a file itself, but also the file's metadata. Metadata is simply data about data. By tracking information like a document's author, its modification time, and other forms of special file data, Spotlight allows you to search for files using much more than a filename.

For example, image files can sometimes be hard to find in the filesystem. Digital cameras have notoriously poor file-naming schemes and scanning through a folder full of thumbnails in the Finder is quite cumbersome. However, if you know that the picture you're looking for was taken on your Olympus digital camera sometime in late October last year, Spotlight can help you quickly narrow down the possibilities, as shown in Figure 8-1.

Figure 8-1. Using the Finder and Spotlight to search for image files

A particularly nice aspect of searching in Tiger's Finder is that its searches are live updating. If you were to import more pictures that met those search criteria, the results window would update with the new files automatically. An even more powerful feature is that the search can be saved for later use. With just a click of a button, these searches become Smart Folders. You access a Smart Folder much like any other folder in the Finder. However, when you're in a Smart Folder, you'll see a gray bar telling you that you're viewing a Smart Folder and offering an Edit button to gain access to the search criteria. Figure 8-2 is an example of a Smart Folder's contents, based upon the search criteria specified in Figure 8-1.

In addition to using the Finder's search functions, you can perform a search using Spotlight itself. While the Finder's search results are composed solely of files and folders, a search in Spotlight reveals items in other parts of the Spotlight store. This makes it easy to search across all of your data for your chosen criteria. Figure 8-3 contains a search of my Home directory for the word "Apple." Spotlight's search window offers several ways to filter and sort the search results, as well as extended information for each item.

Finding Files on the Command Line

While the Spotlight-enabled Finder makes it easy to find files using the GUI, there are times when it's easier (or even necessary) to use the command line. Thankfully,

Figure 8-2. The contents of a Smart Folder

Smart Folders Aren't Really Folders at All

A quick glance in the Terminal reveals that a Smart Folder isn't really a folder at all. Instead, Smart Folders are stored as Property List (*.plist*) files that have a *.savedSearch* file extension. While it's a shame you can't directly access the contents of a Smart Folder using traditional Unix commands, Apple has provided command-line tools for using Spotlight data. You can learn more about these commands later in this chapter.

Since a Smart Folder is simply a Property List, you can edit one using Property List Editor (part of the Xcode Tools and installed in */Developer/Applications/Utilities*) or TextEdit (*/Applications*). Within the file, you'll find the *RawQuery* field, which contains your Spotlight query, and the file path the query scans. Though modifying a Smart Folder by hand doesn't provide the polish of the Finder's GUI, it's a great way to see how Mac OS X handles Smart Folders behind the scenes.

Mac OS X's BSD subsystem includes traditional Unix search tools like *find*, *grep*, and *locate*. Your options for command-line searching are even further broadened by Tiger's Spotlight commands. With so many powerful utilities at your disposal, it can be tough to pick the right command for the job. Here's a breakdown of each to aid your decision.

Figure 8-3. A Spotlight search

find

The aptly named *find* is one of the original Unix file-searching tools and allows you to search for files based on their filenames and other attributes such as when they were last modified. The basic syntax for using *find* is:

```
find pathname conditions
```

where the *pathname* argument indicates where in the filesystem hierarchy the search should occur, and the *conditions* argument indicates the attributes a file must have to match the search. There are more than 40 types of conditions you can use, the most common of which are listed in Table 8-1. However, the option you'll probably find yourself using the most is *-name*.

Table 8-1. Commonly used find conditions

Condition	Description
-group groupname	Find files belonging to the specified group.
-mtime +n | -n | n	Find files that were modified more than *n* (+*n*), less than *n* (-*n*), or exactly *n* (*n*) days ago.
-name pattern	Find files with names matching the given pattern.
-newer file	Find files that have been modified more recently than the given file.
-user username	Find files that belong to the specified user.

Example 8-1 shows how to find all the files that have a *.xls* extension in the directory *~/Documents*.

Example 8-1. Using the find command with the -name argument

```
$ find ~/Documents -name *.xls
/Users/jldera/Documents/Infrastructure Layouts.xls
/Users/jldera/Documents/Jason Deraleau.xls
```

When run, the *find* command scans through every file in the *~/Documents* directory and its subdirectories. Once it's finished, it lists each file with a name matching the pattern **.xls*.

Another useful option is *-mtime*, which lets you search for files that were modified in a particular time frame. Example 8-2 shows how to find all the files that were modified in the last day in the *~/Documents* directory.

Example 8-2. Finding documents based on modification time

```
$ find ~/Documents -mtime  -1
/Users/jldera/Documents/iChats/Fraser Speirs on 2005-04-18 at 09.34.ichat
/Users/jldera/Documents/Infrastructure Layouts.xls
/Users/jldera/Documents/Purchase Requisition.pdf
```

locate

One of the fastest ways to find files—and quite a bit easier to use than *find*—is to use the *locate* command. Unfortunately, on most Macs, this tool won't return any results because it depends on a database (located in the file */var/db/locate.database*) that only gets created if your machine is running at 4:00 a.m. on a Sunday morning. Chapter 13 shows you how to reschedule this task for a better time, but in the meantime, it's possible to create the database manually with the following command:

```
$ sudo /usr/libexec/locate.updatedb
```

When you issue this command, you are prompted to enter an administrator's password. Because you're using *sudo*, you must be an administrative user to execute the command. Since it takes a while to create the *locate* database, you'll want to run this command in its own Terminal window if you plan to continue working in the shell while it is being executed, or add an ampersand (&) at the end of the command to run it as a background process.

Once the database has been created, you can use the *locate* command with the following syntax:

```
locate pattern
```

Example 8-3 shows how to find a file that you can't quite remember the location or name of.

Example 8-3. Using the locate command

```
$ locate 2004Tax
/Users/jldera/Documents/Financial/Taxes/2004/2004TaxReturn.pdf
```

grep

While *find* and *locate* search for files based on their filename, *grep* looks within a file, allowing you to search for something within a file's contents instead of just its filename. You can either search for a string within a single file or a whole group of files. Its basic syntax is:

```
grep pattern file
```

where *pattern* is what *grep* will look for and *file* is the file, or list of files, in which to look. By itself, this command only searches the specified files. Quite often, however, you'll want to search an entire directory. To do so, you can use the *-r* option, which puts *grep* into recursive mode. Example 8-4 shows how to find a document in the *~/Documents* directory that has the word "Appcasting" in it.

Example 8-4. Finding documents based on content with grep

```
$ grep -r Appcasting ~/Documents
/Users/jldera/Documents/Appcasting Article.txt:
Fraser Speirs defines Appcasting as "the practice of using
```

In addition to telling you the name of the file in which that the term is found, the command shown in Example 8-4 gives you the line of text in which the term is found, which is a way to make sure that *grep* has found the document you really want.

mdfind

Unfortunately, not all file formats store data in the same way. While *grep* is an excellent choice for searching text files, it doesn't do as great a job when working with binary files. By using Spotlight commands, you can open up many other types of content for searching. The Spotlight command you'll work with most is *mdfind*. This tool provides command-line access to the Spotlight database. You can search Spotlight with the syntax:

```
mdfind options query
```

There are only three options for use with *mdfind*:

-onlyin
> Limits the search to a given path, much like the *find* command.

-live
> Since one of the beauties of Spotlight is its live updating, you can supply *mdfind* with this option for those same live results, ad infinitum (or you can hit Control-C).

-0
> Directs *mdfind* to print an ASCII NUL character after each result for use with tools like *xargs*; something discussed more in Chapter 14.

When structuring your query, you can either use simple terms, like "Apple" (as shown in Example 8-5), or more advanced search criteria based on Spotlight attributes.

Example 8-5. Searching Spotlight with mdfind

```
$ mdfind -onlyin /Users/jldera "Apple"
/Users/jldera/Library/Preferences/com.apple.print.PrintingPrefs.plist
/Users/jldera/Library/Preferences/com.apple.SetupAssistant.plist
/Users/jldera/Library/Preferences/com.apple.MenuBarClock.plist
/Users/jldera/Library/Preferences/com.apple.HIToolbox.plist
/Users/jldera/Library/Preferences/com.apple.JapaneseAnalysis
/Users/jldera/Library/Mail/Mac-jldera/Archive.imapmbox/Messages/98.emlx
/Users/jldera/Library/Mail/Mac-jldera/Archive.imapmbox/Messages/101.emlx
/Users/jldera/Library/Preferences/com.apple.dashboard.client.plist
```

Unfortunately, there is no master list of the types of metadata available in the Spotlight store. Spotlight's expandability makes creating such a list quite difficult, as each new application built for Spotlight brings its own custom metadata. However, using the *mdls* command discussed later in this chapter, you can view the metadata associated with a file, including the same attribute names used when creating Spotlight queries.

Example 8-6 shows the results of an *mdfind* query similar to that created using the Finder in Figure 8-1.

Example 8-6. Using Spotlight attributes with mdfind

```
$ mdfind -onlyin /Users/jldera/Pictures "kMDItemAcquisitionMake == 'Olympus'"
/Users/jldera/Pictures/iPhoto Library/2004/10/23/PA220010.JPG
/Users/jldera/Pictures/iPhoto Library/2004/10/23/PA220013.JPG
/Users/jldera/Pictures/iPhoto Library/2004/10/23/PA220029.JPG
/Users/jldera/Pictures/iPhoto Library/2004/10/23/PA220033.JPG
/Users/jldera/Pictures/iPhoto Library/2004/10/23/PA220034.JPG
/Users/jldera/Pictures/iPhoto Library/2004/10/23/PA220039.JPG
```

Owners and Access

File ownership in Mac OS X is based directly on the underlying BSD Unix layer and inherits its strengths (as well as a few quirks) from that legacy. On Unix systems, a file has two owners: a user and a group. Each of these owners is separate from the other; there's no requirement that a user who owns a file be a member of the group that owns that same file. This split in ownership is intended to let you be as flexible as possible in the way that you structure access to files. By allowing groups as well as individual users to be associated with a file, you can give users access to an entire set of files simply by adding them to a group, and you can take away access just as easily.

You can see the owner and group for a file in the Finder using the File → Get Info (⌘-I) menu and unfolding the Ownership & Permissions section and the Details subsection, as shown in Figure 8-4. The Inspector tells you what the owner of a file, the users in the group that owns the file, and everybody else can do with the file. In the case of this image file, *jldera* can both read and write to the file (which makes sense), and only members of the group *jldera* can read the files, while everyone else cannot access the file.

Since the file ownership model in Mac OS X comes from Unix, it follows that there is a way to view these permissions from the command line. Example 8-7 shows the use of the *ls* command to view the ownership details for the contents of the *Winter* directory (as seen in Figure 8-4).

Example 8-7. A file listing of the Winter directory

```
$ ls -la
total 9968
drwxr-xr-x  10 jldera  jldera     340 Apr 16 16:23 .
drwxr-xr-x  13 jldera  jldera     442 Apr 17 01:34 ..
-rw-r-----   1 jldera  jldera  769018 Jul  2  2003 earlyfrost1600.jpg
-rw-r-----   1 jldera  jldera  510003 Jul  2  2003 firstsnow1600.jpg
-rw-r-----   1 jldera  jldera  340212 Jul  2  2003 polaris1600.jpg
-rw-r-----   1 jldera  jldera  776794 Jul  2  2003 sleepingforest1600.jpg
-rw-r-----   1 jldera  jldera  261422 Jul  2  2003 snowtop1600.jpg
-rw-r-----   1 jldera  jldera  952634 Jul  2  2003 snowy1600.jpg
-rw-r-----   1 jldera  jldera  773818 Jul  2  2003 valley11600.jpg
-rw-r-----   1 jldera  jldera  706650 Jul  2  2003 valley2k1600.jpg
```

Believe it or not, the line listing the *firstsnow1600.jpg* file gives you the same information as the File Inspector (albeit in a very concise form that is easy enough to read once you know how). Figure 8-5 shows the kinds of data in each column. It's all quite self-explanatory except for the first set of characters, which can be broken down as shown in Figure 8-5.

The Execute Bit and the Finder

Observant Unix veterans will notice that the Finder doesn't offer a way to modify a file's execute permissions. Furthermore, directories (folders) created in the Finder always have the execute permissions set. Usually, this isn't a problem, but if you do want to fine-tune the execute permissions of a file or a directory, you'll need to do so at the command line using *chmod*.

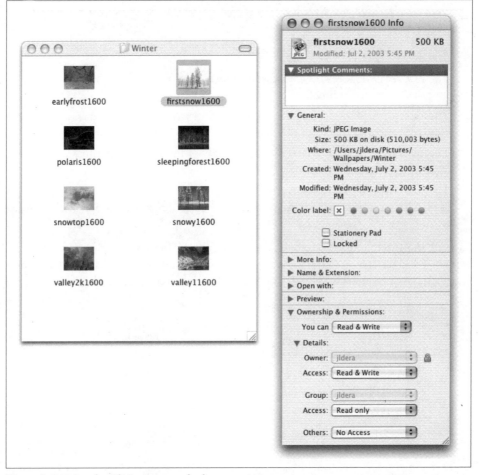

Figure 8-4. Using the File Inspector to look at permissions

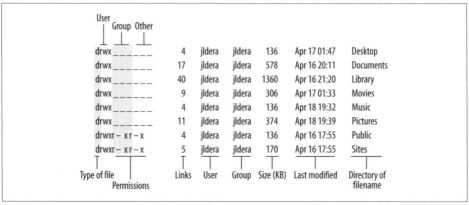

Figure 8-5. Output of ls -l in a user's Home directory

- The first letter denotes the file type. In most cases, this will be either a hyphen (-) for a file or a *d* for a directory.
- The next three letters (characters 2 through 4) indicate the permissions associated with the user owner of the file.
- The next three letters (characters 5 through 7) indicate the permissions associated with the group owner of the file.
- The last three letters (characters 8 through 10) indicate the permissions associated with everyone who is neither the file's user nor a member of the group owner.

Each of the three letter groupings consists of either the letters *r*, *w*, and *x*, or the hyphen (-) character. A letter indicates that permission is allowed, and a hyphen means the permission is withheld. Table 8-2 shows the meanings of these letters.

Table 8-2. File permissions characters

Letter	Meaning for a directory	Meaning for a file
r	Can list the contents of the directory.	Can read the file.
w	Can alter the contents of the directory.	Can write to the file.
x	Can make the directory the current directory (that is, *cd* into it).	Can be executed.
t, T	The directory is "sticky" (see the discussion later in this section).	
S		The executable is either Set UID or Set GID (see the discussion later in this section).

Once you know the secret decoder to the string, it is pretty easy to read the permissions for a file or directory. Using this information, you can read the line describing *firstsnow1600.jpg* in the file listing in Example 8-7 as follows:

- We're looking at a file.
- The user *jldera* has the ability to view and modify the contents of the file.

- Members of the *jldera* group can read the file as well, but not write to it.
- No one else has access to the file.

The permissions for directories work in the same way. The key difference involves the execute bit. To work with the contents of a directory, you must have execute permissions for that directory. So in Figure 8-5, you can see that the *jldera* user has read, write, and execute access to all of the folders. However, most of the folders only allow access to the *jldera* user. The exceptions are Public and Sites. By the nature of their use, these two folders must be accessible by anyone. Thus their permissions have been set to allow read and execute permissions to all.

Table 8-3 shows the most common permission combinations and their meanings.

Table 8-3. Common file permission sets

Pattern	Meaning	Result
---	No access	No activity allowed
r--	Read access only	Lets users read the file
--x	Execute access only	Lets users execute a program
r-x	Read and execute access	Lets users read and execute the file
-wx	Write and execute access	Lets users write to the file, but not read it; useful for Drop Boxes
rwx	Full access	Lets users read, write, and execute the file
rw-	Read and write access	Lets users read from and save to the file

These permissions are reflected in Figure 8-6, which shows another user's Finder view of *jldera*'s Home directory. You can see the "Can't Write" icon in the upper-left part of the window. You can also see that the Desktop, Documents, Library, Movies, Music, and Pictures folders have a "Do Not Enter" symbol on them, indicating that you can't view their contents.

The Sticky Bit

The sticky bit has an odd history. A long time ago it meant an executable file should be kept in memory even after the process using it exited. Most Unix implementations, including Mac OS X, don't use it for this purpose anymore. But, somewhere along the way, it got coerced into another job. When the sticky bit is set on a directory, most file permissions still apply when attempting to read from or write to files within it. However, a user can delete only the files in the directory that belong to him, even if he has access rights to the directory because of a group membership.

For example, consider the */private/tmp* directory is used by Mac OS X and other Unixes for storing temporary files (though most other Unixes simply use */tmp*). Because the directory is used by many different users' processes, the sticky bit is set on */private/tmp* to allow any user to write data to that folder. However, users may

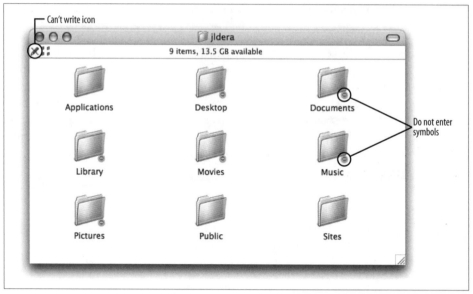

Figure 8-6. Another user's Finder view of jldera's Home folder

only read from and write to the files they create in */private/tmp*. The sticky bit appears in a directory listing like this:

```
drwxrwxrwt  32 root  wheel  1088 Apr 19 20:21 tmp
```

Notice the t at the end of the permission sequence (drwxrwxrwt). It indicates that the sticky bit has been set on the directory. Another directory that has the sticky bit set is */Users/Shared*, as shown in Example 8-8.

Example 8-8. A listing of the /Users directory

```
$ ls -la /Users
total 0
drwxrwxr-t   6 root    admin    204 Apr 19 19:39 .
drwxrwxr-t  29 root    admin   1088 Apr 16 20:48 ..
-rw-r--r--   1 root    wheel      0 Mar 20 18:57 .localized
drwxrwxrwt   6 root    wheel    204 Apr 19 11:50 Shared
drwxr-xr-x  12 alisa   alisa    408 Apr 19 19:46 alisa
drwxr-xr-x  16 jldera  jldera   544 Apr 19 19:45 jldera
```

With the sticky bit set on */Users/Shared*, Mac OS X provides an easy way for users of the system to share files locally. Even though the folder is owned by *root*, the sticky bit signals to the OS that any user can place files in the folder. If user *jldera* saves a document in the */Users/Shared* folder, he can set its permissions to allow others on the system to access the file. However, those users would not have the permissions necessary to delete the file. Only *jldera* (or an administrator) would be able to remove the file from the */Users/Shared* folder.

Set UID and Set GID

Another unique way that Unix uses permissions is through the use of Set UID and Set GID. When you execute an application, it runs as your user and is granted the same permissions to the filesystem as you have. Set UID and Set GID allow you to change this behavior so that a file is always executed as its owner and not necessarily the user who issues the command. While it might not be immediately apparent how this could help you on a day-to-day basis, the need becomes apparent when you look at system commands, such as *sudo*.

As an administrative user, you use the *sudo* command for temporarily gaining superuser privileges. This is often necessary when working with files that are integral to Mac OS X. The dialog box that prompts you for your password when installing software is the graphical equivalent of this practice. To do its job, the *sudo* command needs to be able to run as the superuser. After all, it can't grant you more power than it possesses. This is the directory listing for *sudo*:

```
-r-s--x--x   1 root  wheel  104428 Mar 20 19:03 /usr/bin/sudo
```

The file is executable by anyone. However, no matter who executes the command, it runs as *root* and with *root*'s privileges. This is a powerful tool, but it should be used very cautiously. Notice that *sudo*'s binary has only execute permissions for all users except *root*. This is to prevent outsiders from even reading the file, let alone modifying it for some malicious purpose.

Changing File Ownership and Permissions

If you need to change the ownership of a file, directory, or even a directory tree, you can do so easily from the Finder by using the Inspector. Simply set the various pull-down menus to change the settings for Owner, Group, and Others. To accomplish some of the operations, you'll need to click the padlock icon and authenticate yourself. An administrative user can change ownership for any other user's files. On the command line, you'll need to use the *chown* and *chmod* commands.

chown

The *chown* tool, short for "change ownership," changes the owner of a file. Its basic syntax is:

```
chown owner file
```

where *owner* is the username or user ID of the new owner for the specified *file*. For example, to change the owner of the file *ImportantDocument.doc* to *alisa*, you would use the following command:

```
$ sudo chown alisa ImportantDocument.doc
```

You have to issue this command with *sudo*, because you need to authenticate yourself as an administrator to make this change. After all, you may not want a user to put files under the ownership of somebody else without oversight.

You can also change both the user and group settings for a file by using the following syntax:

```
chown owner:group file
```

where the *owner* and *group* arguments are separated by a colon. For example, to give everyone in the group *sales* access to the document, you would use the following command:

```
$ sudo chown alisa:sales ImportantDocument.doc
```

If you would like to change only the group owner of a file, you can leave the *owner* argument blank. You still must include the separating colon, however, to prevent *chown* from assuming you want to change the file's user owner:

```
chown :group file
```

chmod

The *chmod* tool, short for "change file modes," changes the permissions on a file. Its basic syntax is:

```
chmod access-string file
```

where the *access-string* states the permissions you want to set for the given *file*. The access string has three parts to it: a letter (u, g, o, a), an operation code (+, -, =), and a permission (r, w, x). Table 8-4 gives a summary of what these codes represent.

Table 8-4. Commonly used chmod code summary

String part	Code	Description
Who	u	User
	g	Group
	o	Other
	a	All (default)
Operation	+	Add permission
	-	Remove permission
	=	Assign only this permission, removing others
Permission	r	Read
	w	Write
	x	Execute (file) or search (directory)
	t	Sticky bit

For example, to give everybody write access for a file that you own:

```
$ chmod a+w ImportantDocument.doc
```

To enable execution of a file for everyone in the group that owns the file:

```
$ chmod g+x generatereport
```

To remove the ability to execute a file from all users:

```
$ chmod -x generatereport
```

To remove the ability to read a file from everyone but yourself:

```
$ chmod go-r ImportantDocument.doc
```

Or, if you need to set the sticky bit:

```
$ chmod u+t /Common
```

You can recursively change the permissions of a group of files by using the -R option. For example, if you wanted to allow everybody to see all the documents in your Documents folder, you would use the following command:

```
$ chmod -R +r Documents
```

You can also use commas to set more than one permission at a time. For example:

```
$ chmod a-wx,a+r ImportantDocument.doc
```

Alternatively, you can specify the mode of a file in another format; however, this is a more arcane syntax. To understand this syntax, you have to think in terms of bits and octal notation. A typical mode in this syntax contains three digits—each corresponding to the three levels of permission (user, group, other). Each digit is calculated by adding the octal values shown in Table 8-5.

Table 8-5. Octal values for assigning file permissions

Octal value	Function
4	Read
2	Write
1	Execute
0	No permission

Some common number combinations for setting permissions are shown in Table 8-6. For example, if you wanted to grant read and write permissions for a user and only read permissions for group and others:

```
$ chmod 644 ImportantDocument.doc
```

Here, 644 indicates that the user who created the file has read-write privileges (4 + 2 = 6), and the group and others only get read-only access, as indicated by the 4s.

To grant all permissions to the user and deny all permissions to the group and others:

```
$ chmod 700 ImportantDocument.doc
```

Table 8-6. Commonly used chmod numeric sequences

Number	Result	Description
777	rwxrwxrwx	File can be read, written, or executed by anyone.
774	rwxrwxr-x	File can be read and executed by anyone, but written to only by owner or group.
755	rwxr-xr-x	File can be read and executed by anyone, but written to only by owner.
666	rw-rw-rw-	File can be read and written by anyone, but can't be executed.
664	rw-rw-r--	File can be read by anyone, written by owner or group, and can't be executed.
644	rw-r--r--	File can be read by anyone, written by owner, and can't be executed.
444	r--r--r--	File is read-only.

Access Control Lists

Although the Unix permission model works well in most cases, there are times when it doesn't quite cover all your needs. For example, it isn't possible to grant two members of the same group different types of access to the same file. If you allow one group member to write to the file, all of them can. Similarly, you can't grant a third user access to that one file without making her a part of the group and giving her access to all of the rest of the group's files.

These and similar limitations have plagued the Unix community for years, forcing many Unixes to release their own implementations of *Access Control Lists* (ACLs). Apple has followed suit with the release of Tiger, bringing ACLs to Mac OS X. While they aren't something you'll likely use much on a single Mac, ACLs are a huge feature in network environments. Mac OS X Tiger Server adds ACL support right in the GUI, making it easy and intuitive to manage *Access Control Entries* (ACEs).

The client version of Mac OS X isn't so lucky, however. If you find you've reached the limits of the Unix permissions model, you'll have to delve into the command line to work with the ACLs on your system. The two commands you'll use most when working with ACLs should be familiar to you by now. The *chmod* command is used to set up your ACLs, and *ls* will help you view them. But, before delving into *how* to change your files' ACLs, the next section tells you *what* you can change.

 By default, ACLs are not enabled on the client version of Mac OS X. You can use the command **sudo /usr/sbin/fsaclctl -p / -e** to enable them on the boot volume (/).

Access Control Entries

Access Control Lists are made up of a series of Access Control Entries (ACEs). ACEs are simple rules that specify the user or group involved, whether access is denied or granted, and the type of access in question. When a user requests access to a file, Mac OS X consults each ACE within the ACL, in order, and uses the first matching rule. If it reaches the end of the ACL without a match, Mac OS X resorts to using the

Unix permissions system to determine access privileges. Table 8-7 lists some of the more basic permissions that can be controlled using ACLs. You can find a more detailed list on the *chmod* manpage or in Workgroup Manager on Tiger Server.

Table 8-7. Permissions controlled through ACLs

Permission	Description
read	Read the file's contents
write	Write to the file
delete	Delete the file

Working with Access Control Lists

As mentioned earlier, the two commands you'll use most frequently when working with ACLs are *chmod* and *ls*. Each has been given an extra switch or two for viewing and manipulating a file's ACEs. In the case of *ls*, the *-e* switch has been added to provide a way to look at a file's ACL. In Example 8-9, the file *AnotherDoc.doc* has a single ACE that allows the user *panic* to read the file, despite the fact that the file's Unix permissions would prevent it. If a user besides *panic* (or *jldera*, of course) attempted to read the file, he would be denied access.

Example 8-9. Viewing a file's Access Control Entries

```
$ ls -le
total 121648
-rw------- + 1 jldera  jldera  18931712 Jun 15 14:43 AnotherDoc.doc
 0: user:panic allow read
-rw-r--r--   1 jldera  jldera  43352064 Jun 15 14:43 SomeDoc.doc
```

ACLs are far more flexible than traditional Unix permissions. They offer much finer-grained control over who can do what with a file or folder. Much like traditional Unix permissions, you use the *chmod* command to manipulate a file's ACEs from the command line. Tiger's *chmod* has two new switches: *+a* and *-a*. They are used for adding and removing ACEs, respectively. To add an ACE to a file, use the syntax:

```
chmod +a "user access permission" file
```

where *user* is the user (or group) to whom the entry applies, *access* is either *allow* or *deny*, and *permission* is the type of access you want to restrict or grant. For example, to grant the user *alisa* read access to the file *AnotherDoc.doc*, you would use the command:

```
$ chmod +a "alisa allow read" AnotherDoc.doc
```

Here's is the directory listing for *AnotherDoc.doc* after adding the new Access Control Entry.

```
$ ls -le AnotherDoc.doc
-rw------- + 1 jldera  jldera  18931712 Jun 15 14:43 AnotherDoc.doc
 0: user:alisa allow read
 1: user:panic allow read
```

Removing an ACE is very similar to adding an entry. Note that you should not add a rule that counteracts your undesired rule (that is, a *deny* rule to override an *allow* rule). Instead, remove the unwanted rule using the syntax:

```
chmod -a "user access permission" file
```

Order of Operations

Because Mac OS X processes ACLs in series, it's important that your ACEs are in the correct order. Tiger's *chmod* command has two more switches for removing and inserting rules into a file's ACL. While the *+a* switch normally inserts a rule at the top of the ACL, you can use the *+a# index* switch, where *index* is the position in the ACL where the entry should be inserted. Similarly, the *-a# index* switch allows you to remove the ACE at the specified position in the ACL.

Other Permission Types

Not only has Mac OS X's complex parentage brought a variety of applications and tools, but it has also brought us multiple types of file attributes. Beyond the simple Unix owners, permissions, and ACLs, there are BSD file flags and HFS+ attributes. Both of these methods allow further refinement of access to files, and both also bring their own commands and options.

BSD file flags

There are quite a few different BSD file flags available, but only a handful see frequent use. These can be further broken down into two types: system and user. System flags can be set only by the superuser and may be removed only when the system is in single-user mode (see Chapter 5 for more information on single-user mode). User flags can be set and unset at any time by any user with adequate permissions to access the file being manipulated. Table 8-8 contains a list of the most common file flags.

Table 8-8. Commonly used BSD file flags

Class	Flag	Description
System	*sappnd*	Makes the file append-only
	schg	Makes the file unmodifiable
User	*uappnd*	Makes the file append-only
	uchg	Makes the file unmodifiable

While it is not possible to view a file's flags using the Finder, it's a snap in the Terminal. To view the flags, use the *ls* command's *-lo* options, as shown in Example 8-10.

Example 8-10. A directory listing showing BSD file flags

```
$ ls -lo
total 0
-rw-r--r--   1 jldera  jldera  uappnd 0 Apr 22 11:45 appendonly
-rw-r--r--   1 jldera  jldera  uchg   0 Apr 22 11:52 cantchangeme
```

The *chflags* (change flags) tool is used for modifying BSD file flags. Its syntax is:

```
chflags flag file
```

where *flag* is one of the BSD file flags noted in Table 8-8. If you would like to remove a file flag, preface its name with *no*. For example, to remove the *uchg* flag from the *cantchangeme* file listed in Example 8-10, use this command:

```
$ chflags nouchg cantchangeme
```

HFS+ Attributes

Though UFS is available for use with Mac OS X, most Macs will have their hard drives formatted in HFS+. HFS+ brings its own features and idiosyncrasies (covered in detail in Chapter 9), but the one most relevant to file access is the HFS+ attribute set. These attributes, like BSD file flags, work in concert with the standard file permissions model to provide additional flexibility in controlling who may view, modify, or otherwise work with your data.

The two HFS+ attributes that are most useful when restricting file access are the Invisible and Locked attributes. While the Locked attribute is quite similar to the *uchg* file flag noted earlier, the Invisible flag can be a bit misleading. Files marked with the HFS+ Invisible attribute are not displayed in the Finder; however, they are still plainly visible in the shell.

Table 8-9 contains some common HFS+ attributes. When an attribute's letter is lowercase, that attribute does not apply; when uppercase, the attribute is in effect.

Table 8-9. Commonly used HFS+ attributes

Attribute	Description
A	The file is an alias.
C	The file or folder has a custom icon.
E	The file's or folder's extension is hidden.
L	The file is locked.
V	The file or folder is invisible.

There are two command-line tools available for working with HFS+ file attributes. Though the tools are not a part of the default Mac OS X install, you can easily acquire them by installing the Xcode Tools. With Xcode installed, you can find the pertinent commands in */Developer/Tools*. Remember that if you haven't added the directory *Developer/Tools* to your shell's command path (as discussed in Chapter 4), you must specify a complete path when working with these commands.

To view a file's HFS+ attributes, you'll want to make use of the *GetFileInfo* command. The syntax is pretty straightforward, but reading the output can be tricky. Example 8-11 shows sample output from *GetFileInfo*. The fourth line of the command's output lists all of the file's possible attributes, capitalizing those that are in effect. In the case of *Financial.xls*, the file's extension is hidden (capital "E") and it is locked to prevent modification (capital "L").

Example 8-11. Sample output from the GetFileInfo command

```
$ /Developer/Tools/GetFileInfo Financial.xls
file: "/Users/jldera/Documents/Financial.xls"
type: "XLS8"
creator: "XCEL"
attributes: avbstcLinmEdz
created: 08/25/2004 11:35:49
modified: 01/27/2005 10:36:23
```

GetFileInfo's counterpart is *SetFile*. You'll find it in the same folder as *GetFileInfo*, and the two share a similar syntax. The *SetFile* command is used for changing a file's attributes. If locking *Financial.xls* from changes was not enough to protect it, you can make the file hidden using this command:

```
$ /Developer/Tools/SetFile -a V Financial.xls
```

As mentioned earlier, you'll want to capitalize the letter of any attribute you wish to apply; using a lowercase letter removes the attribute. *GetFileInfo* and *SetFile* also give you access to even more forms of file metadata. These extra bits of file information are used by Mac OS X in some unique ways that are covered in the "Type and Creator Codes" section, later in this chapter.

Metadata and File Attributes

The prefix *meta-* implies a state of transcendence. It's used to describe the derivatives and successors of a lot of different things (think *meta*physics). It should come as no surprise then that metadata is often described as "data about data." What may be surprising, however, is just how much data about your data is available. While the file's owner and filename would be obvious picks, there are many other pieces of metadata embedded in your files.

Take a snapshot from your digital camera as an example. In addition to the basic information that can be derived from the filesystem, even more details are kept in the Exchangeable Image File Format (EXIF) data within the file. This information was added to the file by your digital camera when you snapped the picture. These tidbits of data are not only valuable when working within your imaging software, but they are also indexed in the Spotlight data store for searches down the road.

Spotlight

The introduction of Spotlight technology in Mac OS X Tiger has brought file metadata to the foreground. Spotlight is a powerful tool for searching your data, but it's much more involved than belied by the simple search box presented when you click the Spotlight icon in the menu bar. Spotlight is constantly running in the background, updating its data store whenever the files on your drive change, and making the latest content and metadata available for immediate searching.

At the same time, it is handling search requests from Spotlight-powered applications. As you browse a Smart Folder in the Finder, Spotlight works to populate that folder with the appropriate files. When you're looking through a Smart Mailbox in Mail, Spotlight ensures all messages that meet your criteria are visible. Developers are beginning to make their applications Spotlight aware, extending not only their own software with Spotlight support, but also extending Spotlight itself with support for new file formats and metadata schemas. Spotlight is far more than just a search interface; it's an entire system framework dedicated to helping you find your data as quickly as possible.

Spotlight on Privacy

Sometimes you have data that you don't want to be indexed. Maybe it's a confidential spreadsheet or pictures of that new secret prototype. Either way, you can keep Spotlight from indexing your data through its Privacy preferences. To specify which folders Spotlight should ignore, open System Preferences (⌘ → System Preferences) and select the Spotlight pane.

Once you're in the Spotlight preferences, you'll see a Search Results tab that allows you to control the types of results shown in your Spotlight search window. You'll also see a Privacy tab where you can list folders whose contents you want Spotlight to ignore when indexing.

Apple has provided two useful command-line tools for working with Spotlight data. The *mdfind* command, discussed earlier in the chapter, allows you to search the Spotlight store for all files that meet your criteria. The *mdls* command, however, shows you all Spotlight data for an individual file. Figure 8-7 is a look at some of an audio file's metadata, as reported in iTunes. Example 8-12 shows the metadata for that same file (I've trimmed the output for display purposes), as reported by the *mdls* command.

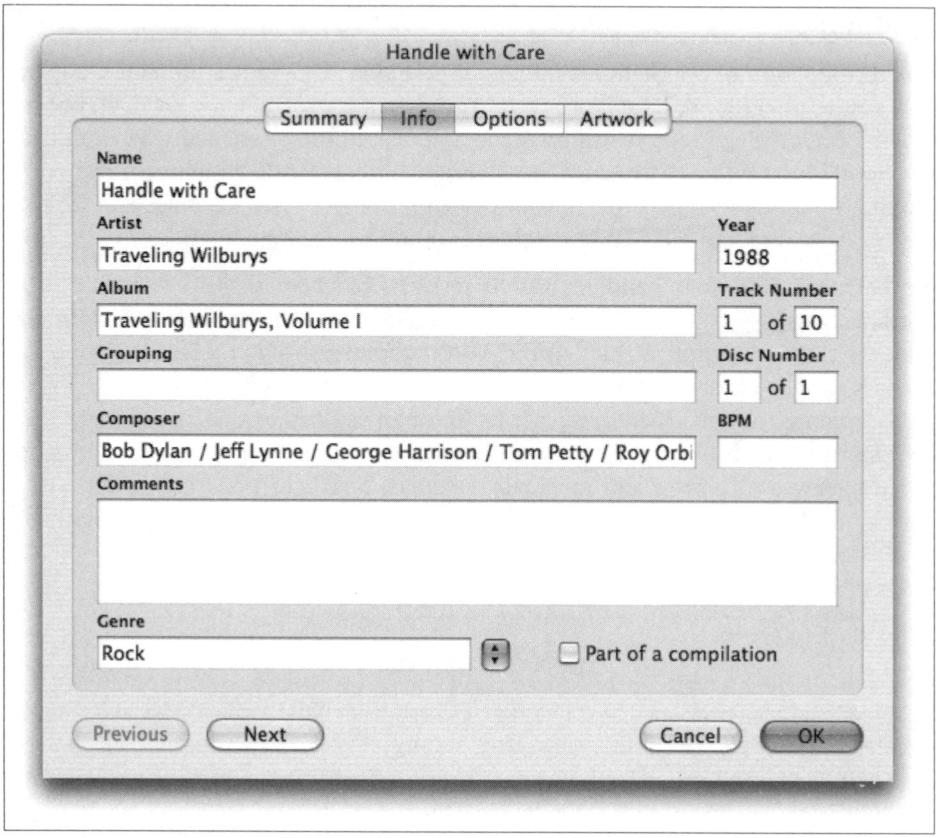

Figure 8-7. An audio file's metadata

Example 8-12. Viewing a file's Spotlight metadata with mdls

```
$ mdls "01 Handle with Care.m4a"
01 Handle with Care.m4a -------------
kMDItemAlbum                    = "Traveling Wilburys, Volume I"
kMDItemAttributeChangeDate      = 2005-04-16 21:17:50 -0400
kMDItemAudioBitRate             = 190672
kMDItemAudioChannelCount        = 2
kMDItemAudioEncodingApplication = "iTunes v4.7, QuickTime 6.5.2"
kMDItemAudioTrackNumber         = 1
kMDItemAuthors                  = ("Traveling Wilburys")
kMDItemCodecs                   = (AAC)
kMDItemComposer                 = "Bob Dylan / Jeff Lynne / George Harrison
                                   / Tom Petty / Roy Orbison"
kMDItemContentCreationDate      = 2004-12-13 08:23:16 -0500
kMDItemContentModificationDate  = 2004-12-13 14:34:40 -0500
kMDItemContentType              = "public.mpeg-4-audio"
kMDItemContentTypeTree          = (
    "public.mpeg-4-audio",
    "public.audio",
```

Example 8-12. Viewing a file's Spotlight metadata with mdls (continued)

```
    "public.audiovisual-content",
    "public.data",
    "public.item",
    "public.content"
)
```

Type and Creator Codes

In Example 8-11, you can see that *GetFileInfo* is telling you much more about the file than its access attributes. While the rest of that information is pretty self-explanatory, the Type and Creator codes may not be familiar to you.

A file's Type code is a case-sensitive, four-character string used by the filesystem to denote the file's type. Type codes can be assigned at file creation and must be four characters in length. Table 8-10 lists some common Type codes. In this table, an underscore means that a space is used where the space character should be (remember, Type codes have to be exactly four characters).

Table 8-10. Common Type codes

File extension	Type code	Type of file
.pdf	PDF_	Portable Document File
.doc	W8BN	Microsoft Word document
.xls	XLS8	Microsoft Excel document
.psd	8BPS	Adobe Photoshop document
.dmg	devi	Disk image
.mov	MooV	QuickTime movie
.jpeg, .jpg	JPEG	JPEG image file

A Creator code is similar to a Type code, except that it denotes the application that was used to create the file. Like Type codes, Creator codes are also exactly four characters in length and are case-sensitive. Table 8-11 lists some common Creator codes.

Table 8-11. Common Creator codes

Creator code	Application
PRVW	Preview
MSWD	Microsoft Word
XCEL	Microsoft Excel
8BIM	Adobe Photoshop

Looking again at Example 8-11, you can see that the file Type is XLS8, which means that it's an Excel document, and the Creator code is XCEL, which means it was created by Microsoft Excel.

Type and Creator codes are used by the Finder to determine the type of a document and the application that should be used to open it. You can see this information in the Finder by choosing File → Get Info (⌘-I).

An Aside on Extensions

Type and Creator codes have been a part of the Mac almost as long as there's been a Mac. They've never been a part of Windows, however, leading to frustrated users on both sides. Microsoft Windows makes use of three-character file extensions to specify a file's type. It then uses file associations to determine which application handles the file. Both get you the same results, though the HFS+ approach offers more finite control, allowing you to specify the handler on an individual file basis.

Unfortunately, the two systems are ignorant of each other, leaving the duty of picking the right application to the user. Inevitably, a Mac user would forget to add that file extension or might encounter an extension she just isn't familiar with. Today it's not as much of a concern: Mac OS X is a much friendlier cross-platform client than its predecessors, providing excellent support of both file extensions and HFS+ Type and Creator codes.

If you still end up coming across an unfamiliar file extension, you'll find some great resources on the Internet for tracking down a compatible application. A search of the file extension will likely yield good results, but you might have better luck searching a site like *http://www.filext.com*.

Further Explorations

To get deeper into the subjects in this chapter, you should refer to the following books:

- *Mac OS X Tiger in a Nutshell*, by Andy Lester, et al. (O'Reilly Media, Inc., 2005)
- *Learning Unix for Mac OS X Tiger*, by Dave Taylor (O'Reilly Media, Inc., 2005)

You may also want to check out the following manpages:

- *find*
- *locate*
- *grep*
- *mdfind*
- *ls*
- *chown*
- *chmod*
- *sticky*
- *chflags*
- *GetFileInfo*
- *SetFile*
- *mdls*

CHAPTER 9

Disks and Filesystems

Mac OS X supports multiple device types that can be accessed as a disk. These include physical disks such as hard drives, FireWire and USB drives, multiple hard drives combined into a RAID, CDs and DVDs, various forms of flash memory (including thumb drives and the iPod Shuffle), network disks residing on a server, and virtual disks that can exist in memory or be derived from files on another filesystem. Even though disks can take many forms, from the user perspective, a disk is a disk is a disk. As long as the disk stores data, and files can be moved and copied between them without too much thought, that's all any user really cares about, right?

To the system, however, two layers mediate between the operating system and disks:

- Device drivers that translate standard system file access calls into a form understood by the disk

- Filesystems that organize data on a drive into a form that can be accessed by a device driver

Mac OS X has device drivers, in the form of kernel extensions (*kexts*), for most of the devices that you will want to use as a disk including FireWire drives, USB flash memory cards, and SCSI disks.

This chapter starts out by introducing the kinds of filesystems that Mac OS X supports and shows you how to examine and work with these filesystems. It then shows you how to work with disks—both physical and virtual—including partitioning disks and moving data safely from one disk to another.

Filesystems

Each device stores data in a form that makes sense for that device. A hard drive usually writes data to the platters using a series of sectors and tracks. A CD writes data in one continuous track that spirals from the inside of the disk out. A compact flash card simply holds data in a matrix of memory cells on the chip. For efficiency reasons, the data that makes up a file may be scattered across various sectors of a hard drive instead of being nicely organized in one lump. The role of a filesystem is to mediate between the world of the device where data resides and the world of the Finder where data shows up in an organized form as files and folders.

The Mac OS Extended Filesystem (HFS+)

The primary filesystem used by Mac OS X is the Mac OS Extended filesystem, also known as HFS+. Introduced in Mac OS 8.1 and upgraded for Panther with journaling features, HFS+ allows long filenames with up to 255 Unicode characters, scales up to 2 TB of data on a filesystem, can handle 2 billion files, and allows for files up to 2 GB in size. In addition, each folder in an HFS+ filesystem can handle a maximum of 32,767 files. When HFS+ was first introduced, the size of these figures was way beyond what the state-of-the-art filesystems of the time could handle.

 Even though it looks like it will be good for the next few years, it's obvious that HFS+ has only a few more years left to it. Apple, in all their infinite wisdom, no doubt realizes this and is probably hard at work devising a new filesystem type for the future; something capable of keeping up with the rapidly growing file sizes we encounter when working with digital audio and video.

One of the quirks of HFS+ is that it is a *case-preserving* and *case-insensitive* filesystem. This means you can't have files named *Readme* and *README* in the same directory. This is similar to the way the filesystems work on Windows, but is different from the traditional Unix case-preserving filesystems where you can have both a *Readme* and *README* file in the same directory. In most cases, this isn't a problem, because people don't tend to place two files with the same name into a directory.

Another difference between the HFS+ filesystem and most others is that HFS+ supports the concept of *resource forks*. Resource forks were used on the old Mac OS to store all sorts of metadata for a file, such as icons. Although resource forks were a good idea, they didn't catch on with the rest of the world. Unix and Windows filesystems don't have an equivalent concept, so Apple adopted a similar policy and recommends that all applications that write files should avoid using resource forks. However, the filesystem still supports resource forks, mainly so older applications that rely on them can run just fine. In all likelihood, many applications will continue to use resource forks to some degree or another. You can read more about resource forks in Chapter 8.

Journaling

If something went wrong with the Mac OS X filesystem in earlier releases, a long and intensive *fsck* process would be run the next time the machine started up. For example, if the machine was powered off incorrectly or if the system crashed, it was pretty

Case Insensitivity and Unix

When Apple's Rhapsody team first brought up the system on top of HFS+, they were concerned that case insensitivity would be a problem. It turned out that the only package in all the various Unix utilities where case insensitivity was a problem was in the Perl source code tree. The problem: there was both a *Makefile* and a *makefile* at the top level of the distribution package. Now that most of the core Perl developers run Mac OS X, this is no longer an issue.

common to wait a long time at the initial gray boot screen. And if the filesystem truly got itself into a bad state, manual intervention was necessary to fix the filesystem.

Journaling, which was first introduced in Mac OS X Server 10.2.2 and has been the default filesystem type since Mac OS X Panther, implements a scheme that keeps the filesystem structure of your disk safe even in the face of an unexpected shutdown or system crash. When your Mac reboots, disk repairs are made as needed. The filesystem does this by keeping a continuous record of changes to the files on a disk in a journal file in a designated area of the disk. If a computer starts up and the disk is in an inconsistent state, the journal is used to quickly restore the disk to its previous known state. This record keeping does come with a slight performance overhead. It typically takes 10 to 15 percent longer to write small files with journaling than without it, but in most cases, the slight performance loss is well worth the safety gained. Journaling also allows other optimizations to be made in the disk I/O system, which more than makes up for the performance penalty.

It is important to note that, in the face of unexpected shutdowns, journaling won't necessarily protect the data being written to disk. By protecting the filesystem, journaling protects all the data that is already on your disk from being lost. Any changes you may have made to a document after its last save, for example, are most likely lost.

Fragmentation

In the past 20 years of personal computing, a common theme with hard disks has been the issue of file fragmentation. Early hard drive formats were extremely susceptible to performance problems manifested over time because file data was often split and scattered across the hard drive. As files grew larger than their original allocation, the filesystem was forced to put parts of those files onto different sectors of the disk. Even more modern formats such as HFS+ can exhibit performance slowdowns over time as a disk is used more.

The following two optimizations to the HFS+ driver were introduced for Mac OS X Panther (v10.3) when using a journaled filesystem:

Automatic file defragmentation
> When opened, if a file has more than eight fragments and is smaller than 20 MB in size, it is defragmented by simply moving the file to a new location on the drive where the file can be written in one contiguous block.

Adaptive hot-file clustering
> Over a period of time, the system keeps track of small files that are read frequently, but never written to. As the system learns which files are used most and which are least likely to change size, it moves them to the fastest part of the drive, where they can quickly be accessed. Files that don't meet the requirements for being in this "hot zone" are moved out to ensure that enough room exists for the files that should be there.

This means—at least for most files most of the time—a separate defragmentation program isn't needed. It also means you should always enable journaling on your drives so you can take advantage of these features. Fortunately, when installing Tiger, the default filesystem type is Mac OS Extended (Journaled), so you should be set.

> These optimizations weren't part of the official advertised feature set for Panther. They were, however, discovered by some programmers while reading the source code for the filesystem drivers available from the Darwin project (*http://developer.apple.com/darwin*).

Other Supported Filesystems

In addition to HFS+, Mac OS X supports several other types of filesystems, each of which has its own unique characteristics:

Mac OS Standard (HFS)
> The standard Mac filesystem prior to the release of Mac OS 8.1, HFS is primarily supported so that older disks can still be accessed.

Unix File System (UFS)
> A variant of the standard BSD Fast File System, UFS is a case-sensitive and case-preserving filesystem provided to ensure that applications needing a case-sensitive filesystem can be run. Some people recommend that Unix software developers use UFS, but experience has shown that HFS+ is a much faster filesystem and case insensitivity isn't the big problem many make it out to be. If you think you have a need for UFS, you'll want to consider your decision carefully because, under Mac OS X, this filesystem doesn't perform as well as HFS+.

Universal Disk Format (UDF)
> The standard format for all DVD media formats including video, DVD-ROM, DVD-RAM, and DVD-RW as well as some writable CD formats.

ISO-9660
> The standard cross-platform file format for CD-ROM data disks.

Audio CD
> The format used by standard audio CDs.

MS-DOS File Allocation Table (FAT)
> The standard filesystem of MS-DOS; widely used by Microsoft Windows. Mac OS X supports both the 16- and 32-bit variants of FAT.

New Technology Filesystem (NTFS)
> Originally developed for Windows NT, NTFS is now the primary filesystem used in the PC world. Mac OS X provides some support for NTFS, but access is limited to read actions; Mac OS X can't write to a locally mounted NTFS volume.

Network-Based Filesystems

In addition to working with physical filesystems, Mac OS X supports a set of network-based filesystem protocols. These are used when you mount a filesystem from a machine elsewhere on the network and, for the most part, make a remote filesystem appear as though it were local to your computer. The network filesystem protocols supported by Mac OS X are:

Apple Filing Protocol (AFP)
> The native network file-sharing protocol for Mac-based computers. Originally designed to work over AppleTalk, it now operates well over IP-based networks. Most connections to Mac-based filesystems will be AFP-based.

Service Message Block (SMB)/Common Internet File System (CIFS)
> The native network file-sharing protocol for Windows-based computers. Known as SMB for most of its life, Microsoft started standardization of the protocol under the CIFS name in the late 1990s, but these efforts were never finalized. This protocol is implemented in Mac OS X by the Samba suite of software (*http://www.samba.org*).

Network File System (NFS)
> An older, Unix-based network filesystem used by Linux, the various BSD systems, Solaris, AIX, and other Unix variants. NFS allows Unix machines to transparently share filesystems in such a way that the Unix user security model is preserved.

Web-Based Distributed Authoring and Versioning (WebDAV)
> A set of extensions to HTTP that allows you to collaboratively edit and manage files on remote web servers. WebDAV is the native protocol used for mounting iDisk shares from .Mac. You can find more information about WebDAV at *http://www.webdav.org*.

File Transfer Protocol (FTP)
> An older protocol, used to transfer files between machines, that's still in use on the Internet. Traditionally, FTP has been used with an FTP client (similar to how the Web is browsed with a web browser), but if you want, you can mount an FTP site as a drive.

Mounting a Network Filesystem

The Finder's Go → Connect to Server menu (⌘-K), shown in Figure 9-1, gives you a simple interface for mounting remote disks locally. There are four ways to connect to a remote server.

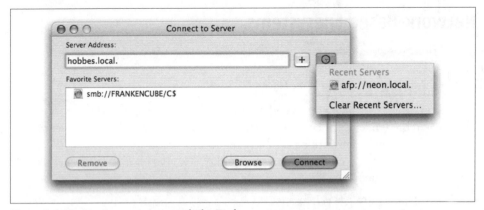

Figure 9-1. Connecting to a server with the Finder

Server Address
> Here you can type the hostname or IP address of the server that you want to connect to. The Finder will assume that you want to connect via AFP if you simply enter a hostname or IP address, but you can also use a URL in this field to connect to the AFP, FTP, SMB, and WebDAV filesystems. Table 9-1 gives the syntax for these URLs.

Favorite Servers
> A list of servers that you can add by clicking the plus (+) button next to the Server Address field. Use this for servers that you connect to frequently.

Recent Servers
> The Clock button gives you access to the servers you have recently connected to. You'll see these recent servers by URL, as shown in Figure 9-1.

Browse
> When you click the Browse button, a Finder view opens, focused on the Network view, as shown in Figure 9-2. This provides you with access to the various Mac- and Windows-based filesystems available on the local network.

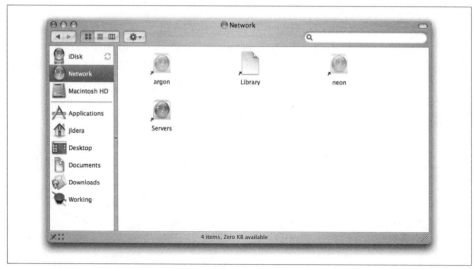

Figure 9-2. The Network browser in the Finder

When you connect to a network-based filesystem using Connect to Server, it shows up as a drive in the Finder and is mounted into the filesystem in the */Volumes* directory. If you want to mount a network-based filesystem into a directory other than */Volumes*, you'll need to use the *mount* command-line utility. The *mount* command has the following general syntax:

```
mount -t filesystemtype url mountpoint
```

The *-t* option lets you specify the type of filesystem you want to mount. The *mountpoint* must be a directory that already exists in the filesystem. For example, to mount a .Mac user's Public folder, issue the following commands:

```
$ mkdir -r /Disks/iDisk
$ mount -t webdav http://idisk.mac.com/runningosx-Public /Disks/iDisk
```

The first command uses *mkdir* to create a directory and subdirectory in the filesystem that you can use for mounting a disk volume. The second command actually mounts the iDisk Public folder, which belongs to the .Mac member named *runningosx*, into the */Disks/iDisk* directory.

There are also specific *mount* command variants for each protocol. These are listed in Table 9-1.

Table 9-1. Network filesystem types, URL syntax, and command-line mount utilities

Protocol	Filesystem type	URL syntax	Command-line mount utility
AFP	afp	*afp://[user]@host/[volumename]*	*mount_afp*
FTP	ftp	*ftp://[user]@host/[path]*	*mount_ftp*
NFS	nfs	*nfs://[user]@host/[path]*	*mount_nfs*

Protocol	Filesystem type	URL syntax	Command-line mount utility
SMB/CIFS	smbfs	*smb://[user]@host/[sharename]*	*mount_smbfs*
WebDAV	webdav	*http://[user]@host/[path]*	*mount_webdav*

Sharing a Network Filesystem

Of course connecting to another machine's filesystem is only half of the equation. You also need a way to share out your Mac's disks to other users. Mac OS X's versatility makes it an excellent solution for cross-platform file sharing. Using System Preferences, you can enable several different protocols that clients can use to connect to your Mac. These protocols can be broken down into two main groups: those that are Internet-based and those intended for Local Area Networks (LANs).

Sharing to Internet users

The two services provided with Mac OS X for Internet sharing are perhaps the most pervasive on the Web: FTP and HTTP. For HTTP, Apple has chosen the extremely popular Apache *httpd* daemon. Easily the most used web server on the Internet, Apache adds Mac OS X as yet another entry in its list of supported platforms. It's a reliable, proven Unix daemon whose complexity is belied by the simplicity of setting it up on your Mac.

Sharing to web users

When you enable Personal Web Sharing (System Preferences → Sharing → Services), the *httpd* web server daemon is started and starts serving pages from the following locations:

- Pages in the */Library/WebServer/Documents* folder are served when you make a request to your machine. For example, to browse the pages on the machine that you are serving from, you can point your web browser at *http://localhost*.

- Pages in each user's *Sites* directory are served for requests to *http://localhost/~username*.

Apache's configuration file is located at */etc/httpd/httpd.conf*. For the most part, this is a standard Apache configuration file, with just a few changes made to adapt it to Mac OS X. Any of the standard Apache configuration directives will work in this file. To access the locally installed documentation on how to configure Apache, browse to *http://localhost/manual/* on your machine after turning on Personal Web Sharing. You can also find this documentation in the */Library/Documentation/Services/apache* directory.

For more information on configuring Apache, see *Apache: The Definitive Guide, Third Edition*, by Ben Laurie, et al. (O'Reilly), or the *Apache Pocket Reference*, by Andrew Ford (O'Reilly).

When adding configuration directives to Apache's configuration, consider creating a file in the */etc/httpd/users* directory that uses the *.conf* extension. Files in this directory that match the pattern **.conf* are automatically included by *httpd.conf*. By making your edits in subfiles, you'll keep your configuration files neater as well as avoid potential conflicts from updated *httpd.conf* files that may be installed as part of future system updates.

HTTP is the workhorse of the Web. For the most part, however, HTTP is intended to send data in a single direction—out. A web browser requests a file, and the HTTP server sends it back. Even though WebDAV and HTML forms allow a user to push a file or information onto the server, the majority of HTTP transactions occur in one direction: server to client. This leaves administrators with a bit of a gap when it comes to putting data on the server.

Long before HTTP came into the limelight, FTP was the primary way files were moved around Internet. Unfortunately, FTP was developed in a time when the Internet was still nascent and the worms, viruses, Trojan horses, and other baddies we see on the Net today were unheard of. Security was never a priority for FTP like it has been for its successors, *sftp* and *rsync*. Luckily, FTP is disabled by default on Mac OS X, and you may want to leave it that way. However, if you want to turn it on, you can in the Sharing preference panel. When you do, you can connect to your Mac with any FTP client, and you'll be able to access the contents of your entire system.

FTP Clients

Over the years, there have been several different FTP clients developed for the Mac. Perhaps the most popular is Panic's Transmit (*http://www.panic.com/transmit*). Transmit offers a very friendly FTP experience to Mac users. The latest release even has a Dashboard Widget for use with Tiger.

If shareware apps aren't within your budget, there are also a number of open source FTP applications available for Mac OS X. As a matter of fact, there's a command-line FTP client included with Darwin named simply *ftp* (take a look at the *ftp* manpage for more information).

Sharing to local network users

The Internet has ushered in a variety of tools for moving files around. Most of them also work on a local area network, but there are still other protocols that lend themselves particularly well to file sharing on a LAN. Mac OS X includes support for two of these protocols that are quite prevalent on today's networks. The Apple Filing Protocol (AFP) has been a part of Mac networking since the beginning. SMB (Server

Message Blocks), implemented with the Samba package, has been the standard protocol for file sharing on Windows networks. This protocol support makes Mac OS X an excellent citizen on just about any kind of network environment you might come across.

Sharing to Mac clients

When you enable Personal File Sharing in the Sharing preference panel, Mac OS X starts the *AppleFileServer* process and sets up Bonjour so that other machines on the local network will be able to see that your machine will accept AFP requests. This makes your machine appear in the */Network* folder in the Finder view of the other Macs on your local network and allows them to connect to your machine.

The *shares* (locations in the filesystem that can be accessed by others) that your Mac exposes to other machines vary depending on how users log into your machine:

- If a user logs into a machine as a Guest, he will see a share for each user on the machine. Each user's share holds the contents of that user's *Public* folder. He won't be able to see any other files on the system.

- If a user logs into a machine as a User with administrative privileges, she will be able to see a share for that user's Home folder as well as a share for each disk attached to the machine, including the boot disk.

- If a user logs into a machine as a Normal User (without administrative privileges), he'll only see a share for that user's Home folder.

Mac OS X's Personal File Sharing feature works quite well on a network composed of all Mac clients. Sadly, such a network isn't nearly as common as some of us might hope. You're far more likely to find yourself on a network filled with Windows clients and servers. If you're behind enemy lines (or maybe just at the corporate office), Mac OS X's Windows Sharing will prove invaluable.

Sharing to Windows clients

When you enable the Windows Sharing checkbox in the Sharing preference panel, your Mac appears in the Network Neighborhood view of Windows Explorer, as shown in Figure 9-3. To connect to a Mac from a Windows machine, simply double-click the machine in Explorer and then enter the name and password of a user on the Mac.

In the Network Neighborhood, you'll find that Windows machines organize themselves within domains or workgroups. Your Mac initially sets its SMB workgroup to be WORKGROUP, but this can be changed using the Directory Access (*/Applications/Utilities*) application. Open Directory Access and select the SMB/CIFS entry, and then click the Configure button. On this sheet, you can configure the SMB workgroup to be used, as well as the Windows Internet Name Service (WINS) server, as shown in Figure 9-4.

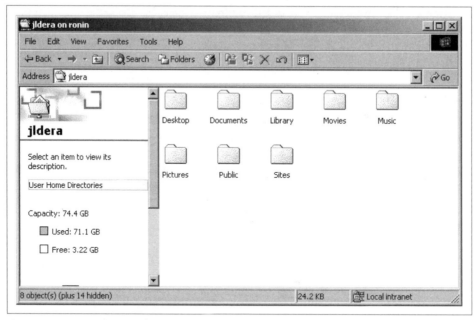

Figure 9-3. Browsing a Mac share using Windows Explorer

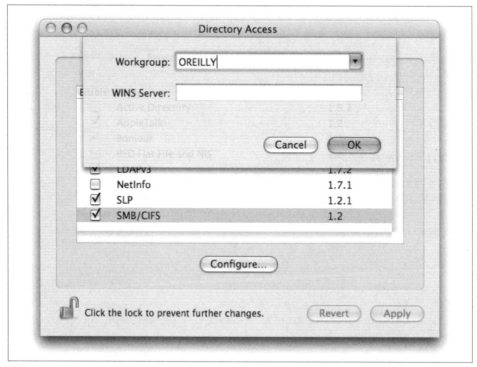

Figure 9-4. Configuring SMB options

By default, when you enable Windows Sharing, only the Home folders of the users on the system will be shared and made available to other machines. You can easily modify this by editing the Samba configuration file located at */etc/smb.conf* on your Mac. To edit the file, you'll need to use a command-line editor, such as *nano*, in conjunction with the *sudo* command to gain the necessary privileges:

```
$ sudo nano -w /etc/smb.conf
```

To share a folder on your Mac, you must create an entry for it in the */etc/smb.conf* file. Example 9-1 shows the basic format for a Samba share's entry. In Example 9-1, the folder */Users/Shared* has been shared out with read/write access. The browseable parameter controls whether the share appears in Windows Explorer. Even if the browseable property is set to no, users can still access the share using the UNC path to the share (e.g., *\\RONIN\SHARED*). Finally, the create mode defines what Unix permissions new files will have on the share when they are created.

 If you want to allow the Windows file-sharing service to share all available disks on your Mac similar to how AFP shares work, you can create a share for the */Volumes* folder. When Mac OS X mounts a disk, disk image, or other volume, it is automatically linked to the */Volumes* folder; however, this is a blanket approach, so be careful that you're not sharing something you'd rather keep private.

Example 9-1. A sample smb.conf entry

```
[shared]
  comment = Shared Directory
  path = /Users/Shared
  read only = no
  browseable = yes
  create mode = 755
```

For more information on configuring Samba, see either *Using Samba*, Second Edition, by Jay Ts, et al. (O'Reilly), or *Samba Pocket Reference*, Second Edition, by Jay Ts, et al. (O'Reilly). You can also find a wealth of information on Samba, including documentation and sample configuration files, at *http://www.samba.org*.

Disk Utility

The primary tool for working with disks and filesystems is the Disk Utility (found in */Applications/Utilities*), shown in Figure 9-5. The Disk Utility can be used to configure, format, eject, and partition disks of all kinds. On the left side of Disk Utility's interface is a list of the disks attached to your machine and the volumes that exist on those disks. Additionally, if you have any disk images mounted, a list of the most recently accessed files appears at the bottom of the left column. On the right side of the interface is a set of panels that give you access to the actions that you can accomplish with a drive. At the bottom of the window is a status display that gives you all sorts of information about the disk or volume you have selected.

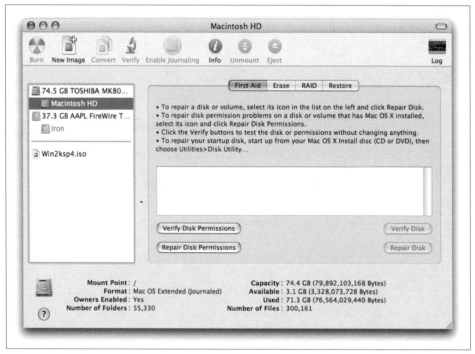

Figure 9-5. Disk Utility

Some of the tasks you can perform with Disk Utility are:

- Mount and eject disks, including hard drives, CDs, and disk images.
- Get the type, format, capacity, and room available for any disk attached to your computer.
- Check and repair disks (other than the boot disk).
- Check and repair disk permissions.
- Erase a disk, including erasure by writing random data to a disk.
- Partition a disk into multiple volumes that subdivide the drive into multiple logical disks.
- Create and work with disk images.
- Restore the contents of a disk image to a disk.
- Set up a Redundant Array of Independent Disks (RAID).

A command-line interface tool called *diskutil* can be used to perform all the features of the Disk Utility program and more. To get a list of the disks attached to your computer, execute the command *diskutil list*, as shown in Example 9-2.

Example 9-2. Getting a list of drives using the diskutil command

```
$ diskutil list
/dev/disk0
    #:                     type name           size       identifier
    0: Apple_partition_scheme                  *74.5 GB   disk0
    1:     Apple_partition_map                 31.5 KB    disk0s1
    2:             Apple_HFS Macintosh HD       74.4 GB    disk0s3
/dev/disk1
    #:                     type name           size       identifier
    0: Apple_partition_scheme                  *1.0 GB    disk1
    1:             Apple_HFS iDisk              1.0 GB     disk1s2
/dev/disk2
    #:                     type name           size       identifier
    0: Apple_partition_scheme                  *37.3 GB   disk2
    1:     Apple_partition_map                 31.5 KB    disk2s1
    2:         Apple_Driver43                  28.0 KB    disk2s2
    3:         Apple_Driver43                  28.0 KB    disk2s3
    4:       Apple_Driver_ATA                  28.0 KB    disk2s4
    5:       Apple_Driver_ATA                  28.0 KB    disk2s5
    6:         Apple_FWDriver                  256.0 KB   disk2s6
    7:     Apple_Driver_IOKit                  256.0 KB   disk2s7
    8:          Apple_Patches                  256.0 KB   disk2s8
    9:             Apple_HFS Iron              37.3 GB    disk2s9
```

This view gives you much more information than the list of drives and volumes on the left side of the Disk Utility application. In particular, it shows you that more than just a single volume is associated with a disk. In fact, there are several parts, sometimes called *slices*, to a disk, each with an identifier. The first slice of the disk holds the partition map. This is a key to where everything is located on the rest of the disk. Then a group of other partitions follows. In the case of Example 9-2, slices 2 through 8 of *disk2* hold disk drivers used by Mac OS 9, and slice 9 is the actual HFS+ volume of the drive. The Mac OS 9 drivers are installed by default when you a format a disk. If you format an internal boot drive without the OS 9 drivers, you'll see something like the output listed for *disk0*.

Examining a Disk

To take a closer look at a device attached to your computer or a volume associated with a device, select the disk or volume and then click the Info button in Disk Utility's toolbar. A window pops up listing all sorts of information about the device or volume, as shown in Figure 9-6. The following are some of the fields that you'll see in the Info window for a disk:

Name
> The name of the device or volume. In the case of a volume, this is the name you gave the volume and is that which appears in the Finder. In the case of a device, this is the hardware name of the disk, such as Hitachi IC25N080ATMR04-0.

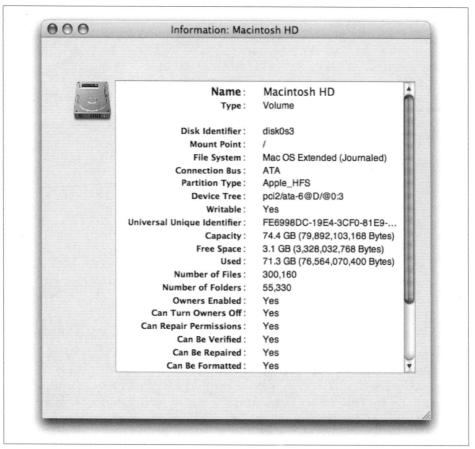

Figure 9-6. Disk Utility's Disk Info window

Disk Identifier

The label by which the operating system refers to the disk. For example, the primary boot disk in most Macs is identified as *disk0*. A volume on the drive has an additional set of characters identifying the partition on the drive it occupies, such as *disk0s9*. The disk identifier is also the filename in the */dev* directory under which programs may access the drive directly.

Connection Bus

The kind of bus that the device is attached to. The internal disk in a PowerBook will show "ATA" for this field while an external FireWire drive will show "FireWire."

Device Tree

The identifier in the system's device tree that the device occupies. This is the same identifier that shows up in the Open Firmware device tree.

Writable
> Indicates whether the device can be written to.

Ejectable
> Indicates whether the device can be ejected.

Total Capacity
> The amount of data that the device can hold.

S.M.A.R.T. Status
> Many disks made in the last few years contain a set of onboard diagnostic functions known as S.M.A.R.T., which stands for *Self-Monitoring, Analysis, and Reporting Technology*. These disks monitor disk calibration, cyclic redundancy check (or CRC) errors, disk spin-up time, rotation speed of the disk, distance between the head and the disk, and the temperature of the drive. The values you see in this field are either "Verified," which means everything is okay; "About to Fail," which means the disk needs to be replaced immediately; or "Not Supported," which means the drive doesn't support S.M.A.R.T.

If you examine a volume on a disk with the Info button, you'll see more information about the disk, including:

File System
> The type of filesystem that the volume is formatted to use.

Capacity, Free Space, Used
> The total amount of data that can be stored on the volume, the amount of additional data that can be stored on the volume, and how much space the current contents of the volume occupy.

Number of Files, Number of Folders
> The number of files and folders on the volume.

Permissions Enabled, Can Turn Permissions Off, Can Repair Permissions
> Indicates whether the system keeps and enforces permission information on files. This setting will always be "Yes" for the internal boot drive of your machine and is usually "No" for external drives where it is expected that you'll be moving data between machines. For disks that support permissions, the "Can Repair Permissions" setting indicates whether you can use Disk Utility to set the permissions of a disk to work with the current system.

Supports Journaling, Journaled
> Indicates whether the volume supports journaling and whether it is enabled.

You can also get information on a disk by using the *diskutil* tool. Two commands that can be used with *diskutil* are:

```
diskutil info device
diskutil info mountpoint
```

The first command uses a disk identifier, such as *disk0*, to locate the disk to obtain the information on. The second command uses the location in the filesystem where the device is mounted, such as /. Example 9-3 shows the result of running *diskutil info* against the boot drive of a machine.

Example 9-3. Getting disk information for the boot drive by using the disk identifier

```
$ diskutil info disk0
Device Node:        /dev/disk0
   Device Identifier:  disk0
   Mount Point:
   Volume Name:

   Partition Type:     Apple_partition_scheme
   Bootable:           Not bootable
   Media Type:         Generic
   Protocol:           ATA
   SMART Status:       Verified

   Total Size:         74.5 GB
   Free Space:         0.0 B

   Read Only:          No
   Ejectable:          No
   OS 9 Drivers:       No
   Low Level Format:   Not Supported
```

Example 9-4 shows the information about the volume mounted at /.

Example 9-4. Getting disk information for the root volume by using the mountpoint

```
$ diskutil info /
Device Node:        /dev/disk0s3
   Device Identifier:  disk0s3
   Mount Point:        /
   Volume Name:        Macintosh HD

   File System:        Journaled HFS+
                       Journal size 8192 k at offset 0x256000
   Owners:             Enabled
   Partition Type:     Apple_HFS
   Bootable:           Is bootable
   Media Type:         Generic
   Protocol:           ATA
   SMART Status:       Verified
   UUID:               FE6998DC-19E4-3CF0-81E9-FC3BE0318265

   Total Size:         74.4 GB
   Free Space:         3.1 GB

   Read Only:          No
   Ejectable:          No
```

From this output, you can see that the filesystem is formatted as Journaled HFS+, and that the journal size is a mere 8192 KB. Even though it is modest in size, the journal has a large impact on the integrity of the filesystem and allows for many performance optimizations.

Verifying and Repairing Disk Permissions

One of the most common things that can go wrong with a disk is that the permissions for the various files and directories on it get set incorrectly. Although the permissions for a disk should never get out of whack, quite a few installers that require an administrator's password seem to set the permissions on various directories of your disk to what they think they should be. This is one reason why many system administrators abhor old-style software installers and prefer to install software distributed on disk images, which can be drag-and-dropped into the Applications folder without harm.

To see if the permissions on your disk are correct for your system, select the disk or volume you want to check and click the Verify Disk Permissions button in the First Aid panel of the Disk Utility interface. This determines what the correct file permissions are for your system and then checks your disk against those permissions. If your permissions are not set correctly, you should strongly consider repairing them by clicking the Repair Disk Permissions button.

To check permissions from the command line, use the following syntax to *diskutil*:

```
diskutil verifyPermissions [diskid | mountpoint]
```

For example, to verify the permissions of the boot volume, you would use the following command:

```
$ diskutil verifyPermissions /
```

To repair permissions, use the following:

```
$ diskutil repairPermissions /
```

 Disk Utility determines the correct permissions by examining data left by Mac OS X's Installer (found in the */Library/Receipts* folder). Because drag-and-drop installation and custom application installers do not make use of Mac OS X's Installer, Disk Utility cannot determine if the permissions are set properly for programs installed by other means. Additionally, since user files and data also aren't handled by Mac OS X's Installer, the permissions on a user's data are not taken into account.

Verifying and Repairing Disks

To ensure that the filesystem on a disk is working correctly, select the disk or volume that you want to check and click the Verify Disk button. This scans the various parts of the filesystem to make sure they are intact. If any problems are reported, you should use Disk Utility's Repair Disk button to correct the issues.

To verify or repair a disk, Disk Utility must first unmount the drive, which removes the ability to access the files on the disk while it performs its work. This means you can't verify or repair the disk you booted from, and in most cases, that's the disk that you want to verify. There are two solutions to this problem, and they work equally well:

- Boot off Mac OS X Tiger's install DVD. When the Installer shows up, select Installer → Open Disk Utility from the menu bar so you can work on the local disk.

- Put your machine into FireWire target disk mode by booting the machine and holding down the T key. Then plug the machine into another Mac using a FireWire cable and use Disk Utility on the other machine to verify and repair the disk.

If Disk Utility runs into a problem it can't handle, you'll need to enlist the help of another application such as Drive 10 from Micromat (*http://www.micromat.com*) or Disk Warrior from Alsoft (*http://www.alsoft.com/DiskWarrior*).

To verify and repair a disk from the command line using *diskutil*, you can use one of the following:

```
diskutil verifyDisk [diskid | mountpoint]
diskutil repairDisk [diskid | mountpoint]
```

Example 9-5 shows the command you should use to repair a FireWire disk named *Backup*.

Example 9-5. Repairing a disk using the diskutil command

```
$ diskutil repairDisk /Volumes/Backup
Started verify/repair on disk disk1s3 Backup
Checking HFS Plus volume.
Checking Extents Overflow file.
Checking Catalog file.
Checking Catalog hierarchy.
Checking volume bitmap.
Checking volume information.
The volume Backup Alpha appears to be OK.
Verify/repair finished on disk disk1s3
```

If for some reason you don't have Tiger's Install DVD or another computer to connect to your Mac, you can attempt to fix filesystem problems using *fsck*. The filesystem checker is a traditional Unix tool that performs many of the same tasks of *diskutil*'s *repairDisk* mode. To use *fsck*, you'll first need to boot your Mac into single-user mode (discussed in Chapter 5). Once you're at the command-line prompt, enter the command:

```
# /sbin/fsck -fy /
```

This forces *fsck* to check the boot volume for errors and to automatically correct them. If any issues crop up during the check, *fsck* notifies you that the filesystem was modified. If no problems are found, *fsck* tells you that the volume appears to be OK. You may need to run *fsck* several times before it comes back clean.

Erasing and Formatting Disks

There are many times when you want to "start over" with a drive, such as when you are upgrading your Mac OS X installation and would rather start from scratch, or when you want to make sure that all of your data is removed from a FireWire drive. Erasing a disk with the Disk Utility is very simple, almost too simple considering the fact that all the data on the disk will be obliterated.

The Erase tab of Disk Utility, shown in Figure 9-7, lets you erase and format a disk with the following options:

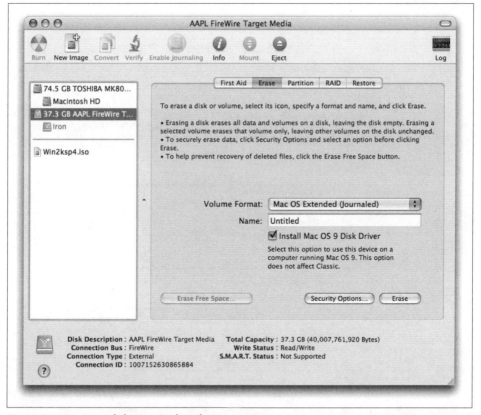

Figure 9-7. Erasing a disk using Disk Utility

Volume Format

The Volume Format pull-down list lets you select the filesystem you want to place on the device. For most purposes, you'll want to use Mac OS Extended (Journaled).

Name

Lets you name the volume that will be created on the disk.

Install Mac OS 9 Disk Driver

Installs the necessary drivers for using the disk with a Mac OS 9 system.

There are additional options hiding behind the Security Options button, shown in Figure 9-8. When you write data to a disk, there is still a faint magnetic remnant of the original data on the drive. Very sophisticated equipment can detect these magnetic traces and re-create data that was once on the drive but erased. Each time data is written to a spot on a disk, the traces from previous data at that spot get covered up and fade. Using the 7-Pass or 35-Pass Erase options, you can be sure (or really, really sure in the case of the 35-Pass) that no data *whatsoever* is left on the drive.

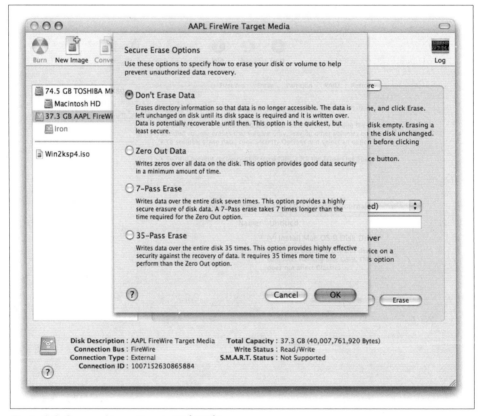

Figure 9-8. Secure erase options in Disk Utility

To use the *diskutil* command to erase a disk, use one of the following commands:

```
diskutil eraseDisk [format] newName [diskid | mountpoint]
diskutil zeroDisk [diskid | mountpoint]
diskutil randomDisk [numberOfPasses] [diskid | mountpoint]
```

For example, to format an external FireWire disk that had the device ID of *disk1*, use the following:

```
$ diskutil eraseDisk "Journaled HFS+" Backup disk1
```

To write zeros across the entire filesystem of a FireWire disk named *Backup*, use the following:

```
$ diskutil zeroDisk /Volumes/Backup
```

> One thing to keep in mind when either zeroing or performing the 7- or 35-Pass Erase of a disk is that they take quite a while to run, especially on large disks. After issuing the command, you might want to go off and refinance your house; the commands might be done by the time you get back.

Partitioning Disks

For the most part, you'll want to assign a single volume to each of your hard drives. It's quick, easy, and is usually the most efficient use of space. However, there are times when you might want to have more than one volume on a drive. For example, while working with the first few releases of a new version of Mac OS X, you might want to have a test partition for the new version while keeping a stable, known version available. Or you might want to keep an old copy of Mac OS 9 available on a separate partition from your Mac OS X installation for running Classic.

> The best and only time to partition your disk is when you're installing the operating system. Once the system is installed, you can't go back later and partition the drive or adjust the partition sizes. So, if you want to partition your drive, you must first back up all your critical data to another drive, and then do a clean install of Mac OS X using the Disk Utility on the Install DVD. For details on partitioning and installing Mac OS X, see Chapter 2.

To create multiple volumes on a disk, select the disk that you want to divide and click the Partition tab. This brings up an interface that lets you configure how much space to give each volume on a disk, as shown in Figure 9-9. From the volume scheme pop-up menu choose the number of partitions you want and size them however you want by either using the graphical tool or typing sizes for each partition. Then click the Partition button to commit the changes. This erases all the data on the disk, creates the volumes, and then creates the filesystems for each volume.

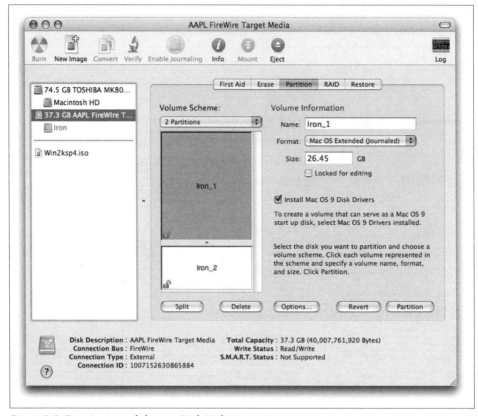

Figure 9-9. Partitioning a disk using Disk Utility

Adding a Disk Drive

For the most part, adding an internal disk drive to your computer is as easy as making sure that you get a drive with an interface that your computer supports (IDE drives for most G3 and G4 machines, Serial ATA for the newer G5 machines) and that will fit into your Mac. Adding an external FireWire drive is even easier; you simply plug it in. If the FireWire drive is formatted properly, it should automatically appear in your Finder and in Disk Utility. If the drive is not formatted, it won't appear in the Finder, but it will appear in Disk Utility.

When you first add a drive to a machine, you should make sure that it is formatted the way you want. Often, new hard drives arrive from the factory preformatted as MS-DOS FAT. If you encounter this with a new drive, you will need to reformat the drive as Journaled HFS using the Disk Utility. The only exception to this rule is if you want to share an external FireWire drive with a Windows machine, in which case you'll want to leave the drive formatted as MS-DOS FAT.

RAID

Another feature that Disk Utility and its related command-line tools enable is the use of Redundant Array of Independent Disks (RAID), where multiple physical disks are combined into one virtual disk. In general, RAID solutions are designed for increased data availability and integrity. They trade the overhead of maintaining data across a set of disks for the fault tolerance that using multiple drives can provide.

There are several types of RAID in use today. These are:

RAID 0

Data is striped across two or more disks giving increased I/O performance; if each disk is on a separate disk controller, this allows for large virtual disks. This type of RAID provides no protection against disk failure. If a disk fails, all the data on the disk set is lost.

RAID 1

Data is mirrored across two drives, giving complete data redundancy. If one disk fails, the other still has all the data needed to keep going.

RAID 3, RAID 4, RAID 5

Multiple disks (three or more) are used to both stripe data for performance and to keep parity information to provide for redundancy in case a disk fails. Because data is split and duplicated among many disks, this type of RAID requires significant computation power.

Mac OS X provides support for RAID 0 (striping) and RAID 1 (mirroring). Both types of RAID can be performed with acceptable performance in software. The other forms of RAID are not supported in software, as the increased overhead would create too large a performance hit to be worthwhile. If you require RAID 3, 4, or 5, you should take a close look at hardware solutions such as Apple's Xserve RAID, which has dedicated processors to handle the extra overhead, or other third-party RAID solutions.

Figure 9-10 shows Disk Utility's RAID panel. Using this panel, you can perform the majority of tasks involved with using RAID. To create a RAID set using Disk Utility, drag the disks that you want to be part of your RAID to the Disk table, select the RAID scheme, and then click the Create button. If your RAID set is having problems, you may need to rebuild it by clicking the Rebuild button on the RAID panel. Lastly, if you wish to destroy the RAID array, click the Delete Set button.

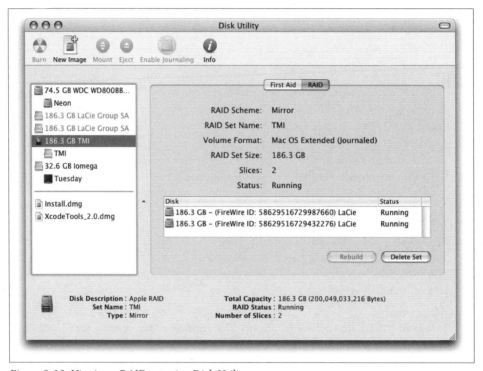

Figure 9-10. Viewing a RAID set using Disk Utility

You can also use the *diskutil* command to manipulate RAID sets from the command line. For example, to create a RAID set using the command line, use the *diskutil createRAID* command as follows:

```
diskutil createRAID [mirror|stripe] setname filesystemtype diskids...
```

Example 9-6 shows how to create a striped RAID set using two disks with the device IDs of *disk2* and *disk3*.

Example 9-6. Creating a RAID set using the command line

```
$ diskutil createRAID stripe RAID "Journaled HFS+" disk2 disk3
The RAID has been created successfully
```

Disk Images

Disk images (files with a *.dmg* extension) have become a frequent part of life on Mac OS X. Originally created to store the block-for-block contents of a floppy disk for ease of duplication, the disk images created and used by Mac OS X are based on a format called Universal Disk Image Format (UDIF). UDIF allows the storage of the same partition tables, disk drivers, and volumes found on physical disks, which lets disk images serve as intermediaries in the duplication of any kind of disk, including CDs and DVDs.

Beyond their origin as a disk duplication format—and because of their ease of use— disk images are used by many software vendors, including Apple, as a distribution format instead of *.sit* (StuffIt), *.tar*, or *.zip* files. When you double-click a disk image (or use Disk Utility to open it), Mac OS X uses the contents of the image as the data for a disk that it mounts into the filesystem, which shows up in the Finder as shown in Figure 9-11; Figure 9-12 shows the same disk image in Disk Utility.

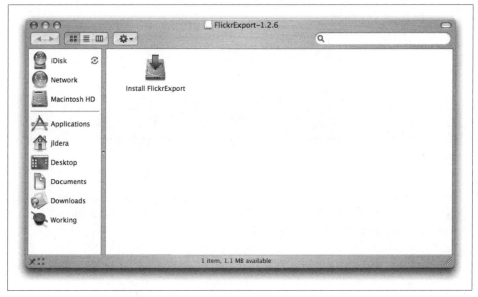

Figure 9-11. A disk image mounted in the Finder

Types of Disk Images

Because they can be used for many different purposes, disk images have several different types. These are:

Read/write disk image
> A fixed-size disk image that doesn't just contain data but also allows data to be written to it. These disk images are useful if you want to have an encrypted data

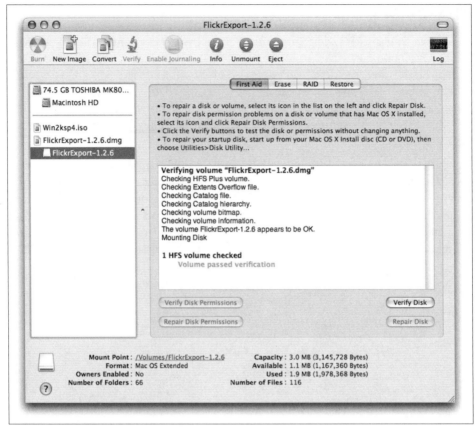

Figure 9-12. A disk image mounted in Disk Utility

storage point, or if you want to set up the contents of a disk image before converting it to one of the other types. This kind of disk image occupies the same amount of space on a disk as its capacity.

Read-only disk image

A fixed-size disk image that only allows data to be read from it. This kind of disk image occupies the same amount of space on a disk as its capacity.

Compressed disk image

A read-only disk whose contents have been compressed, resulting in the size of the disk image being much less than its capacity. This is the preferred format for distributing software across the Internet.

CD/DVD master disk image

A disk image whose internal format uses either ISO-9660 or UDF so its contents can be directly burned to a CD or DVD. CD and DVD master disk images end with the *.cdr* extension, though you may also find the *.iso* extension in use.

Sparse disk image

A read/write disk image format that starts out smaller on disk than its original capacity. The disk image grows in size as needed up to either its capacity or the size of the disk it is located on, whichever is less. Sparse disk images end with the *.sparseimage* extension.

Encryption and disk images

One attribute that disk images don't share with their physical cousins is that all the data on a disk image can be encrypted. This enables you to store data on public disks that can't be accessed by anybody who doesn't have the proper password. For example, you could store valuable data on a keychain USB flash drive using an encrypted disk image with the knowledge that if somebody gains access to your keys, he won't be able to gain access to the data stored on the USB drive. These encryption features are also used by FileVault to protect your Home directory, if you enable this feature in System Preferences.

FileVault Implementation

Mac OS X's FileVault, which encrypts all the data in your Home folder, uses disk images under the covers to perform its magic. When you enable FileVault for a user, all the user's data is placed into an encrypted sparse disk image. When a user logs into the machine, the image holding her data is mounted into the */Users* folder. When she logs out, the disk image is unmounted, making any data in the user's Home directory inaccessible.

When you enable FileVault for a user, the data that was in her original Home folder is erased. It is, however, the same kind of erase that happens when you drag files to the Trash. This means that any data that was in a user's Home folder before FileVault was enabled could potentially be recovered. The best time to enable FileVault for a user is before any sensitive data is placed into her Home folder.

Working with Disk Images on the Command Line

In addition to Disk Utility, Mac OS X provides the *hdiutil* command-line tool to work with disk images. This tool has a wealth of options to create and manipulate disk images, many of which venture into very arcane territory. Some of the more commonly used features of *hdiutil* are covered here, so you can see how to manipulate disk images from the command line.

To mount a disk image from the Terminal, use the following command:

```
hdiutil mount imagename
```

This command mounts the contents of the disk image into the */Volumes* folder and it appears as a disk in the Finder's Sidebar. Example 9-7 shows a disk image named *FlickrExport-1.2.6.dmg* being mounted.

Example 9-7. Mounting a disk image using hdiutil

```
$ hdiutil mount FlickrExport-1.2.6.dmg
/dev/disk2          /Volumes/FlickrExport-1.2.6
```

When you mount a disk image, you'll see several items that should be familiar from looking at disks. There is a series of slices to the disk, including a partition map. The output of the *hdiutil* command also gives you the filesystem location where the disk image was mounted.

You aren't limited to mounting disk images into the */Volumes* folder. The following command can be used to mount the contents of a disk image into any directory in the filesystem:

```
hdiutil mount -mountpoint directory imagename
```

The only catch here is that the directory you are mounting the disk drive into has to exist in the filesystem first. The contents of the directory that you are mounting the disk image into will also be hidden by the contents of the disk image. Example 9-8 shows an example of this command.

Example 9-8. Mounting a disk image into the filesystem

```
$ hdiutil mount -mountpoint /Foo test.dmg
Password:
Initializing...
Verifying...
Checksumming DDM...
DDM: verified CRC32 $70362E53
Checksumming Apple (Apple_partition_map : 0)...
Apple (Apple_partition_map : 0): verified C
RC32 $DFA2282D
Checksumming (Apple_Free : 1)...
(Apple_Free : 1): verified CRC32 $00000000
Checksumming Apple_HFS_Untitled_2 (Apple_HFS : 2)...
.....................................................................
Apple_HFS_Untitled_2 (Apple_HFS : 2): verified CRC32 $2877B09E
Checksumming (Apple_Free : 3)...
(Apple_Free : 3): verified CRC32 $00000000
Verification completed...
verified CRC32 $3CAEE635
Attaching...
Finishing...
Finishing...
/dev/disk5 Apple_partition_scheme
/dev/disk5s1 Apple_partition_map
/dev/disk5s3 Apple_HFS /Foo
```

To unmount a disk image, use the following command:

```
hdiutil unmount mountpoint
```

Here, the *mountpoint* is the path of the folder where the disk image is mounted.

Creating a New Disk Image

To create a new empty read/write disk image using Disk Utility:

1. Use Disk Utility's File → New → Blank Disk Image menu, or the New Image button on Disk Utility's toolbar. A dialog window opens, as shown in Figure 9-13.

2. Select the size of the disk image. This size governs the disk image's capacity. As with hard drives, keep in mind that the size of a disk image doesn't equal how much data it can actually hold because of filesystem overhead.

3. Select whether you want to encrypt the disk image.

4. Select the kind of disk image to create. When you create a new disk image, you have your choice of a read/write disk image or a sparse disk image. For most purposes, the standard read/write disk image is appropriate.

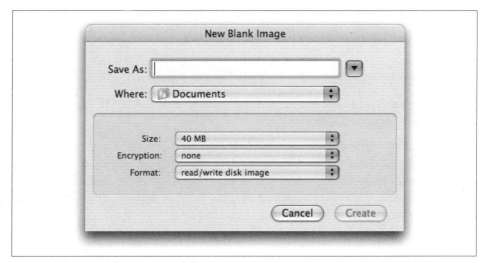

Figure 9-13. Options for creating a disk image

When you hit the Create button, a disk image is created and mounted in the Finder and into the filesystem in */Volumes*. By default, the disk image contains a single HFS+ volume. To change the format of the volume to HFS or to UFS, simply highlight the volume in Disk Utility and use the Erase tab, just as you would with an actual physical disk.

To create a disk image on the command line, use the following *hdiutil* command:

```
hdiutil create -volname volumename -fs fstype -size size imagename
```

where *volumename* is the name of volume you want to create, *fstype* is one of the file-system types listed in Table 9-2, and *size* is the size of the disk image expressed as a number followed by either *b* (which stands for sectors, not bytes), *k* (for kilobytes), *m* (for megabytes), *g* (for gigabytes), *t* (for terabytes), *p* (for pentabytes), or *e* (for exabytes).

Table 9-2. Filesystem type codes used by hdiutil

Filesystem type code	Description
HFS+J	Journaled HFS+
HFS+	HFS+ (non-journaled)
HFS	Original HFS
MS-DOS	The FAT filesystem used by MS-DOS
UFS	The Unix filesystem (Berkeley Fast File System)

Example 9-9 shows how to create a 10 MB disk image.

Example 9-9. Creating a new disk image

```
$ hdiutil create -volname Foo -fs HFS+ -size 10m foo.dmg
Initializing...
Creating...
..............................................................
Finishing...
created: /Users/duncan/foo.dmg
```

To create an encrypted disk image, add the *-encryption* argument to the command. Applied to the command in Example 9-9, it looks like:

```
hdiutil create -encryption -volname Foo -fs HFS+ -size 10m foo.dmg
```

By default *hdiutil create* creates read/write disk image files. Creating other kinds of disk image files requires the use of the *-format* argument along with a four-letter code. The complete list of codes is given in Table 9-3. For example, to create a sparse disk image, you would use the following command:

```
diskutil create -format UDSP -voname Foo -fs HFS+ size 10m foo.dmg
```

Table 9-3. diskutil disk image format codes

Code	Description
UDRW	Read/write
UDRO	Read-only
UDZO	Compressed
UDTO	DVD/CD master

Creating a Disk Image from a Folder

To create a disk image that holds the contents of a folder using Disk Utility:

1. Use Disk Utility's File → New → Disk Image From Folder, or the New Image button on Disk Utility's toolbar. An Open dialog window appears, giving you the chance to select a folder to create the disk image. Select the folder you want to create an image from and hit the Open button.

2. A dialog window, confusingly titled Convert Image, opens, letting you set the options for the disk image, as shown in Figure 9-14.

3. Select the kind of image to create. Since you are creating an image with data, you can select from read-only, compressed, DVD/CD master, and read/write.

4. Select whether you want to encrypt the contents of the disk image.

When you hit the Create button, the disk image is created. Unlike when you create an image, it will not be mounted.

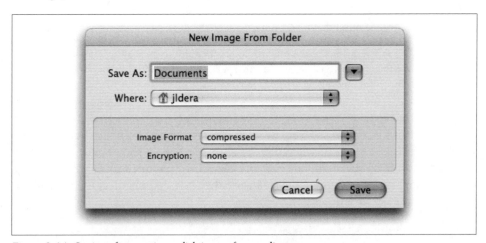

Figure 9-14. Options for creating a disk image from a directory

To create a disk image from a folder on the command line, use the following *hdiutil* command:

```
hdiutil create -srcfolder folder imagename
```

where *folder* is the path to the folder that you want to image and *imagename* is the name of the resulting image. Example 9-10 shows the creation of a disk image from the Documents directory in the Home directory.

Example 9-10. Creating a disk image with the contents of a directory

```
$ hdiutil create -srcfolder ~/Documents Documents.dmg
..............................................................
created: /Users/jldera/Documents.dmg
```

By default, the disk images that *hdiutil* creates from a directory are read-only. To create a read/write disk image, use the following syntax for the *hdiutil* command:

```
hdiutil create -srcfolder folder -format UDIF imagename
```

Creating a Disk Image from a Device

Since disk images can hold all the data on a disk drive, including the partition map, it's natural that you can create a disk image directly from either a disk drive or a volume on it. By creating a disk image from a drive, you can later restore that image back onto the drive or onto any other drive. You can use this for backup purposes or to create a master disk image for a department or company, making it easy for you to clone one installation onto every machine. To create a disk image from a disk drive using Disk Utility, select the drive and then select File → New → Disk Image from *diskname* from the menu bar. Here, *diskname* is the name of the volume you've selected in Disk Utility's left pane.

 Keep in mind that if you want to clone the drive or partition that contains your installation of Mac OS X, you shouldn't use Disk Utility to accomplish this task while the system is running. Instead, you should either boot from Tiger's Install DVD, or put your Mac into target mode and mount its drive(s) via FireWire on another system.

Creating an image of a device from the command line is a bit trickier. There isn't a direct command in *hdiutil*, so you have to use the *convert* command and convert from the disk's device in the */dev* directory. Example 9-11 shows how to create a compressed disk image of an external FireWire drive mounted at */dev/disk1*. Since this command accesses the raw device of the disk, the command must be run by a user with administrative privileges.

Example 9-11. Creating a disk image from a device

```
$ sudo hdiutil convert /dev/disk1 -format UDZO -o /FirewireBackup.dmg
Preparing imaging engine...
Reading DDM...
(CRC32 $70362E53: DDM)
Reading Apple_partition_map (0)...
(CRC32 $DFA2282D: Apple_partition_map (0))
Reading Apple_Free (1)...
(CRC32 $00000000: Apple_Free (1))
Reading Apple_HFS (2)...
................................................................
(CRC32 $15DC1C94: Apple_HFS (2))
Reading Apple_Free (3)...
................................................................
(CRC32 $00000000: Apple_Free (3))
Terminating imaging engine...
Adding resources...
```

Example 9-11. Creating a disk image from a device (continued)

```
...........................................................................
Elapsed Time: 11.784s
(1 task, weight 100)
File size: 1433395 bytes, Checksum: CRC32 $43A4EE39
Sectors processed: 58605120, 62161 compressed
Speed: 2.6Mbytes/sec
Savings: 100.0%
created: FirewireBackup.dmg
```

Converting a Disk Image

Once you have worked with a disk image in one format, such as read/write, you may want to convert it to read-only format, so that it is compressed and ready to post to the Internet, or convert it into a CD master that is ready for duplication. To convert an image using Disk Utility, use the Images → Convert menu option, select the disk you want to convert, and then use the Covert Disk dialog box that appears to select the kind of image you want to convert it to. This dialog box is shown in Figure 9-15.

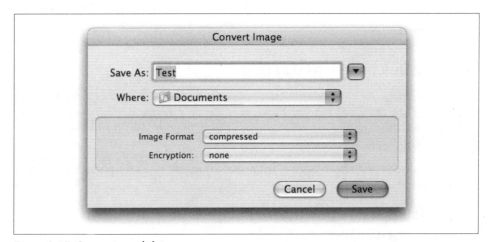

Figure 9-15. Converting a disk image

To convert a disk image on the command line, use the *hdiutil convert* command as follows:

```
hdiutil convert -format format -o outputfile imagefile
```

where *format* is the four-letter code that the disk image will be converted to, *outputfile* is where the new disk image will be saved, and *imagefile* is the disk image to convert. Example 9-12 shows how to use this command to convert a disk image to a compressed disk image.

Example 9-12. Converting a disk image to a compressed disk image

```
$ hdiutil convert -format UDZO -o Compressed.dmg Documents.dmg
Preparing imaging engine...
Reading DDM...
(CRC32 $EEB3C0C1: DDM)
Reading Apple_partition_map (0)...
(CRC32 $5A2C9F73: Apple_partition_map (0))
Reading Apple_HFS (1)...
.................................................................
(CRC32 $C7097C7F: Apple_HFS (1))
Reading Apple_Free (2)...
.................................................................
(CRC32 $00000000: Apple_Free (2))
Terminating imaging engine...
Adding resources...
.................................................................
Elapsed Time: 23.061s
(1 task, weight 100)
File size: 48394357 bytes, Checksum: CRC32 $79BEA1E4
Sectors processed: 258898, 238321 compressed
Speed: 5.0Mbytes/sec
Savings: 63.5%
created: Compressed.dmg
```

Burning a Disk Image to CD or DVD

Burning an image to CD or DVD from Disk Utility is simple; just select the disk image and click the Burn button. Make sure that the image doesn't contain more data than the disc you are burning to can hold. CDs can hold up to 700 MB and DVDs can hold up to 4.7 GB.

Burning to disc is just about as easy from the command line. Simply use the *hdiutil burn* command as shown in Example 9-13.

Example 9-13. Using the hdiutil burn command

```
$ hdiutil burn Documents.dmg
Please insert a disc:
Preparing data for burn
Opening session
Opening track
Writing track
.................................................................
Closing track
Closing session
Finishing burn
Verifying burn...
Verifying
.................................................................
Burn completed successfully
.................................................................
hdiutil: burn: completed
```

Restoring a Disk Image to a Drive

To restore the contents of a disk from a disk image, use Disk Utility's Restore panel, as shown in Figure 9-16, and use the following process:

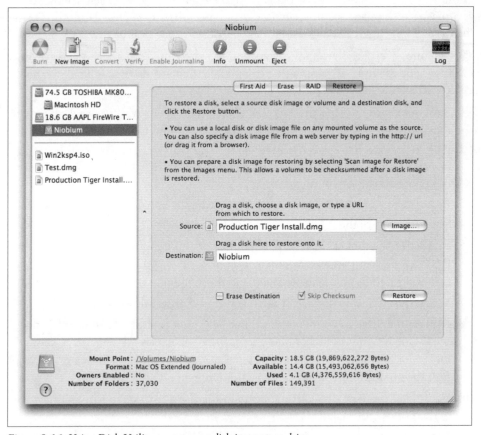

Figure 9-16. Using Disk Utility to restore a disk image to a drive

1. Either drag a disk image to the Source text field or click the Image button and select the image you want to restore from.

2. Drag the disk that you want to restore to from the left column to the Destination text field.

3. Optionally, check the Erase Destination checkbox if you want to replace the contents of the disk with the disk image.

4. Click the Restore button.

 You should be aware that it is possible to restore the contents of a drive to another drive that is either larger or smaller than the original drive. As long as there is enough space on the target drive to hold the data being moved to it, Disk Utility will take care of the rest.

Moving the Contents of One Drive to Another

You can use the Restore panel of Disk Utility to copy one disk to another. This is useful when you want to move a perfect copy of your boot disk to another drive. For example, you could copy a disk to an external FireWire drive and then use that drive as a master disk image for restoring the disk onto other machines. To do this using the Restore panel, select a disk as the source instead of a disk image.

This feature is especially handy when you want to upgrade the boot drive in a machine. For example, if you wanted to upgrade the hard drive in your PowerBook, you could use the following process:

1. Boot your system using the Mac OS X Install DVD. Instead of proceeding with the install, use the Utilities → Disk Utility menu option to launch Disk Utility.

2. Plug in an external FireWire drive (either one that you own or have begged or borrowed from someone). Make sure that the FireWire drive is large enough to hold the contents of your hard drive.

3. Click the Restore tab of Disk Utility (refer to Figure 9-16).

4. Set the Source of the restore to your internal boot drive.

5. Set the Destination of the restore to your external FireWire drive.

6. Click Restore and go have a coffee at your local coffee shop while Disk Utility copies the data from the internal drive to the external.

7. When Disk Utility is done, exit the Installer and power down your system.

8. Replace the drive in your computer. For help, you should refer to Apple's documentation for your model of Mac.

9. Once the new drive is installed, boot your system with the Mac OS X Install DVD again. And once again, launch Disk Utility.

10. Verify that the new disk drive appears in the drive list. Make sure that it is formatted to use Journaled HFS+.

11. Using the Restore tab, make the external FireWire drive the Source and the new internal hard drive the Destination.

12. Click Restore and go have some more coffee.

When Disk Utility finishes, you're almost done. You just need to check to make sure that your disk is set up to boot. Usually Disk Utility does the right thing if each disk has only a single partition on it, but when you are moving data around on disks with multiple partitions, things might not always work out so well. You can check the boot status of your drive with the Startup Disk tool. To open the Startup Disk tool, select Utilities → Startup Disk. Here, make sure that the correct Mac OS install is chosen and then click the Restart button to boot the system and test out the restoration process.

Further Explorations

If you find yourself using the tools in this chapter extensively, you should consult the following manpages for more information:

- *diskutil*
- *hdiutil*
- *mount*
- *umount*

## CHAPTER 10

Printing

The Mac's impressive printing capabilities date back 20 years to the introduction of the PostScript-based LaserWriter printer in 1985. During the transition to Mac OS X, Apple redesigned the printing system to make it easier for printer manufacturers to develop drivers, and also made it more flexible and robust. This was by no means a seamless transition, as it took time for printer manufacturers to rewrite their drivers for the new system. But, the payoff for this work has been realized: seamless printing from any application to any Mac- or Windows-based printer and beyond to PDF generation and built-in fax capabilities. What once was difficult, if not impossible, is now very easy to do.

This chapter gives you an overview of how Mac OS X's print system works, how to add and configure local and network printers, and how to work with printers from the command line.

Print System Overview

Mac OS X's printing system makes use of the following technologies:

- Quartz and PDF for creating print-ready output from applications.
- Common Unix Printing System (CUPS) for managing printers, printer drivers, and print jobs. CUPS also accepts print jobs using the Internet Printing Protocol (IPP). The CUPS project can be found on the Internet at *http://www.cups.org*.
- Samba 3 for connecting to Windows SMB-based printers and for receiving print jobs from Windows clients. Additional information on Samba can be found at *http://www.samba.org*.
- Open Directory for locating printers with LDAP, NetInfo, Bonjour, and SMB.

Generally the printers that you will use come in two varieties:

Locally attached
> Printers that are directly connected to your machine via USB or FireWire. You can always access these printers and, if you choose, share them with other computers on the network by going to System Preferences → Print & Fax → Sharing and enabling it.

Network accessible
> Printers that are either connected directly to the network (such as many laser printers in office environments) or are attached to other computers that have enabled printer sharing. Because Mac OS X understands a variety of network protocols, it can connect to printers hosted by Windows- and Unix-based machines as well as by other Macs.

In addition, there are two virtual types of printers that are built into the print system:

Fax
> From any print dialog, you can press the Fax button and fax a document with the modem built into your Mac.

PDF
> Instead of printing to hardcopy, you can easily generate PDF files.

Managing Printers

The Printer Setup Utility (*/Applications/Utilities*) is the principal application used to define and manage printers from the GUI. Even though you'll find buttons to add and otherwise manage printers in the Print & Fax preference panel, these buttons call upon the Printer Setup Utility to do the dirty work. When launched, the Printer Setup Utility displays a list of the printers you can use, as shown in Figure 10-1.

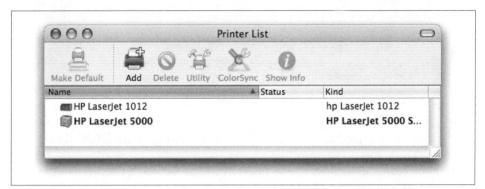

Figure 10-1. The Printer Setup Utility window

Each printer in the list shows whether it appears in Print dialog's menu, the name of the printer, its current status, and the kind of printer it is. Additional printer properties can be shown by enabling them using the View → Columns menu.

In Figure 10-1, two printers are set up on the machine, both HP LaserJets. The default printer, which is shown in bold in the Printer Setup Utility, is used automatically by the system whenever a document is printed. You can change the default printer by highlighting the name of another printer and clicking the Make Default button.

Double-clicking a printer in the printer list brings up a window showing the print queue (a list of pending print jobs) for that printer along with the status of the printer, as shown in Figure 10-2.

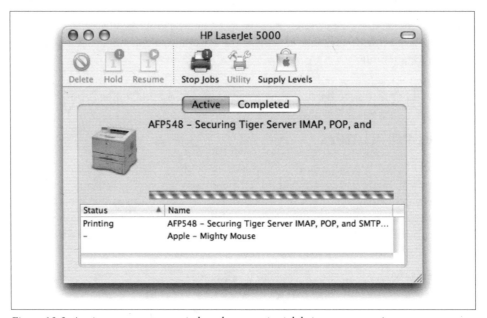

Figure 10-2. A printer queue status window shows a print job being sent to a printer

You can get more information about a printer by highlighting it in the Printer Setup Utility list and clicking the Show Info button, or by going to the Printers → Show Info (⌘-I) menu. This brings up the dialog box shown in Figure 10-3. The dialog box shows the name and location of the printer (both fields can be edited for a local printer), the name of the print queue (used by the underlying CUPS system to route print jobs) for the printer, and the host the printer is located on. This window also contains a pull-down menu that gives you access to additional information about the printer model as well as any installable options, such as duplexer, extra paper trays, and installable memory available to the printer.

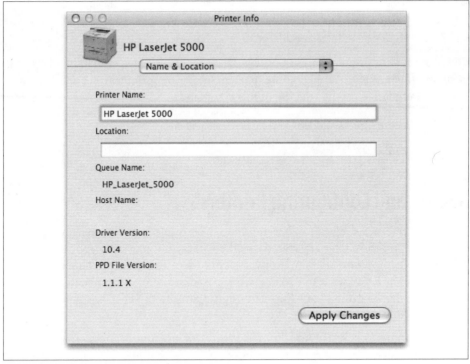

Figure 10-3. The Printer Info window

To retrieve the list of printers that your Mac knows about, go to the command line and use the *lpstat -a* command as shown in Example 10-1.

Example 10-1. Seeing the printers attached to a Mac

```
$ lpstat -a
HP_LaserJet_1012 accepting requests since Jan 01 00:00
HP_LaserJet_5000 accepting requests since Jan 01 00:00
```

The output from the *lpstat -a* command lists the printers by queue name and, in the case of a printer located on a remote machine, the name of the machine that hosts the print queue for the printer.

 Two items may show up in the output from *lpstat -a* that don't appear in the Printer Setup Utility. These are labeled Internal_Modem and Bluetooth-Modem. These devices are used by the underlying print system to handle faxing from applications via the Print Dialog box.

To see the default printer from the command line, use the *lpstat -d* command, as shown in Example 10-2.

Example 10-2. Seeing the default printer from the command line

```
$ lpstat -d
system default destination: HP_LaserJet_5000
```

To set the default printer that is in use by the system from the command line, use the *lpoptions -d* command, supplying the queue name of the printer to set as the default queue. Example 10-3 shows the use of this command.

Example 10-3. Setting the default printer from the command line

```
$ lpoptions -d HP_LaserJet_1012
job-sheets=none,none printer-info='HP LaserJet 1012'
```

Adding and Configuring Printers

Many printers, including those that are directly connected to your machine via USB or FireWire and those that are shared by other Macs, automatically appear in the list of printers in the Printer Setup Utility, making them ready to use almost immediately. However, if you want to use a network-based printer that isn't shared by a Mac or use a printer for which your Mac can't figure out the driver to use automatically, you'll have to add it yourself.

To add a printer, click the Add Printer button (or use the Printers → Add Printer menu item). After a few moments, a window pops up that allows you to Browse for the printer you'd like to add (as shown in Figure 10-4), or specify the details to add an IP Printer manually (shown in Figure 10-5). The pull-down menu at the top of the dialog has the following options to choose from:

AppleTalk
> Lets you add and configure a printer using the legacy AppleTalk protocol. You can select from printers on the local AppleTalk zone and from any other zones that your computer knows about.

IP Printing
> Lets you add and configure a printer connected to a server (either a standalone machine or an embedded server inside the printer) using an IP-based protocol. These protocols include: LPD/LPR, a Unix-based printing protocol that has become a de facto industry standard; Internet Printing Protocol (IPP), a newer protocol based on HTTP that is intended to provide better interoperability over Internet-based networks; and HP's Jet Direct protocol, widely deployed in HP network-enabled printers. Since they are IP-based, these protocols can be used to communicate with printers beyond your local network.

> The version of CUPS that ships with Mac OS X Tiger implements a change that causes some older LPD/LPR print servers to reject jobs. If you have this problem, you can find a solution at MacOSXHints.com (*http://www.macosxhints.com/article.php?story=20031118180912371*).

Figure 10-4. Browsing for printers

Open Directory
  Lets you add a printer defined in the various directory services that your computer has access to. For example, if your network administrator set up information about the computers on your network in an LDAP server that your machine connects to, that information shows up here.

Bonjour
  Lets you add Bonjour-enabled printers that don't automatically show up in your printer list but that exist on the network.

  If you are using a USB printer attached to an AirPort Extreme base station, the printer will show up in the Bonjour section.

USB
  Lets you add any USB printer that isn't already set up on your machine. Typically, only USB-based printers for which Mac OS X can't figure out the proper driver to use appear here instead of being automatically added to the list of printers.

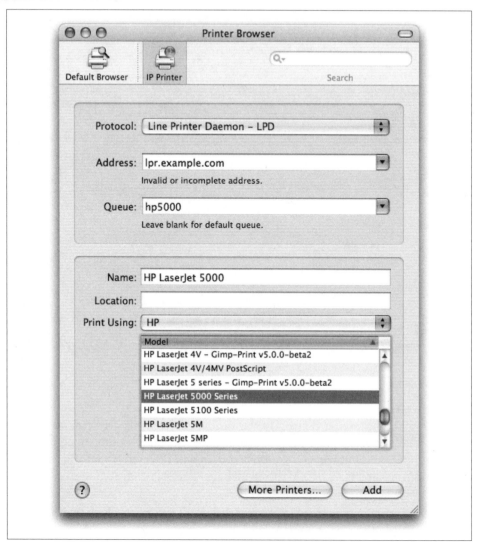

Figure 10-5. Adding a printer by address

Windows Printing

Lets you connect to any printer that is being shared by a Windows or Windows Server machine. The list of printers is organized by workgroup or domain; you can select the workgroup or domain to look for printers.

No matter which type of connection is used to connect to a printer, you'll need to select the printer model by using the Printer Model pull-down menu at the bottom of the Add Printer dialog. This sets the print system to use the correct driver for the printer. Mac OS X Tiger ships with drivers for printers from Apple, Brother, Canon,

Epson, HP, Lexmark, Tektronix, and Xerox. For drivers for other printers, you'll need to check the printer manufacturer's web site.

Support for many printers that were previously unsupported under Mac OS X has been added thanks to CUPS and Gimp-Print, a set of open source printer drivers for many older (as well as newer) printers. You can even find a driver for the original Epson 9-pin dot matrix printer by looking under ESP in the Printer Model pull-down in the Add Printer dialog. You can find more information on Gimp-Print at *http://gimpprint.sourceforge.net*.

Once a printer has been added, you need to make sure that it is configured properly. There are many settings, such as whether a printer has a duplexer for two-sided printing, or how much memory it has installed; these items can't always be automatically configured for you. To examine the configuration for a printer, select it in the list and click the Info button, or select Printers → Show Info (⌘-I) from the menu bar.

Determining IP-Based Print Queue Names

To add an IP-based printer, you'll need to know the IP address or hostname of the server, possibly the name of the queue for the printer you want to use if the server handles more than one printer, and the model of the printer. To get the name of a queue for a printer, you can either ask a network administrator or use the *lpstat -a -h* command, as shown in Example 10-4.

Desktop Printers

Users familiar with Mac OS 9 may miss having a printer on the desktop; you know, the little desktop printer alias that let you just drag, drop, and print. Fear not, for Mac OS X still offers this feature, it's just buried in the Printer Setup Utility. To add a desktop printer, select the desired printer in the Printer Setup Utility, and then select Printers → Create Desktop Printer (Shift-⌘-D) from the menu bar. You'll be prompted with a name and a location to save the printer shortcut. Once you've created the desktop printer, you can drag and drop a file onto the printer icon to immediately send the job to the printer. You can also double-click the icon to view and manage its print queue. You can drag the desktop printer icon to your Dock, which makes it easier to access.

Example 10-4. Using lpstat -a -h to list queue names on a machine

```
$ lpstat -a -h TiBook.local
HP_LaserJet_1012 accepting requests since Jan 01 00:00
```

The output from *lpstat* may contain more printers than those connected to the machine from which the information was requested. It also includes the other shared printer queue names on the network and indicates the hostnames that those queues are on.

Vendor-Specific Connections

Depending on the drivers you have installed, there may be several additional items in the Add Printer pull-down menu. These are provided by printer manufacturers to handle situations that aren't covered by the built-in capabilities of Mac OS X.

Faxing

As mentioned earlier, Mac OS X includes a virtual printer that uses your Mac's modem to fax print jobs. In addition, Mac OS X can be configured to listen for incoming faxes, which can then be saved, printed, or even emailed to you. To configure faxing, switch to the Faxing tab in the Print & Fax preferences, as shown in Figure 10-6.

Anatomy of a Print Job

Every print job starts as output from an application. The first step, albeit one that is already performed for you, is to produce output from an application and tell it what size paper you want to use and the orientation of that paper. In most applications, this is usually accomplished by using the standard File → Page Setup (Shift-⌘-P) command, which brings up the dialog shown in Figure 10-7. Most of the time, you'll

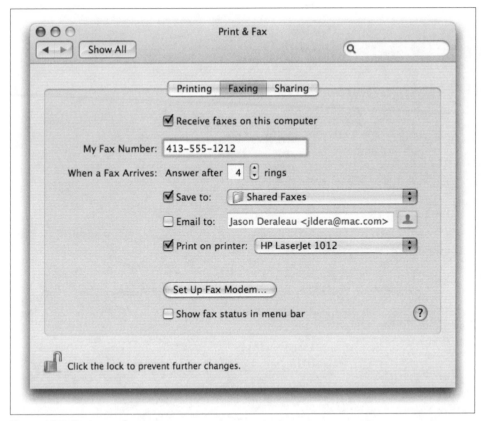

Figure 10-6. Faxing preferences

want to leave the default settings in this dialog or just change the orientation of your page. However, if you are printing a 4×6 photo or an envelope, you'll want to select a printer attached to your system that gives you access to the page sizes it can handle.

 Not all applications have a Page Setup dialog box, and those that do don't always have the Shift-⌘-P keyboard shortcut.

The second step in getting output from an application is to print a document using the standard File → Print (⌘-P) command, which brings up the dialog shown in Figure 10-8. From here, you can print to a printer, save to a PDF file, or fax documents anywhere in the world. This rather simple dialog gives access to a wealth of options that can be performed by both the system and by individual printer drivers. The dialog lets you select the printer to print to, listing both local printers and remote printers. It also gives you the opportunity to choose a preset setting and to customize the printer- and, possibly, application-specific settings.

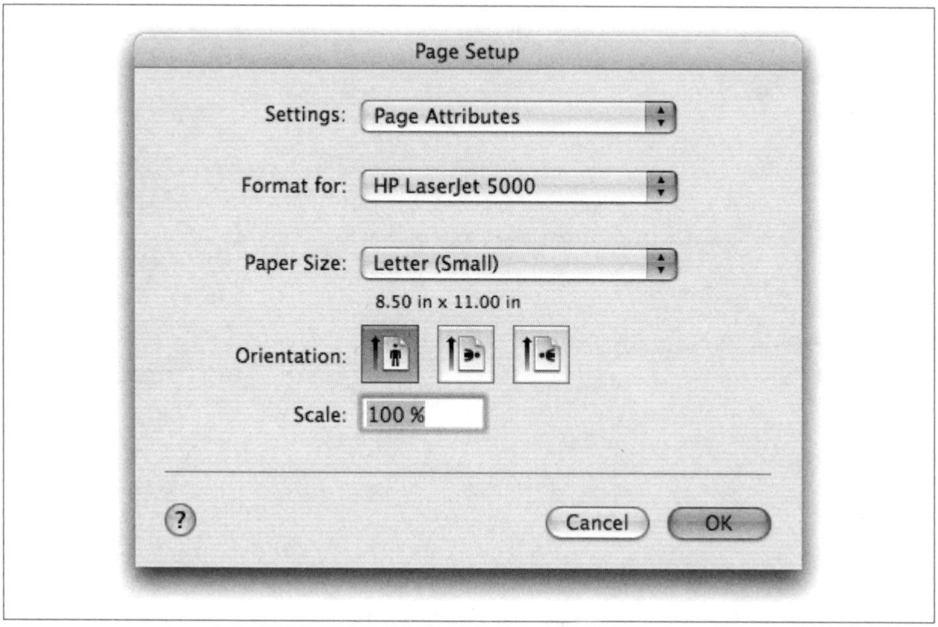

Figure 10-7. The Page Setup dialog box

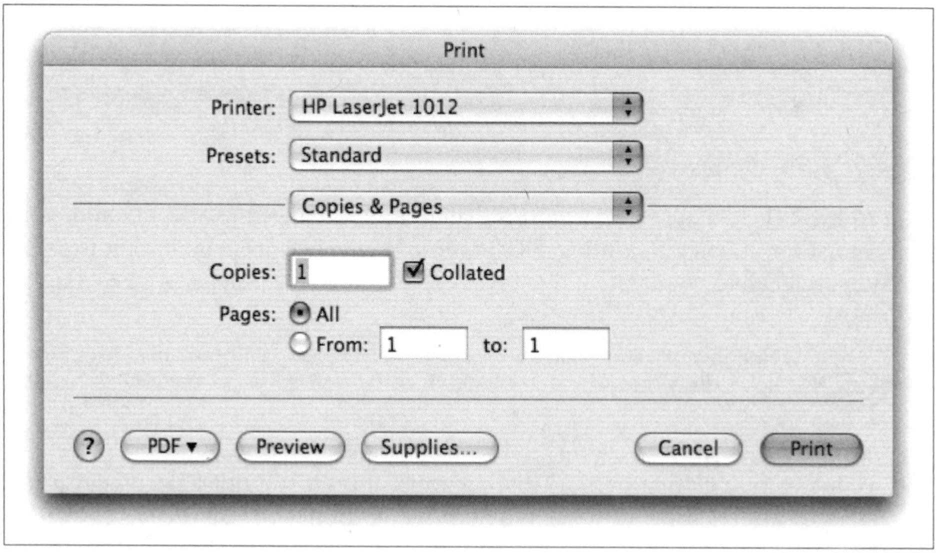

Figure 10-8. The standard Print dialog

The following settings are always available:

Copies & Pages
> Lets you specify how many copies of a document you want to print. Some applications put additional controls into this pane to allow you to specify what content to print in terms that make sense for the application. For example, when you print from Microsoft Excel, you have control over the sheets to print out of a workbook.

Layout
> Gives you the ability to print up to 16 pages on one side of a sheet of paper and the option to print on both sides of the sheet, if your printer supports duplex two-sided printing. Confusingly enough, you can't control the orientation of printing here—you have to set that using the Page Setup dialog before you print.

Scheduler
> Lets you schedule a print job to be printed at some time in the future. You can even place a job on the printer queue, and hold it indefinitely until a time when you are ready for it to be printed. This last option is useful for when you are traveling and don't have access to your printer back at the office, but want to create print jobs before arriving at your destination.

Paper Handling
> Lets you control how the pages are ordered when printed, or to print only even- or odd-numbered pages. This is handy when you want to manually print two-sided documents on a printer that doesn't support duplex printing.

ColorSync
> Sets whether you want the transformation from the document's color space to the printer's to be performed by the printer. Usually you want Mac OS X to perform this work unless you have already modified the colors in the document to print correctly on the target printer. This pane also gives you access to filters—such as applying a sepia tone or converting a grayscale document to black and white—that are performed by Quartz.

Cover Page
> Allows you to print a cover page with your document, including the type of cover page and whether it prints before or after your document.

Summary
> Gives a text representation of all the current settings for a print job.

In addition to these standard settings, many printer drivers add options to this menu. For example, the HP LaserJet printer driver adds panes to let you select which paper tray to use, whether or not to generate a cover page, and the resolution you want to print at. As another example, the Epson Stylus Photo printer drivers add panes allowing you to select the kind of paper you are printing on since different papers react differently to photographic printing.

Sometimes you have to look carefully here for a setting you want to use. For example, the driver for HP's InkJet printers that support duplex printing don't allow you to set up two-sided printing using the Layout pane; instead, a separate two-sided printing pane is provided and accessible via the lower pull-down menu. Of course we can't test and detail the quirks of each printer model here, but the point is, you'll need to check out all the options that your printer driver gives you.

Saving Print Settings

The Print dialog's Presets menu lets you create presets of your chosen settings across all the option panes, allowing you to quickly set up a print job. For example, you might want to provide a Double-Sided setting so you can quickly opt for duplex printing. Another good idea is a Photo preset that sets the paper type and ColorSync options for your particular printer.

To save a set of print settings, simply use the pull-down menu and select the Save As option. Once applied, the name that you choose for a group of print settings will always appear in this menu.

The Simplified Print Panel

Some applications that aim for an ease-of-use interface, such as iPhoto, can choose to present a simplified print panel, as shown in Figure 10-9. This panel presents several of the settings located in the various sections in a single interface, which omits many of the more complex settings of the regular print panel. You can get to all the options by clicking the Advanced Options button.

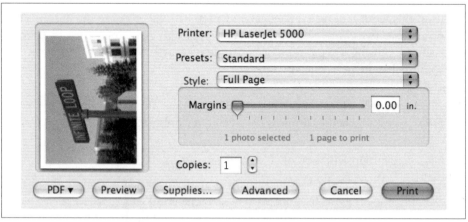

Figure 10-9. The simplified print panel

PDF Services

A nice feature of Mac OS X's print system is its tight integration with Adobe's Portable Document Format (PDF). Earlier versions of Mac OS X had a simple Save as PDF button in the lower-left corner of the print sheet. With Tiger, the Save as PDF button has been replaced with a PDF menu that allows you to perform several different PDF-related tasks. The PDF menu also provides easy access to PDF *workflows*, which are scripts and programs designed to automate common tasks when working with PDFs:

Save as PDF

The first—and simplest—is the Save as PDF option. Select it, give your new PDF a name, and Mac OS X does the rest of the work. The end result is a PDF version of what your document would look like on paper.

Save PDF as PostScript

Selecting the Save PDF as PostScript option performs a very similar process to the Save as PDF option, you just end up with a file in the PostScript format (*.ps*) instead of a PDF.

Fax PDF

As mentioned earlier in this chapter, Mac OS X Tiger has added fax support to the OS. This option is how you make use of that fax functionality. Selecting this option will pop up a new sheet for entering the fax recipient, cover page information, and other fax-related settings.

Compress PDF

The Compress PDF option is the first of several Automator workflows that Apple has included with Mac OS X. You can examine this action yourself by double-clicking it in the */Library/PDF Services* folder. The workflow contains a single action, which compresses all image files in the PDF to keep its file size down.

Encrypt PDF

This workflow also contains only one Automator action. When you choose this option, you will be prompted for a password with which to encrypt the file. The PDF is then encrypted to secure its contents from prying eyes.

Mail PDF

Selecting this option causes the print job to be saved as a PDF file that is then attached to a new Mail message.

Save as PDF-X

PDF/X is a subset of the PDF standard that is geared toward the publishing industry. It is designed to have fewer problems between different PDF implementations and between different types of publishing equipment. This option will take the print job and turn it into a file that meets the PDF/X specification.

Save PDF to iPhoto

Upon choosing this option, the print job is saved to a PDF file that is then imported into iPhoto.

Save PDF to Web Receipts Folder

A handy option for online shoppers, selecting this will create a PDF that is then saved in a folder named *Web Receipts*, which is within the *Documents* folder. If you don't have a *Web Receipts* folder, it will be created upon use.

The included Automator workflows are great examples of what is possible using Automator and PDF Services. You can add some workflows of your own by creating a PDF Services folder within your user Library folder. Not sure what kind of workflows to create? Take a look at Chapter 13 for some more sample workflows and to get an idea of what's possible.

Printing from the Command Line

Since the Mac OS X printing infrastructure is built on top of various Unix tools, it should be no surprise that you can print from the command line. You can print plain-text, PDF, and PostScript files from the command line by using the following command:

```
lp filename
```

You can print the following kinds of files from the command line to any printer:

- Plain text
- PDF
- PostScript

Because Mac OS X supports all these technologies in its print system, you don't have to worry about sending PostScript to a non-PostScript printer—even if the printer is an old dot matrix printer. For example, to print out the contents of a PostScript file named *requirements.ps*, you would use the command shown in Example 10-5.

Example 10-5. Printing a text file to a printer

```
$ lp requirements.ps
request id is HP_LaserJet_5000-6 (1 file(s))
```

CUPS tells you that the job has been submitted and provides you with an *identifier* for the job. The identifier is composed of two parts: the name of the printer that the job will be printed on—in this case, HP_LaserJet_5000—and a sequence number—in this case, the number 6 indicates that this is the sixth job printed from this machine since CUPS was launched.

When called by itself, *lp* prints to the default printer on the system. To print to another printer, you have to specify its queue to the *lp* command. But how do you know the names of the printers attached to your computer? Use the *lpstat* command (refer back to Example 10-1 to see this in action).

Armed with this information, you can use the *lp* command with the *-d* option, as shown in Example 10-6. The *-d* option tells *lp* which printer to select as its destination.

Example 10-6. Printing a PDF file to a specific printer

```
$ lp -d HP_LaserJet_1012 test.pdf
request id is HP_LaserJet_1012-7 (1 file(s))
```

Working with PostScript

Panther has added several features for working with PostScript files. For example, you can open PostScript files (which usually have the *.ps* extension) using Preview. When you do, Preview converts the PostScript to PDF and then displays the result in its window.

There's also a command-line tool, *pstopdf*, which you can use to convert a Post-Script file to PDF. For example, to convert a PostScript file named *stats.ps*, you would use the following command:

```
$ pstopdf stats.ps
```

This creates a *stats.pdf* file. To specify a different output filename, use the *-o* option:

```
$ pstopdf stats.ps -o results.pdf
```

Another helpful utility is *enscript*, which converts plain-text files to PostScript. This command uses the following syntax:

```
enscript outputfile filename
```

where the *outputfile* argument is the name of the file to save PostScript data to and the *filename* argument is the plain-text file to convert. For example, to convert your *.bash_profile* file to PostScript, you could use the following command:

```
$ enscript -p profile.ps .bash_profile
```

If you call *enscript* without the *-p* option, it prints the converted PostScript output directly to the default printer on the system. A nice feature of the *enscript* command's *-p* switch is that you can send its output to STDIN by specifying a hyphen (-) as the *outputfile*. Team this up with *pstopdf*'s *-i* switch, which instructs *pstopdf* to take its input from STDIN, and you can go from a plain-text file to a PDF with a quick stop in PostScript on the way. For example, to make a PDF version of your *.bash_history* file, enter this command:

```
$ enscript -p - .bash_history | pstopdf -i -o History.pdf
```

Command-Line Printing to AppleTalk-Based Printers

For the most part, printing to an AppleTalk printer from the command line is as easy as printing to any other printer, as long as you have set up the printer using the Printer Setup Utility so it has a print queue on your system. If you don't have the AppleTalk printer set up on your system, the first thing you should do is either set it up or find a shared print queue for that printer on another system. (Life is much simpler when CUPS takes care of things.)

If you don't, or can't, set up the AppleTalk printer using the Printer Setup Utility, then you'll need to use the *atprint* command. Unlike *lp*, the *atprint* command doesn't work with files. Instead, it takes its input from the output of other commands and sends it either to a printer that you specify or to the default AppleTalk printer (which is not the same as the default printer for the system set in the Printer Setup Utility). You also have to be careful to send the right kind of data to the printer. In the case of most AppleTalk printers, this means that you have to send PostScript data. Example 10-7 shows how to send a PostScript file to a printer using *atprint*.

Example 10-7. Sending a PostScript file to an AppleTalk printer

```
$ cat manuscript.ps | atprint
Looking for PET:LaserWriter@*.
Trying to connect to PET:LaserWriter@*.
atprint: printing on PET:LaserWriter@*.
```

If the data you want to send isn't in PostScript format, you'll need to convert it first (if possible) using *enscript*. Example 10-8 shows how to print the contents of a plain-text file to an AppleTalk printer named PET.

Example 10-8. Printing a plain-text file to an AppleTalk printer

```
$ cat .bash_profile | enscript -p - | atprint PET
Looking for PET.
Trying to connect to PET:LaserWriter@*.
[ 1 pages * 1 copy ] left in -
atprint: printing on PET:LaserWriter@*.
```

The *at_cho_prn* command is used to set the default printer for use by *atprint*. You'll need to execute this command as *root*, as shown in Example 10-9.

Example 10-9. Setting the default atprint printer

```
$ sudo at_cho_prn
Password:
Zone:*???????????^@???????????`?????????` ?
1: ff01.04.9dtPET:LaserWriter
ITEM number (0 to make no selection)? 1
Default printer is:PET:LaserWriter@*
status: idle
```

All in all, while the *atprint* command is handy in a pinch, the right thing to do is to set up the printer in the Printer Setup Utility and leverage the power of CUPS and the rest of the Mac OS X printing system to your advantage.

Print Sharing

Since the earliest AppleTalk networks, the Mac OS has focused on simplicity in its printer sharing. Mac OS X continues this tradition by including a print system that makes sharing your printers with others quite simple. It even lets you share printers with Windows and Unix users, just as easily as sharing them with another Mac.

There are two ways to enable printer sharing on Tiger. You can either enable Printer Sharing in the Sharing preference panel (System Preferences → Sharing → Services → Printer Sharing), or you can check the box on the Sharing tab of the Print & Fax preferences (as shown in Figure 10-10). The latter offers you a bit more control; you can choose which printers are shared out, as well as enable others to send faxes through your Mac. If you'd like to share your printers with Windows machines, you'll have to go one step further: make sure that Windows Sharing is enabled in the Sharing preferences, and Windows users will then see your Mac's printers in their Network Neighborhood.

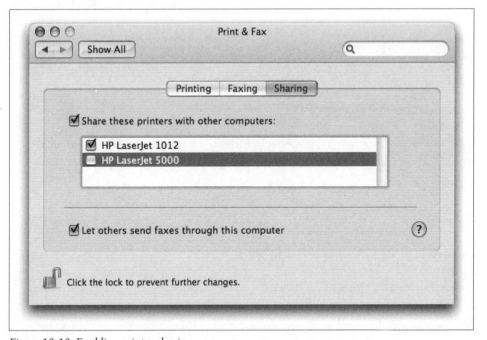

Figure 10-10. Enabling printer sharing

Connecting to the Shared Printers

Sharing out your Mac's printers is the easy part. Things get more complicated when it's time to connect to the shared printer from another machine. Adding the printer to another Mac is a pretty simple process, just add it using Bonjour as discussed in the Adding and Configuring Printers section earlier in this chapter. For those Windows and Unix users, you'll find instructions for adding the printer to your system in the next section.

Connecting from a Windows machine

As mentioned earlier, you'll need to have both Windows Sharing and Printer Sharing enabled for Windows users to be able to print through to your Mac. Once that's done, you can navigate through the Windows Network Neighborhood, where your Mac sits side by side with the other Windows machines on your network.

Double-clicking the Mac shows you its shares in Windows Explorer (as shown in Figure 10-11), including your shared printers. To add a shared printer to the Windows machine, double-click it in Windows Explorer and use the Add Printer wizard to confirm the make and model of the printer. If your printer model is not listed, you may need to acquire the appropriate driver from the printer's manufacturer. Once you've completed the wizard, the printer is available for use on the Windows machine.

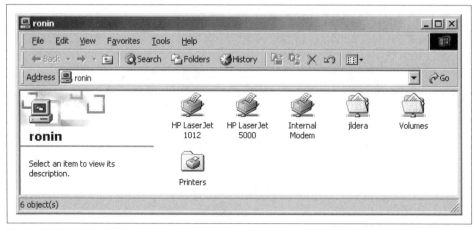

Figure 10-11. A Mac's shares viewed from Windows Explorer

Connecting from a Unix client

The same CUPS software that is included with Mac OS X also forms the print system of most Unix and Linux operating systems. Unix clients can connect to a Mac OS X printer using either IPP or LPD. To add a printer using CUPS, open a web browser on the Unix machine and navigate to *http://localhost:631/*. Using the web interface, select Manage Printers and then click the Add Printer button, as shown in Figure 10-12.

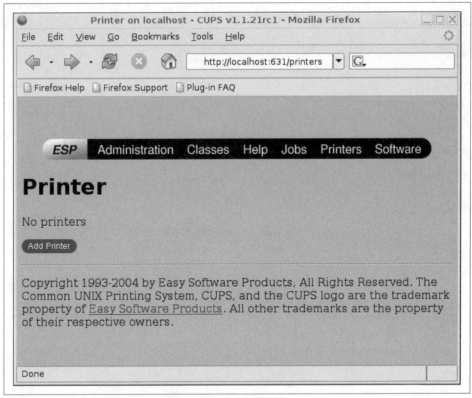

Figure 10-12. Adding a printer using the CUPS web interface

After entering the necessary credentials, you'll be prompted for some information about the printer. Enter the printer's name, location, and a brief description, and then click the Continue button. CUPS then asks you for the type of device to use. Select LPD/LPR Host and click Continue once again. On this page, you'll need to enter the IP address of your Mac and the queue name for the desired printer.

After entering the address information for the printer, CUPS prompts you for the make and model of the printer. Finally, CUPS confirms that the printer was added successfully. At this point, you can click over to the Printers tab to double-check that the printer was added properly by printing a test page to it.

Further Explorations

To learn more about CUPS, you can access the CUPS documentation on your Mac by opening Safari and browsing to *http://localhost:631/documentation.html*. You may want to explore the following manpages for more information about how to use the printing system from the command line:

- *lp*
- *lpstat*
- *lpoptions*
- *pstopdf*
- *enscript*
- *atprint*
- *at_cho_prn*

## CHAPTER 11

Networking

Networking has always been easy on the Mac. The original Macintosh shipped with AppleTalk, which made it easy to connect a group of computers and printers. Historically, other systems have had a harder time: using a variety of standards that were sometimes proprietary and that did not always work well together. The rise of the Internet, however, has meant that, for all practical purposes, there is now one primary network standard that all machines use: the suite of protocols based on the Internet Protocol, more commonly known as IP. In the development of Mac OS X, Apple has gone to great lengths to make IP as easy to use as possible, approaching the ease of use of AppleTalk. For the most part, the system will try to autoconfigure itself to work with whatever network is available, making it easy to use in this day of café computing. (Would you like WiFi with your latte?)

This chapter gives a fundamental view of how IP works and how to examine the various networking settings as well as monitor your network from both the command line and the GUI. Also, you'll see how dial-up networking, virtual private networks (VPNs), and firewalls can be configured.

The Internet Protocol

IP is the dominant network standard in use today because its namesake, the Internet, was successful in connecting the world's various networks together. IP is built on a set of assumptions that break the problem of networking into a set of layers, as shown in Figure 11-1. Each layer acts independently of the ones above and below it, allowing flexibility in how each layer is implemented.

 Figure 11-1 is actually a simplified view of the abstract seven-layer networking model that you'll find in many books on IP networking. In practice, however, most people usually simplify things to the four-layer view presented here.

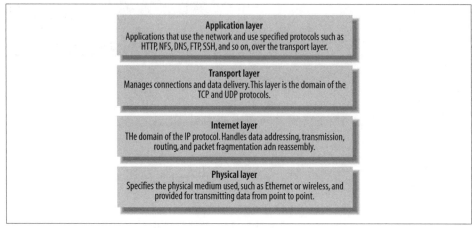

Application layer
Applications that use the network and use specified protocols such as HTTP, NFS, DNS, FTP, SSH, and so on, over the transport layer.

Transport layer
Manages connections and data delivery. This layer is the domain of the TCP and UDP protocols.

Internet layer
THe domain of the IP protocol. Handles data addressing, transmission, routing, and packet fragmentation adn reassembly.

Physical layer
Specifies the physical medium used, such as Ethernet or wireless, and provided for transmitting data from point to point.

Figure 11-1. A conceptual view of the networking stack

In addition to this layered approach, IP breaks data into separate self-contained pieces, known as *packets*, which are transmitted individually from their point of origin to their destination. Each packet can, if needed, take a different route from its origin to its destination. This lets information flow even in the face of changing network topologies. The connections between networks can go down or change, but as long as the network can find a new route, the packets eventually find their way through.

By using a layered model, and by using packets that flow over virtually any kind of transmission infrastructure, IP runs over a variety of media including wired Ethernet, wireless 802.11, fiber-optic lines, FireWire, and more. It's been joked that IP would work just fine over slips of paper carried by carrier pigeon (you can read the full joke at *http://www.ietf.org/rfc/rfc1149.txt*).

IP is also *routable*, which means multiple networks can connect to each other and that packets can be routed across those networks to reach their final destination. This is how the Internet was built in the first place: as a collection of networks at universities and government laboratories that had interconnections placed between them.

Above IP are two protocols that the applications on your machines use to access the network:

Transmission Control Protocol (TCP)
Known as TCP/IP, or TCP over IP, this protocol specifies how packets of data should be transmitted over IP in a reliable fashion. TCP makes sure that all the data transmitted between two machines is presented to an application in the order in which it was transmitted and received. This is very important because IP doesn't guarantee that packets will be transmitted in any particular order; usually they are sent in the order in which they are generated, but because of

changing network conditions, they may arrive in any order. TCP also performs error checking. If a packet is corrupted or doesn't arrive, TCP automatically requests retransmission of the data from the sender without intervention of the application. This means application writers don't have to worry about the way in which data is transported across the network. To an application, a network connection can be regarded as a consistent stream of data when in fact that data is being split into several parts and moved across the network in individual units.

User Datagram Protocol (UDP)
UDP sends data between computers with a minimum of overhead. Unlike TCP, it doesn't guarantee that the order in which packets arrive is the same as when they were transmitted, and it doesn't request redelivery of bad packets. Because of this, UDP is considered an unreliable protocol, but don't let the negative connotation of the word *unreliable* fool you. UDP is used extensively where performance needs are paramount and the data errors being transmitted can be worked around or even ignored. For example, UDP is used by many video conferencing applications, such as iChat AV. Because of its low overhead and the fact that if a data frame representing a moment in time isn't received, there is no need to retransmit it as it is no longer valid.

In conjunction with IP, two other important protocols work at the lower layers of the protocol stack:

Internet Control Message Protocol (ICMP)
ICMP is used by the network, at the Internet layer, to send messages to itself. For example, the various parts of a network can inform each other that errors have occurred or that a particular network segment is congested with too much traffic. It can also determine whether a particular network address is being used. In addition, ICMP is often used to test the connections between networks.

Address Resolution Protocol (ARP)
At the physical layer, an entirely different set of network addresses is used. For example, each Ethernet card has a unique Media Access Control (MAC) address to identify it. ARP is used to map the IP addresses used by the Internet layer of the network stack into the physical addresses used by the equipment on the local network segment.

Network Addressing and Masks

Every device, or *host*, that uses the IP networking stack has an address so that packets can be sent to it. This address has to be unique to the network that the computer is part of. A traditional Internet network address (also known as an IPv4 address) is a sequence of 32 bits (4 bytes), usually written as a series of four dot-separated values in the form #.#.#.#, where each # is a decimal integer between 0 and 255 representing one of the four bytes of the address. For example, 66.93.174.29 is a valid IP address.

An IPv4 address is also composed of two parts, albeit indirectly. The first part identifies the local network while the second part identifies the host in that network. Confusingly, the boundary between these two parts in an IPv4 address varies depending on the network. A network mask is used to delineate between the network and host parts of the address. Network masks can come in many forms, but typically, you'll see the following three network masks in use (listed both in dotted notation and in the hexadecimal form that you'll see in some of the command-line utilities):

255.255.255.0 or 0xffffff00

> Known as a Class C mask, this indicates that the first three bytes of the address are the network address. There can be 254 hosts on a Class C network. This is the most common mask you'll see in day-to-day use.

255.255.0.0 or 0xffff0000

> Known as a Class B mask, this indicates that the first two bytes of the address are the network address. There can be up to 65,000 hosts on a Class B network.

255.0.0.0 or 0xff000000

> Known as a Class A mask, this indicates that the first byte of the address is the network address and the remaining bytes identify the host on the network. There can be up to 16.7 million hosts on a Class A network.

Network addresses for hosts connected directly to the Internet must always come from an official source, your Internet Service Provider (ISP). Your ISP owns the rights to use a block of addresses on the Internet and assigns your computer an IP address, or block of IP addresses, as part of your connection to the Internet.

Examining Network Settings

There are several ways to see what IP address (or addresses, if you have multiple interfaces active) you are using. The first, but not the most convenient, place most people go to find this information is the Network preference panel (System Preferences → Network), shown in Figure 11-2. When you first open the Network panel, you're given a quick heads-up of the various network settings and the order in which network connections are attempted. In this panel, you'll see one of three colored dots next to the network connections on your system:

- Green dots indicate a working network connection
- Red dots indicate a service that is currently off or not yet configured
- Yellow dots indicate a service that is set up, but is not able to connect for some reason

For example, if your PowerBook is connected to an AirPort or wireless network, you'll see a green dot next to AirPort in the Network Status view of the Network panel. Likewise, if your PowerBook is attempting to connect to an unknown AirPort network, you'll see a yellow dot next to AirPort.

IPv6 Addresses

The IPv4 addressing scheme was created at a time when there were relatively few computers running TCP/IP. The original designers didn't imagine that the Internet would expand to the point it has today, where you can easily access it from most of the countries on the planet. Because of this expansion, as well as the anticipation that in the near future there will be an explosion of devices such as mobile phones and home entertainment centers that will access the Internet, a new addressing scheme known as IPv6 is starting to be deployed.

IPv6 addresses are 128 bits long and are written as a series of eight colon-separated, 16-bit values written in hexadecimal form, such as the following:

    fe80:0000:0000:0000:0203:93ff:feef:baa5

Unlike IPv4 addresses, IPv6 addresses don't require a separate network mask.

IPv6 isn't in wide use yet, at least in most of the networks that you are likely to find yourself using. But due to the limited number of IPv4 addresses, many networks, especially in Asia where the IPv4 address allocations have already run out, are starting to move to IPv6. In addition, many of the primary Internet backbone service providers are moving their networks to IPv6 in preparation for a full deployment.

Mac OS X natively supports IPv6 addresses and, even though you might not be using an IPv6 network for a few more years, you'll see these addresses as you work with the various network tools.

A better place to look is the Network Utility (*/Applications/Utilities*) application, as shown in Figure 11-3. Network Utility displays the information about the network interface that is currently being used to connect to the network, also known as the *default interface*. You can select from the various network interfaces by using the pop-up menu.

The information you'll see in the Network Utility's display consists of the following:

Hardware Address
> Displays the physical MAC address of the interface. This is the address used at the physical layer to move data to and from the network.

IP Address
> Displays the IP address of the interface.

Link Speed and Link Status
> Provides the speed of the connection as well as whether it is active.

Vendor and Model Version
> Provides the maker of the physical interface as well as any version information in the firmware of the interface.

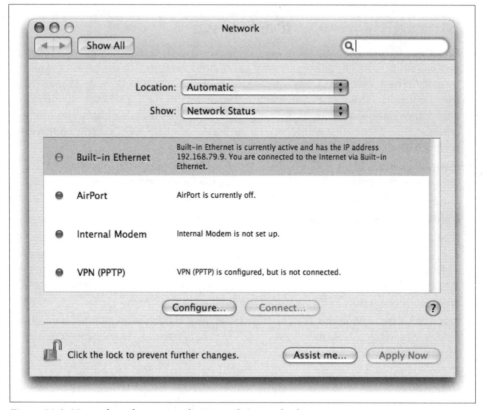

Figure 11-2. Network preference panel's Network Status display

Transfer Statistics

Provides some information on how the interface is performing. Typically as you use the network, you'll see the sent and received packets counters increasing. You shouldn't see any errors or collisions unless something is wrong with your network.

On the menu, you'll notice designators like *(en0)*, *(en1)*, or *(fw0)*. The operating system uses these internal identifiers to track the various interfaces. The identifiers you might see are:

lo0

This is the loopback interface, which allows network-aware programs to communicate with other programs on the system without sending packets onto the network. This interface always has the IPv4 *(inet)* address of 127.0.0.1 and the IPv6 *(inet6)* address of ::1.

en0

The primary Ethernet interface of your machine. This is always the built-in Ethernet controller for your Mac.

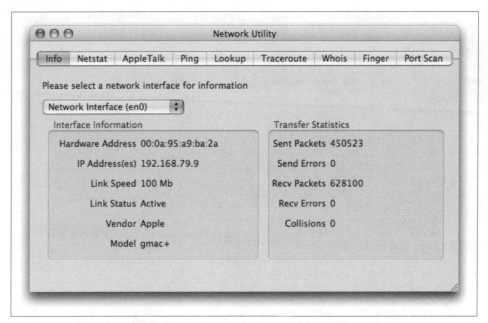

Figure 11-3. Network Utility showing information on an active network interface

en1

> An Ethernet interface. Typically *en1* is an AirPort card in your computer (if you have one) or a second Ethernet card. In addition to the IPv6 (*inet6*) and IPv4 (*inet*) addresses, the MAC address is given using the ether parameter.

fw0

> The FireWire interface for your machine. This interface is disabled until you manually turn on FireWire as a networking option in the Network preference panel.

gif0

> This is the generic interface tunnel, used to tunnel network packets from one machine to another, most often to connect two IPv6 networks over a link that uses the IPv4 protocol or to connect two IPv4 networks over a link that uses the IPv6 protocol. By default, this interface is not active. See *man gif* for more information.

stf0

> The 6to4 tunnel interface allows IPv6 hosts on one network communicate transparently with IPv6 hosts on another network over an IPv4 link. By default, this interface is not enabled and is used only when a machine is used as a router between an IPv6 and an IPv4 network. See *man stf* for more information.

To get more detailed information about the current state of all the network adapters connected to your Mac, use the *ifconfig* command-line tool, as shown in Example 11-1.

Example 11-1. Using ifconfig to look at network connection status

```
$ ifconfig
lo0: flags=8049<UP,LOOPBACK,RUNNING,MULTICAST> mtu 16384
        inet 127.0.0.1 netmask 0xff000000
        inet6 ::1 prefixlen 128
        inet6 fe80::1%lo0 prefixlen 64 scopeid 0x1
gif0: flags=8010<POINTOPOINT,MULTICAST> mtu 1280
stf0: flags=0<> mtu 1280
en0: flags=8863<UP,BROADCAST,SMART,RUNNING,SIMPLEX,MULTICAST> mtu 1500
        inet 192.168.79.9 netmask 0xffffff00 broadcast 192.168.79.255
        ether 00:0a:95:a9:ba:2a
        media: autoselect (100baseTX <full-duplex>) status: active
        supported media: none autoselect 10baseT/UTP <half-duplex> 10baseT/UTP <full-
duplex> 10baseT/UTP <full-duplex,hw-loopback> 100baseTX <half-duplex> 100baseTX <full-
duplex> 100baseTX <full-duplex,hw-loopback>
en1: flags=8863<UP,BROADCAST,SMART,RUNNING,SIMPLEX,MULTICAST> mtu 1500
        ether 00:0d:93:7f:42:48
        media: autoselect (<unknown type>) status: inactive
        supported media: autoselect
fw0: flags=8863<UP,BROADCAST,SMART,RUNNING,SIMPLEX,MULTICAST> mtu 2030
        lladdr 00:0a:95:ff:fe:a9:ba:2a
        media: autoselect <full-duplex> status: inactive
        supported media: autoselect <full-duplex>
```

The output from *ifconfig* lists the information for each interface using its identifier.

Looking at addresses on the local network

The system keeps a table of the MAC addresses of the various computers that are on the local network segment and their IP addresses. To see this table, use the *arp -a* command, as shown in Example 11-2.

Example 11-2. Using arp to display host information for your local network

```
$ arp -a
gateway.example.com (192.168.79.1) at 0:0:d1:f0:67:9 on en0 [ethernet]
ronin.example.com (192.168.79.5) at 0:3:93:d7:3d:c0 on en0 [ethernet]
? (192.168.79.255) at ff:ff:ff:ff:ff:ff on en0 [ethernet]
```

There are three lines in *arp*'s output in Example 11-2. The first two are hosts, showing the name of the network, the network's IP and MAC addresses, and the port on which the hosts are connected (*en0*, or Ethernet). The third item in *arp -a*'s output is special because the IP address ends with 255. This means that this is the broadcast address and is primarily used to send packets to all the hosts on a network. Since it is a network address and isn't associated with a host, there isn't a MAC address that corresponds to it (as indicated by ff:ff:ff:ff:ff:ff).

Configuring IP Addresses

When IP was first used, every computer on a network had to be hand-configured with a static IP address and a netmask address before it could communicate with other machines. While it's nice to have a static IP address, it also meant that it was possible to run out of IP addresses assigned to a domain. This often forced sysadmins to restrict certain users from access to network services (file sharing, printing, even the Internet) by not assigning an IP address to a certain class of machines or users, with dedicated "network" computers in each group from which the network could be accessed. As you can imagine, that was a real pain.

Fortunately for today's users, most networks provide Dynamic Host Configuration Protocol (DHCP) services. These services allow computers to be configured automatically with an IP address and netmask for that particular network. DHCP also helps conserve IP addresses by letting a potentially large number of computers share a smaller number of active IP addresses. DHCP services are provided by a separate server on the network or can be built into the hardware, known as a *gateway router*, providing access to the Internet via an ISP.

When you plug your computer into a DHCP-enabled network, your machine sends out a low-level request to the DHCP server for configuration information. The DHCP server responds by sending the IP address, netmask, router, and DNS information that the computer needs to connect to the network. Your computer uses this information to configure itself and becomes a fully functional node on the network.

DHCP works only when the network has been configured properly. In the absence of a DHCP server, Mac OS X uses a link local address, which is part of Bonjour. This is a private network address in the range 169.254.1.0 to 169.254.254.255. By assigning itself an address when no other address information is present, your Mac can still interact with other hosts on the network that also have self-assigned IP addresses. This is perfect for setting up ad hoc networks—such as when you want to connect two laptops together with an Ethernet or FireWire cable. This address won't work for accessing the Internet, but it works for connecting a group of computers together to share data, compile code, and the like.

 IP over FireWire (IPoFW) was introduced with Mac OS X Panther (Version 10.3). The benefit of IPoFW is it often offers higher data transfer rates (up to 400 MB per second for standard FireWire, or 800 MB per second between FireWire Extreme–equipped Macs) over traditional Ethernet connections (either 10 or 100 MB per second).

Manually Configuring IP Information

If you need to manually configure your IP information so your Mac can access a network or the Internet, the place to do so is in the Network preference panel, shown in

Figure 11-4. You'll need the following pieces of information from your network administrator or ISP:

- The IP address assigned to your computer
- The subnet mask for the address
- The router, also called a *gateway* by many admins, that your computer should use to communicate with the Internet
- The DNS servers your computer should use

 While it is possible to configure your IP information using *ifconfig*, it is not recommended. Settings made with *ifconfig* are not reflected in the Network preference panel and will be overridden by any changes made in the GUI. If you want to use a command-line tool, you should take a look at *ncutil* by Jeff Frey. You can find it online at *http:// deaddog.duch.udel.edu/~frey/darwin/ncutil/*.

After entering the information for your network connection, you'll need to click the Apply Now button for the settings to take effect. Check your connection's status by going to the Show pop-up and select Network Status from the menu. If you see a green dot, your connection is working; a red dot, as mentioned earlier, means that your connection isn't working properly.

Naming and DNS

IP addresses, especially IPv6 addresses (see the sidebar "IPv6 Addresses," earlier in this chapter), aren't something that you ever really want to deal with directly; hostnames are much more convenient to use. However, every operation that involves a hostname has to involve looking up an IP address for that hostname. For example, when you point Safari or Firefox to *www.oreilly.com*, the system translates that hostname into an IP address using the Domain Name System (DNS), a distributed naming system that resolves hostnames to an IP addresses.

For the most part, DNS is transparent. All you need to have is a DNS server defined in your network configuration, and you can use hostnames in your applications. Without DNS, all you'll be able to do is surf the Net by IP address, which is possible but not a very fun experience.

If your computer obtained its IP address through DHCP, it should also be configured with the correct DNS server. However, if you have to configure your IP address manually, you'll need to provide valid values for a DNS server. If you have to configure your own DNS servers, make sure you use a DNS server that is close to you on the network. After all, every connection to a host on the Internet requires the resolution of hostname to IP address. The closer you are to the server, the better.

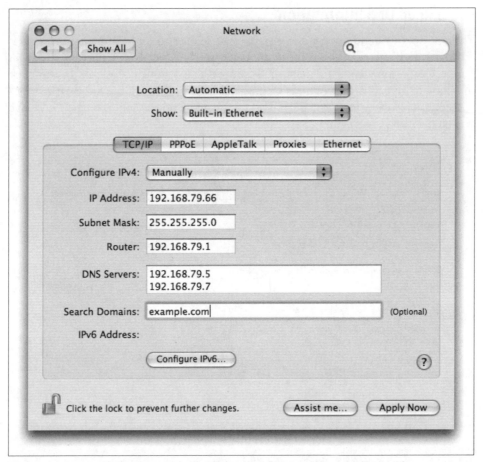

Figure 11-4. Manually configuring network settings in the Network preference panel

The DNS servers that your machine is currently using are shown in the Network preference panel. You can also find them in the */etc/resolv.conf* file, as shown in Example 11-3.

Example 11-3. Examining the contents of the resolv.conf file

```
$ cat /etc/resolv.conf
domain example.com
nameserver 192.168.79.5
nameserver 192.168.79.7
```

On other Unix systems, you can directly edit the *resolv.conf* file to change your nameserver configuration. However, this file is automatically updated by the networking system in Mac OS X, so any changes you make to it will be lost the next time you change networks.

Looking up DNS Information

To look up an IP address for a hostname yourself, or to find the hostname associated with an IP address, you can use the Lookup tab of Network Utility, as shown in Figure 11-5. Simply enter the host or IP address that you want to look up and click the Lookup button. Other options are available to you through the information pop-up menu. However, for most purposes, the default information setting should give you all the information you need.

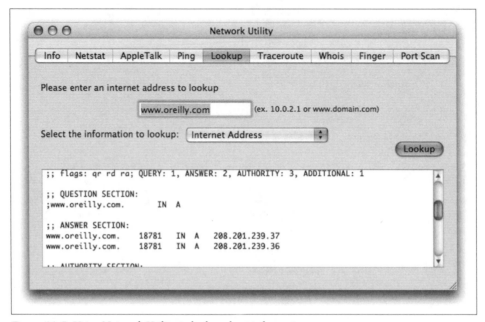

Figure 11-5. Using Network Utility to look up host information

On the command line, you can use the *host* command to determine the IP address for a host or vice versa, as shown in Example 11-4.

Example 11-4. Using host to look up DNS information

```
$ host www.oreilly.com
www.oreilly.com has address 208.201.239.37
www.oreilly.com has address 208.201.239.36
$ host 208.201.239.36
36.239.201.208.in-addr.arpa domain name pointer www.oreillynet.com.
```

Multicast DNS

Even without a configured DNS server, there is another component of Bonjour known as *multicast DNS* (mDNS). mDNS lets computers on a local network know each others' names so that you can access a computer using a human-readable name instead of an IP address. For example, for a machine named Hobbes, you should be able to browse a web server running on it from another machine on the local network by entering into Safari *Hobbes.local*.

 By default, when you install Mac OS X, the name of your machine will be based on the full name given when setting up the first account. For example, the default name of my machine after installing Tiger was "Jason Deraleau's Computer." You should change this to be something a bit shorter and more personalized (throughout this book you'll see Ronin and Hobbes, the names of two of my machines) in the Sharing preference panel.

The combination of mDNS and self-assigned IP addresses provides the foundation for Bonjour to work its magic. With mDNS, Bonjour-enabled computers not only let each other know their names, but they can also advertise the services they offer. When you enable iTunes music sharing or iChat, a description of that service is broadcast via mDNS, allowing any other Bonjour machine to see it.

Wide-Area Bonjour

A feature of Tiger that hasn't gotten much attention is wide-area support in Bonjour. Normally, Bonjour is limited to the local subnet for advertising and discovering network services. Wide-area Bonjour extends the convenience of Bonjour beyond the LAN and brings it to the WAN. This part of Bonjour isn't enabled by default, but some savvy developers have put together a Bonjour preference pane that lets you configure wide-area Bonjour. The preference pane is a free download available at *http://www. dns-sd.org/ClientSetup.html*.

Ports and Services

The various services provided by a host, such as HTTP for serving web pages or SMTP for handling email, are each exposed to other computers on a separate port: a network connection endpoint in the IP stack identified by a number. For example, HTTP is defined to run on port 80. This means whenever you browse to a page on the server, your web client is opening a connection to port 80 of the server to make its request.

Most services use ports numbered less than 1024; these are known as the *well-known ports*. Table 11-1 lists the various services and ports built into Mac OS X's firewall. Table 11-2 lists some more common services and their ports. You can also find an extensive listing of well-known services in the */etc/services* file.

Table 11-1. Well-known ports found in Mac OS X's firewall

Service	Ports
Personal File Sharing	548/tcp, 427/tcp
Windows Sharing	139/tcp, 137/udp, 138/udp
Personal Web Sharing	80/tcp, 427/tcp, 443/tcp
Remote Login	22/tcp
FTP Access	21/tcp
Apple Remote Desktop	3283/tcp, 5900/tcp, 3283/udp, 5900/udp
Remote Apple Events	3031/tcp
Printer Sharing	631/tcp, 515/tcp
iChat Bonjour	5297/tcp, 5298/tcp
iTunes Music Sharing	3689/tcp
iPhoto Bonjour Sharing	8770/tcp
Network Time	123/udp

Table 11-2. More well-known services and their ports

Service	Ports
Telnet	23/tcp
SMTP	25/tcp
DNS	53/tcp, 53/udp
POP3, POP3S	110/tcp, 995/tcp
NNTP	119/tcp
IMAP, IMAPS	143/tcp, 993/tcp
LDAP, LDAPS	389/tcp, 636/tcp

Private Networks and NAT

Because IPv4 addresses are relatively scarce, each address typically costs money to use. You may not pay directly for an IP address, but your ISP has a limited supply of them and will use some mechanism to control their use. To allow multiple machines to run behind a limited supply of IP addresses, many networks use a block of private addresses as well as Network Address Translation (NAT).

Supported by most routers, NAT processes all packets bound for the Internet from a private network, transforming the original IP addresses into an address that is reachable from the Internet, before sending the packets on. In effect, packets from the private network appear to be coming from the router running NAT (Figure 11-6). When packets arrive back at the router that corresponds to a connection already in progress, the NAT translates them into a form usable on the private network and sends them back to the original host.

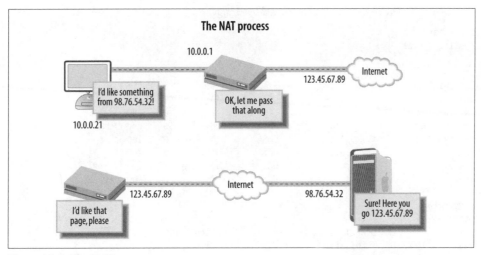

Figure 11-6. The NAT process

You can tell if you are on a private network when your IP address is in one of the following ranges:

- 10.0.0.0 through 10.255.255.255
- 169.254.1.0 through 169.254.254.255
- 172.16.0.0 through 172.31.255.255
- 192.168.0.0 through 192.168.255.255

Using NAT creates two follow-on effects:

- Since NAT relays only packets from the Internet that were requested by a computer on the private network, NAT acts as a basic firewall concealing the machines on the private network.
- With no way to directly address a machine on a private network, it's harder to set up a machine on the private network to act as a server. Some NAT routers let you forward specific ports from their external IP address to various machines on the private network.

You'll need to consult the information about your router to be sure.

Routing

To see the routing table used by the system, you can use the Netstat tab of the Network Utility application, click the Display routing table information radio button, and then hit the Netstat button, as shown in Figure 11-7. This outputs the same routing table information as the *netstat -r* command, shown in Example 11-5.

Example 11-5. The routing table as displayed by netstat -r

```
$ netstat -r
Routing tables

Internet:
Destination      Gateway          Flags    Refs      Use  Netif Expire
default          192.168.79.1     UGSc      19       13   en0
192.168.79       link#4           UCS        6        0   en0
192.168.79.1     0:0:d1:f0:67:9   UHLW       5        0   en0   1178
192.168.79.9     127.0.0.1        UHS        0        0   lo0
127              127.0.0.1        UCS        0        0   lo0
127.0.0.1        127.0.0.1        UH        13   259841   lo0
169.254          link#4           UCS        0        0   en0

Internet6:
Destination      Gateway          Flags    Netif Expire
::1              link#1           UHL       lo0
fe80::%lo0/64    fe80::1%lo0      Uc        lo0
fe80::1%lo0      link#1           UHL       lo0
ff01::/32        ::1              U         lo0
ff02::/32        ::1              UC        lo0
```

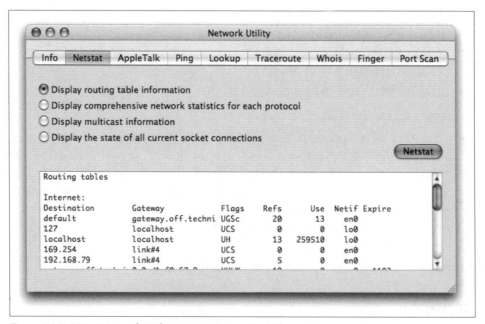

Figure 11-7. Using Network Utility to examine routing information

There are two parts to the routing table: the first is the *Internet* table for routing packets to IPv4-based networks; the second is the *Internet6* table for routing packets to IPv6-based networks. Each part contains a set of entries. Here's what the first few entries in the Internet table mean:

- The first line indicates that the default destination for all packets is 192.168.79.1, a router to the Internet. The packets should be sent via the en0 interface.

- The second line indicates that packets for the 192.168.79 network should use the en0 interface.

- The third line indicates that packets to 192.168.79.1 (the address of the router) should be sent to the device with the MAC address 0:0:d1:f0:67:9 using the en0 interface.

- The fourth line indicates that packets to 192.168.79.9 (in this case, the local machine) should be sent to the localhost on the lo0 interface. The system puts this route into place so that any packets for the local machine that use the external IP address aren't sent to the network.

The *Internet6* table, shown in Example 11-5, contains the same sort of information but with IPv6 instead of IPv4 addresses.

The most useful entry in these tables is the default route. When you are having problems connecting to the network, you can quickly check to see whether the system has a default route. Example 11-6 shows the output of *netstat -r* when all the network connections on a machine are down. As you can see, the only machine that packets can get to is localhost. You can also see that when the network interfaces are all down, there is no default route, as traffic is not able to leave the machine.

Example 11-6. The routing table with no external routes

```
$ netstat -r
Routing tables

Internet:
Destination      Gateway          Flags      Refs        Use  Netif Expire
127              127.0.0.1        UCS           0          0   lo0
127.0.0.1        127.0.0.1        UH           16     259946   lo0
224.0.0/4        127.0.0.1        UCS           2          0   lo0
224.0.0.2        127.0.0.1        UHW           1          1   lo0
224.0.0.251      127.0.0.1        UHW           1          7   lo0

Internet6:
Destination      Gateway          Flags      Netif Expire
::1              link#1           UHL        lo0
fe80::%lo0/64    fe80::1%lo0      Uc         lo0
fe80::1%lo0      link#1           UHL        lo0
ff01::/32        ::1              U          lo0
ff02::/32        ::1              UC         lo0
```

Active Network Connections

To dig a bit deeper, you can take a look at all the active network connections on your machine. To do this, use the same Netstat tab in Network Utility, click the radio button next to "Display the state of all current socket connections," and the hit the Netstat button. It usually takes a few seconds to generate the result, which is shown in Figure 11-8. This displays the same information as typing *netstat -a* into a Terminal window, shown in Example 11-7.

Example 11-7. Some output from netstat -a

```
$ netstat -a
Active Internet connections (including servers)
Proto Recv-Q Send-Q  Local Address          Foreign Address        (state)
tcp4      0      0  192.168.79.9.50836     192.168.79.5.993       ESTABLISHED
tcp4      0      0  192.168.79.9.49932     192.168.79.5.993       CLOSE_WAIT
tcp4      0      0  192.168.79.9.49894     192.168.79.5.5900      ESTABLISHED
tcp4      0      0  192.168.79.9.49593     17.250.248.64.993      ESTABLISHED
tcp4      0      0  *.*                    *.*                    CLOSED
tcp4      0      0  192.168.79.9.49225     205.188.7.200.5190     ESTABLISHED
tcp4      0      0  *.*                    *.*                    CLOSED
tcp4      0      0  127.0.0.1.1033         127.0.0.1.925          ESTABLISHED
tcp4      0      0  127.0.0.1.925          127.0.0.1.1033         ESTABLISHED
tcp4      0      0  *.*                    *.*                    CLOSED
tcp46     0      0  *.6942                 *.*                    LISTEN
tcp4      0      0  *.6942                 *.*                    LISTEN
```

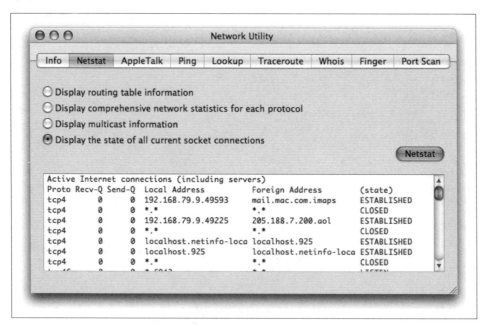

Figure 11-8. Using Network Utility to examine network connections

Each item in the list shows the local and remote addresses and ports in the form *host.port* where the port name is translated, if known, into a service name such as *http* or *imap*. In Example 11-7, the first connection listed is from the local machine to a server at *mac.com*. The connection is using the secure IMAP protocol.

AppleTalk

When the Mac was developed in the early 1980s, an easy-to-use networking protocol called AppleTalk allowed multiple users to share files and devices, such as printers and scanners. AppleTalk went through several changes, including the ability to route AppleTalk packets between networks (called *Zones* in AppleTalk parlance) and run AppleTalk over Ethernet. Because AppleTalk has been around since the introduction of the Mac, large numbers of networks still support AppleTalk, and many AppleTalk-only devices still exist.

Mac OS X continues to support AppleTalk even though IP is its primary networking protocol. When you have an Ethernet or AirPort connection, AppleTalk is automatically running by default so any available AppleTalk devices on the network can be used. You can control whether AppleTalk is active for a network connection by using the Network preference panel.

From the command line, you can check the status of AppleTalk on your machine by running the *appletalk -s* command, as shown in Example 11-8.

Example 11-8. Getting the status of AppleTalk

```
$ appletalk -s
AppleTalk interface............. en1
Network Number ................. 65420 (0xff8c)
Node ID ........................ 122 (0x7a)
Current Zone ................... *
Bridge net ..................... 0 (0x0)
Bridge number .................. 0 (0x0)
DDP statistics:
Packets Transmitted ............ 64
Bytes Transmitted .............. 2751
Best Router Cache used (pkts) ... 0
Packets Received ............... 79
Bytes Received ................. 3644
Packets for unregistered socket . 0
Packets for out of range socket . 2
Length errors .................. 0
Checksum errors ................ 0
Packets dropped (no buffers) .... 0
```

The output from *appletalk -s* shows the network interface AppleTalk is active on, the numeric network and node identifiers, and some statistics about the packets being transmitted via AppleTalk.

You can see the AppleTalk hosts and services on the network by using the *atlookup* command, as shown in Example 11-9.

Example 11-9. Looking up AppleTalk hosts and services using atlookup

```
$ atlookup
Found 3 entries in zone *
ff8c.7a.80 Ronin:Darwin
ff8c.7a.80 Ronin:AFPServer
ffee.44.80 Hobbes:Darwin
ffee.44.81 Hobbes:AFPServer
```

The first column in the output is composed of three dot-separated hexadecimal numbers. The first two numbers identify the host's network number and ID. The third number identifies the service being provided. The second column is composed of the name of the host as well as the name of the service being provided. In Example 11-9, the first two lines indicate that there is a Darwin-based (Mac OS X) machine on the network named Ronin and that its Apple Filing Protocol (AFP) service is running. The next two lines describe the same for the host Hobbes.

Locations

You can use the Network preference panel to create and manage several independent profiles of network configuration information, known as *Locations*. This is handy when you have to manually configure your network settings for the office but want to use your computer easily on DHCP-based networks at home or at the local coffee house. Locations are managed using the Location menu in the Network preference panel, shown in Figure 11-9.

By default, all Mac OS X systems have a location named *Automatic*. To create a new location, select New Location from the Location menu. After naming the location, it appears in the pop-up menu. When you choose a location, you can configure it as needed. When you hit Apply Now, your changes are applied and your Mac attempts to connect to that network location.

Once you have defined multiple locations, you can switch between them without going into the Network preference panel; instead, you use the → Location menu. This menu also gives you a quick shortcut to the Network preference panel.

If all the networks you move between assign IP addresses with DHCP, you can probably get away with not setting different locations. Instead, just use the Automatic location setting.

Using a Dial-Up Connection

Compared to the simplicity of using Ethernet or AirPort, connecting to a network through a modem requires a bit more effort in configuring your computer to dial into a server. This can be done either on-demand when your computer wants to access the network, or only when you wish to. To use a dial-up network, you'll have to set

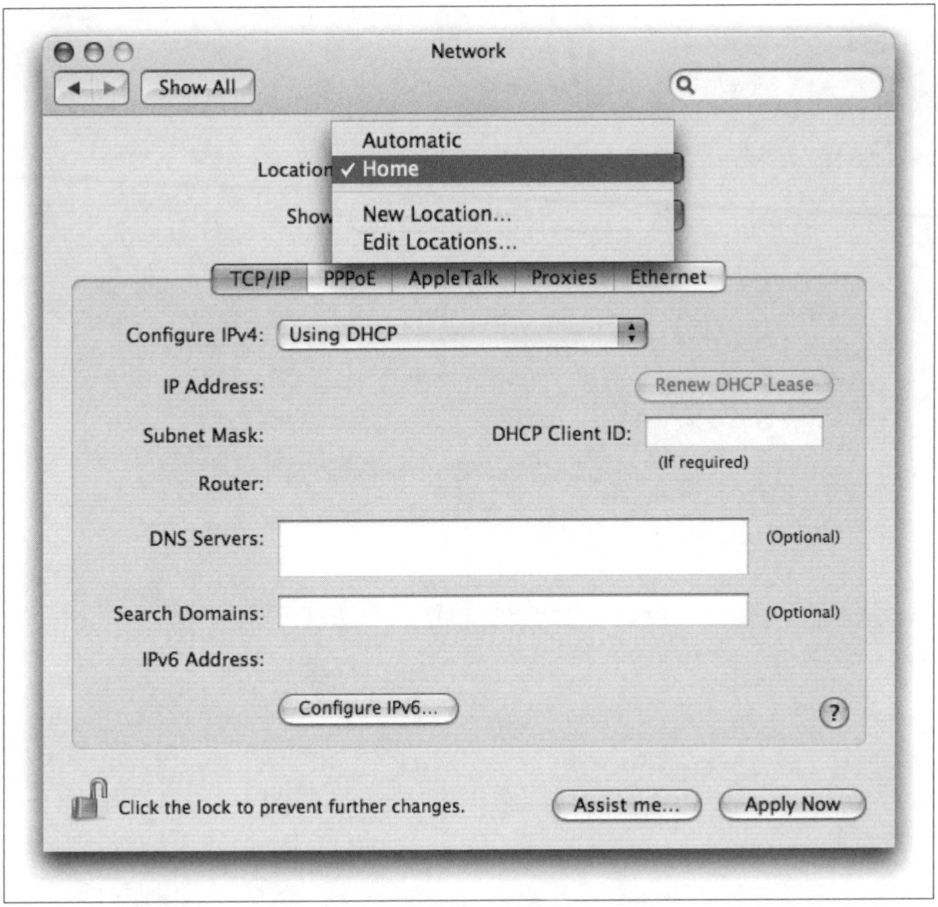

Figure 11-9. Using the Location pull-down menu in the Network preference panel

up some additional information in the PPP tab of the Network preference panel for a modem, as shown in Figure 11-10. For most dial-up networks, using the information given to you by your ISP will work here.

If you need to set up additional configuration items, you can click the PPP 'Options button and get the sheet displayed in Figure 11-11. Some options of interest here:

Connect automatically when needed

If this box is checked, your computer will try to dial your network provider when any program makes a request that needs connectivity. For example, if you were offline but opened Safari, the system would automatically connect so you could use Safari to surf the Web. This also happens with Mail.app and the Backup utility included with .Mac memberships. If this box is checked and you have Backup scheduled to run a backup to your iDisk and your Mac isn't online, your Mac will connect to your ISP so Backup can get its job done.

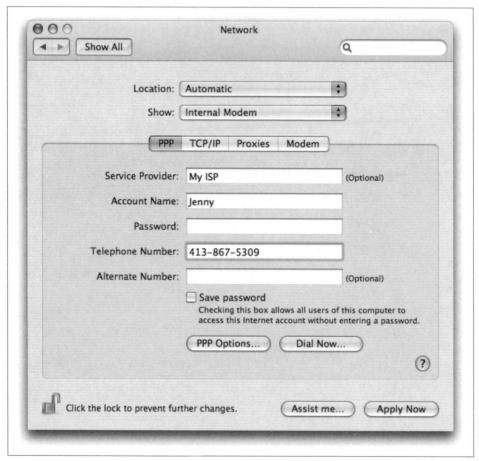

Figure 11-10. Configuring dial-up networking using the Network preference panel

Prompt every nn minutes to maintain connection

This option is geared to those who don't want to unnecessarily tie up their phone line or are billed by the hour for Internet usage. Enabling this option results in a small dialog box appearing every time the designated interval has passed. The window asks you to confirm you want to stay online and, if you haven't confirmed the connection, automatically disconnects you from the Internet.

Disconnect if idle

This setting controls how long your connection will be idle before the computer disconnects from the Internet automatically; that is how long the connection is held if you aren't sending or receiving any data.

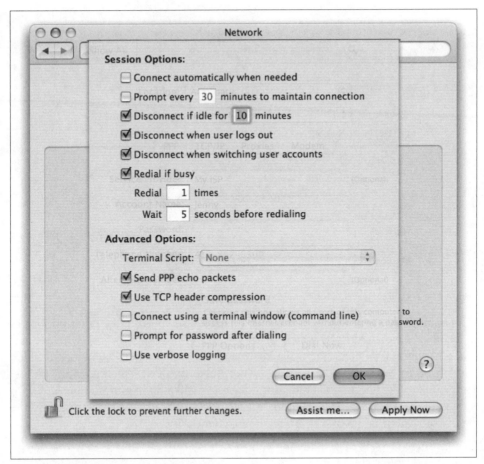

Figure 11-11. Advanced PPP options

Connect using a terminal window (command line)

> If checked, this causes a simple terminal window (not related to the Terminal application) to open so you can manually dial in to the PPP server. Usually this isn't required, as most PPP servers use a standard login process that your Mac can deal with seamlessly. However, some older networks may require the use of this option.

In addition to using the Network preference panel, you can use Internet Connect (*/Applications*), shown in Figure 11-12, to connect to a dial-up networking provider. Internet Connect also allows you to manage multiple numbers, which is handy if you are traveling between cities and want to easily connect to the right dial-up number. To add a configuration, use the Configuration pop-up menu and select Edit Configurations.

Figure 11-12. Using Internet Connect to manage dial-up connections

Observant readers will note that Internet Connect also sports a few other options in its toolbar. One is AirPort, which provides you with details on any wireless networks within range, including a signal strength meter. Another is Bluetooth, which allows you to connect to the network via a Bluetooth device such as a cell phone. Unfortunately, connecting via Bluetooth devices is still a bit of a mysterious art, with wildly different procedures depending on your device. Your best bet is to dig on the Internet for information on how to configure your device.

The last item is a VPN tab, allowing you to access a Virtual Private Network, which is discussed later in this chapter.

FireWire Networking

Another method for connecting your Mac to a network is through its FireWire port. Originally released as a developer beta, FireWire networking has become a core feature of Mac OS X. To connect two computers together for blazing-fast, 400+ Mbps file transfers, you only need a FireWire cable. Connect each end into one of the machines and then make your way into the Network preferences (System Preferences → Network).

Another great FireWire trick is Target Disk Mode, discussed more in Chapter 5.

The FireWire network interface is not enabled by default, so select Network Port Configurations from the Show menu. The resulting window will look something like Figure 11-13.

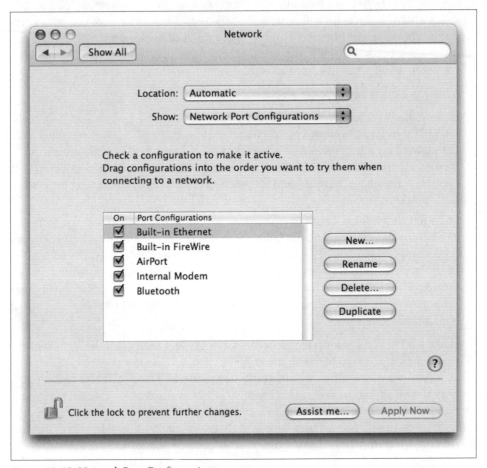

Figure 11-13. Network Port Configurations

Once the Built-in FireWire interface is enabled, it is added to the Show menu and available for configuration. At this point, Bonjour kicks in, and each machine gives itself an IP address, sets up mDNS, and begins advertising available services. After that's all working, connecting to your other Mac is as easy as using the Finder's Network browser and logging in.

IP over FireWire is quick and capable. The FireWire interface behaves like any other network interface in your system. You can even enable Internet Connection Sharing for the FireWire interface and use it to get onto the Internet.

Virtual Private Networks

In a nutshell, a VPN is an encrypted logical network connection, also known as a *tunnel*, which runs over a physical connection such as the open Internet. When you establish a VPN connection with a server, all the network packets between your computer and the server are encrypted and remain safe from prying eyes. This means you can access resources on another network, such as your corporate network, from anywhere in the world without compromising your corporate network's security.

Mac OS X supports two types of VPNs:

Point-to-Point Tunneling Protocol (PPTP)
> A VPN standard developed by Microsoft and supported by many manufacturers of networking equipment. All you need to connect via PPTP is the address of the server, an account name, and a password or an RSA Secure ID card (a gizmo that displays a random number and is synchronized with a similar gizmo on the server side).

Level 2 Tunneling Protocol (L2TP)
> L2TP is a newer VPN standard that uses IPSec, a standard for encrypting data over an IP connection. To make an L2TP connection, you'll need the address of the server, an account name, a password or an RSA SecurID card, and a shared secret. The *shared secret* is a key that the administrator of the L2TP server gives you along with the account name and password. It is used in the initial setup of the tunnel.

To make a VPN connection, open Internet Connect and then click the VPN button. When you first attempt to configure a VPN, you'll have to make a choice as to whether you want to configure your computer to use L2TP or PPTP for the connection, as shown in Figure 11-14. Once you've selected the type of connection, you'll see the Internet Connect VPN window, shown in Figure 11-15. This window works the same way the dial-up window does, in that you can configure Internet Connect so you can select from one of many different VPN configurations.

To enter the shared secret of an L2TP connection, you'll need to edit its configuration, as shown in Figure 11-16. Here you will also find many other options to configure, including the types of authentication and encryption used for the connection. In Tiger, a new option for VPN access has been added. Using VPN on demand, you can specify domains and hosts that are present on the remote network. When Tiger encounters a request bound for one of the specified addresses, it establishes a connection to the VPN automatically. For example, if you need to connect to a corporate VPN to check email, anytime you launch Mail.app, the VPN connection is automatically made for you.

AirPort
Your computer needs to be set up to make VPN connections.
To continue with setup, choose which kind of VPN you'd like to configure, and then click Continue. Check with your network administrator if you are unsure which to choose.
L2TP over IPSec
PPTP
Cancel
Continue
Show AirPort status in menu bar
Status: AirPort link status not available
Status not available

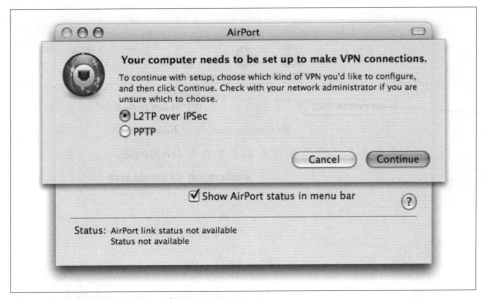

Figure 11-14. Selecting the type of VPN to use

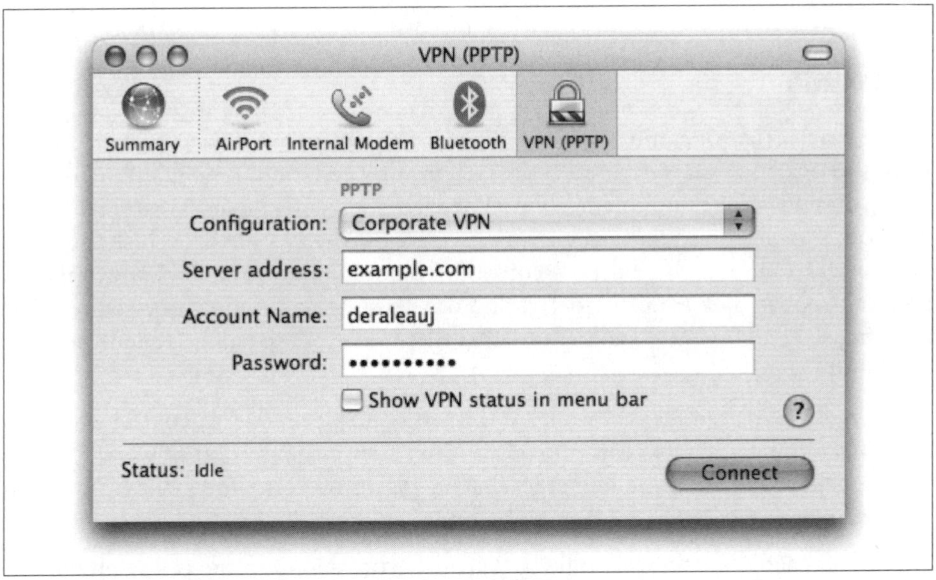

VPN (PPTP)
Summary
AirPort
Internal Modem
Bluetooth
VPN (PPTP)
PPTP
Configuration: Corporate VPN
Server address: example.com
Account Name: deraleauj
Password: ••••••••••
Show VPN status in menu bar
Status: Idle
Connect

Figure 11-15. Managing VPN connections with Internet Connect

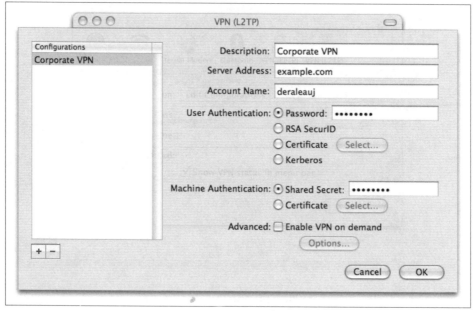

Figure 11-16. Managing VPN configurations with Internet Connect

Firewalls

Unlike many other operating systems, Mac OS X ships in a secure state with all network services disabled. This means you can be fairly certain that no matter what network you find yourself on, the likelihood of somebody cracking into your machine is very low. However, as you turn on various services, such as file or web sharing, the ports used to support those services on your computer are opened up, which means they can receive data from the network. For the most part, Apple does a good job releasing security updates, making sure that these services are patched as soon as vulnerabilities are discovered.

If you are truly paranoid and want to take every step possible to control access to your Mac, you can enable Mac OS X's built-in firewall, based on *ipfw*, which performs packet filtering at the kernel level. You can turn on the firewall by using System Preferences → Sharing → Firewall, as shown in Figure 11-17.

When you enable the firewall, only packets that correspond to the rules that you set up in the Allow list are allowed into your machine. All other packets are dropped. The default rules are set up so that any services that you share are allowed. However, other ports, such as those needed to use iChat over Bonjour, are closed by default. To allow these ports, you can enable the corresponding rule for the service you want to allow.

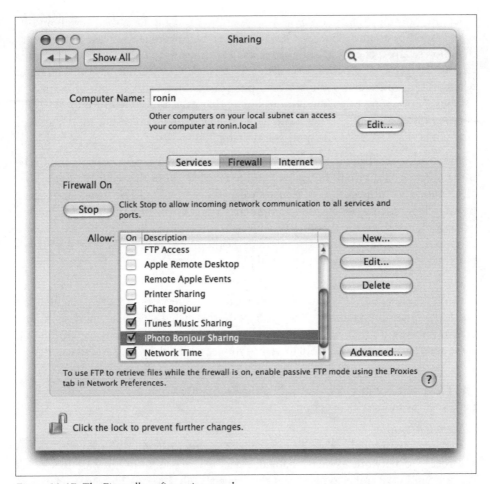

Figure 11-17. The Firewall configuration panel

To open ports for services not listed, you'll need to create rules. Clicking the New button in the firewall pane brings up the sheet shown in Figure 11-18. Several default services are listed in the Port Name pull-down menu for easy selection. However, only a limited number of services that you might want to enable are listed. For example, the ports used by iChat during a voice or video chat aren't listed in the default rules or in the list of rules to add. You'll have to add the ports yourself using the Other option in the pull-down menu.

Information about which ports to open for iChat AV can be found in Apple Knowledge Base article 93208 (*http://docs.info.apple.com/article.html?artnum=93208*). A list of the well-known ports used by Apple software is contained in Apple Knowledge Base article 106439 (*http://docs.info.apple.com/article.html?artnum=106439*). You can also find a list of the ports commonly used on Mac OS X in Table 11-1.

Since the firewall is based on *ipfw*, it is possible to manipulate the firewall and its rules from the command line. However, doing so is dangerous. It is easy to craft rules that look secure, yet can make things worse than they were to begin with. This gives you a false sense of security. It is also easy to lock yourself out of your computer when editing rules remotely or even to put your computer in an unusable state by tweaking the wrong rule. The bottom line is that even though you can go into the depths of firewall configuration using *ipfw*, you're strongly urged not to. It's an area where it is way too easy to do more harm than good.

If you need more flexibility in your firewall than the GUI gives you, you should be using an external firewall. In fact, if you are worried about the security of your system enough to turn on the built-in firewall, you really should be using an external firewall. It is much more effective to have network security performed in a dedicated external device than it is to configure a piece of software on the machine that, if compromised, can give access to the internals of the machine. This is as true of third-party, add-on firewall products as it is of *ipfw*.

When you want to secure your machine in a network environment that you don't control, such as in a café, you should turn off all the services that your machine has on in the Sharing preference pane, make sure that iChat's Bonjour mode is turned off, and make sure that you aren't sharing your iTunes music library. By turning off these services, you've done more to secure your machine than any firewall can do.

For Tiger, Apple added a few small enhancements to the built-in firewall. You can find these new options by clicking the Advanced button on the Firewall pane, revealing a sheet with these new options:

Block UDP Traffic
> As was mentioned earlier, UDP is one of the two primary IP protocols used to access a network. When enabled, Mac OS X's built-in firewall blocks all inbound TCP connections except those specifically allowed. However, its default configuration does nothing to block UDP traffic. By enabling this option, the firewall blocks all inbound UDP traffic, except that which has been specifically allowed.

Enable Firewall Logging
> The beauty of Mac OS X's firewall is that, consistent with Apple's other creations, it just works. You enable it and it runs in the background, never to disturb you again. However, it isn't very forthcoming, either. By default, the firewall does not log the connections it denies. Upon enabling this advanced option, Mac OS X logs unauthorized network access attempts to */var/log/ipfw. log*. You can view the log by clicking the Open Log button, which opens Mac OS X's Console (*/Applications/Utilities*) to the appropriate logfile.

Third-Party Firewall Software

Portable users are quick to point out that there are often times when you have no way to insert a hardware device between your Mac and the Internet. The convenience of wireless networking belies its security risks, especially on public access points. You might find yourself wanting a more configurable software firewall to protect your Mac for those situations when a hardware solution just isn't possible.

Luckily, several third-party solutions are available. Two popular packages are Fire-Walk X (*http://www.pliris-soft.com/products/firewalkx/index.html*) and BrickHouse (*http://personalpages.tds.net/~brian_hill/brickhouse.html*). Both offer a variety of enhancements to Mac OS X's built-in firewall at a nominal cost. There are also trial versions available for both of the firewall enhancers, making it easy to decide which one works best for your particular needs.

While Mac OS X does a great job of blocking undesired inbound traffic, it does nothing to filter outbound traffic. *Egress filtering*—that is, filtering outbound connections—has become a necessary consideration with today's crop of software phoning home to its developers. Even though spyware is virtually nonexistent on Mac OS X, there are still legitimate software applications that may disclose more personal information than you'd like.

Once again, a third-party solution is available to enhance this aspect of the Mac OS X firewall. Objective Development's Little Snitch (*http://www.obdev.at/products/littlesnitch/index.html*) is a System Preferences panel that adds egress filtering to Mac OS X. It works by monitoring which applications are attempting to access network resources and then presenting the user with a confirmation dialog. The user can then allow or deny the application's access to that resource, either for a specific connection or for all connections meeting those criteria. Little Snitch is a shareware application, and a demo version is available from the developer.

Finally, packet filter firewalls do a great job of keeping most nasties out, but for those who are a little more security conscious, look no further than HenWen (*http://seiryu.home.comcast.net/henwen.html*). HenWen is an open source application that aims to make the popular Network Intrusion Detection System (NIDS) Snort (*http://www.snort.org/*) simple to configure and use on Mac OS X. A NIDS examines traffic that does make it past the firewall, searching for patterns of malicious traffic. HenWen does an excellent job of putting Snort to work protecting your Mac.

Enable Stealth Mode

When Mac OS X blocks a connection, it specifically notifies the offending host that the connection has been denied. With Stealth Mode enabled, the firewall still blocks the connection, but it does not notify the offender. To an attacker, this makes it seem as if your computer does not exist on the network.

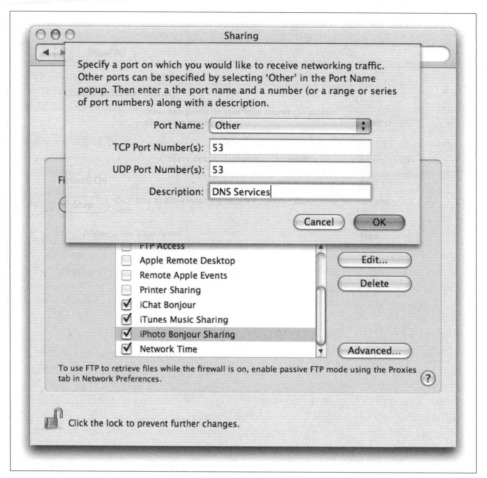

Figure 11-18. *Adding a rule to the firewall*

While Stealth Mode deters many attackers, a savvier miscreant will see through the façade. When a host is truly not there, Internet standards require that the last router before the destination host respond with an ICMP message indicating that the host or network is unavailable. Stealth Mode simply doesn't respond, signaling to the attacker that *something* must still be there.

Internet Connection Sharing

Building on top of the various tools and concepts, such as DHCP and NAT, covered in this chapter, Mac OS X provides an easy-to-use mechanism for sharing one of its network connections to networks on any of its other network connections. For example, if you are in a meeting room and have only one Ethernet jack, but everyone has Wi-Fi cards in their laptops, you can plug your Mac into the Ethernet and then share that connection with everyone else in the room over a private wireless network managed by your computer—regardless of whether the others are running Mac OS X, Windows, or Linux. Essentially, you can turn your Mac into the equivalent of an Internet gateway.

 You shouldn't activate Internet Sharing on a network segment that already has an operational DHCP server. If you do, your Mac interferes with the DHCP server on the network, resulting in confusion among users and drawing the ire of the network administrator. In short, don't share to existing networks. Always make your own private network to share your public network connection with.

To enable Internet Connection Sharing, simply use the Internet tab of the Sharing preference panel, shown in Figure 11-19.

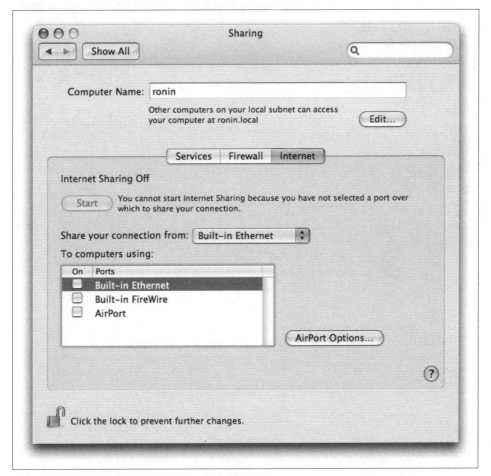

Figure 11-19. Setting up Internet Connection Sharing

Use the pull-down menu to select which of your network connections you want to share—that is the connection that is connected to the Internet. Then click the checkboxes to select which network connections you want your machine to act as a router for. If you want to share via AirPort, you'll want to click the AirPort Options button to configure the wireless network that will be set up. Once everything is configured to your liking, click the Start button, and you'll be the star of the room.

Further Explorations

If you would like to get a deeper knowledge of how networking works, you should investigate the following:

- *TCP/IP Network Administration,* Third Edition, by Craig Hunt (O'Reilly Media, Inc., 1992)
- *Virtual Private Networks,* Second Edition, by Charlie Scott, et al. (O'Reilly Media, Inc., 1998)
- *Building Internet Firewalls,* Second Edition, by Elizabeth D. Zwicky, et al. (O'Reilly Media, Inc., 2000)

Also, you can investigate the following manpages on your system:

- *ip*
- *ifconfig*
- *netstat*
- *appletalk*
- *ipfw*

## CHAPTER 12

Monitoring the System

The Mac, as well crafted as it is, hides a lot of complexity under its hood. This is unavoidable given what it does. Much to Apple's credit, the Mac works a lot smoother than most computers, but it's still a complex beast underneath the Aqua interface. In a lot of ways, the Mac is similar to a smooth running car. There's a set of well laid out controls, including a steering wheel, accelerator, and brake, but underneath the hood, it's a bit more complicated than that. There's system after system that works together to make it all happen.

This chapter shows you how to get under the hood and find out what kind of hardware, such as how much RAM and the kind of hard drives, is in your Mac. It also shows you how to view the software that is installed, how to watch the software running, and how to see what resources it is using. Finally, a couple of ways to remotely access your Mac are discussed to help you monitor and administer it from a distance.

About This Mac

The first place to go to get information about your system is the → About This Mac menu, which brings up the panel shown in Figure 12-1. This simple panel shows you the kind of processor (or processors) in your Mac, the amount of memory you have installed, and your Mac's Startup Disk. You can even find out the exact build of Tiger you are running. Click the Version string in the panel, and it will change to the build number, such as 8C46. Click again, and you'll get the serial number of your system—a valuable piece of information when you are on hold with AppleCare. But the information here is only the surface details. Click the More Info button and System Profiler will launch.

System Profiler

The System Profiler (*/Applications/Utilities*) gives you a great deal of insight into the kind of hardware that is installed and connected to your system and the software it's

Figure 12-1. The About This Mac panel

running. It gives fast answers to the questions: "How much memory do I have?" or "What version of Safari do I have installed?" In fact, it does such a thorough job that a System Profiler report is often the first thing Apple's support folks will ask you for when you have a problem or report a bug. Figure 12-2 shows what System Profiler looks like when you first launch it.

System Profiler has another face as well. The command-line version, */usr/sbin/system_profiler*, is discussed later in this chapter.

The column on the left side is divided into three principal parts:

Hardware

Gives a detailed listing of the hardware in and connected to your system including memory, PCI and AGP cards, ATA and SCSI devices (such as hard drives), USB- and FireWire-connected devices, AirPort card, and modem. Each item displays all the information known to the system about the device such as its model number and firmware revisions.

Network

Gives a complete list of all the network connections on your machine and the configuration information, such as IP address, subnet mask, router address, and Ethernet address for each connection.

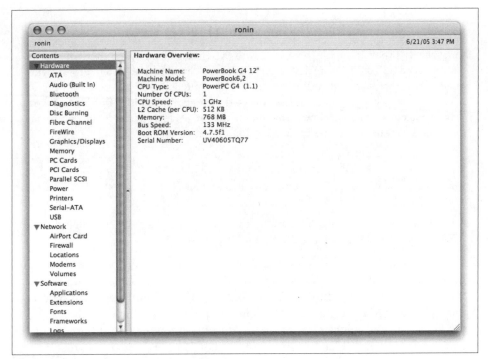

Figure 12-2. The System Profiler main window

Software

> Provides a detailed list of the applications in the */Applications* folder as well as the frameworks and kernel extensions on your system. Each item includes the name of the software component, its version number, and the date on which it was last modified.

The amount of information that the System Profiler gives you access to can be overwhelming. Thankfully, the interface does a much better job than its predecessor did in previous versions of Mac OS X by letting you drill down to the information you want to see.

Creating a System Profile Report

Occasionally, you may be asked by Apple or some other software company to send a report from System Profiler so they can see the details of your system and troubleshoot a problem for you.

There are a variety of ways to generate this information:

- Save an XML document containing all the information in a format that can be opened later with the System Profiler application. To do this, use the same File → Save (⌘-S) command that you would in any other application. This is Apple's preferred format for receiving system profiles.

- Export the data to a plain text or rich text file (RTF) using the File → Export menu.
- Print the file, but instead of sending it to your printer, save it as a PDF file using File → Print → PDF → Save as PDF.

To vary the detail level of the information in the report (as well as the size of the files generated), you can choose the level of detail you want to display using the View menu and then save, export, or print the report. When sending problem reports to Apple, it is best to err on the side of sending too much information rather than too little. However, you might want to be careful if you are actually printing out the reports—a full, extended report can run upward of 75 pages.

System Profiler on the command line

The *system_profiler* command-line tool allows you to get the same information from the command line that System Profiler gives you access to. When run with no arguments, *system_profiler* generates a full report, the beginning of which is shown in Example 12-1.

Example 12-1. The start of output from system_profiler

```
$ system_profiler
Hardware:

    Hardware Overview:

      Machine Name: PowerBook G4 12"
      Machine Model: PowerBook6,2
      CPU Type: PowerPC G4  (1.1)
      Number Of CPUs: 1
      CPU Speed: 1 GHz
      L2 Cache (per CPU): 512 KB
      Memory: 768 MB
      Bus Speed: 133 MHz
      Boot ROM Version: 4.7.5f1
      Serial Number: UV40605TQ77

...
```

Filing a Bug with Apple

One of the most valuable things you can do when something goes wrong with Mac OS X—which is a heck of a lot more productive than just complaining to your friends—is to file a bug with Apple. The easiest way to send feedback is to use the form on Apple's web site at *http://www.apple.com/macosx/feedback*. Even better is to use the Apple Developer Connection's bug report site at *http://bugreport.apple.com*. You'll have to have an ADC membership (free for the lowest tier) to use this form, but in return, you'll be able to track the progress of your issue after you submit it.

The full report that *system_profiler* outputs is quite long. You might want to save it as a file so that you can view it using a text editor, or so that you can send it to Apple or another software vendor as part of a bug report. To do this, use the following command:

```
$ system_profiler > ~/Desktop/MySystemProfile.txt
```

 You could take this tip a step forward and add it to your *crontab* (see Chapter 13) so that you always have an up-to-date inventory of your system. System administrators can use this tip to keep track of machines across their networks.

To limit the amount of information that *system_profiler* generates, you can pass a data type as an argument. You can get the list of data types for your system by using the *-listDataTypes* argument, as shown in Example 12-2.

Example 12-2. Listing the data types that system_profiler can report

```
$ system_profiler -listDataTypes
Available Datatypes:
SPHardwareDataType
SPNetworkDataType
SPSoftwareDataType
SPParallelATADataType
SPAudioDataType
SPBluetoothDataType
SPDiagnosticsDataType
SPDiscBurningDataType
SPFibreChannelDataType
SPFireWireDataType
SPDisplaysDataType
SPMemoryDataType
SPPCCardDataType
SPPCIDataType
SPParallelSCSIDataType
SPPowerDataType
SPPrintersDataType
```

```
SPSerialATADataType
SPUSBDataType
SPAirPortDataType
SPFirewallDataType
SPNetworkLocationDataType
SPModemDataType
SPNetworkVolumeDataType
SPApplicationsDataType
SPExtensionsDataType
SPFontsDataType
SPFrameworksDataType
SPLogsDataType
SPPrefPaneDataType
SPStartupItemDataType
```

Armed with this information, if you wanted to see the status of the network connections of your Mac, you could use the *SPNetworkDataType* argument, as shown in Example 12-3.

Example 12-3. Using system_profiler to get network interface data

```
$ system_profiler SPNetworkDataType
Network:

    Built-in Ethernet:

      Type: Ethernet
      Hardware: Ethernet
      BSD Device Name: en0
      Has IP Assigned: Yes
      IPv4 Addresses: 192.168.79.60
      IPv4:
          Addresses: 192.168.79.60
          Configuration Method: DHCP
          DHCP Client ID: ronin
          Interface Name: en0
          Router: 192.168.79.1
          Subnet Masks: 255.255.255.0
      DNS:
          Server Addresses: 192.168.79.5, 192.168.79.7
      DHCP Server Responses:
          Domain Name Servers: 192.168.79.5,192.168.79.7
          Lease Duration (seconds): 0
          DHCP Message Type: 0x05
          Routers: 192.168.79.1
          Server Identifier: 192.168.79.5
          Subnet Mask: 255.255.255.0
      Proxies:
          FTP Proxy Enabled: No
          FTP Passive Mode: Yes
          Gopher Proxy Enabled: No
          HTTP Proxy Enabled: No
```

```
        HTTPS Proxy Enabled: No
        RTSP Proxy Enabled: No
        SOCKS Proxy Enabled: No
    Ethernet:
        MAC Address: 00:0a:95:a9:ba:2a
        Media Options: Full Duplex
        Media Subtype: 100baseTX
```

Monitoring System Activity

Once you know what is installed on your system, it's always helpful to see how your system is running. The System Profiler report gives access to two logs (console and system) that provide a little bit of information, but two tools, Console and Activity Viewer (both found in */Applications/Utilities*), can provide you with quite a bit more information about what's going on in your system, such as how much memory is available, what processes are tying up system resources, and what kind of network activity is going on.

Console

The Console application (shown in Figure 12-3) lets you view all the *logfiles* on your computer. A logfile is a simple text file that software applications use to report their status. Logfiles are sequential, with new entries appended to the log and timestamped as they occur. Depending on the application, the log might be used solely for error reporting or it might list every mundane task the software performs.

When you launch Console, it gathers the system logs, and any logs from your Home directory, and displays them in the left pane, making it easy to navigate between the logs. If you don't see the left pane, click the Logs icon in the Console's toolbar (or select View → Show Log List from the menu bar) to reveal it.

The first two logs you'll see are the system and console logs, but that's just the warm-up. Console also gives you the following areas in which to see the logs:

~/Library/Logs
> Contains the logs that are associated with a user. These include the various CrashReporter logs, which give the gory details of any application crashes that you might have experienced. You'll also find the MirrorAgent log detailing the activities of synchronizing your iDisk.

/Library/Logs
> Contains logs that are associated with the system at large. For example, you'll find that CrashReporter reports on components that are being run by the system (instead of applications you run) and, if you are unlucky enough to experience a kernel panic, the log for that is found here, too.

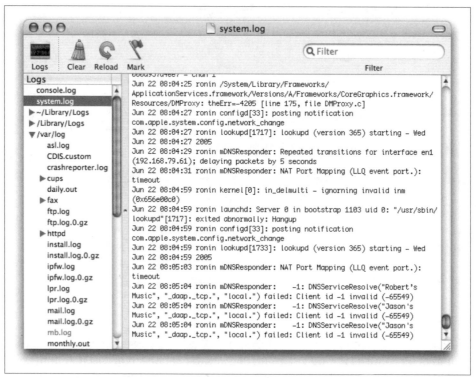

Figure 12-3. The Console application displays the various logs available in a sidebar on the left

/var/log

> Contains the logs of the various BSD Unix utilities and daemons running on your system. For example, you'll find the logs for the Apache *httpd* web server and the *ipfw* firewall here.

With such an extreme amount of data at your fingertips, how can you sort through it all? This is where Apple's use of the Filter box in the menu bar comes in handy. Figure 12-4 shows an example of the user searching for any lines containing "kernel" in the *system.log*. The quick filtering abilities of the Console utility make it easy for you to look for needles in a haystack. A great use of this feature is to scan your web server's logs to search for requests from a particular IP address.

Another useful tool in the toolbar is the Mark button, which inserts a separator of text, along with the current date and time, into the log view. This allows you to bring up the Console, make a mark in a log, do something with another part of the system, and then come back to see what has happened since you made the mark.

For example, if you're having problems synchronizing your iDisk, you can select the *~/Library/Logs/MirrorAgent.log* file in Console, click Mark to stamp it with the current date and time, and then attempt another sync. As MirrorAgent (the process in

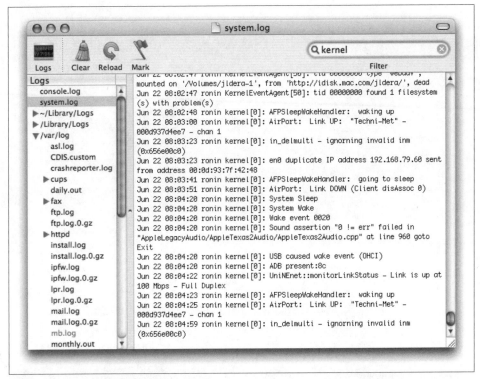

Figure 12-4. Filtering for "kernel" in the system log

charge of iDisk synchronization) contacts the .Mac servers and begins synchronizing, you'll see the log entries pop up in Console.

After the synchronization has completed (or failed, in this case), use Mark to stamp the log again. At this point, the information between your two Marks would prove invaluable to the .Mac support team. As you can see, the Mark feature makes it easy to distinguish a particular series of log entries from the rest of the logfile. It's a way for you to make a checkpoint in the logfile before attempting to troubleshoot a problem.

Activity Monitor

To view what's going on with your system right now, nothing beats the Activity Monitor, shown in Figure 12-5. For example, say that Word is taking an awfully long time to open a new file; you could pop open the Activity Monitor to see what the holdup is. Maybe it's just sucking up more memory than what's available? The Activity Monitor gives real-time measurements of resources in use on the system, the processes that are taking up the most memory or CPU cycles, and the system's disk and network activity.

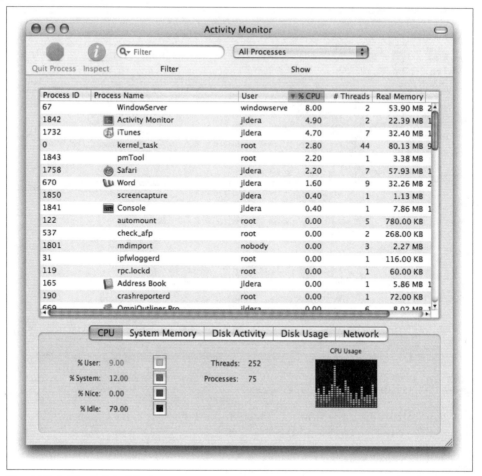

Figure 12-5. The Activity Monitor

The top part of the Activity Monitor window contains a table list of the processes on your system along with the various attributes of those processes. Unlike the Dock or the Force Quit panel (⌘ → Force Quit), the Activity Monitor lets you see every process running on your system. The processes in the main window can be filtered either with the text box or the pull-down menu in the menu bar.

The "All Processes, Hierarchically" option provides an interesting view. Using this view, you can see how all the processes on your system are owned by the *launchd* process, as discussed in Chapter 5. You can also see how GUI applications are owned by the *WindowServer* process and, if you have a Terminal window open, you can see the various processes owned by it, including the *bash* shell.

Not only can you monitor every application on the system from the Activity Monitor, but you can also terminate applications. When you select a program and then press the Quit Process button (or use View → Quit Process, or Option-⌘-Q), a dialog sheet will appear giving you the option of politely quitting the application (this works the same as going to that application and selecting File → Quit, or ⌘-Q) or using Force Quit.

Figuring Out What a Process Does

It's pretty easy to figure out what many of the processes that show up in Activity Monitor do, particularly with applications like Safari or iTunes, which show up with their icon and name. Others such as *slpd*, *rpc.lockd*, or *netinfod*, however, aren't as easy to figure out simply by looking at them. These are usually the processes that take care of various system functions. If you are curious about what a particular process is, try looking at its manpage. For example, the manpage for *netinfod* tells you that it is the NetInfo database daemon.

Interpreting process information

The impact of a process on your system can be in the amount of memory it consumes, the processor activity, or in the amount of disk I/O that it causes. Some processes can be running without using any processor time and can consume large amounts of memory. Others can consume your processor without any impact on memory usage. The process view gives quite a bit of this information to you all at once. Table 12-1 lists the various columns in the top part of the window and what they mean. The most useful columns to use are %CPU and Real Memory. If you notice your system is sluggish, click the %CPU heading to find out which process is using the most processing power.

Table 12-1. Process attributes reported in the Activity Monitor main window

Attribute	Description
PID	The numerical id of the process
Process Name	The name of the process
User	The user to whom this program belongs
%CPU	The amount of CPU time that the process is taking on your system
# Threads	The number of threads that the process is running
Real Memory	The amount of physical memory used by the process
Virtual Memory	The total amount of memory addressed by the process

To get more detail on a process, select the process in the top part of the window and then hit the Inspect button or select View → Inspect Process (⌘-I). This brings up a detailed Inspector window (see Figure 12-6) that gives you more information about the process such as the Mach ports in use by the application, the number of messages being sent via the Mach ports, the files that the application is using, and the various memory statistics, such as faults and page-ins for the process. Many of these statistics are of use only to developers, but they can give you a good idea of the kinds of resources that your applications are using.

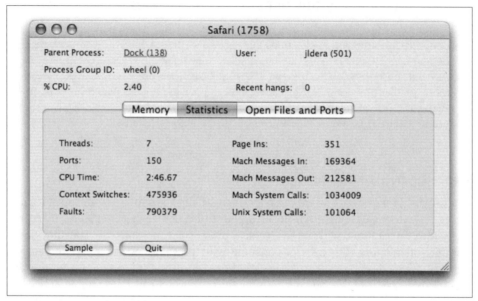

Figure 12-6. Inspecting Safari's process

Sampling an application

The Process Inspector window gives access to a powerful feature that is of interest mainly to developers who want to take a peek into the inner operation of an application. From the Inspector, hit the Sample button, and another window pops open (shown in Figure 12-7), allowing you to see the call stack of an application, the amount of time spent in each function of an application, and other related information that only a developer could want to see. You can also sample a process from the main Activity Monitor window by selecting View → Sample Process (Option-⌘-S).

Monitoring Processes from the Command Line

As good as the Console and Activity Monitor are, sometimes the best tool for a job is the Unix command line, particularly when you are logged into a machine remotely

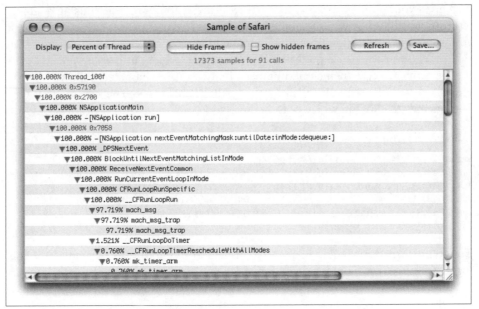

Figure 12-7. Sampling Safari's process using the Activity Monitor's Process Viewer

via *ssh* (the Secure Shell). Fortunately, there is an abundance of great Unix utilities in Mac OS X, many of which served as the inspiration for their GUI counterparts.

Working with logfiles

To work with logfiles on the command line, your primary tools of choice are *grep* and *tail*. Named after "get regular expression," *grep* allows you to quickly search through and return lines in a file that contain a pattern of text. Think of it as the command-line version of the Console's Filter box (discussed earlier), although *grep* predates the Filter box by a few decades. Example 12-4 shows the use of *grep* to perform a search for the term "kernel" in the system log (the same search as before, giving you a point of comparison).

By default, *grep* will search for the exact term you specify, including the letter case. If you're not sure whether the file will contain AirPort, Airport, or AiRpOrT, use *grep*'s *-i* option to have it ignore case.

Example 12-4. Searching the system log for the pattern "kernel"

```
$ grep kernel /var/log/system.log
Jun 16 11:15:21 ronin kernel[0]: in_delmulti - ignorning invalid inm (0x656e0000)
Jun 16 11:15:24 ronin kernel[0]: in_delmulti - ignorning invalid inm (0x656e00c0)
Jun 16 17:03:02 ronin kernel[0]: UniNEnet::monitorLinkStatus - Link is down.
Jun 16 17:03:06 ronin kernel[0]: AirPort:  Link DOWN (Client disAssoc 0)
```

grep gives you quite a bit more power than just the ability to search using a simple term. It actually gives you the ability to use *any* regular expression. For example, if you wanted to find all the lines that contained the words "kernel" and "AirPort" (in that order), you could use the *kernel.*AirPort* regex, which, in human, means "look for the term 'kernel,' then some number of any kind of characters followed by the term 'AirPort.'" Example 12-5 shows the result of this regex. You can see that *grep* outputs only the lines in which both the words "kernel" and "AirPort" appear.

Example 12-5. Using a more detailed regexp with grep

```
$ grep kernel.*AirPort /var/log/system.log
Jun 19 14:32:53 ronin kernel[0]: AirPort: Link UP: "lifeHertz" - 0011240087dd -
Jun 19 14:33:30 ronin kernel[0]: AirPort: Link DOWN (Client disAssoc 0)
Jun 19 14:33:37 ronin kernel[0]: AirPort: Link UP: "lifeHertz" - 0011240087dd -
Jun 19 14:35:36 localhost kernel[0]: AirPortPCI: Ethernet address 00:0d:93:7f:42:48
Jun 19 14:35:46 ronin kernel[0]: AirPort: Link UP: "lifeHertz" - 0011240087dd -
```

To monitor what's changing in a logfile, instead of trying to read through the whole logfile from the top, Unix gives you the *tail* command for looking at just the last part of a file. Example 12-6 shows the use of *tail* on the system log.

Regular Expressions

Regular expressions (also known as *regexes*) make up a small, highly specialized language for processing text strings. They can be a bit scary to use at first because of their extremely concise syntax. which makes them look confusing and complicated to the uninitiated. Here are a few of the most commonly used characters in regular expressions:

Character	Description
.	Matches any single character
*	Matches zero or more occurrences of the character immediately preceding it
^	Matches the beginning of a line
$	Matches the end of a line
/	Used to quote the following character, for example, to find a $ character

To learn all about regular expressions, you should pick up *Mastering Regular Expressions*, Second Edition, by Jeffrey E. F. Friedl (O'Reilly).

Example 12-6. Using tail to view the end of the system log

```
$ tail /var/log/system.log
Jun 22 08:04:59 ronin configd[33]: posting notification
com.apple.system.config.network_change
Jun 22 08:04:59 ronin lookupd[1733]: lookupd (version 365) starting - Wed Jun 22
```

Example 12-6. Using tail to view the end of the system log (continued)

```
08:04:59 2005
Jun 22 08:05:03 ronin mDNSResponder: NAT Port Mapping (LLQ event port.): timeout
Jun 22 08:05:04 ronin mDNSResponder:    -1: DNSServiceResolve("Robert's Music",
"_daap._tcp.", "local.") failed: Client id -1 invalid (-65549)
Jun 22 08:05:04 ronin mDNSResponder:    -1: DNSServiceResolve("Jason's Music",
"_daap._tcp.", "local.") failed: Client id -1 invalid (-65549)
Jun 22 08:05:04 ronin mDNSResponder:    -1: DNSServiceResolve("Jason's Music",
"_daap._tcp.", "local.") failed: Client id -1 invalid (-65549)
Jun 22 08:55:01 ronin sudo:   jldera : TTY=ttyp3 ; PWD=/Users/jldera ; USER=root ;
COMMAND=/opt/local/bin/port install gimp
Jun 22 08:58:48 ronin ntpd[96]: time reset 0.220736 s
Jun 22 10:46:22 ronin kernel[0]: IOAudioStream[0x1c61900]::clipIfNecessary( ) -
Error: attempting to clip to a position more than one buffer ahead of last clip
Jun 22 10:46:22 ronin kernel[0]: IOAudioStream[0x1c61900]::clipIfNecessary( ) -
adjusting clipped position to (8f,2cd9)
```

By default, *tail* displays the last 10 lines of the file you apply it to. To change this behavior, you can use the *-n* option to specify how many lines to go backward into the file. Example 12-7 shows this in action.

Example 12-7. Using the -n argument of tail

```
$ tail -n 2 /var/log/install.log
Jun 21 12:13:37 ronin Software Update[694]: It took 0.011676 seconds to process
the volume "Macintosh HD"
Jun 21 12:13:37 ronin Software Update[694]: It took 0.005440 seconds to perform
the Installation Check
```

If you want to see the system log as it changes (for example, if you want to monitor the firewall's log on the command line), you can use the *-f* option to *tail*, as shown in Example 12-8.

Example 12-8. Using tail -f on the system log

```
$ tail -f -n0 /var/log/system.log
Jun 22 15:27:02 ronin ipfw: 12190 Deny TCP 192.168.79.1:2446 192.168.79.60:80 in
Jun 22 15:27:05 ronin ipfw: 12190 Deny TCP 192.168.79.1:2446 192.168.79.60:80 in
Jun 22 15:27:11 ronin ipfw: 12190 Deny TCP 192.168.79.1:2446 192.168.79.60:80 in
```

To exit from *tail* when running with the *-f* option, hit Control-C.

Finding open files

When working with your Mac, you may occasionally encounter an error when trying to open a file that's already in use. In most cases, closing all of your applications or restarting your machine will free up the file, but what if you wanted to track down which program was keeping the file open? Activity Monitor gives you plenty of information about a process's memory and CPU usage, but gives little detail about the files a program is accessing.

Mac OS X's BSD layer includes the *lsof* tool for just this purpose. This complex command lists open files on the system, as well as the user, process, and full path of each of the open files. *lsof*'s output can be overwhelming at first, but a few command-line switches can help you sort through all of those open files for just the ones you're curious about. To see which files a specific application is using, use *lsof*'s *-c* switch with this syntax:

```
lsof -c processname
```

Example 12-9 shows *lsof* listing the files that are in use by iPhoto.

Example 12-9. Using lsof to view a process's open files

```
$ lsof -c iPhoto
COMMAND PID  USER   FD   TYPE   DEVICE SIZE/OFF    NODE NAME
iPhoto  474 jldera  cwd  VDIR    14,2     1122       2 /
iPhoto  474 jldera  txt  VREG    14,2  3746104  472267 /Applications/iPhoto
iPhoto  474 jldera  txt  VREG    14,2    17688    3320 /System/Library/Core
iPhoto  474 jldera  txt  VREG    14,2    81316    3321 /System/Library/Core
iPhoto  474 jldera  txt  VREG    14,2   352454    3319 /System/Library/Core
iPhoto  474 jldera  txt  VREG    14,2    19336  250427 /Library/Caches/com.
iPhoto  474 jldera  txt  VREG    14,2  5425091    5907 /System/Library/Fram
iPhoto  474 jldera  txt  VREG    14,2  2244215    4315 /System/Library/Font
iPhoto  474 jldera  txt  VREG    14,2  9826240   11314 /usr/share/icu/icudt
iPhoto  474 jldera  txt  VREG    14,2   925696 1237911 /Library/Caches/com.
iPhoto  474 jldera  txt  VREG    14,2   991360    4312 /System/Library/Font
```

Another handy *lsof* option is *-u*. When called with the *-u* option, *lsof* displays all open files by processes owned by a specified user. For example, to see all files that the user *jldera* has open, issue the following command:

```
$ lsof -u jldera
```

You can find much more information about *lsof*'s parameters and capabilities from its manpage. It's a very flexible tool, especially in light of the fact that most Unix input and output operations are handled through a filesystem call. For example, since network sockets are considered a type of file in Mac OS X, they appear open on your system. That means you can use *lsof*'s *-i* switch to see which network connections are open, much like was shown in Chapter 11 using *netstat*. Example 12-10's output is quite similar to that shown back in Example 11-7.

Example 12-10. Some output from lsof -i

```
$ lsof -i
COMMAND    PID  USER   FD   TYPE   DEVICE SIZE/OFF NODE NAME
Microsoft  124 jldera  35u  IPv4 0x0340cc6c      0t0  TCP *:3994 (LISTEN)
Microsoft  124 jldera  37u  IPv4 0x01c88ad0      0t0  UDP *:rockwell-csp2
iChatAgen  235 jldera   6u  IPv4 0x031cb6c0      0t0  UDP localhost:60971->local
iChatAgen  235 jldera   7u  IPv4 0x0264f81c      0t0  TCP 192.168.79.60:52636->2
Mail       268 jldera  25u  IPv4 0x03409ac0      0t0  TCP 192.168.79.60:59775->m
SubEthaEd  345 jldera   8u  IPv4 0x0341ac6c      0t0  TCP *:6942 (LISTEN)
SubEthaEd  345 jldera  12u  IPv6 0x01c8d820      0t0  TCP *:6942 (LISTEN)
```

Example 12-10. Some output from lsof -i (continued)

```
OmniOutli   346 jldera   16u   IPv4 0x01efddd0        0t0   UDP *:65080
OmniOutli   346 jldera   17u   IPv4 0x031cbee0        0t0   UDP *:62050
ARDAgent  27536 jldera   16u   IPv4 0x01c88a00        0t0   UDP *:net-assistant
AppleVNCS 27537 jldera   23u   IPv4 0x01e1cb08        0t0   TCP *:5900 (LISTEN)
```

When reading *lsof*'s output for network connections, there are a few items that might need some explanation. The NODE column indicates whether a given connection is using TCP or UDP. The NAME column contains most of the information you'll use to determine what is happening on your system. You'll find two types of entries in the NAME column: entries where the software has already established a connection and entries where the software is waiting for a connection.

When an application is waiting for an incoming network connection, it's said to be *listening* on a given port. In *lsof*'s output, an app that's listening for a connection will have an entry showing what network address it's listening on, as well as the port it's listening on, separated by a colon. In Example 12-10, the SubEthaEdit application is listening on all network addresses (represented by the asterisk) and on port 6942. To further distinguish the entries that are awaiting connections, *lsof* adds (LISTEN) to the end of the entry.

> You might have noticed that some of the network connections in Example 12-10 have words like net-assistant instead of numbers like 5900. This is because *lsof* has used the */etc/services* file to display the ports by name instead of by number. Those entries that still show a number do not have a corresponding entry for their port in */etc/services*. To force *lsof* to show only the port numbers, use its *-P* switch. The same can be done for IP addresses being represented by DNS entries if you supply the *-n* switch.

For those applications that have already established a connection, the entry in *lsof*'s output will be a bit different. Established connections will show the network address and port being used for the connection locally (again, separated by a colon), followed by an arrow pointing to the remote end of the connection. The remote host will also have its address and port shown.

Monitoring Users

You can see who's logged in to the machine right now using the *who* command, as shown in Example 12-11.

Example 12-11. Using the who command

```
$ who
jldera   console  Jun 11 12:28
jldera   ttyp1    Jun 11 15:04
```

Example 12-11. Using the who command (continued)

```
jldera    ttyp2    Jun 11 15:26
panic     ttyp3    Jun 11 15:27 (localhost)
```

The console entry is the GUI shell that you are logged into. The ttyp entries are created by active Terminal windows.

The *w* command outputs a different format of this information, as shown in Example 12-12.

Example 12-12. Using the w command

```
$ w
15:28  up  3:07, 4 users, load averages: 0.96 0.68 0.55
USER    TTY      FROM            LOGIN@  IDLE WHAT
jldera  console  -               12:28   2:59 -
jldera  p1       -               15:04   - w
jldera  p2       -               15:26   1 bash
panic   p3       localhost       15:27   - bash
```

As well as listing the users logged into the system, the *w* command gives the system uptime and load averages on the CPU.

You can see who has been logged into the system (as well as see when the system has been rebooted) by using the *last* command, as shown in Example 12-13.

Example 12-13. Using the last command

```
$ last
panic     ttyp3    localhost      Sat Jun 11 15:27   still logged in
jldera    ttyp2                   Sat Jun 11 15:26   still logged in
jldera    ttyp2                   Sat Jun 11 15:26 - 15:26  (00:00)
panic     console  ronin.local    Sat Jun 11 15:25   still logged in
jldera    ttyp1                   Sat Jun 11 15:04   still logged in
jldera    ttyp1                   Sat Jun 11 15:04 - 15:04  (00:00)
panic     console  ronin.local    Sat Jun 11 13:58 - 14:04  (00:06)
jldera    console  ronin.local    Sat Jun 11 12:28 - 13:58  (01:30)
reboot    ~                       Sat Jun 11 12:21
```

Working with Processes

The *ps* command (short for *process status*) outputs information about the various processes on your system. However, if you just execute *ps* by itself on the command line, you'll see only the process information about the shell process you are running. For information about all the processes that belong to you, use the *ps -x* command, as shown in Example 12-14.

Example 12-14. Listing all the processes that belong to a user

```
$ ps -x
  PID TT  STAT     TIME COMMAND
   71 ??  Ss    0:23.61 /System/Library/Frameworks/ApplicationServices.framework/
   72 ??  Ss    0:13.62 /System/Library/CoreServices/loginwindow.app/Contents/Mac
  131 ??  Ss    0:00.44 /System/Library/CoreServices/pbs
  138 ??  S     0:42.75 /System/Library/CoreServices/Dock.app/Contents/MacOS/Dock
  139 ??  S     0:40.96 /System/Library/CoreServices/SystemUIServer.app/Contents/
  145 ??  Ss    0:36.46 /System/Library/CoreServices/MirrorAgent.app/Contents/Mac
  147 ??  Ss    0:00.36 /System/Library/PrivateFrameworks/DMNotification.framewor
  157 ??  S     0:53.75 /Users/jldera/Library/PreferencePanes/Growl.prefPane/Cont
  159 ??  S     0:00.55 /Applications/iTunes.app/Contents/Resources/iTunesHelper.
  160 ??  S     0:01.02 /Applications/iCal.app/Contents/Resources/iCalAlarmSchedu
  161 ??  S     0:32.99 /Applications/iCal.app/Contents/MacOS/iCal -psn_0_1572865
```

When combined with *grep*, you'll find that *ps* is just the process you are looking for. Example 12-15 shows a command to return the process information for Safari.

Example 12-15. Looking for Safari using ps and grep

```
$ ps -x | grep Safari
1758 ??  S    23:46.64 /Applications/Safari.app/Contents/MacOS/Safari -psn_0_17301505
 422 p2  R+    0:00.00 grep Safari
```

To see all the processes running on the system, use the *-ax* option. This produces quite a bit of content, so it's best to use this option with *grep* to narrow down the results to only what you want to see. For example, if you want to see all the processes running as *root*, you would use:

> `$ ps -aux | grep root`

Another useful command for monitoring your system is *top*. In fact, it's almost certain that *top* provided the inspiration for the Activity Monitor's process view. When you execute *top*, your Terminal window fills up with a list of processes as well as the percentage of processor time and memory they are using, as shown in Figure 12-8. When you are done with *top*, use Control-C to quit, or use the Mac standard ⌘-. command.

> Invariably, *top* displays too much information in a standard Terminal window. One helpful hint is that you might want to resize the Terminal window *before* you run *top* so you can see everything it has to offer.

Killing Processes

Unfortunately, there are times when you have to manually intervene and end the execution of a process. Maybe it is a buggy program that has stopped accepting user input (like when you see the "Spinning Beach Ball of Death" when an application freezes), or maybe the program is just consuming a huge dataset and you've decided

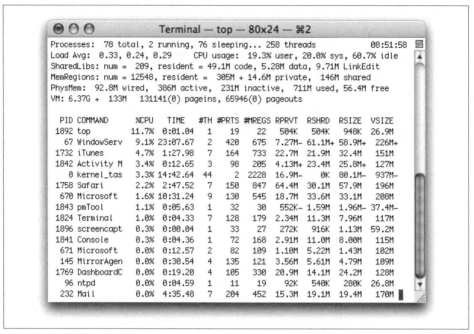

```
  ⊖ ⊖ ⊖            Terminal — top — 80x24 — ⌘2
Processes:  78 total, 2 running, 76 sleeping... 258 threads        08:51:58
Load Avg:  0.33, 0.24, 0.29     CPU usage: 19.3% user, 20.0% sys, 60.7% idle
SharedLibs: num =  209, resident = 49.1M code, 5.28M data, 9.71M LinkEdit
MemRegions: num = 12548, resident = 305M + 14.6M private,  146M shared
PhysMem:  92.8M wired,  386M active,  231M inactive,  711M used, 56.4M free
VM: 6.37G +  133M   131141(0) pageins, 65946(0) pageouts

  PID COMMAND      %CPU   TIME    #TH #PRTS #MREGS RPRVT  RSHRD  RSIZE  VSIZE
 1892 top         11.7% 0:01.04   1    19    22   504K   504K   948K   26.9M
   67 WindowServ   9.1% 23:07.67  2   420   675  7.27M- 61.1M+ 58.9M+  226M+
 1732 iTunes       4.7% 1:27.98   7   164   733  22.7M  21.9M  32.4M   151M
 1842 Activity M   3.4% 0:12.65   3    98   205  4.13M+ 23.4M  25.8M+  127M
    0 kernel_tas   3.3% 14:42.64 44     2  2228  16.9M-    0K  80.1M-  937M-
 1758 Safari       2.2% 2:47.52   7   150   847  64.4M  30.1M  57.9M   196M
  670 Microsoft    1.6% 10:31.24  9   130   545  18.7M  33.6M  33.1M   208M
 1843 pmTool       1.1% 0:05.63   1    32    30   552K- 1.59M  1.96M- 37.4M-
 1824 Terminal     1.0% 0:04.33   7   128   179  2.34M  11.3M  7.96M   117M
 1896 screencapt   0.3% 0:00.04   1    33    27   272K   916K  1.13M  59.2M
 1841 Console      0.3% 0:04.36   1    72   168  2.91M  11.0M  8.00M   115M
  671 Microsoft    0.0% 0:12.57   2    82   109  1.10M  5.22M  1.43M   102M
  145 MirrorAgen   0.0% 0:30.54   4   135   121  3.56M  5.61M  4.79M   109M
 1769 DashboardC   0.0% 0:19.20   4   105   330  20.9M  14.1M  24.2M   128M
   96 ntpd         0.0% 0:04.59   1    11    19    92K   540K   280K   26.8M
  232 Mail         0.0% 4:35.48   7   204   452  15.3M  19.1M  19.4M   170M
```

Figure 12-8. top running in a Terminal window

you can't wait for it to finish the task. Or as an administrator, you might need to log into a remote system to kill a user's errant process or even reboot a server. Whatever the reason, here are the ways in which you can stop a process's execution.

Force Quit

The easiest way to kill off an application while logged in to the system is with the Force Quit Applications window, shown in Figure 12-9. You can open this window by choosing the → Force Quit menu item or using the Option-⌘-Escape keystroke. The Force Quit window contains a list of all active GUI applications, with hung applications appearing in red (sometimes with the words "Not Responding" next to them in parentheses). Simply select the application you want to kill and click the Force Quit button.

> Only GUI applications show up in the Force Quit window. To quit non-GUI applications, you'll need to use the Activity Monitor, as described in the next section, or the Unix *kill* command.

You can also Force Quit an application using its icon on the Dock. If you Control-Option-click an application's icon in the Dock (or click and hold the mouse button down for a second or two), a contextual menu pops up. Select Force Quit from that contextual menu, and the application that's causing you problems quits instantaneously.

Figure 12-9. The Force Quit Applications window

The Difference Between Quit and Force Quit

What's the difference between Quit and Force Quit? Quit makes a request to the application to terminate. This is essentially the same action you would take if you brought the application to the foreground and triggered the ⌘-Q keyboard shortcut.

Force Quit isn't so polite. It instructs the system to immediately terminate the process—with no-holds barred. This ensures that the process goes away, but does so without giving it a chance to save files or perform any other clean up.

Using the Activity Monitor

The Activity Monitor also provides a way to force applications to quit, including those processes that aren't visible on the display. To quit an application this way, simply highlight the process and then use the Quit Process button or the View → Quit Process menu item (Option-⌘-Q). This brings up a dialog box allowing you to Quit or Force Quit an application.

Using the command line

As always, there is a command-line tool waiting for you if you can't use the GUI tools. Appropriately enough, it's named *kill*. To kill a process, you need to first get its process ID via the *ps* tool. Then you just pass that process ID to *kill*, as shown in Example 12-16.

Example 12-16. Using the kill tool

```
$ ps -x | grep Safari
 1758  ??  S     24:38.16 /Applications/Safari.app/Contents/MacOS/Safari -psn_0_173
  468  p2  R+     0:00.00 grep Safari
$ kill 1758
```

If a process is being unruly, you can tell the system to kill it without prejudice by using the *-KILL* option. Example 12-17 shows this in action.

Example 12-17. Using kill -KILL to terminate a process without prejudice

```
$ ps -x | grep iTunes
 1732  ??  S     17:44.61 /Applications/iTunes.app/Contents/MacOS/iTunes -psn_0_170
  498  p2  R+     0:00.00 grep iTunes
$ kill -KILL 1732
```

 You should exercise great care when killing errant processes, especially when using the *kill* command, as it's easy to create problems when doing so. For example, every system administrator has a story about executing *sudo kill -KILL 1* instead of *sudo kill -KILL 128*. Unfortunately, the *launchd* process has the ID of 1, which causes this command to hang the system.

kill has another commonly used switch, *-HUP*. When you kill a process using the *-HUP* option, the process reloads its configuration files and reinitializes itself. Not all processes will correctly interpret this command, however. It's mostly used for reinitializing Unix daemons like *named* or *httpd*.

Kill 'Em All

Some applications such as the Apache web server create multiple child processes when they run. When Apache is running, there are several *httpd* daemons loaded to handle requests. It can become quite tedious to find and kill all these processes individually, so it wasn't long before Unix developers implemented a *killall* command. The *killall* command works much like the *kill* command, with the exception that you pass it a process's *name* instead of its process *ID*. *killall* then kills each process, and any child processes, that match the specified name.

Remote Maintenance

In today's world of high-speed connections, Virtual Private Networks (VPNs), and ubiquitous Internet access, it's become quite common to have your computer constantly connected to a network. Sometimes, you'll find yourself needing a file from your Mac and you know it's out there on the Internet waiting for you, if you could just get to it. Luckily, Mac OS X has several different tools that allow you to securely connect to your Mac, even when you're far, far away.

The two most commonly used tools for remote maintenance on Mac OS X are Virtual Network Computing (VNC) and the Secure Shell (SSH). Much like many other Mac OS X offerings, you are given a graphical (VNC) and a command-line (SSH) tool. Given that most Mac OS X maintenance tasks can be performed in either environment, pick the one you're most comfortable with, as described in the following sections.

Virtual Network Computing

Virtual Network Computing, or VNC, is a software package designed to enable a user to remotely connect to a graphical session on another computer. Originally developed by AT&T, VNC is an open source alternative to tools like Symantec's pcAnywhere and Microsoft's Remote Desktop. The VNC package is made up of two components: a server and a client. The server runs on the machine that is hosting the graphical session, while the VNC client is run by the user to connect to the VNC server from a remote location, similar to Figure 12-10.

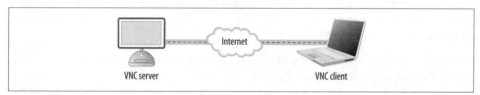

Figure 12-10. The VNC client-server relationship

One of the nice things about VNC is that it has been ported to a variety of computing platforms. What's more, each of these platforms can interact with another's clients and servers. For example, a Macintosh user could use a Mac VNC client to connect to a Windows XP machine running a Windows-based VNC server. The platform differences simply don't come into play and you can easily work with Windows, Linux, and other Mac OS X machines using a single VNC client on your Mac.

Apple has taken the VNC suite and reworked it for integration with Mac OS X. Unfortunately, it takes the form of another product known as Apple Remote Desktop (ARD; see *http://www.apple.com/remotedesktop*). While ARD is a very powerful tool for administering multiple Macs, it's a bit expensive ($299) for just one Mac. However, ARD is really made up of two components. One component—the administration software—is what Apple charges you for. The other—the client portion of the software—is a part of every Mac OS X installation. Bundled with that ARD client software is Apple's enhanced VNC server, ready for your use.

Third-Party VNC Servers

Given VNC's open source nature, it comes as no surprise that several different VNC solutions are available on the Internet. The Mac is no exception, with a variety of VNC servers and clients being developed for Mac OS X. Though Apple's VNC solution is more than sufficient for most purposes, you might want to try some of the other VNC packages out there.

A quick search on VersionTracker (*http://www.versiontracker.com*) or MacUpdate (*www.macupdate.com*) reveals many different choices, including the most popular non-Apple VNC server for the Mac, Share My Desktop (*http://www.bombich.com/software/smd.html*), by Mike Bombich (creator of lots of useful Mac tools, including Carbon Copy Cloner).

Enabling the VNC server

Apple has placed the configuration settings for Apple Remote Desktop in the Sharing panel of System Preferences. To enable ARD, launch System Preferences and then go to Sharing → Services and turn on Apple Remote Desktop. If this is the first time ARD has been enabled on the system, you are presented with the Access Privileges sheet, shown in Figure 12-11.

Most of the options on the Access Privileges sheet are irrelevant unless you are specifically using the Apple Remote Desktop management software. The only option you'll need to configure is listed as "VNC viewers may control screen with password." Enable it and enter a memorable password in the corresponding text field. Once your changes are complete, click OK to put them into effect.

Connecting to VNC

Now that your Mac is listening for VNC connections, you'll need a VNC client to access it. As mentioned earlier, there are a variety of VNC clients available for just about every platform out there. A popular one for Mac OS X is Chicken of the VNC (*http://sourceforge.net/projects/cotvnc/*). To connect using Chicken of the VNC, just enter your Mac's IP address in the Host field and then enter the password you set in the ARD Access Privileges sheet, as shown in Figure 12-12. Once you've connected via VNC, you can control your Mac the same as if you were sitting at it.

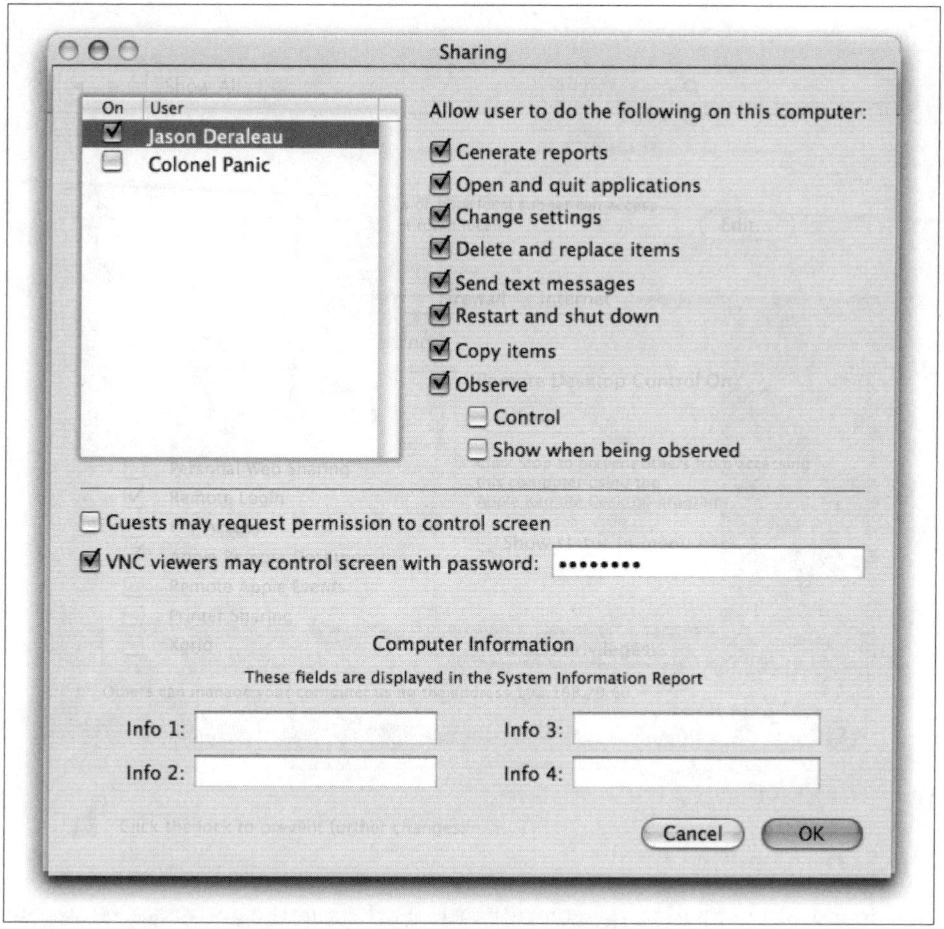

![Sharing dialog window. Title bar: Sharing. Left list with "On / User" columns: Jason Deraleau (checked, selected), Colonel Panic (unchecked). Right side: "Allow user to do the following on this computer:" with checked items: Generate reports, Open and quit applications, Change settings, Delete and replace items, Send text messages, Restart and shut down, Copy items, Observe; unchecked sub-items: Control, Show when being observed. Below: unchecked "Guests may request permission to control screen"; checked "VNC viewers may control screen with password:" with password field dots. Computer Information section with "These fields are displayed in the System Information Report" and Info 1-4 text fields. Cancel and OK buttons.]

Figure 12-11. The Apple Remote Desktop Access Privileges sheet

Of course, the remote system needs to be turned on, connected to the Internet, and you'll need to know its IP address ahead of time, but that should go without saying. Just keep that in mind for times when you plan to travel. Some things you'll need to do to the server system include:

- Leave the system on and set Energy Saver preferences to Never (System Preferences → Energy Saver → Sleep) so the system doesn't put your computer to sleep when it is inactive.

- Set the Energy Saver preferences so the display goes to sleep after an amount of time that sounds reasonable to you.

- Jot down the IP Address from the TCP/IP tab of the Network preferences panel.

- Pack your bags and hit the road.

With your Mac at home set up so it doesn't sleep, you'll be able to connect to your machine and do whatever it is you need to do, even if the display is asleep.

Figure 12-12. Establishing a VNC connection

The Secure Shell

Also found in the Sharing preference panel, the Remote Login service is used to enable Mac OS X's Secure Shell server (*sshd*). SSH is a protocol for using key-based encryption to allow secure communication between machines. To connect to a machine running *sshd*, simply use the following command:

    ssh machinename

For example, to connect to a machine named *Hobbes.local*, you would use the following:

    $ ssh Hobbes.local

The *ssh* program uses the username with which you are logged into the Terminal to connect to the server. If you want to use a different username, prepend the machine name with *username*. For example:

    $ ssh panic@Hobbes.local

And thanks to Bonjour, you can also connect to *ssh* servers on your local network easily by selecting File → Connect to Server (Shift-⌘-K) in the Terminal. This brings up a dialog from which you can see the local machines you can connect to, as shown in Figure 12-13.

Figure 12-13. The Terminal's Connect to Server dialog

Upon establishing a connection to your Mac's Remote Login service, you'll be presented with a shell session much like the one you'd find when using Terminal. Using the command line and SSH, you can easily work with your Mac remotely without the overhead of a graphical session. It might not be as pretty as the VNC connection, but an SSH session offers all of the power and flexibility of the command line.

For more information about SSH, see *SSH, The Secure Shell: The Definitive Guide*, by Daniel J. Barrett, et al. (O'Reilly).

Further Explorations

To get more information about the tools in this chapter, check out the following manpages:

- *grep*
- *kill*
- *killall*
- *last*
- *lsof*
- *ps*
- *ssh*
- *system_profiler*
- *tail*
- *top*
- *w*
- *who*

## CHAPTER 13

Automating Tasks

Mac OS X Tiger has an unprecedented number of tools for automating tasks on your machine. From the ease of Automator to the intricacies of shell scripting, this chapter discusses using Tiger's tools to take the tedium out of using your Mac. It also covers using iCal and *cron* to schedule tasks to be executed automatically, never to be accidentally forgotten again.

The Importance of Time

Without having the time accurately set on your machine, it's pretty hard to schedule tasks. Using the Date & Time preference panel (System Preferences → Date & Time), you can set the time and date on your computer, as shown in Figure 13-1. However, if you're using a broadband connection or otherwise spend any amount of time connected to the Internet, you can have your computer set the date and time using a network time server.

A network time server is nothing more than a machine that has an accurate clock and that understands the Network Time Protocol (NTP). NTP is designed to keep large numbers of machines synchronized with an accurate clock. Apple ships Mac OS X with the addresses of their own NTP servers. Apple has servers for the Americas, Asia, and Europe.

In some network environments, you might find an NTP server locally. If you're using Mac OS X Server on your network, it includes an NTP server. Also, many Unix administrators have set up NTP servers for their local network. Finally, there are many publicly accessible NTP servers on the Internet; you can find a list of them at *http://ntp.isc.org/bin/view/Servers/WebHome*.

To take advantage of an NTP server, enable the "Set date & time automatically" checkbox in the Date & Time preferences and either select one of Apple's servers or

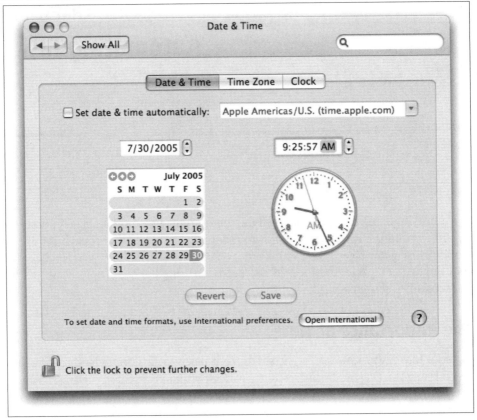

Figure 13-1. The Date & Time preference panel

enter the address information for another NTP server. When you set up a time server, the system does the following:

- Sets the time server that is being used in */etc/ntp.conf*.

- Makes sure that the *ntpd* process is running. This process checks the time server periodically to make sure your clock is set correctly.

- Sets the TIMESYNC line in */etc/hostconfig* to -YES-, ensuring that *ntpd* starts when the system reboots.

Using iCal to Schedule Tasks

iCal is the personal calendaring application that comes with Mac OS X. iCal features multiple calendars that can be published to other computers and synchronized with .Mac. To schedule something in iCal, you create an *event*, which is an entry on the calendar that is at a specific time with a specific duration. Events can be one-time occurrences, or they can repeat.

Each event can have an alarm that can display a notice on your computer screen, open a file, or even launch an application at a certain time prior to the event so that it can be ready for you. In addition, alarms can go off even if iCal is not running. iCal uses the iCal Helper application (stored in */Applications/iCal.app/Contents/Resources*) to keep track of events and fire them off on schedule whether or not iCal itself is running.

You can use iCal's alarms along with AppleScript to execute just about any kind of task you'd like. To do so requires only three simple steps:

1. Create an AppleScript application that performs the functionality you want and save it somewhere.

> One logical place to store your scripts is in *~/Library/Scripts*. Anything that you store here will show up in the Script menu, once you've enabled it. To enable the Script menu, open up the AppleScript Utility (*/Applications/AppleScript*) and enable the "Show Script Menu in menu bar" option. If you also enable "Show Library Scripts," the Script menu will be populated with the scripts found in */Library/Scripts* as well as those you place in *~/Library/Scripts*.

2. Create a one-time or a repeating event in iCal (see Figure 13-2).

3. Set the alarm properties on that event to open your AppleScript application.

> For some sample scripts to run using iCal, take a look at the "AppleScript" and "Automator" sections found later in this chapter.

cron

The primary tool for scheduling tasks on the command line is the venerable *cron*. This tool is started automatically by *launchd* (as required) and runs continuously in the background. When loaded, *cron* wakes up every minute to consult a set of tables to see if there is anything to be executed at that time. If so, it takes care of executing it. These tables, known as *crontab* files, are located in two places on the filesystem:

/etc/crontab
> The *crontab* file for the system at large. Each entry in this table represents a command that will be run by the *root* user and the time that it will be run. Anybody can read this file, but only the *root* user can edit it. Starting in Tiger, most of the tasks that were once launched by *cron* have made their way to *launchd*. Thus, *crontab* is somewhat deprecated from Apple's standpoint, but it's still there if you want it.

Figure 13-2. Setting a repeating event in iCal to execute a script

/var/cron/tabs/

> This directory contains the user *crontab* files for each user on the system who is using *cron*. These files are hidden and are visible only to the *root* user, so that other users on the system can't look at each other's *crontab* files.

The *launchd* daemon loads *cron* only if a *crontab* is set up on the system. In a default Tiger install, this means *cron* is not running at all. However, once you install a *crontab* for your user or make changes to the system *crontab*, *launchd* notices the change and launches *cron*.

What About at, batch, atq, and atrm?

If you're coming to Mac OS X from another Unix system, you may be familiar with using the *at*, *batch*, *atq*, or *atrm* commands for scheduling tasks. These commands exist in Mac OS X, but they have been disabled by Apple due to power management concerns. If you really need these commands, you must enable the *atrun* by tweaking its *launchd* configuration in */System/Library/LaunchDaemons/com.apple.atrun.plist*.

The System crontab File

The *crontab* file format is similar to that of many other Unix utilities. Any line beginning with the hash character (#) is a comment. Each entry in a *crontab* file consists of five numbers defining the time pattern at which a particular task is to run. The end of the line contains the command to run. In the case of the system *crontab*, the command also contains the name of the user under which to run the command. Figure 13-3 describes the settings for each of these fields. In addition to numbers, each field can contain an asterisk (*) character, which means match every possibility for that field.

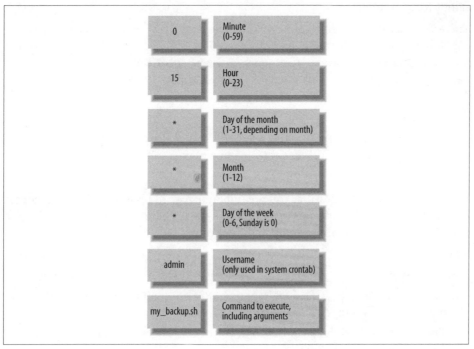

Figure 13-3. The crontab file format

For each of the fields, you can also specify a list or range of numbers. For example, if you wanted to run a command every 15 minutes, you could use the following line:

```
0,15,30,60 * * * * command
```

Or, if you wanted a command to only run at 5:00 p.m. on weekdays, you could use the following:

```
0 5 * * 1-5 command
```

The User crontab

To set up tasks that will get executed, you have to edit your own personal *crontab*. You can take a look at what you already have in your *crontab* file by using the *crontab* command:

```
$ crontab -l
crontab: no crontab for jldera
```

This output means nothing has been scheduled yet. By default, a user account won't have a *crontab* when it is first set up.

Editing a user crontab

There are two ways to edit your *crontab*. The first involves using whatever editor you've set up on the command line (for example, *vi*, Emacs, and *nano*). The second involves using any editor you want (such as TextEdit or BBEdit) and loading a text file as your *crontab*. To edit your file on the command line, use the following command:

```
$ crontab -e
```

For your first *crontab* entry, let's add a line that will make your computer say "hello" every minute. To do this, add the following line to your *crontab* file:

```
* * * * * osascript -e 'say "hello"'
```

If you get stuck in an editor that you are unfamiliar with, remember that you can get out of *vi* by typing :q! and out of Emacs by typing Control-X then Control-C. See Chapter 4 for more info about command-line editors.

Now, every minute of every day that your machine is on, it will say "hello" to you, which could become annoying indeed. There are a couple things going on here:

1. The osascript -e 'say "hello"' command is being issued by your system every minute, based on the five preceding asterisks.

2. The command uses the default system voice set in the Speech preference panel to speak the word "hello" on cue.

But now that you've got a *crontab* file installed, you can use *crontab* to list the file:

```
$ crontab -l
* * * * * osascript -e 'say "hello"'
```

The other way to create a *crontab* file is to use an editor like TextEdit or BBEdit. To get the current *crontab* out in a form that you can open with any editor, save the file on your hard drive, and then execute the *crontab* command as follows:

```
$ crontab mycrontabfile
```

This also gives a way to quickly reset the *crontab* file for a user. By passing the */dev/ null* file into *crontab*, the user's *crontab* will be set to an empty file.

Using the *crontab* command to specify a file is also a good way to accidentally lose any *cron* settings that you have in place. Be sure to check your *crontab* before loading in a new *crontab* file.

To retrieve your *crontab* for editing, you can direct the output using the following command:

```
$ crontab -l > mycrontabfile
```

Finally, if you want to get rid of your *crontab* altogether, enter the command:

```
$ crontab -r
```

Additional configuration settings

The *cron* command on Mac OS X has been enhanced compared to those found on some other Unix variants. For example, you can use the following more readable entries in the time field:

- Days of the week can be indicated by their abbreviated names: sun, mon, tue, wed, thu, fri, or sat.
- Months can be indicated by their abbreviated names: jan, feb, mar, apr, may, jun, jul, aug, sep, oct, nov, or dec.
- You can indicate step values by using a fraction notation such as 8-17/2 which, if it were in the hours field, would mean "every two hours between the hours of 8 a.m. and 5 p.m."

Some special strings can be used in *crontab* files. Table 13-1 has a list of these strings. Except for the last one, all these strings replace the time fields. The last, @AppleNotOnBattery, can be used in front of a command to prevent it from running when your laptop is disconnected from AC power. This ensures that you don't run disk-intensive tasks when you need your battery the most. For example, if you write a script that copies all your files from your *~/Documents* folder to some safe storage location that you want to run only when your PowerBook is plugged in, you would use the following *crontab* entry:

```
0 * * * * @AppleNotOnBattery ~/bin/copyfiles
```

Table 13-1. Special strings that can be used in a crontab

String	Description	Equivalent to
@reboot	Runs when the system reboots	
@yearly	Runs at midnight of January 1	0 0 1 1 *
@monthly	Runs at midnight on the first of the month	0 0 1 * *
@weekly	Runs at midnight each Sunday	0 0 * * 0
@daily	Runs every day at midnight	0 0 * * *
@hourly	Runs every hour at the top of the hour	0 * * * *
@AppleNotOnBattery	Prevents command from running if the system is on battery	

Sleep and cron

The *cron* system won't execute while your system is asleep. This is because the CPU is powered down and there's just enough happening in your machine to keep the contents of memory ready when you want to wake the system up.

Sometimes this isn't a big deal. For example, if you use a *crontab* line to remind you to stretch every hour, then you won't mind it not running. However, for other tasks that you would like to have run, it can create a bit of a problem. The best piece of advice is to time tasks that need to be run when your system is less likely to be in sleep mode.

Automator

One of the most touted new features in Mac OS X Tiger is Automator (*/Applications*). Automator brings the power of scripting to the masses. It's an easy way to automate repetitive tasks that you'd normally have to perform by hand. Using drag-and-drop simplicity, you add various *actions* to a *workflow*, crafting the order they are processed to suit the task at hand.

Automator ships with a library full of actions. Actions are the individual steps that are processed in a workflow. Each application is responsible for providing actions that perform a function within that app. For example, Apple's Mail includes about a dozen actions that do everything from checking for new mail to sending birthday cards. Not all applications have Automator actions yet, but there are more available each day. To see some of the latest actions, visit Apple's Automator Actions site: *http://www.apple.com/downloads/macosx/automator/*.

Creating Workflows

Now that you're a bit more familiar with Automator actions, let's take a look at workflows. Workflows are simply an ordered set of actions. To create a new workflow, select File → New. Automator opens a blank workflow, as shown in Figure 13-4.

The Automator window is broken up into four main panels. The Library panel lists all of the applications with available actions, as well as some sample workflows and any workflows you might have saved. Selecting an application from the list will filter that app's actions in the Action panel.

The Action panel contains the actions available for that particular app, organized by relevancy. As you create workflows, different actions will float to the top as their relevancy increases. Selecting an action causes the description pane to display information about the selected action, such as what it does, what it expects for input, and what kind of output it creates.

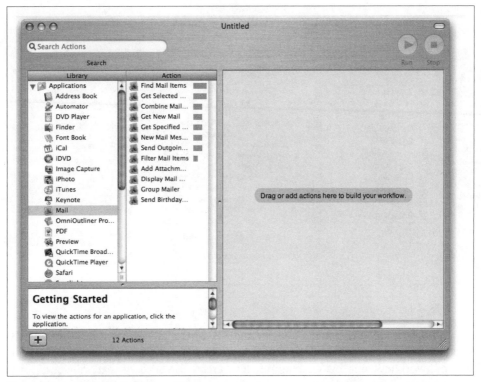

Figure 13-4. A new Automator workflow

The type of input and output are important, because you should only tie actions together if they use compatible data types. For example, the Finder's "Get Selected Finder Items" action outputs the Files/Folders data type. This data type would work quite well if you connected it to Mail's "Add Attachments to Front Message" action. However, connecting an action such as Address Book's "Get Contact Information" would cause problems. The workflow may not work properly because the actions aren't compatible.

Figure 13-5 shows two compatible options (note the input/output markers are connected and are of the type Files/Folders). Figure 13-6 shows two incompatible Automator actions.

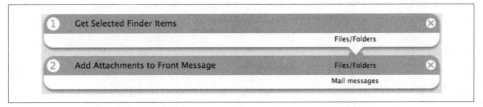

Figure 13-5. Compatible Automator actions

Figure 13-6. Incompatible Automator actions

Finally, the empty gray panel along the right is where you build your workflow. To build a workflow, start by dragging an action from the Action panel and dropping it into the workflow area. As an example, let's create a workflow that will send birthday greetings to our friends.

> For this workflow to function, you must have entered your contacts' birthdays in Address Book.

First, select Address Book from the Library panel. Next, drag the action named "Find People with Birthdays" out of the Action panel and drop it in the workflow area. Then, select Mail from the Library panel and track down the "Send Birthday Greetings" action. Drag the action out and drop it below the "Find People with Birthdays" action in the workflow area.

At this point, you have the bare necessities for an Automator workflow. You might want to tweak it a bit and make it more personal. Most actions allow you to configure certain aspects of their operation. In the case of the "Find People with Birthdays" action, you can select whether you want to search for anyone whose birthday is Today, Tomorrow, This Month, etc. For the "Send Birthday Greetings" action, you can customize the greeting text and the birthday image that's sent with the message.

Once you've played with the settings a bit and settled on a message, the resulting workflow looks something like Figure 13-7.

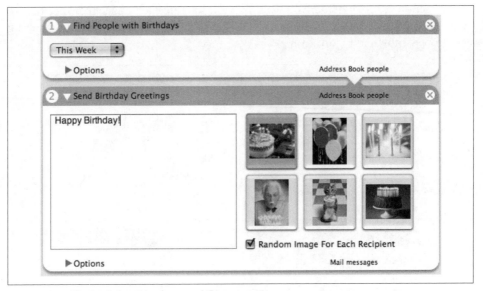

Figure 13-7. The Birthday Greetings workflow

To execute your new workflow, click the Run button. Automator will process each step of the workflow and, if anyone in your Address Book has a birthday coming up, send out some mail messages. Assuming you don't have any problems and you're happy with the flow of the workflow, you can save the workflow for later use. For extra convenience, you can create a repeating iCal event that runs your Birthday Greetings workflow every week to send out the messages for you. See the section "Using iCal to Schedule Tasks. earlier in this chapter, for more information.

Running Workflows

There are many different ways to run your workflows. You can have them run by iCal on a scheduled basis. You can add them to your Script menu by saving them in *~/Library/Scripts*. Workflows can be saved as double-clickable applications. You can even attach them to folders and use them as *folder actions*.

The folder actions option is particularly powerful. Using folder actions, you tie an Automator workflow to a particular folder. Any files that are placed in that folder are then processed by your workflow. Let's take a look at setting up a folder action workflow. This particular workflow can be used to make thumbnails of image files that are copied to the folder.

First, create a new workflow by selecting File → New. The first action you want to use is the Finder's "Rename Finder Items" action. Configure the action so that it adds the text *_thumb* to the end of each file's name. Next, add Preview's "Scale

Image" action. Select whether you want Preview to scale each image to a specific size or based on a percentage, as well as the desired size or percentage. The resulting workflow is shown in Figure 13-8.

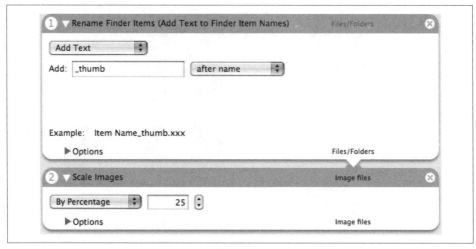

Figure 13-8. The Thumbnailer workflow

Here comes the tricky part. Save the workflow by selecting File → Save as Plug-In. Give the workflow a name, like "Thumbnailer," and then select Folder Actions from the "Plug-in For" pop-up. Next, use the "Attached to Folder" pop-up to choose the folder you want to use for processing the thumbnails (e.g., create a new folder named *Thumbnailer* in the *Pictures* folder of your Home directory and attach the action to that). Finally, click Save to put everything into place.

Now when you drag an image file into your new *Thumbnailer* folder, the file will be renamed and resized to your specified dimensions. Just remember to copy the file to the folder instead of moving it. Otherwise, you'll lose the original full-scale file.

PDF Services

Another way to use Automator workflows is with Mac OS X's PDF Services. PDF Services are a convenient way of using Adobe's Portable Document Format (PDF) to create print-ready documents from within any application. The PDF menu found on Mac OS X's print dialog gives easy access to a variety of workflows for creating PDFs. You can find out more about PDF Services—and printing in general—in Chapter 10.

As discussed in Chapter 10, Apple has included several Automator workflows for use with PDF Services. You can take a look at these workflows yourself by looking in the */Library/PDF Services* folder. Figure 13-9 is of one of Apple's included workflows: Compress PDF.

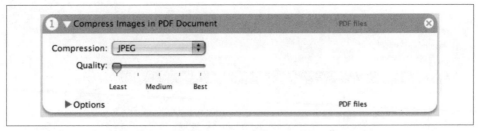

Figure 13-9. The Compress PDF workflow

As you can see, most of the PDF-oriented workflows included with Mac OS X are rather simple. The only thing that makes a PDF Service workflow different from any other is that it's geared toward PDFs and is kept in the *PDF Services* folder (either */Library/PDF Services* or *~/Library/PDF Services*). When you save a PDF workflow, use the Save as Plug-In option and select Print Workflow as the plug-in type. Figure 13-10 and Figure 13-11 show PDF workflows that you can create and use yourself.

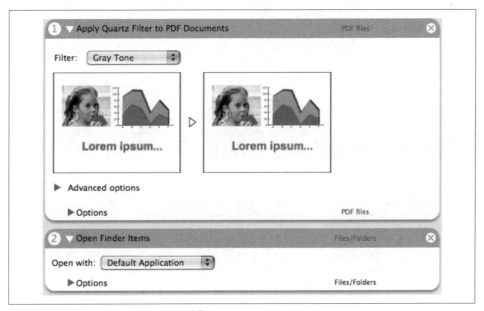

Figure 13-10. The Grayscale PDF workflow

Scripting

In addition to Automator, Mac OS X has several scripting languages to help you automate tasks on your machine. At first glance, creating your own scripts may seem like a daunting task. The goal of this section is to take some of that dread away by introducing you to scripting in a friendly manner. There are some concepts that can

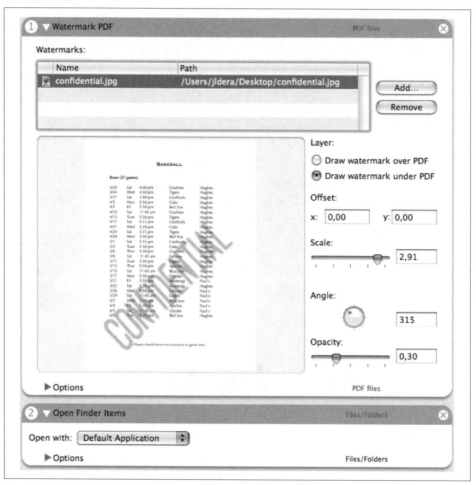

Figure 13-11. *The Confidential Watermark workflow*

be a bit hard to grasp at first, especially if you've never programmed before. But with a bit of luck and some know-how gained from the following sections, you'll be writing your own scripts in no time.

Scripting Languages

Picking a scripting language can be one of the most difficult parts of scripting, especially when you have as many choices as those supplied by Mac OS X. Sometimes, a certain language just works better for a job. For example, when you're working with text, Perl will prove much more versatile than AppleScript. It's the nature of the language—its included features and functions—that helps you determine if it's up to the task.

Mac OS X comes with quite a few different scripting languages: Perl, Python, Ruby, AppleScript, C shells, Bourne shells...the list goes on. Some of these languages are much more sophisticated than others. Entire books have been dedicated to each, but in this chapter, we're just going to dabble with two: AppleScript and Bourne shell (that is, *bash*) scripting. These two languages are easier to grasp and flexible enough to accomplish a wide array of tasks.

Essential Programming Concepts

When you're writing a program—and a script is really a small program—there are certain concepts that you'll frequently encounter. The terminology might seem a little strange at first, but once you understand what they do and when to use them, these concepts are applicable across languages.

Variables
> Variables are perhaps the most basic idea you'll need to grasp. A variable is simply a placeholder for a value. The value might be hardcoded into the script when you write it, determined at runtime by some sort of process or equation, or by getting input from the user. Variables come in many different shapes and sizes, usually determined by the language you're using to write the script.

Operators and functions
> The operators found in scripting are similar to those found in mathematics. Addition, subtraction, multiplication, and division are all operators that you're probably quite familiar with. Operators are a form of function. Functions are *subroutines*—small blocks of code written for a specific purpose—that return some sort of value after being processed.

Conditionals
> A conditional is a comparative statement in code. The statement might compare two variables to each other, a variable against a specific value, whether a variable contains a value, etc. Conditionals usually take the form of if *condition* then *action*. Conditionals may also employ the else keyword, which will be processed if the conditional is not true. Another type of conditional is a case statement, where a condition is compared to several possible values with different actions.

Loops
> Loops are blocks of code that are processed repetitively. Loops come in two main forms: incremental and conditional. In an incremental loop, the loop is processed a predetermined number of times. For example, a loop might use a counter that goes from zero to four, resulting in the loop code being processed five times. In a conditional loop, the loop code is processed until the desired condition is met.

Now that you're a little more familiar with the terminology, the following sections discuss how to put these concepts to practical use.

Shell Scripting

Chapter 4 discussed some of the basics behind shell scripts, but shell scripts can actually be quite complicated. The *bash* scripting language is pretty flexible, and there are a variety of command-line tools to help you accomplish just about any task. The major difference between scripting for the command line and scripting in an environment like AppleScript is that shell scripts are really just a bunch of commands saved in a file. The same commands that you enter at the command line can be strung together and saved for later use as a shell script.

 The nice part about that is that it's easy to extend the commands available to your shell scripts by installing a few new tools. Take a look at Fink and DarwinPorts for some help; they're discussed in Chapter 2.

A simple script

To make a shell script, launch a basic text editor, such as *nano*, and kick things off with a *shebang*. "Shebang" is Unix parlance for a hash symbol (or number sign), followed by a bang (or exclamation point): #!. A shebang tells the shell which *interpreter* should be loaded to process the script. An interpreter is a program capable of processing the code found in the script. Conveniently, the interpreter for *bash* shell scripts is *bash*. So, the first line of any *bash* script you write should start with a shebang, followed by the path to the *bash* executable:

```
#!/bin/bash
```

In programming circles, it's customary to have one's first program simply print "Hello, World!" to the screen. On the Unix command-line, there's a utility called *echo* that prints whatever arguments you supply it out to the screen. So, for our Hello World example, we need only two lines of code:

```
#!/bin/bash
echo 'Hello, World!'
```

Once you've typed these two lines of code into *nano*, press Control-O to save the file. Give it a name like *HelloWorld.sh* (The *.sh* extension will help you remember it's a shell script). After you've saved the file, press Control-X to exit *nano* and return to the command line.

You've just created a shell script. It might not be a particularly complicated shell script, but all of your future shell scripts will be created in a similar fashion. However, your shell script isn't quite ready to go yet. You must first set its execute bit, to indicate to the shell that the script is a valid command to be used on the command line. To set the execute bit on your script, use the *chmod* command:

```
$ chmod +x HelloWorld.sh
```

Commenting and the Hash

Strangely, the first line of a shell script is only processed by the shell. To the script interpreter, a line starting with a # represents a comment. Everything after the hash symbol is ignored. It's a good idea to comment your scripts. As you grow more familiar with scripting, you'll find that the code is often self-explanatory. However, the logic behind your script may not be as obvious as its syntax. Some well-placed comments can help you remember what a block of code does when you need to revisit a script after a lengthy hiatus.

After its execute bit has been set, the script can be called like any other command. Because the script has been saved to your Home directory and not a directory that is in your shell's PATH, you must specify the absolute path to the script to run it, as shown in Example 13-1.

Example 13-1. Running the HelloWorld.sh script

```
$ ./HelloWorld.sh
Hello, World!
```

Tying in variables

Chapter 4 also discussed the concept of *environment variables*. If you recall, an environment variable is a value stored in memory that is used to set certain runtime parameters for shell commands. The variables found in scripts are used for similar purposes, with the exception that they only exist while the script is running and within the context of that script. Even though a script can view and manipulate environment variables, other scripts running in the same environment cannot see other scripts' variables. This is what is known as the *scope* of a variable.

To create a variable for your script, you must use an assignment statement. An assignment statement starts with the name of the variable you'd like to instantiate, an equals sign to indicate the assignment, and then the value you'd like to assign. For example, to assign the value "Hello, World!" to a variable named MESSAGE, use this statement:

```
MESSAGE="Hello, World!"
```

The resulting variable, $MESSAGE, can be substituted for the original message in the *HelloWorld.sh* example. Remember that to use a variable, you must preface its name with a dollar sign. So, the *HelloWorld.sh* script rewritten to use a variable is:

```
#!/bin/bash
MESSAGE='Hello, World!'
echo $MESSAGE
```

A nice thing about variables is that they can be assigned a value that is the result of a command (or series of commands). Using *command substitution*, you can call one command and have its results placed in a variable (or even used as a parameter for another command). Command substitution is processed using one of two code conventions. You can use either $(*command*) or `command` (note that a back tick is used, not a single quote). For example, to have the results of calling the *whoami* command placed in the variable ME, use the statement:

```
ME=$(whoami)
```

The command is processed when the interpreter encounters your assignment statement, and the command results are placed in your variable. This variable can then be used just like any other. Expanding upon our *HelloWorld.sh* example:

```
#!/bin/bash
ME=$(whoami)
MESSAGE="Hello, $ME!"
echo $MESSAGE
```

The value from *whoami* can also be entered directly into the MESSAGE variable without assigning it to the ME variable:

```
MESSAGE="Hello, $(whoami)!"
```

Or, you can skip the variables altogether:

```
echo "Hello, $(whoami)!"
```

Single Quotes Versus Double Quotes

When you want to group several different words together as a single value, you should surround the words with quotation marks. Depending on if you use single quotes or double quotes, the shell will interpret the grouping differently. In the case of single quotes, the content is used in its literal form. For double quotes, the shell interacts with the content.

For example, *echo "$PATH"* (double quotes) will return the contents of your PATH environment variable. Entering the command *echo '$PATH'* (single quotes) simply prints $PATH to the screen without interpreting the PATH variable.

Conditionals in bash

Now that you know how to assign a value to a variable, you're probably wondering about ways to access that value. In most cases, you'll use a variable either in some form of output (like the *echo* statements discussed in the previous section) or in a conditional statement. As mentioned in the "Essential Programming Concepts" section, conditionals are used to perform an action based on the value of a condition.

When writing shell scripts, the most common type of conditional you'll use is the if statement. Using if statements, you can determine whether your desired condition evaluates to true. If it does, then the shell will follow the code until an else or fi statement is encountered. The else statement is used to define alternate actions that should be performed if your desired condition evaluates to false. Finally, the fi statement marks the end of the conditional logic. Example 13-2 shows a simple if statement.

Example 13-2. A block of conditional code

```
if [ "$UID" == "0" ]; then
  # It's true, do something as root
  echo "You're root! "
else
  # It's false, the user is not root
  echo "Sorry, you're not root. "
fi
```

The other major conditional statement available in *bash* is the case statement. A case statement allows you to test a condition for several possible values. Each value has its own block of logic to be processed if the condition equals that value. A case statement starts out by calling case and supplying your condition, followed by the keyword in. Each possible outcome is then listed, with the potential value, the block of code to be processed, and two semicolons to mark the end of that value's code. Finally, the esac keyword marks the end of all of the case conditional logic.

Example 13-3 shows a case statement with three possible outcomes.

Example 13-3. A case statement with three potential outcomes

```
case "$UID" in
        0)      # The UID is 0, do something as root
                echo "You're root!"
                ;;
        501)    # The UID is 501; the first user
                echo "You're the first user on this machine."
                ;;
        *)      # Some other user
                echo "You're not root nor the first user."
                ;;
esac
```

You might have noticed that the last potential value is an asterisk (*). In a case statement, the asterisk branch of code is used if the condition does not trigger one of the other code branches. The case statement is an excellent alternative to using nested blocks of if and else statements.

When creating a conditional, *bash* offers many different types of tests to perform. For example, you can check whether the value stored in a variable is equal to another value. You can check whether a file or directory exists. You can determine if you have read access to a file. These tests enable you to create scripts that react to a variety of different scenarios. Table 13-2 shows some of the more useful tests. To see what else is available, take a look at the manpage for *test*.

Table 13-2. Some useful bash tests

Test	Purpose
[-a *FILE*]	True if *FILE* exists
[-d *FILE*]	True if *FILE* is a directory
[-r *FILE*]	True if *FILE* is readable
[-w *FILE*]	True if *FILE* is writable
[-x *FILE*]	True if *FILE* is executable
[-s *FILE*]	True if *FILE* has a file size greater than zero
[*STRING1* == *STRING2*]	True if *STRING1* and *STRING2* are equal
[*STRING1* != *STRING2*]	True if *STRING1* does not match *STRING2*

Send in the loops

Loops are where the real power of scripting comes into play. Being able to perform a series of commands on a series of files with just a few keystrokes can turn a tedious project into an easy job. Loops (and scripting in general) shift the burden of monotonous tasks onto the computer. As mentioned earlier, there are two types of programming loops. For incremental loops, *bash* uses the for command. For conditional looping, there are two options: while and until.

The *bash* shell handles for loops a bit differently from most other programming languages. It's still used for iterating through a block of code a certain number of times. The main difference, however, is that *bash*'s for is designed to step through a series of values within a string. Chapter 4 provided an example of such a loop, which is repeated here in Example 13-4.

Example 13-4. A simple for loop

```
for i in $(ls ~/Desktop/*.txt); do
    say -f $i
done
```

The earlier discussion of command substitution mentioned that the resulting value can be used as an argument for another command. That's exactly what's happening in Example 13-4. The *ls* command is run first, and its results are then supplied to the for loop. Example 13-5 applies the command substitution and shows what the resulting values might look like.

Example 13-5. The command substitution expanded

```
for i in "/Users/jldera/Desktop/One.txt /Users/jldera/Desktop/Two.txt"; do
    say -f $i
done
```

The for loop then takes the first value from the list and inserts it into the variable i. The shell considers a blank space to be the demarcation between entries, so in the first iteration of the loop, i would have a value of /Users/jldera/Desktop/One.txt. Subsequent iterations of the loop step through the list of values until the entire list has been processed.

The other two loop commands, while and until, are based around the use of conditionals. They have a similar syntax, and both operate under the same basic principle. A conditional statement is checked and the loop either processes again or it doesn't. Depending on which command you're using, the when and why of stopping is handled differently. For the while command, the code inside the loop is processed as long as the condition holds true. Example 13-6 shows a while loop.

Example 13-6. T.G.I.F. while loop

```
while [ $(date +%a) == "Fri" ]; do
    # As long as it's Friday...
    osascript -e 'say "T G I F"'
    sleep 360
done
```

An until loop is the reverse. The loop code is processed while the condition is *not* true. Example 13-7 shows a simple until loop.

Example 13-7. An until loop

```
# Use the shell's random number generator
VALUE=$RANDOM

until [ $VALUE -lt 1000 ]; do
    # We do this til the value is less than 1k
    echo Nope, $VALUE is greater than 1000.
    VALUE=$RANDOM
Done

# Now print something after the loop is done
echo Success! $VALUE is less than 1000.
```

Interacting with the user

Another important aspect of scripting is the ability to get parameter information and other feedback from the user. The *read* command and some special script environment variables are more than up to the task of supplying interaction with the user. When a script is launched, it has a few variables that are defined and populated with information about how the script was called. These variables can be used in your scripts just like any other variable. They just contain data that is supplied by the shell.

To get some information about the command-line execution of your script, look no further than the positional parameter variables. These variables start with the name of the script itself in position 0. Position 1 will contain the first parameter; position 2, the second; and so forth. You refer to the variable by using its numerical position, prefaced by a dollar sign. For example, the first parameter is $1. For positions beyond $9, enclose the number in curly brackets; e.g. ${13}.

There are a few other variables related to the positional parameters. The $* variable contains all of the position parameter values, combined into a single value. The $@ variable contains all of them as well, but the parameters are passed as individual values. Finally, the $# variable contains the number of command-line arguments that were supplied.

For those scripts that want more interaction with the user than command-line arguments offer, the *bash* shell includes the *read* command. Using *read*, the shell will wait for keyboard input from the user. Once the user presses Enter, the input is stored in the variable specified in the read call. For example, to get input from the user and store it in the variable AGE, use code like that in Example 13-8.

Example 13-8. Reading keyboard input

```
echo -n "Please enter your age: "
read AGE
echo "Your age is $AGE!"
```

Getting Secure Input

If you're using the *read* command to solicit a password from the user, you should turn off the local echo of keyboard input. This prevents the user's password from being displayed on the screen and to any passers-by. To turn off the local echo, use read like this:

```
stty_backup=$(stty -g)
stty -echo
read PASSWORD
stty $stty_backup
```

Sample scripts

Nothing beats experience. If you haven't already, go back and try out some of the code examples. Most of them should work for you with few—if any—changes. The best way to learn to script is to jump in headfirst. Start out by trying a couple of little tests, even if they aren't practical. Even just working on redirecting output and piping when using the Terminal can help you build your scripting foo.

Here are a few scripts for you to pick apart and try out. Feel free to use them as a starting point for your own scripting efforts.

The script in Example 13-9 uses piping and the *grep* command to display information about a hard disk.

Example 13-9. Report essential information about a disk

```
#!/bin/bash
# disk_info.sh: Displays summary data about a disk

DISK=/dev/disk0                    # The disk to check

echo "Drive status for $DISK:"
diskutil info $DISK | grep "SMART" # Display SMART status

echo; echo "Mount points:"
mount | grep $DISK                 # Display mount points

echo; echo "Disk Space:"
df | head -n 1                     # Print out the column headers
df | grep $DISK                    # Display only relevant results
```

Example 13-10 is a script that redirects the output from the *system_profiler* command into a file. It then uses the *diff* command to compare the output from the current run and output from the prior run. If a difference is found, it notifies the user and then displays the differences.

Example 13-10. Alert user to changes in system hardware

```
#!/bin/bash
# watch_profiler.sh: Alerts user if basic hardware is changed

# Store the data from System Profiler temporarily
system_profiler -detailLevel mini > /tmp/newest_system_profile

# Check for changes
if [ -f ~/.last_system_profile ]; then
    DIFF=$(diff -s /tmp/newest_system_profile ~/.last_system_profile |
        grep -c "identical")

    # We have a change
    if [ $DIFF == 0 ]; then
        echo There have been changes to the hardware!
        diff /tmp/newest_system_profile ~/.last_system_profile
    fi

fi

# Setup for the next run
mv /tmp/newest_system_profile ~/.last_system_profile
```

The script in Example 13-11 uses command substitution to get the current *date*, create a temporary directory using *mktemp*, and find out the directory path for a file. It also uses the *find* command to locate files that have been modified within the past day. After *find*'s output is stored in a file, a while loop uses the *read* command to read the file back in. The results are then copied to the temporary folder, after which the *hdiutil* command is invoked to create a disk image of the workspace and place it on the desktop. Finally, the script removes its workspace to keep the disk clean.

Example 13-11. A simple backup script

```
#!/bin/bash
# daily_diskimage.sh: Creates a disk image of files found in
#        FOLDER that have changed within the past day.
#        The image is then placed in OUTDIR.

FOLDER=~/Documents                          # The folder to search
OUTDIR=~/Desktop                            # Where to place image

TODAY=$(date +"%Y%m%d")                      # Get today's date
WORK=$(mktemp -d /tmp/diskimage.XXXXXX)      # Create a work path

find $FOLDER \( -mtime 1 -or -ctime 1 \) -and -type f \
    -print >> $WORK/.BackupList              # Find files to backup

# Copy our files to the work directory
while read FILE; do
    DEST="$WORK"$(dirname "$FILE")
        mkdir -p "$DEST"
    cp -v "$FILE" "$DEST"
done<"$WORK/.BackupList"

# Create a disk image of the work directory
hdiutil create -fs HFS+ -srcfolder $WORK -volname $TODAY \
    "$OUTDIR"/$TODAY.dmg

# Remove our workspace
rm -rf $WORK
```

As you can see, shell scripts can perform a variety of tasks and have a wide number of commands at their disposal. For more information on scripting, take a look at some of the books and manpages mentioned in the "Further Explorations" section at the end of this chapter.

AppleScript

Long before Mac OS X and its scriptable shell, the tool with which Mac power users automated their systems was AppleScript. AppleScript has persisted as a part of today's Mac OS, Tiger. In Tiger, AppleScript is still going strong, with more and more functionality and refinement being built into the language itself, its editor, and its interaction with the OS and user.

Commenting AppleScripts

For commenting in AppleScript, preface your comments with two hyphens (--). AppleScript also supports block commenting, which allows you to write lengthy comments easily. To use block commenting, start the block with (* and end it with *). You can use block commenting to disable a block of code for debugging purposes.

Another simple script

Unlike shell scripts, which are simply text files with a series of commands, AppleScripts have a special file format. So, to work with AppleScripts, you need to use a special editor, called Script Editor (*/Applications/AppleScript*), shown in Figure 13-12.

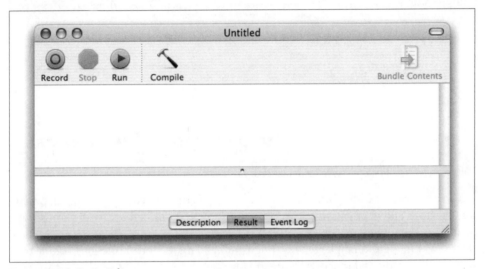

Figure 13-12. Script Editor

Much like shell scripts, the commands available to AppleScript are dependent on what software you have installed. When you install an application that supports AppleScript—which isn't all Mac applications, but many of them—the application implements an AppleScript dictionary. Using the app's dictionary, you can determine what kind of tasks you can perform in your script by calling that application. Figure 13-13 shows the Finder's dictionary.

To open an application's dictionary, open up Script Editor and click File → Open Dictionary. A dialog box containing all of the available dictionaries will appear, allowing you to select the one you're interested in. You can keep as many dictionaries open as you'd like, which is convenient when you're looking up commands for multiple applications.

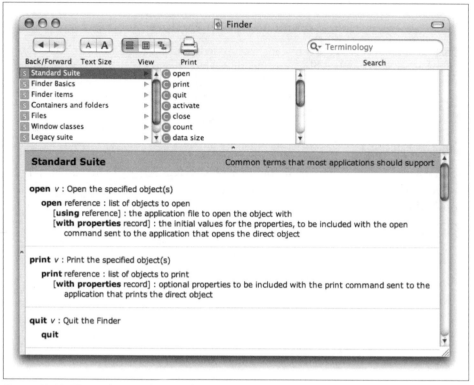

Figure 13-13. The Finder's AppleScript dictionary

Now that you're a little more familiar with AppleScript, its editor, and its dictionaries, let's take a look at its syntax. AppleScript is often described as a very verbose language. In their quest to make AppleScript more accessible to new users, Apple's developers made the language very English-like. This is both a blessing and a burden, as the code is far easier to read, but can be a bit more tedious to write. Example 13-12 is our Hello World script, revised for AppleScript.

Example 13-12. Hello World, AppleScript style

```
display dialog "Hello, World!"
```

Once you've entered that line of code into your script in Script Editor, click the Run button to execute it. A dialog like that shown in Figure 13-14 is displayed, letting you know it worked.

Variables: AppleScript style

Like any good scripting language, AppleScript has variables as well. AppleScript has more variable types than most shells, however, allowing you to store different types

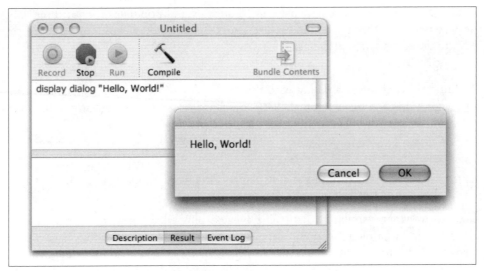

Figure 13-14. The Hello World script in action

of values more efficiently. Assigning a variable in AppleScript is done using the *set* command, followed by the variable name, the keyword *to*, and then the value to assign to the variable. For example:

```
set message to "Hello, World!"
```

assigns the value "Hello, World!" to the variable message. So, the Hello World script rewritten with a variable is:

```
set message to "Hello, World!"
display dialog message
```

Depending on the type of value you're storing and how you're going to use it, you can specify a variable type in its declaration. As an example, to declare the message variable as a string, use:

```
set message to "Hello, World!" as string
```

You can also change a variable's type on the fly as follows:

```
set num to 3 as number
set message to (num as string) & " is a magic number."
display dialog message
```

In addition to individual variables, variables can be combined into *lists* and *records*. A list is simply a series of values stored in a single list variable (often called an "array" in programming parlance). You can refer to individual items in the list, add items to the list, etc. For example, to create a new list, define it as follows:

```
set animals to {"cat","dog","dogcow")
```

This line of code creates a new list named *animals* and populates it with three values. To refer to a specific item in the list, use the *item...of* keyword. For example, to refer to the second item in the list:

```
display dialog item 2 of animals
```

The line above displays a dialog with the word "dog," which is the value stored in the second position of the animals list. To change a specific element in the list, use the *item...of* keyword in conjunction with the *set* command:

```
set item 2 of animals to "horse"
display dialog item 2 of animals
```

This time around, the resulting dialog displays the word "horse," since the first line has replaced the "dog" value in position two with "horse".

Records are quite similar to lists. The biggest difference between them is that a record stores multiple *properties*. Properties are essentially variables that have a persistent value. Most programmers would call such variables *constants*. Some properties are defined by an application (and thus listed in its dictionary). Others are user-defined using the *property* keyword, similar to using *set*.

The other unique quality of records is that their values are stored in name-value pairs. This allows you to then refer to a given property within a record by its name, instead of using a positional number. For example, here is a definition of a simple record:

```
set pet to {name: "Charlie", owner: "Jason", type: "Turtle"}
```

Instead of using the *item...of* keyword, you'll want to refer to the property using its name. To get the owner property out of the pet record, use the statement:

```
display dialog owner of pet
```

AppleScript conditionals

Also like the *bash* shell, AppleScript includes conditionals for diverting program logic. AppleScript has a variety of comparison operators, all of which can be easily used with an English-like syntax. Here are some example comparisons, each on a separate line:

```
if type of pet is equal to "Turtle" then display dialog "Turtle!"

if num is greater than 5 then display dialog "It's bigger than 5!"

if passwd is not equal to "secret" then display dialog "Sorry,
wrong password."
```

When working with strings, records, and lists, there are some special comparisons at your disposal. These comparisons make it easy to look for a specific substring or value. The starts with comparison is used to examine the beginning of a string. The reverse of starts with is the ends with comparison; use it to check the end of a

---

string. Lastly, the contains comparison evaluates true when the substring is found within your variable. Here are some examples using these comparisons:

```
if name of pet starts with "C" then display dialog "The name starts
with a C"

if animals ends with "dogcow" then display dialog "Clarus was here"

if owner of pet contains "Jobs" then display dialog "Are you Steve's
relative?"
```

Looping in AppleScript

In AppleScript, all loops are defined using the repeat keyword. Depending on whether you want the loop to be incremental or conditional, the syntax for using repeat is a little bit different. For example, to create an incremental loop in Apple-Script, use code similar to Example 13-13.

Example 13-13. An incremental AppleScript loop

```
set nums to ""
repeat with i from 1 to 10
    set nums to nums & " " & (i as string)
end repeat
display dialog nums
```

Like *bash*, there are two ways to use a conditional loop in AppleScript. Conveniently, the keyword and purpose for both types are the same as those found in the shell. Example 13-14 uses a while loop.

Example 13-14. A loop using while logic

```
set today to the current date
repeat while (today as string) starts with "Monday"
    display dialog "Sounds like somebody's got a case of the Mondays"
    set today to the current date
end repeat
```

Example 13-15 shows a loop using until logic.

Example 13-15. Using until logic in a loop

```
set WorldPeace to false as boolean        -- Sad, but true
repeat until WorldPeace is equal to true
    display dialog "All we are saying is, give peace a chance."
end repeat
```

User interaction

AppleScript is much more flexible than shell scripts when it comes to interacting with the user. Though it is not possible to use parameters quite the way you would with a command line, it is possible to use several different dialog windows for soliciting information from the user.

In the previous code examples, the *display dialog* command has been used to provide feedback about a script's progress. This command can also be used to obtain basic text input from the user. For example, to get some text from the user and store it in a variable called nom, use this code:

```
display dialog "Please enter your name" default answer ""
set nom to text returned of the result
```

 Since variables cannot have the same name as an AppleScript keyword, this example uses nom instead of name.

You can also give the user up to three different buttons to accompany the text input (or, just use the buttons for input and skip the text). To do this, use the buttons parameter of the display dialog command, as follows:

```
set reply to display dialog "Enter pet's name and type" default
answer "" buttons {"Dog", "Cat", "Turtle"}
set nom to the text returned of reply
set type to the button returned of reply
display dialog nom & " is a " & type
```

If you want to offer the user more than three choices, you can use the choose command and implement a list. For example, to have the user choose an option from a list of fruits, use the command:

```
choose from list {"apple", "orange", "pear", "banana"} with prompt
"Pick one:"
set fruit to the (result as string)
display dialog fruit & "s are good"
```

The choose command offers several other dialog windows for different types of choices. The file keyword is used for files, folder for folders, and application for applications. As an example, you can have the user pick a file with the command:

```
choose file with prompt "Pick a PDF file:" of type {"PDF"}
```

Sample scripts

Here are a couple of simple AppleScripts to help you get started on your own scripting projects.

Example 13-16 is an excellent candidate for a script to tie to iCal. The script activates iTunes and then plays a playlist named "Wake-Up." To use this script, create the playlist in iTunes and name it "Wake-Up." Populate the playlist with your desired tracks and then use this script as a musical alarm clock for iTunes.

Example 13-16. iTunes playlist script

```
-- Opens up iTunes and plays a playlist named "Wake-Up"
tell application "iTunes"
    activate
    play playlist "Wake-Up"
end tell
```

Example 13-17 is an example of a folder action. Using folder actions, you can create a script that is launched upon changes to the folders contents. Example 13-17 displays a simple dialog window that notifies you when a file has been placed in a folder. This is a great script to use with your Mac's Drop Box. To configure the folder action, you'll first need to save your script in *~/Library/Scripts/Folder Action Scripts*. Then, use the Folder Action Setup tool (*/Applications/AppleScript*) to select the folder to attach the script to, followed by your new script. Figure 13-15 shows a folder and its associated action scripts.

Example 13-17. A folder action

```
-- Displays a simple dialog whenever a file is added to the folder
on adding folder items to this_folder after receiving added_items
    display dialog "Someone has placed an item in " & this_folder
end adding folder items to
```

Figure 13-15. Configuring folder action scripts

Bridging the Gap

A convenient command for moving between the AppleScript and shell script worlds is *osascript*. Using *osascript*, you can execute an AppleScript from the command line, either by specifying the path to an existing script or using *osascript*'s *-e* switch to enter the AppleScript line by line.

Example 13-18 is a script that will control iTunes playback.

Example 13-18. A script to control iTunes playback

```
#!/bin/bash
osascript - <<EOF
tell application "iTunes"
    playpause
end tell
EOF
```

Further Explorations

For more information about the technologies in this chapter, see the following resources:

- *AppleScript: The Definitive Guide*, by Matt Neuburg (O'Reilly Media, Inc., 2006)
- *AppleScript: The Missing Manual*, by Adam Goldstein (Pogue Press/O'Reilly Media, Inc., 2005)
- *Unix Power Tools*, Third Edition, by Shelley Powers, Jerry Peek, et al. (O'Reilly Media, Inc., 2002)

You may also be interested in consulting the following manpages:

- *cron*
- *crontab*
- *date*
- *diff*
- *find*
- *for*
- *grep*
- *hdiutil*
- *ls*
- *mktemp*
- *osascript*
- *read*
- *test*
- *until*
- *while*

## CHAPTER 14

Preferences and Defaults

Whenever you customize the behavior of a Mac OS X application, such as changing the default font or colors or the windows that are visible, the various changes you make are saved into a preference file for that application. This is in contrast with Windows where application preferences typically are saved into the monolithic registry. And because each application stores its preferences in a separate file, the overall system is more robust than if all the preferences were in one big file. If a preference gets corrupted, it is less likely to affect the system and typically affects only the application that uses that preference. The designated location for preference data is the *Library/Preferences* folder in each of the filesystem domains. (Review Chapter 3 for more information about filesystem domains.)

Many Mac OS X applications, including all the applications Apple provides, go beyond just using the *Library/Preferences* directory and store their preferences in the *defaults system*. This system, which is often referred to as the *defaults database*, is made of each application's preferences stored in an XML-based property list (*plist*) file in the Preferences folder. By using the defaults system, applications can use code in the operating system to manage preferences instead of having to provide their own preference-handling code. Additionally, you can use the *defaults* command in the Terminal to read and write data into the defaults database.

Property Lists

A property list (*plist*) file is a file that contains all kinds of data in a structured form. There are three formats for a property list file: an older ASCII-based property list format, the XML-based property list format used in earlier versions of Mac OS X, and the new binary format used in Tiger. We saw an example of the older ASCII property list format in Chapter 5 when we looked at Startup Items. This is one of the few places where you'll see the older format in use. In most places, including the defaults database, you'll see the new binary format. In still other places, the XML format may still be used. A simple XML property list used by the battery menu extra is shown in

Example 14-1. If you've ever looked at HTML or other XML dialects, the basic structure of this file should look somewhat familiar.

 For the sake of explanation, most of the following discussion assumes you're looking at property list files that are either still in the XML-based format used in Panther or have been converted from the binary format into XML-based format using *plutil* (as described later).

Example 14-1. The com.apple.menuextra.battery.plist file

```
<?xml version="1.0" encoding="UTF-8"?>
<!DOCTYPE plist PUBLIC "-//Apple Computer//DTD PLIST 1.0//EN"
"http://www.apple.com/DTDs/PropertyList-1.0.dtd">
<plist version="1.0">
<dict>
    <key>ShowPercent</key>
    <string>NO</string>
    <key>ShowTime</key>
    <string>YES</string>
</dict>
</plist>
```

The binary files aren't nearly as interesting to look at from the command line; unfortunately, they are not human-readable. Luckily, Apple includes a tool to convert between the binary and XML formats. This tool, *plutil*, makes it quite a bit easier when you want to tweak *.plist* files by hand. To convert from the new binary format to the XML format used in earlier versions of Mac OS X, use the *xml1* (XML followed by the numeral 1) format option for *plutil*'s *-convert* switch:

```
$ plutil -convert xml1 com.example.myprogram.plist
```

Once you're done making changes to the file while it's in XML form, you can convert it back to binary format with the *binary1* format option, as in:

```
$ plutil -convert binary1 com.example.myprogram.plist
```

Before you convert it back, however, you may want to check the syntax of your changes. The *plutil* tool can help you with that as well; just call it using its *-lint* switch:

```
$ plutil -lint com.example.myprogram.plist
```

The structure of a property list file contains a plist root element that contains one or more data elements. In Example 14-1, as in all property lists used by the defaults system, the child element of plist is named dict (which stands for *dictionary*—a mapping between names and values) and contains a set of key and string elements. Each set of key and string elements defines a name-value pair. In essence, the example file can be interpreted as "this file contains a dictionary in which the key ShowPercent is set to NO and the key ShowTime is set to YES."

Unless you have modified the battery menu extra, you may not have the file shown in Example 14-1 or many other *plist* files that are mentioned in this chapter. The *plist* files for a preference domain typically are created only on demand.

The XML elements that can appear in a property list file are listed in Table 14-1. One thing you might notice in Example 14-1 is that even though there are the true and false values that can appear as tags in the XML file, the ShowPercent and ShowTime keys have string values set to NO and YES, respectively. It's unfortunate, but this inconsistency crops up in many of the defaults keys used by applications and is something you should be aware of.

Table 14-1. Property list elements

Element	Description
plist	Root element of a property list.
dict	A dictionary to hold other data elements in key value form. The contents of this element are a set of <key> elements, followed by the data associated with the key.
array	Contains a set of data values in a particular order. The contents of these elements are simply a list of data elements.
string	Contains a data value as a string.
real	Contains a data value as a real number, such as 8.14.
integer	Contains a data value as an integer, such as 10 or −9.
date	Contains data that represents a date in ISO 8601 (a standard format for dates), such as 2003-10-24T08: 00:00Z which represents 8:00 p.m. October 24th, 2003 (the time Panther was released to the public).
true	Indicates that the value is true.
false	Indicates that the value is false.
data	Contains arbitrary data.

Where Preferences Are Stored

As mentioned earlier, the defaults database stores preference data in files located in the *Library/Preferences* folder of a filesystem domain. For example, when a preference applies to a single user, it is written to the *~/Library/Preferences* folder. If the preference applies to all users on a system, it is written to the */Library/Preferences* folder.

Each of the files in the defaults database takes a unique name, known as a *preference domain*, determined by the application that uses it. The Apple-recommended naming convention for preference domains is to use the reverse Internet domain name of an application's vendor, followed by the name of the application. For example, all the *plist* files used by the various Apple-supplied applications use filenames that begin with *com.apple*, followed by the name of the application, followed by the *.plist* extension. Example 14-2 shows a partial command-line listing of the *~/Library/ Preferences* directory for a freshly created user:

Example 14-2. The ~/Library/Preferences directory

```
$ ls -l
total 296
drwx------   3 panic  panic    102 Jun  9 20:52 ByHost
drwx------   3 panic  panic    102 May 16 16:27 Explorer
drwxr-xr-x   3 panic  panic    102 Jun  9 20:53 Macromedia
-rw-r--r--   1 panic  panic   8611 Jun  9 20:52 QuickTime Preferences
-rw-------   1 panic  panic    234 Jun  9 21:04 com.apple.AddressBook.plist
-rw-------   1 panic  panic    443 May 16 16:38 com.apple.BezelServices.plist
-rw-------   1 panic  panic    483 Jun  9 20:52 com.apple.Bluetooth.plist
-rw-------   1 panic  panic     98 May 16 16:34 com.apple.HIToolbox.plist
-rw-------   1 panic  panic    239 May 16 16:34 com.apple.MenuBarClock.plist
-rw-------   1 panic  panic   1603 Jun  9 21:24 com.apple.Preview.plist
-rw-------   1 panic  panic   1561 Jun  9 21:31 com.apple.Safari.plist
-rw-------   1 panic  panic     71 Jun  9 21:22 com.apple.Syndication.plist
```

When you look into your own *~/Library/Preferences* directory, you'll see more files than this, but by applying the naming convention rules, you should be able to easily sort out which property list file belongs to which application.

Preferences are written into the *Library/Preferences* folder of a filesystem domain. When an application searches for the value of a preference, it can be given a value from the User, Local, Network, or System filesystem domains. This means general settings that apply to all users can be defined at the Local or Network domain level. Settings that apply to a single user are written to the User domain so that they remain separate from the preferences of other users.

Backing Up Preferences

Before the transition to Mac OS X, users used to back up their preferences regularly to a floppy disk. This was done because the preferences would get corrupted at the drop of a hat. By having a stable backup floppy at the ready, it was pretty easy to get everything back to the way it was supposed to be simply by copying the preferences back into place. With Mac OS X, even though preferences don't tend to get corrupted as often, nor do they have as devastating an effect when they do, it is still easy to make quick backups of the *~/Library/Preferences* directory. For example, you can drag the *~/Library/Preferences* folder to a USB key fob, upload them to your iDisk, or even use Backup (part of the .Mac toolset) to back them up to your iDisk or a CD or DVD. In fact, you should do this regularly. Then, whenever you need to restore the preferences for an application, they are easy to find.

Host-Based Preferences

Because Mac OS X can mount Home folders from a server and a user might log into several different machines with her account, the defaults database provides a mechanism for applications to store information on a per-machine basis. This allows applications, such as the one that provides iDisk synchronization, to keep distinct settings depending on which machine you are using. To keep these settings distinct, they are kept in a *ByHost* folder within the *Library/Preferences* folder. They too use a naming convention consisting of the reverse Internet domain name of the vendor, the application name, the Ethernet MAC address of the host, and then the *plist* file extension. Example 14-3 shows a list of the files you might find in the *ByHost* folder.

Example 14-3. The contents of the ByHost folder

```
$ ls ~/Library/Preferences/ByHost
RSS Visualizer.000a95a9ba2a.plist
com.apple.DotMacNotifications.000a95a9ba2a.plist
com.apple.HIToolbox.000a95a9ba2a.plist
com.apple.ImageCapture2.000a95a9ba2a.plist
com.apple.ImageCaptureExtension2.000a95a9ba2a.plist
com.apple.MIDI.000a95a9ba2a.plist
```

Global Preferences

In addition to the preferences that you can see in Example 14-2, a hidden file named *.GlobalPreferences.plist* in the *~/Library/Preferences* folder contains preferences used by all applications. It contains data that affects all applications equally, such as the locale of the system in use. Example 14-4 shows this file for a freshly created user (converted into XML format first, of course).

Example 14-4. The .GlobalPreferences.plist file

```
<?xml version="1.0" encoding="UTF-8"?>
<!DOCTYPE plist PUBLIC "-//Apple Computer//DTD PLIST 1.0//EN"
"http://www.apple.com/DTDs/PropertyList-1.0.dtd">
<plist version="1.0">
<dict>
<key>AppleAntiAliasingThreshold</key>
<integer>8</integer>
<key>AppleLanguages</key>
<array>
    <string>en</string>
    <string>ja</string>
    <string>fr</string>
    <string>de</string>
    <string>es</string>
    <string>it</string>
    <string>nl</string>
    <string>sv</string>
    <string>no</string>
    <string>da</string>
```

Example 14-4. The .GlobalPreferences.plist file (continued)

```
    <string>fi</string>
    <string>pt</string>
    <string>zh_CN</string>
    <string>zh_TW</string>
    <string>ko</string>
</array>
<key>AppleLocale</key>
<string>en_US</string>
</dict>
</plist>
```

These preferences correspond to some of the settings you can apply in the System Preferences application. For example, Example 14-4 shows the array of strings associated with the AppleLanguages key. The strings in the array correlate to the language packages you can choose from in the International preference panel (shown in Figure 14-1).

Non-Defaults-Based Preferences

Application preference files that aren't part of the defaults database can also be stored in the *~/Library/Preferences* folder. These preferences tend to be written in a proprietary format and are not easily readable except through the application that wrote them.

Typically, applications that write non–defaults database preferences are older Carbon-based applications that migrated to Mac OS X from Mac OS 9 and already have their own preference-handling code. These applications are truly antisocial because they can only run in Classic mode, and they write their opaque preference files into Mac OS 9's */System Folder/Preferences* folder.

Reading and Writing Preferences

There are three ways in which to read and write information in the defaults database:

- With the Property List Editor (*/Developer/Applications/Utilities*) installed as part of the Xcode Tools
- From the command line using the *defaults* command-line utility
- Converting the file to XML format using *plutil* and then using TextEdit (found in */Applications/Utilities*) or another plain-text editor to modify the file by hand

Property List Editor

The Property List Editor, shown in Figure 14-2, is a GUI application installed with the Xcode Tools that lets you view and edit property list files. When you first open a property list with the Property List Editor, you'll notice that the top root element is

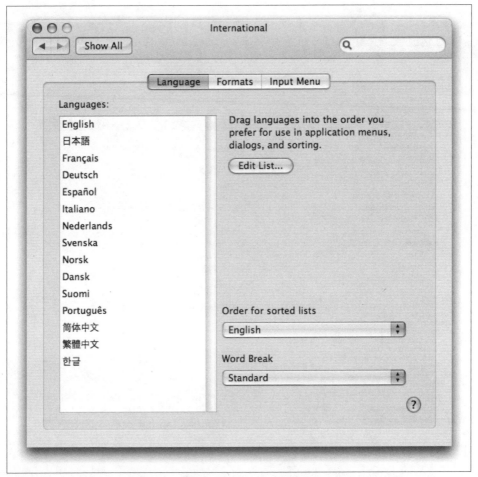

Figure 14-1. The Language section of the International Preference panel

collapsed. Click the disclosure triangle next to it, and you can drill through the various preferences.

As shown in Figure 14-2, there are three columns to the Property List Editor. These are:

Property List
> Lists the keys of the property list; that is, the contents of the <key/> tags of a *plist* XML file.

Class
> Lists the classes available for each key definition. This affects the value tags in the XML file as defined in Figure 14-1.

Value
> Contains the value for the preference key.

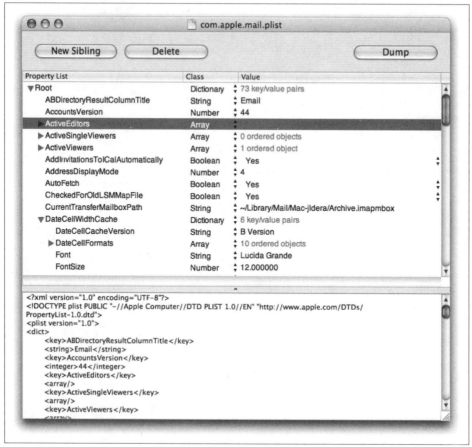

Figure 14-2. The Property List Editor application

To view the XML version of the *plist* file, click the Dump button in the upper-right corner of the Property List Editor's window. You can't edit the XML source here, but you can see the effects of the changes that you make in the top part of the window.

To edit an item, double-click the item's name that you want to edit, type in the new value, and then hit Return to accept the new value.

The defaults Command-Line Tool

The *defaults* tool gives you easy access to the defaults system from the command line, letting you read and write the preferences for any Mac OS X application on the system. As with any command-line utility, you can write shell scripts to run several defaults commands automatically, enabling you to set an application's behavior any way you'd like in an instant.

Since *defaults* provides a simple way to read and write preferences on the command line, you can easily integrate it with your shell scripts. Chapter 13 has more information on putting *defaults* to use in your scripting projects.

Reading preferences

The basic usage of the *defaults* command for reading an application's preferences is:

```
defaults read domain [key]
```

where *domain* is the property domain that you want to read the preference from, and *key* is an optional key name that lets you see the value of a single key for a preference domain. Since a preference key can contain many different kinds of data, the output from this command will vary depending on the kind of data that is associated with a preference key. Example 14-5 shows the output from reading the preferences for a domain.

Example 14-5. Using the defaults command

```
$ defaults read com.apple.menuextra.battery
{ShowPercent = NO; ShowTime = YES; }
```

Example 14-6 shows how to read a single key from a domain, in this case, a Boolean value.

Example 14-6. Using the defaults command specifying a key

```
$ defaults read com.apple.menuextra.battery ShowPercent
NO
```

Strings and numbers are shown as Boolean values. The only caveat is that a string containing a space is surrounded by quotes. An array associated with a property key is output as a list of items within a set of parentheses, and the items themselves are comma-delimited. Example 14-7 shows the most recently used folders as stored in the *com.apple.finder* preference domain.

Example 14-7. Recent folders stored in the com.apple.finder domain

```
$ defaults read com.apple.finder AppleRecentFolders
(
    "file://localhost/Macintosh%20HD/Developer/Applications/Utilities/",
    "file://localhost/Volumes/Macintosh%20HD//Users/jldera/Documents/Downloads/",
    "file://localhost/Volumes/Macintosh%20HD//Users/jldera/Documents/"
)
```

A dictionary associated with a key is output as a set of name-value pairs surrounded by curly braces. Example 14-8 shows a dictionary associated with the InboxViewerAttributes preference in the *com.apple.mail* preference domain.

Example 14-8. A dictionary of values associated with a preference

```
$ defaults read com.apple.mail InboxViewerAttributes
{
    DisplayInThreadedMode = yes;
    SortOrder = "received-date";
    SortedDescending = NO;
}
```

You'll also see this format used when you output all of the defaults for a preference domain. Example 14-9 shows the contents of the *com.apple.systemuiserver* domain, which controls the menu extras shown in the upper-right corner of the screen.

Example 14-9. A dictionary output of the preferences in the com.apple.systemuiserver domain

```
$ defaults read com.apple.systemuiserver
{
    "NSWindow Frame NoTimeLeft" = "274 440 475 163 0 0 1024 746 ";
    "__NSEnableTSMDocumentWindowLevel" = 1;
    menuExtras = (
        "/System/Library/CoreServices/Menu Extras/Script Menu.menu",
        "/System/Library/CoreServices/Menu Extras/iChat.menu",
        "/System/Library/CoreServices/Menu Extras/AirPort.menu",
        "/System/Library/CoreServices/Menu Extras/Battery.menu",
        "/System/Library/CoreServices/Menu Extras/User.menu",
        "/System/Library/CoreServices/Menu Extras/Clock.menu"
    );
}
```

You can also read the preferences for an application by using its name instead of trying to figure out its preference domain. The syntax for this is:

```
defaults read -app appname
```

For example, to read the preferences for Mail, you would use the following command:

```
$ defaults read -app Mail
```

Writing preferences

The basic syntax to write preferences to the defaults database is:

```
defaults write domain key value
```

where *domain* is the preference domain to write the preference to, *key* is the preference name, and *value* is the content to associate with that key. For example, to configure the Terminal so it uses a blinking cursor, you would issue the following command:

```
$ defaults write com.apple.terminal BlinkCursor YES
```

If you enter this command into a Terminal window and then open a new window, you'll see the cursor blinking. To reverse this setting, use the following command:

```
$ defaults write com.apple.terminal BlinkCursor NO
```

You can use two commands to write properties to an array. The first associates an array with a preference key and replaces any previous values associated with that key. This command has the syntax:

```
defaults write domain key -array element1 element2 element3...
```

To add new elements to the end of an array for a key without replacing all the elements in the array, use the *-array-add* option with the following syntax:

```
defaults write domain key -array-add element1 element2...
```

 You should always make sure that the application for which you are writing preferences isn't running when you use the *defaults* command. A running application might write something to the defaults database that overwrites any changes you may have made.

Reading and writing host-specific preferences

To work with host-specific preferences, you can use the *-currentHost* or *-host* options to the *defaults* command. For example, to read the preference from the *com.apple. idisk* preference domain on the machine that you are working on, you would use the following command:

```
$ defaults -currentHost read com.apple.idisk
```

Reading and writing global preferences

To access the global preferences (those associated with all applications) use the *-g* options with the *defaults* command, as shown in Example 14-10.

Example 14-10. Reading global preferences

```
$ defaults read -g
{
    AppleAntiAliasingThreshold = 8;
    AppleCollationOrder = en;
    AppleID = jldera;
    AppleLanguages = (en, ja, fr, de, es, it, nl, sv, nb, da, fi, pt, "zh-Hans", "zh-
Hant", ko);
    AppleLocale = "en_US";
    AppleScrollAnimationEnabled = 1;
    AppleScrollBarVariant = Single;
    NSFavoriteStyles = {
        Bold = {NSFontTrait = 2; };
        Italic = {NSFontTrait = 1; };
        Outlined = {NSStrokeWidth = 3; };
...
```

Using TextEdit

As mentioned earlier in the chapter, Tiger's new binary format for *plist* files makes you jump through an extra couple of hoops if you want to work with the files using a text editor. Fortunately, the *plutil* command makes those hoops pretty easy to navigate. Once you've used *plutil* to convert the file into XML format, you can open it up in TextEdit (*/Applications/Utilities*) and modify the preference data by hand, as shown in Figure 14-3.

```
<?xml version="1.0" encoding="UTF-8"?>
<!DOCTYPE plist PUBLIC "-//Apple Computer//DTD PLIST 1.0//EN" "http://
www.apple.com/DTDs/PropertyList-1.0.dtd">
<plist version="1.0">
<dict>
        <key>AppleAntiAliasingThreshold</key>
        <integer>8</integer>
        <key>AppleID</key>
        <string>jldera</string>
        <key>AppleLanguages</key>
        <array>
                <string>en</string>
                <string>ja</string>
                <string>fr</string>
                <string>de</string>
                <string>es</string>
                <string>it</string>
                <string>nl</string>
                <string>sv</string>
                <string>nb</string>
                <string>da</string>
                <string>fi</string>
                <string>pt</string>
                <string>zh_Hans</string>
                <string>zh_Hant</string>
                <string>ko</string>
        </array>
```

Figure 14-3. Modifying a plist file using TextEdit

This is perhaps the riskiest way to work with data in the defaults database, as an error in the file will prevent it from being properly processed, most likely resulting in lost preferences. Once you're done making your changes in TextEdit, make sure you use *plutil*'s -*lint* switch to check the file out. Otherwise, your changes won't have the desired effect.

Determining Preference Keys

Editing preferences in the defaults database is a chicken-and-egg problem. Without knowing the key to set a preference for, it's hard to customize an application's behavior. Setting preference keys randomly won't accomplish much except to fill your defaults database with useless data. To determine which keys can be set, you have to do a bit of research. Three methods will help you determine the preference keys an application might use:

- Looking at the preference *plist* files after you've customized an application
- Searching the Web
- Digging into the application itself

The first of these methods is fairly self-explanatory. Simply fiddle with the various settings of the application and watch the *plist* file to see what changes. Once you have an idea of the ways that keys are named, you can use the *defaults find* command. This command searches through the defaults database and returns the preference file and data associated with any particular string. For example, if after tweaking the opacity of your Terminal windows, you searched for the string *Opaque*, you would find the key in the *com.apple.Terminal* domain, as shown in Example 14-11.

Example 14-11. Searching for a string in the defaults database

```
$ defaults find Opaque
Found 1 keys in domain 'com.apple.Terminal': {TerminalOpaqueness = 0.7783334; }
```

If other applications used keys with the string *Opaque*, they would also be listed.

The second of these methods is also straightforward—using the Web. The Mac OS X Hints web site (*http://www.macosxhints.com*) has a wealth of information on ways to hack the defaults database. Google searches (*http://www.google.com*) can turn up quite a lot of useful information as well.

The third of these methods is a bit more difficult and requires looking inside the application's bundle and using the *strings* command. The *strings* command examines a binary file and prints out all the strings it finds in a binary. For example, to look inside the Dock's executable, you would use the command shown in Example 14-12.

Example 14-12. Examining a binary for preference keys

```
$ strings /System/Library/CoreServices/Dock.app/Contents/MacOS/Dock
__dyld_mod_term_funcs
__dyld_make_delayed_module_initializer_calls
The kernel support for the dynamic linker is not present to run this program.
showhidden
showshadow
DoesPointToFocusCursorUpdate
ClientMayIgnoreEvents
com.apple.finder
en_US
trashlabel
owensdock
dock
```

Example 14-12. Examining a binary for preference keys (continued)

```
.dock
AppleShowAllExtensions
AppleShowAllFiles
notfound
trashfull
trashempty
finder
...
```

The result is a large number of strings, which probably don't have anything to do with preference settings at all. But many of these strings are used as preference keys and values in the *plist* file. This method becomes a sleuthing game that is boring for some and immensely interesting to others.

If you locate undocumented preferences, keep in mind that they may go away or be renamed in a future version of the application, something that has been known to happen in the past (especially when clever hackers have unearthed settings that Apple would really rather keep private).

Further Explorations

For more information about the defaults system, see the PDF book titled *System Overview*, located at */Developer/Documentation/MacOSX/Conceptual/SystemOverview/SystemOverview.pdf*.

You may also want to consult the following manpages:

- *defaults*
- *strings*
- *plutil*

Boot Command Keys

It seems like the people who truly know how their Mac works inside and out can do odd things with it by holding down a key, or a combination of keys, as the machine boots. Table A-1 lists the known boot keys that can be used when Mac OS X is starting up.

Table A-1. Keyboard shortcuts used for starting, restarting, logging out, and shutting down

Key command	Description
C	Holding down the C key at startup boots from a CD or DVD (useful when installing or upgrading the system software).
N	Attempts to start up from a NetBoot server.
R	Resets the display for a PowerBook.
T	Holding down the T key at startup places your Mac into Target mode as a mountable FireWire drive. After starting up, your screen will have a blue background with a floating yellow FireWire symbol. Target mode makes the hard drive(s) of your Mac appear as mounted FireWire drives when connected to another system.
	To exit Target mode, press the Power-On button to turn off your Mac. After your Mac has shut down completely, press the Power-On button again to restart your Mac.
X	Holding down the X key at startup forces your Mac to boot into Mac OS X, even if Mac OS 9 is specified as the default startup disk.
⌘-S	Boots into *single-user mode* (something you'll only need to do when troubleshooting your system, or if you're a system administrator).
⌘-V	Boots into *verbose mode*, displaying all the startup messages on screen. (Linux users will be familiar with this.)
Shift	Holding down the Shift key at startup invokes Safe Boot mode, turning off any unnecessary kernel extensions (*kexts*) and ignoring anything you've set in the Accounts preferences panel.
Option	Holding down the Option key at startup opens the Startup Manager, which allows you to select which OS to boot into.

Table A-1. Keyboard shortcuts used for starting, restarting, logging out,
and shutting down (continued)

Key command	Description
Mouse button	Holding down the mouse button at startup ejects any disk (CD, DVD, or other removable media) that might still be in the drive.
Shift-Option-⌘-Q Option + ⌘ → Log Out Option–Power-On	Logs you off without first prompting you.
Option + ⌘ → Shut Down	Shuts down your system without first prompting you.
Option + ⌘ → Restart	Restarts your machine without first prompting you.
Control-⌘–Power-On button	Forces an automatic shutdown of your system; this should be used only as a last resort, because it could mess up your filesystem.
Control-Eject (F12)	Opens a dialog box that contains options for Restart, Sleep, and Shutdown.
Control-Option-⌘-Eject (F12)	Quits all applications and shuts down the system. If there are any application windows open with unsaved changes, you will be prompted to save the changes before the application is forced to quit.

Other Sources of Information

The following is a list of resources for Mac OS X users, including books, magazines, mailing lists, and web sites.

Books

The following books are available for Mac users, administrators, and developers.

User and Administrator Focus

- *iMovie HD & iDVD 5: The Missing Manual*, by David Pogue (Pogue Press/O'Reilly Media, Inc., 2005)
- *iPhoto 5: The Missing Manual*, by David Pogue and Derrick Story (Pogue Press/O'Reilly Media, Inc., 2005)
- *iPod and iTunes: The Missing Manual*, by J. D. Biersdorfer (Pogue Press/O'Reilly Media, Inc., 2005)
- *Learning the bash Shell*, by Cameron Newhan (O'Reilly Media, Inc., 2005)
- *Learning Unix for Mac OS X Tiger*, by Dave Taylor (O'Reilly Media, Inc., 2005)
- *Mac OS X 10.4 Tiger*, by Robin Williams (Peachpit Press, 2005)
- *The Macintosh Bible,* Eighth Edition, by Clifford Colby, Marty Cortinas, et al. (Peachpit Press, 2002)
- *Mac 911*, by Christopher Breen (Peachpit Press, 2002)
- *Mac OS 9: The Missing Manual*, by David Pogue (Pogue Press/O'Reilly Media, Inc., 2000)
- *Mac OS X: The Missing Manual, Tiger Edition*, by David Pogue (Pogue Press/O'Reilly Media, Inc., 2005)
- *Mac OS X Disaster Relief*, by Ted Landau and Dan Frakes (Peachpit Press, 2002)

- *Mac OS X Tiger for Unix Geeks*, by Brian Jepson and Ernest E. Rothman (O'Reilly Media, Inc., 2005)
- *Mac OS X Tiger in a Nutshell*, by Andy Lester (O'Reilly Media, Inc., 2005)
- *Mac OS X Tiger Killer Tips*, by Scott Kelby (New Riders Publishing, 2005)
- *Mac OS X Tiger Pocket Guide*, by Chuck Toporek (O'Reilly Media, Inc., 2005)
- *Mac OS X Tiger Unleashed*, by John Ray and William C. Ray (Sams, 2005)
- *Office X for Macintosh: The Missing Manual*, by Nan Barber, David Reynolds, Tonya Engst (Pogue Press/O'Reilly Media, Inc., 2002)
- *Secrets of the iPod*, by Christopher Breen (Peachpit Press, 2002)
- *Switching to the Mac: The Missing Manual*, by David Pogue (Pogue Press/ O'Reilly Media, Inc., 2001)
- *Using csh & tcsh*, by Paul DuBois (O'Reilly Media, Inc., 1995)

Developer Focus

- *AppleScript: The Definitive Guide*, by Matt Neuburg (O'Reilly Media, Inc., 2006)
- *AppleScript: The Missing Manual*, by Adam Goldstein (Pogue Press/O'Reilly Media, Inc., 2005)
- *AppleScript for Applications: Visual QuickStart Guide*, by Ethan Wilde (Peachpit Press, 2001)
- *Carbon Programming*, by K. J. Bricknell (Sams, 2001)
- *Cocoa Programming*, by Scott Anguish, Erik Buck, and Donald Yacktman (Sams, 2002)
- *Cocoa Programming for Mac OS X*, by Aaron Hillegass (Addison Wesley, 2001)
- *Cocoa Recipes for Mac OS X: The Vermont Recipes*, by Bill Cheeseman (Peachpit Press, 2003)
- *Learning Carbon*, by Apple Computer, Inc. (O'Reilly Media, Inc., 2001)
- *Learning Cocoa with Objective-C,* Second Edition, by James Duncan Davidson and Apple Computer, Inc. (O'Reilly Media, Inc., 2002)
- *Objective-C Pocket Reference*, by Andrew M. Duncan (O'Reilly Media, Inc., 2002)
- *Programming Objective-C*, by Stephan Kochan (Sams, 2003)
- *REALbasic: The Definitive Guide,* Second Edition, by Matt Neuburg (O'Reilly Media, Inc., 2001)

Magazines

The following print magazines are available for Mac users:

MacAddict
> Published monthly, *MacAddict* is a magazine for users and power users. Each issue contains hardware and software reviews, and is accompanied by a CD containing free and shareware applications, as well as demo versions of games and many popular graphics applications. Available online at *http://www.macaddict.com*.

Mac Design
> Published monthly, *Mac Design* is a magazine for Mac-based graphic designers. Available online at *http://www.macdesignonline.com*.

macHOME
> Published monthly, *macHOME* is a magazine for home-based Mac users. Each issue contains articles and tutorials on how to use your Mac. Available online at *http://www.machome.com*.

MacTech
> Published monthly, *MacTech* is a magazine for Macintosh developers. Each issue contains articles and tutorials with code examples. Available online at *http://www.mactech.com*.

Macworld
> Published monthly, each issue of *Macworld* contains hardware and software reviews, as well as tutorials and how-to articles. Available online at *http://www.macworld.com*.

Mailing Lists

The following mailing lists can help you learn more about the Mac.

Apple-Run Mailing Lists

The following mailing lists are run by Apple. For information on how to subscribe to these and other Apple-owned mailing lists, see *lists.apple.com*.

 Apple also maintains a listing of miscellaneous Mac-related mailing lists at *lists.apple.com/cgi-bin/mwf/forum_show.pl*; click the "Non-Apple Mailing Lists" link.

Applescript-studio
> For scripters and developers who are using AppleScript Studio to build AppleScript-based applications for Mac OS X.

applescript-users
> For scripters who are working with AppleScript.

Carbon-development
> For Carbon developers.

Cocoa-dev
> For Cocoa developers.

Java-dev
> For Java developers.

Mac-games-dev
> For Mac-based game developers.

Macos-x-server
> For network and system administrators who are running the Mac OS X Server.

Bonjour
> Discussions on how to develop applications and devices that use Bonjour.

Scitech
> Discussions on Apple's support for science and technology markets.

Studentdev
> For student developers.

Weekly-kbase-changes
> Keep informed of weekly changes to Apple's Knowledge Base (KB).

Omni Group's Mailing Lists

The following mailing lists are run by the Omni Group. For more information on how to subscribe to these and other Omni lists, see *http://www.omnigroup.com/developer/mailinglists.*

macosx-admin
> A technical list for Mac OS X system administrators

Macosx-dev
> A moderated list for Mac OS X application developers

Macosx-talk
> A list for general discussions about the Mac OS X operating system

Web Sites

These are just a few of the many URLs every Mac user should have bookmarked.

Apple Sites

Web site	Address
Apple's Mac OS X page	www.apple.com/
Software Downloads page	www.apple.com/downloads/macosx
Apple's Support page	www.apple.com/support
Apple's Knowledge Base	kbase.info.apple.com
Apple Developer Connection (ADC)	developer.apple.com
Apple Store Locator	www.apple.com/retail
Bug Reporting Page	developer.apple.com
.Mac page	www.mac.com

Developer Sites

Web site	Address
Cocoa Dev Central	www.cocoadevcentral.com
Cocoa Dev Wiki	www.cocoadev.com
Mac DevCenter (by O'Reilly Network)	www.macdevcenter.com
Stepwise	www.stepwise.com

Discussions and News

Web site	Address
Applelust	www.applelust.com
Apple Slashdot	apple.slashdot.org
As the Apple Turns	www.appleturns.com
MacCentral	www.maccentral.com
MacInTouch	www.macintouch.com
Mac Minute	www.macminute.com
Mac News Network	www.macnn.com
MacSlash	www.macslash.org

Rumor Sites

Web site	Address
Apple Insider	www.appleinsider.com
Fly on the Mac	www.flyonthemac.com
MacRumors	www.macrumors.com

Web site	Address
RumorTracker	*www.rumortracker.com*
SpyMac	*www.spymac.com*
Think Secret	*www.thinksecret.com*

Software

Web site	Address
AquaFiles	*www.aquafiles.com*
Bare Bones Software	*www.barebones.com*
Fun with Fink	*www.funwithfink.com*
MacUpdate	*www.macupdate.com*
The Omni Group	*www.omnigroup.com*
Version Tracker	*www.versiontracker.com/macosx*

Tips, Tricks, and Advice

Web site	Address
Mac OS X FAQ	*www.osxfaq.com*
Mac OS X Hints	*www.macosxhints.com*
Google Apple/Mac Search	*www.google.com/mac.html*

Index

Symbols

> (angle bracket, right), 97
   console command, 109
>> (angle brackets, right), 84
* (asterisk), 75
! (bang), 83
[ ] (brackets), 75
^ (caret), 91
: (colon), 80
$ (dollar sign), 68
   PATH environment variable and, 80
. and .. (parent directories), 71
.Mac, 15
   .Mac synchronization, 22
.bash_history file, 84
.bash_profile file, 80
.bashrc file, 80
/ (forward slash), 70
(hash mark), 321
-- (hyphens), 329
% (percent sign), 86
| (pipe character), 84
+ (plus) button, 119
? (question mark), 75
" (quotes, double), 322
' (quotes, single), 322
#! (shebang), 320
~ (tilde), 72

Numbers

1984 commercial, 2
6to4 tunnel interface, 249
680x0, 8

A

About This Mac menu, 277
absolute path, 70
Access Control Entries (see ACEs)
Access Control Lists (see ACLs)
Accounts preference panel, 119
ACEs (Access Control Entries), 174
ACLs (Access Control Lists), 174
Active Directory, 132, 145
active network connections, 259
Activity Monitor, 285–288
   killing processes, 297
adaptive hot-file clustering, 187
ADC (Apple Developer Connection), 20, 66
Address Book, 15
administrative users, 117
AFP (Apple Filing Protocol), 188
agents, 103
AIM (AOL Instant Messenger), 15
AirPort, 246, 249
aliases, 81
   alias command, 82
AOL Instant Messenger (AIM), 15
Apache web server, 191
   starting and stopping, 108
appending output, 84
Apple Developer Connection (ADC), 20, 66
Apple Filing Protocol (AFP), 188
Apple II and Apple III, 1
Apple merger with NeXT, 5
Apple Password Server, 132
Apple Remote Desktop (ARD), 299
AppleCare, 27

We'd like to hear your suggestions for improving our indexes. Send email to *index@oreilly.com*.

About the Authors

James Duncan Davidson is a freelance author, software developer, and consultant focusing on Mac OS X, Java, XML, and open source technologies. He is the author of *Learning Cocoa with Objective-C* (O'Reilly) and is a frequent contributor to the O'Reilly Network online web site. He is also the publisher of his own web site, x180 (*http://www.x180.net*), where he keeps his popular weblog.

Duncan was the creator of Apache Tomcat and Apache Ant and was instrumental in their donation to the Apache Software Foundation by Sun Microsystems. While working at Sun, he authored two versions of the Java Servlet API specification as well as the Java API for XML Processing.

Jason Deraleau has been a computer enthusiast since the Commodore 64. Having spent time focusing on DOS, Windows, Linux, and FreeBSD, his newest passion is the Macintosh and Mac OS X. Currently residing in Western Massachusetts, he works as a systems administrator by day, IT consultant and technical writer by night. Jason was a presenter at O'Reilly Mac OS X Conference 2004 and is a contributing author on the O'Reilly Network.

Colophon

Our look is the result of reader comments, our own experimentation, and feedback from distribution channels. Distinctive covers complement our distinctive approach to technical topics, breathing personality and life into potentially dry subjects.

The animal on the cover of *Running Mac OS X Tiger* is a Siberian tiger. The Siberian tiger is the largest member of the cat family, including lions. A male averages 7 to 9 feet in length, and it usually weighs about 500 pounds. A female weighs slightly less, averaging about 300 pounds. This animal is native to Siberia and parts of China. Its fur color ranges from yellow to orange, with black stripes, although a few white tigers with black stripes have been spotted. The fur is long and thick, to help the animal survive its native cold climates. An interesting fact about tiger stripes is that the pattern of each tiger's stripes is unique to that tiger. Therefore, stripes are a useful tool for identifying different tigers.

The Siberian tiger is endangered. Although there are about 1,000 living in captivity, only about 200 to 300 live in the wild. This is partly due to industrial encroachment on its natural habitat, limiting the tiger's hunting resources. Poaching is also a serious problem; in some areas of the world, tiger parts are thought to have great medicinal value, so these parts bring great financial gain to sellers.

Adam Witwer was the production editor and Linley Dolby was the copyeditor for *Running Mac OS X Tiger*. Sada Preisch proofread the text. Colleen Gorman and Darren Kelly provided quality control. John Bickelhaupt wrote the index.

Emma Colby designed the cover of this book, based on a series design by Edie Freedman. The cover image is an original illustration by Susan Hart. Karen Montgomery produced the cover layout with Adobe InDesign CS using Adobe's ITC Garamond font.

David Futato designed the interior layout. This book was converted by Andrew Savakis to FrameMaker 5.5.6 with a format conversion tool created by Erik Ray, Jason McIntosh, Neil Walls, and Mike Sierra that uses Perl and XML technologies. The text font is Linotype Birka; the heading font is Adobe Myriad Condensed; and the code font is LucasFont's TheSans Mono Condensed. The illustrations that appear in the book were produced by Robert Romano, Jessamyn Read, and Lesley Borash using Macromedia FreeHand MX and Adobe Photoshop CS. The tip and warning icons were drawn by Christopher Bing. This colophon was written by Mary Brady.

Better than e-books

Buy *Running Mac OS X Tiger* and access the
digital edition FREE on Safari for 45 days.

Go to www.oreilly.com/go/safarienabled
and type in coupon code 2LJR-5GLK-HZH2-9CKP-MHRU

Search
thousands of
top tech books

Download
whole chapters

Cut and Paste
code examples

Find
answers fast

Search Safari! The premier electronic reference
library for programmers and IT professionals.

Related Titles from O'Reilly

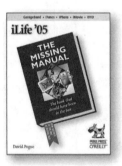

Macintosh

AppleScript: The Definitive Guide

AppleScript: The Missing Manual

AppleScript Language Pocket Reference

Appleworks 6: The Missing Manual

The Best of the Joy of Tech

FileMaker Pro 8: The Missing Manual

GarageBand 2: The Missing Manual

iBook Fan Book

iLife '05: The Missing Manual

iMovie HD & iDVD 5: The Missing Manual

iPhoto 5: The Missing Manual

iPod Playlists '05

iPod Shuffle Fan Book

iPod & iTunes: The Missing Manual, *3rd Edition*

iWork '05: The Missing Manual

Mac Annoyances

Mac OS X Tiger in a Nutshell

Mac OS X Tiger Pocket Guide

Mac OS X Panther Power User

Mac OS X: The Missing Manual, *Tiger Edition*

Mac OS X Unwired

Modding Mac OS X

Office 2004 for the Macintosh: The Missing Manual

Revolution in The Valley: The Insanely Great Story of How the Mac was Made

Switching to the Mac: The Missing Manual, *Tiger Edition*

Mac Developers

Building Cocoa Applications: A Step-By-Step Guide

Cocoa in a Nutshell

Essential Mac OS X Panther Server Administration

Learning Carbon

Learning Cocoa with Objective-C, *2nd Edition*

Learning Unix for Mac OS X Tiger

Mac OS X for Java Geeks

Mac OS X Panther Hacks

Mac OS X Tiger in a Nutshell

Mac OS X Tiger for Unix Geeks

Objective-C Pocket Reference

RealBasic: The Definitive Guide, *2nd Edition*

Running Mac OS X Tiger

Our books are available at most retail and online bookstores.

To order direct: 1-800-998-9938 • *order@oreilly.com* • *www.oreilly.com*

Online editions of most O'Reilly titles are available by subscription at *safari.oreilly.com*